W9-ADG-226

American Bibliography

A Preliminary Checklist

for

1817

Items 39907-42993

Compiled by

Ralph R. Shaw

and

Richard H. Shoemaker

The Scarecrow Press, Inc.

New York   1963

Copyright 1963 by Ralph R. Shaw
and Richard H. Shoemaker

L. C. Card No. 58-7809

A

Abbadie, Jacques, 1658-1727
The deity of Jesus Christ essential to the Christian religion...Charlestown, Mass., A. Brown, 1817. 290 p. CSansS; CSmH; CtW; CtY; ICP; KWiU; KyLoS; MB; MH; MNF; MWA; MWiW; NNC; Nh; VtU.   39907

Abbot, Abiel
A discourse, delivered before the Bible society of Salem and its vicinity...June 11, 1817...Salem, Mass., Pr. by Thomas C. Cushing, 1817. 24 p. MHi; MWA; MeHi; NjPT.   39908

[Abbot, John Emery]
A catechism of the New Testament. Salem, Mass., Pr. by T. C. Cushing, 1817. 20 p. MSaE.   39909

Abernethy, Andrew
The pocket chronological directory; or, compend of general history, in the form of questions and answers. 1st ed. Hartford, Pr. by Peter B. Gleason & co., 1817. 176 p. Ct; CtHi; CtY; IaDL; LU; MH; MWA; MDedHi; MDeeP; NjR; OClWHi; RPB; ScCMv.   39910

Academy of natural sciences of Philadelphia.
Journal of the Academy of natural sciences of Philadelphia. v. 1- Philadelphia, 1817- . CtHT-W; DLC; IaDaM; IaDaP; MNBedf; MdBP; MdHi; NIC; NhD; RNR.   39911

Account of the battles of the late war, with adventures of Corporal Samuel Stubbs (a Kentuckian) Boston, 1817. Brinley 5072.   39912

Account of Sir Matthew Hale. [Hartford, Hartford
Evangelical Tract Society, Feb. 1817] 4 p. (Hartford
Evangelical Tract Society. Publications. no. 15a)
CtHi.   39913

An account of the doctrines of the New Jerusalem
Church. According to the writings of Baron Sweden-
borg. With a sketch of the life of Baron Swedenborg.
From Bishop Hurd's History of all religions. New
York, Pr. by Charles N. Baldwin, 1817. 23 p. MiD-B.
                                                         39914
Accum, Friedrich Christian
    A practical essay on chemical re-agents... Phila-
delphia, M. Carey & Son, 1817. 204 p. MWA; NcD.
                                                         39915
The actress of the present day. [New York] Harper,
1817. 3 v. (Ingpen & Co. (Lond.), catal. 32 (1935),
item 76)   39916

Adam, Alexander, 1741-1809
    Roman antiquities; or, An account of the manners
and customs of the Romans... Designed chiefly to illus-
trate the Latin classics... Rev., cor., and illus. with
notes and additions by P. Wilson. 2d Amer. ed. New
York, 1817. 648 p. CtW.   39917

Adams, Daniel, 1773-1864
    The scholar's arithmetic; or, Federal accountant...
Stereotype ed., rev., cor., with additions. Keene,
N.H., John Prentiss, 1817. MB; MDeeP; MH; MLit;
MPeHi; MWA; NNC; Vt; VtMiM; VtMiS.   39918

-- The thorough scholar: Or the nature of language...
4th ed., imp. Montpelier, Vt., Pr. [by E.P. Walton]
for Lucius Q. C. Bowles, 1817. 131 p. CtHT-W; DLC;
MBAt; MH; NN; NNC; MWA; Vt; VtU-W; WU.   39919

Adams, Hannah, 1755-1831
    Close communion contrary to the Gospel. Dedham,
1817. 12 p. MWA.   39920

-- A dictionary of all religions and religious denominations, Jewish, heathen, Mahometan and Christian, an-

cient and modern. ...Ed. 4, with cor. and lge. addi-
tions. New York, James Eastburn; Cummings and
Hilliard, Boston, 1817. 376 p.   CtW; DLC; GColu;
GEU; ICMe; ICU; LNH; LU; MA; MAm; MH; MWA;
MWHi; MdBJ; MdW; MnM; NHi; NR; NRU; Nh-Hi;
OClWHi; PMA; RP; UPB.   39921

Adams, Joel T.
    The birth and life...by himself.   Lynchburg, Va.,
1817. 14 p.   MWA.   39922

Adams, John
    Flowers of ancient history; comprehending, on a
new plan, the most remarkable and interesting events,
as well as characters, of antiquity...Baltimore, Pr. by
Pomeroy & Toy, for the booksellers, 1817. 288 p.
CtY; IaCrM; MB; MW; MdBE; MdHi; RP.   39923

Adams, John Quincy, 1767-1848
    Report upon weight and measures.   Prepared...in
obedience to a resolution of the Senate of the third
March, 1817.   Washington, D.C., Gales & Seaton,
1817. 245 p.   PPM.   39924

Adams, Robert
    The narrative of Robert Adams, an American sail-
or who was wrecked on the western coast of Africa, in
the year 1810; was detained three years in slavery by
the Arabs of the great desert...Boston, Wells and Lilly,
1817. 200 p.   AU; CSfCW; CSmH; CU; CtHC; CtY;
DLC; MB; MBBC; MBC; MDeeP; MH; MHi; MW; MWA;
MWal; Me; NHi; NNS; NcD; NcU; NcWsHi; NcWS; NhD;
NjR; OAU; OC; PMA; RPB; ScCC; TNF; WHi.   39925

[Adams]
    School atlas to Adam's geography.   Boston, Lin-
coln & Edmands, 1817. MWA.   39926

An address delivered by a member of the Manumission
Society, on Aug. 17, 1816, and again on the last of
January, 1817...Knoxville, Tenn., Pr. by Heiskell &
Brown, 1817. 21 p.   TMaryC.   39927

Address of a minister to his parishioners on prayer.
[Hartford, Conn., Hartford Evangelical Tract Society,
Hudson & Co., Printers, Dec. 1817] 4 p. (Hartford
Evangelical Tract Society. Publications. No. 11) CtHi.
                                                      39928
An address of the Board of Managers of the United Fo-
reign Missionary Society of the three denominations
united in this institution. New York, Pr. by J. Sey-
mour, 1817. 11 p. PLT.   39929

Address of the Corresponding committee of the county
& city of Philadelphia to the people of Pennsylvania.
Philadelphia, Pr. by the Chronicle, 1817. 8 p. PU.
                                                      39930
Address to Christians on the primitive government of
the Christian church, as proved by the Holy Scriptures.
New Haven, Pr. by Steele & Gray, 1817. 52 p. CtHi;
MWA; NcD.   39931

Address to mothers. Simsbury, Conn., Pr. for the
mothers in Simsbury [1817?] MWiW.   39932

An address to the emigrants from Connecticut, and
from New England generally, in the new settlements in
the United States. Hartford, Pr. by Peter B. Gleason
& Co., 1817. 16 p. CtY; MiDMCh; NHi; NjPT; OClWHi.
                                                      39933

An address to the free electors of the commonwealth of
Pennsylvania. [Philadelphia] 1817. 8 p. DLC. 39934

An address to the good people of Connecticut...[Middle-
town, Conn., 1817] MWA.   39935

An address to the inhabitants of the state of Vermont,
on the use of ardent spirits; by a committee appointed
for that purpose, at a meeting of members of the Legislature, and others from various parts of the state, at
Montpelier, Oct. 1817. Montpelier, Pr. by E.P. Walton, 1817. 13 p. MWA; NNUT; OCHP; Vt; VtMiS.
                                                      39936
An address to the members of the Legislature of Maryland concerning the establishment of a Loan office for

the benefit of the land owners of the state. [Annapolis,
1817] 31 p. MdHi.   39937

An address to the people of Maryland on the necessity
of establishing a bank for the benefit of agriculturalists.
By a freeholder. Annapolis, Pr. by J. Green, July
1817. 16 p. NN.   39938

Address to the people of Pennsylvania. [Philadelphia,
1817] 12 p. DLC.   39939

Address to the people of Pennsylvania, upon a great
public question. By a meeting of freeholders held at
Philadelphia, March 15, 1817. [Philadelphia, 1817?]
9 p. PHi.   39940

An address to the Roman Catholics of the United States
of America. By a Catholic clergyman. New York, Pr.
by Clayton & Kingsland, for David Longworth, 1817.
120 p. InID.   39941

Adventurer's almanack, or, the Daily Visitant and
Friendly Prompter, for 1818. Boston, Parmenter &
Norton [1817] MH; MWA.   39942

The adventurer's almanack...for the year of our re-
demption 1818...Boston, Pr. by Parmenter & Norton,
for Lincoln & Edmands [1817] [38] p. MWA; MWeyHi.
                                                                    39943
The adventures of old Dame Trudge and her parrot.
Part I...Philadelphia, Wm. Charles, 1817. [16] p.
MWA; PP.   39944

The Aeolian harp; or, Songster's cabinet, being a selection of songs and recitation. New York, 1817. 124 p.
RPB.   39945

Aesopus
    Fabulae Aesopi Selectae...Baltimore, Pr. by J.
Robinson, for Fielding Lucas, Jr., 1817. MWA. 39946

-- -- ...or, Select fables of Aesop; with an English
translation, more literal than any yet extant, designed

for the readier instruction of beginners in the Latin
tongue...Ed. 9, cor. and amended. Baltimore, J.
Cushing, 1817. 161 p. MWA; MdBE; MdHi.   39947

-- -- Baltimore, Pr. by Joseph Robinson, 1817. 161 p.
CtY; DLC; MH; MWA; MdBE; MdHi.   39948

African Methodist Episcopal Church
     The doctrines and discipline of the African Method-
ist Episcopal Church...1st ed. Philadelphia, Pr. by
John H. Cunningham, for Richard Allen and Jacob Tap-
sico and the African Methodist connection in the United
States, 1817. 192 p. NNMHi.   39949

[Agg, John] fl. 1816
     Pilgrimage to the Holy Land, a poem--in two can-
tos. To which is added, The tempest, a fragment...
Philadelphia, Pr. by J. Maxwell, for M. Thomas,
1817. 65 p. DLC; MWA; PHi; PPL.   39950

Agricultural almanack, for 1818...Philadelphia, Solomon W. Conrad, 1817. MWA.   39951

Agricultural and economical almanac, for 1818. Astron.
by Elijah Middlebrook. New Haven, T. G. Woodward
[1817] [36] p. CtHi; MWA; NjR.   39952

Agricultural Society of Albemarle, Charlottesville, Va.
     [Organization and program]. Extract from the Pro-
ceedings, November 14, 1817. [Richmond, Va., 1817]
Broadside. [2] p. ViU.   39953

Agriculture and Manufacturing Society. Jefferson County,
Ohio.
     [Constitution, Steubenville, 1817] (Amer. Imprint
Inventory no. 17 (363))   39954

Aikin, John, 1747-1822
     The farm yard journal...New Haven, Pr. by Sid-
ney's press, 1817. 31 p. CtY; MWA.   39955

Albany Bible society, N. Y.
     Report of the Board of managers... February 1817

... Albany, Pr. by Websters and Skinners, 1817. DLC;
MWA; MPiB; NjPT; NjR.   39956

Albany County Bible Society
    Annual report of... 1816.   Albany, 1817. MB.
                                                  39957
[Albany County Sabbath School Society]
    Constitution of the Albany Sunday School Society,
formed on the twenty-first of April, 1817.   Also, the
rules to be observed in the institution and management
of the schools.   Albany, Pr. by G.J. Loomis & Co.,
for the Society, 1817.   8 p. MWA; N.   39958

The Albany directory, for the year 1817... Albany, Pr.
by Packard & Van Benthuysen, 1817.   NN.   39959

Alden, Timothy
    Memoirs of the late Reverend Karl Wilhelm Colson.
[1817?]   MWA.   39960

Ali Baba
    The forty thieves... Philadelphia, Wm. Charles,
1817.   MWA.   39961

Allen, Benjamin Franklin
    An oration, pronounced before the students of
Brown university... July 4, 1817... Providence, Pr. by
Jones & Wheeler, 1817.   MWA; RPB.   39962

Allen, John
    The fathers, the reformers, and the public formu-
laries, of the Church of England in harmony with Calvin, and against the Bishop of Lincoln... By a layman.
Preface... by an American clergyman.   Philadelphia,
P.H. Nicklin and A. Small, 1817.   203 p. MWA; MiU.
                                                  39963
Allen, Paul
    History of the American revolution.   Baltimore,
1817.   2 v.   CtHT-W.   39964

Allen, Samuel Clesson
    Eulogy on the Hon. John Wheelock, LL.D. late
president of Dartmouth University... pronounced in the

University Chapel Aug. 27, 1817...Hanover, N.H., Pr.
by David Watson, Jun., 1817. 19 p. MA; MWA; OCHP.
39965

Allen, Mrs. Sarah
    A narrative of the shipwreck and unparalleled suf-
ferings of Mrs. Sarah Allen, (late of Boston) on her
passage in May last from New-York to New Orleans.
...Ed. 2. Boston, Pr. by Henry Trumbull, 1817. 24 p.
DLC; MWA.   39966

Allen, William, 1784-1858
    A farewell sermon, preached at Pittsfield, Feb. 23,
1817, being the last Sabbath of his ministry...Pitts-
field [Mass.] Pr. by Phinehas Allen, 1817. 16 p.
CSmH; CtY; PPL.   39967

[--] Thoughts on the importance of religion...Philadel-
phia, Pr. [by J.R.A. Skerrett] for Benjamin & Thomas
Kite...1817. 12 p. MWA; NbU.   39968

Allen's New-England almanack, for the year of our
Lord 1818...By A. Allen, Philo...Hartford, Pr. by P.
B. Gleason & Co. [1817] 24 p. Ct; CtHi; MWA; MWHi;
NjR.   39969

American academy of the fine arts, New York.
    Charter and by-laws...with an account of the
statues, busts, paintings, prints, books and other property belonging to the academy. New York, The Academy, 1817. 34 p. MH; MWA; NBLiHi; NN; PHi;
PPAmP.   39970

American almanac...1818. Philadelphia, T. Desilver,
[1817] MWA; PHi.   39971

The American Baptist magazine, and missionary Intelligencer. New series...Vol. 1- Boston, James Loring
and Lincoln & Edmands, 1817- CSmH; ICMBI; IU;
MBeHi; MH; NIC; NjR; TxHuT; ViRU.   39972

American Baptist Society for Propagating the Gospel.
    The constitution of the American Baptist Society,
for the Propagating the Gospel, established January 1,

1817. (Published by order of the Society) 8 p. NRAB.
39973

American Bible society.

The first annual report of the Board of managers of the American Bible society, presented May 8, 1817 ...New-York, Pr. by J. Seymour, for the Society, 1817. 57 p. CSmH; DLC; GDC; InID; MH; MHi; NjR; OCl; OMC; PHi; PPAmP; PHC; PPL; PCC; PP; PU.
39974

American board of commissioners for foreign missions.

Report of the American board of commissioners for foreign missions: compiled from documents laid before the board, at the eighth annual meeting, which was held at Northampton, Mass., Sept. 18, 19 and 20, 1817. Boston, Pr. by Samuel T. Armstrong, 1817. 59 p. MWA; MeB; MiKC; N; TxFwSB. 39975

American colonization society.

Annual report of the American colonization society, with the minutes of the annual meeting and of the board of directors...Washington, 1817-1890. M. 39976

-- A view of exertions lately made for the purpose of colonizing the free people of colour, in the United States, in Africa, or elsewhere. City of Washington, Pr. by Jonathan Elliot, 1817. 23 p. DLC. 39977

-- -- City of Washington, Pr. by Jonathan Elliot, 1817. 22 p. DLC. 39978

American convention for promoting the abolition of slavery, and improving the condition of the African race.

Minutes of the proceedings of the fifteenth American convention...Philadelphia, Pr. by Merritt, 1817. MWA.
39979

American Eagle. Sag Harbor, N.Y., Samuel A. Seabury, Oct. 18, 1817, 1st issue. Weekly newspaper. MWA. 39980

American Education Society

Address of the directors. Boston, S.T. Armstrong, 1817. 7 p. CtY; MWiW. 39981

American Journal. Ithaca, N.Y., Mack and Shepard, Aug. 20, 1817. 1st issue. Weekly newspaper. MWA.
39982

American Monthly Magazine and Critical Review. New York, H. Biglow, May, 1817, 1st issue. CtW; MC; NUtHi.
39983

The American ready reckoner, and traders' infallible guide, in dollars and cents; with a variety of useful tables. Baltimore, William Warner, and F. Lucas, jun., 1817. 155 p. DLC; MWA; MdBE; MdHi; PU.
39984

The American register; or, Summary review of history, politics, and literature... Philadelphia, Pr. by William Fry, for Thomas Dobson and son, 1817. 2 v. CSmH; DLC; ICN; MB; MS; MoSHi; MoSM; MoSpD; NWM; PEaL; RP; ViRVal.
39985

American School for the deaf.
    Report of the Committee of the Connecticut Asylum, for the education and instruction of deaf and dumb persons, exhibited 1st June, 1817. Hartford, Pr. by Hudson and Co., 1817. 15 p. CtHT-W; CtY; CtHC; CtHT; DLC; ICU; KHi; MB; MdFred; MoS; N; NAuT; NN; NNNAM; NNS; OC; OMC; WHi.
39986

American society for educating pious youth for the Gospel ministry.
    Address of the directors... Boston, Pr. by Samuel T. Armstrong, 1817. 7 p. CSt; MWA; NjR.
39987

American society for the encouragement of domestic manufactures.
    Address of the American society for the encouragement of domestic manufactures, to the people of the U-nited States. New-York, Pr. by Van Winkle, Wiley & Co., 1817. 32 p. DLC; DeGE; MB; MWA; MdHi; NjPT.
39988

American Society for evangelizing the Jews.
    An account of the origin and formation of the American Society for evangelizing the Jews; with its constitution, and an address to the public. New-York, Pr. by

George Forman, for the Society, 1817. 15 p. DLC.
                                             39989
American Society for meliorating the condition of the
Jews.
    Account of the origin and formation.   New York,
1817. 15 p. MBC.   39990

American society of New York for promoting domestic
manufactures.
    Extracts from an address...[Philadelphia? 1817?]
MWA.   39991

American speaker, a selection of popular, parliament-
ary and forensic eloquence; particularly calculated for
the seminaries in the United States. Ed. 4. Philadelphia, Small, 1817. 371 p. MWA; PHi; PU.   39992

The American star. Being a choice collection of the
most approved patriotic & other songs. Together with
many original ones, never before published. Ed. 2.
Richmond, Pr. [by Shepherd & Pollard] for Peter Cottom, 1817. 215 p. CtHT-W; DLC; IaU; MB; MH;
MWA; NBuG; NcH; RPB; Vi.   39993

American star. Petersburg, Va., T.W. Lorrain and
M.W. Dunnavant, 1817. Tri-weekly newspaper. Brigham, p. 1130.   39994

American Yeoman. Brattleboro, Vt., Simeon Ide, Feb.
4, 1817, 1st issue. Weekly newspaper. MWA; Vt.
                                             39995
Americanischer Stadt- und Land- Calender. Auf das
Jahr...1818. Zum zweytenmal herausgegeben. Baltimore, Pr. by Schaffer u. Maund [1817] Seidensticker
p. 200.   39996

Americanischer Stadt und Land Calender auf das 1818te
Jahr Christi. Philadelphia, Pr. by Conrad Zentler,
[1817] MWA; PHi.   39997

Anacreon
    Select odes of Anacreon. Translated...by William
Biglow. Cambridge, Mass., Univ. Press...Hilliard &

Metcalf, 1817. MWA; RPB.   39998

Ancient and Honorable Artillery Company, Boston.
    Rules and regulations of the Ancient and Honorable
Artillery Company. Boston, Pr. by E. G. House,
1817. 23 p. MWHi.   39999

Andover theological seminary.
    The constitution and associate statutes of the Theo-
logical seminary in Andover. Andover, Mass., Pr. by
Flagg and Gould, 1817. 40 p. CSmH; DLC; MB; MWA;
MWiW; NjR; RPB.   40000

-- Laws of the Theological Institution in Andover.
Andover, Mass., Pr. by Flagg and Gould, 1817. 16 p.
MWA.   40001

Andrewes, Lancelot, bp.
    The devotions of Bishop Andrews... Philadelphia,
Pr. by A. Walker, for D. Hogan, 1817. 148 p. MBAt;
MH-AH; MWA; NNS.   40002

[--] New manual of private devotions... 3d Amer. ed.
New York, T. & J. Swords, 1817. MWA.   40003

Andrews, William
    A sermon, delivered at Danbury, Nov. 13th, 1817;
being the day appointed for the execution of Amos
Adams... New Haven, Pr. by T. G. Woodward, 1817.
20 p. CtHC; CtHi; MHi; MWA; NjPT.   40004

Andros, Thomas
    Discourses on several important theological sub-
jects... Boston, Samuel T. Armstrong, 1817. 224 p.
MBC; MTaHi; MWA.   40005

-- The scriptures liable to be wrested to men's own
destruction... Taunton, Mass., Pr. by A. Danforth,
1817. MWA.   40006

Animal creation; or, Juvenile history of beasts and
birds. By a parent. New-York, S. Wood & sons,
1817. 71 p. DLC; NN.   40007

Annual visitor and citizen and farmer's almanac for
1818. Astronomical calculations by Joshua Sharp.
Wilmington, Del., James Wilson [1817] 30 p. DeWI;
MWA.   40008

Anthony, Daniel
   The gauging inspector, and measurer's assistant;
shewing the most common errors in the practice of
gauging, and how to correct them... Providence, Pr. by
Miller & Hutchens, 1817. 70 p. DeGE; MWA. 40009

Anthony, John Hopkins
   The school's instructor, and scholar's catechism
...Hudson, N. Y., Pr. for the author, 1817. 48 p. NNC.
                                                    40010
An appeal to the Church in her own behalf... 1817.
MWA.   40011

An appeal to the people of New Hampshire... Exeter,
N. H., Pr. by Henry A. Ranlet, 1817. MWA.   40012

Appleton, Jesse
   A sermon, delivered at Freeport, November 6,
1816, at the ordination of the Reverend Enos Merrill...
Portland, Me., Pr. by A. & J. Shirley, 1817. 28 p.
MWA; MeB; MiD-B; NjPT.   40013

-- A sermon, delivered at Northampton, September 18,
1817, before the American board of commissioners for
foreign missions... Charlestown, Mass., Pr. by Samuel
Etheridge, 1817. 31 p. C; CSmH; MA; MBAt; MH-AH;
MNe; MSaE; MWA; MeB; MeBaT; MeHi; MiD-B; PHi;
PPPrHi; VtMiM.   40014

Arbouin, James
   Dissertations on the regenerate life; in harmony
with the theological views of Baron Swedenborg, the un-
doubted messenger of our Lord's second advent...
Philadelphia, Anderson & Meehan, 1817. 102 p. PBa.
                                                    40015
Aristotle [pseud.]
   Aristotle's master-piece... New York, Pr. for the
Company of Flying Stationer, 1817. 114 p. MWA. 40016

The arithmetical tables. Most of which must neces-
sarily be committed to memory, before any consider-
able progress can be made in learning arithmetic.
Philadelphia, Kimber & Sharpless, 1817. [20] p. PP
                                                    40017
-- ...for the use of schools. New-York, Samuel Wood
& sons, 1817. 24 p. MWA; NNMuCN; TxSaWi. 40018

Armata; a fragment. Ed. 2, with additions. New
York, 1817. (An early romance of a political Utopia)
(The Burnham Antique Book Store, List 8, May, 1939.
No. 48.   40019

Arnold, Samuel James
    The devil's bridge; an opera, in three acts. New-
York, D. Longworth, 1817. 57 p. MH; MWA; NN; PU.
                                                    40020
Arrangements for the reception of the President of the
United States (James Monroe), in Salem. July 8, 1817.
Broadside. MHi; MSaE.   40021

The art of domestick happiness, and other poems: by
the recluse, author of The independency of the mind,
affirmed... Pittsburgh, Pa., Robert Patterson, 1817.
316 p. CSmH; DLC; ICU; MB; MH; MWA; NBLiHi;
NN; OCHP; OClWHi; O; PPiU; PHi; PPL; PPi; PPPrHi;
PWW; RPB.   40022

The articles of belief, professed by the followers of
Calvin, Luther, & Arminus... Middletown, Conn., Pr.
by T. Dunning, 1817. 12 p. MWA; PReaHi.   40023

Artiguenave, Joseph Linna
    Morceaux divers de prose ou de poesie... Boston,
Pr. by T. G. Bangs, 1817. MB; MBAt; MH; MHi;
MWA.   40024

-- -- [New York?, 1817?] MWA.   40025

-- Quatrième seance de déclamation... Boston, Pr. by
T. G. Bangs, 1817. 23 p. DLC; MH; MWA; MiD-B.
                                                    40026

Asbury, Francis
   The causes, evils, and cures of heart and church
divisions...New York, J. Soule and T. Mason, 1817.
MWA.   40027

Associate Church in North America. Associate Synod
of North America.
   A book of church government and discipline, a-
greed upon, and enacted by the Associate synod of
North America, at Pittsburgh, June 6, 1817. Pittsburgh, Pa., Butler & Lambdin, 1817. 66 p. ICP;
MWA; NNUT; PPiXT; PPi; PPPrHi.   40028

-- Extracts from the minutes...Carlisle, Pa., Pr. by
A. Loudon, 1817. MWA.   40029

Associate Reformed Church of North America. Carolinas and Georgia.
   Circular letter of the Synod of the Associate Reformed Church in the Carolinas and Georgia. Columbia, S.C., Pr. at the Telescope Press, 1817. 8 p.
NcMHi.   40030

-- General Synod.
   Extracts from the minutes of the proceedings...
Philadelphia, Pr. by J. Price & co. ...1817. 67 p.
MWA; PLT.   40031

Association for the Relief of Respectable Aged Indigent
Females.
   The fourth annual report...New-York, Pr. by Geo.
Largin, for the Society, 1817. 17 p. NN; NNG. 40032

Association of Friends for the Printing and Distribution of Tracts.
   Abstract of the first annual report of the committee of management of the Association of Friends for
the Printing and Distribution of Tracts on Moral and
Religious Subjects. To which is subjoined the constitution, with a list of contributors, etc. Philadelphia,
Pr. by J.R.A. Skerrett, for the Association, 1817.
12 p. PPM.   40033

Der Astrologische Wahrsager...1817. MWA.   40034

An astronomical diary, or almanack, for the year of our Lord and Saviour 1818...Calculated for the meridian of Andover [Mass.]...Exeter, N.H., Pr. by H.A. Ranlet, for Charles Norris, [1817] [24] p. MB; MWA; NCH; NhHi.   40035

The Athenaeum of Philadelphia
      Charter and by-laws...Philadelphia, Pr. by W. Fry, 1817. MWA.   40036

Atheneum or Spirit of the English magazines. Boston, Munroe & Francis, January, 1817, 1st issue. MPlyP; MiD; NRU.   40037

Auburn, N.Y. Presbyterian Church
      Articles of faith and covenant, adopted by the Presbyterian Church, in Auburn, November, 1817. [Auburn, 1817] 8 p. NAuT.   40038

Auctions inconsistent with regular trade, and injurious to the city. Addressed to the people of New-York. New-York, Pr. by Van Winkle, Wiley & co., 1817. 16 p. DLC; MHi; MWA; MiU-C; NNS.   40039

Augusta Patriot. Augusta, Maine, James Burton, Jr., Mar. 7, 1817, 1st issue. Weekly newspaper. MWA.   40040

Auxiliary Bible Society. Cayuga County.
      The constitution of the Auxiliary Bible Society of the county of Cayuga. Adopted 12th June, 1817. Auburn, Pr. by Skinner & Crosby, 1817. 8 p. NAuHi; NAuT.   40041

Auxiliary New-York Bible and Common prayer book society.
      The first annual report...New York, Pr. by T. & J. Swords, 1817. 15 p. MWA; MiD-B; NjR.   40042

B

Bailey's Rittenhouse almanac for the year of our Lord,

1818. Philadelphia, [1817] Tuttle. XB 6682. 40043

Baker, Mrs. Caroline (Horwood) fl. 1800
The deserted boy; or, Cruel parents. A tale of
truth... Philadelphia, Wm. Charles, 1817. 12 p. DLC;
NNC. 40044

Baker, J. W.
A grammar of moral philosophy, and natural the-
ology: with a summary of the evidences of Christianity.
Abstracted chiefly from the works of Dr. Paley... 1st
Amer. ed. New York, D. Longworth, 1817. 248 p.
DLC; InI; MH; MWA; N; NN. 40045

Balcom, D. A.
Confession of the prince of darkness, concerning
his devices, in politics and religion... Ed. 2. Leesburg, Va., Pr. for the author at the office of the
Genius of liberty, 1817. 48 p. DLC; NN. 40046

-- The devil on politics... 1817. MWA. 40047

Baldwin, Thomas, 1753-1825
A catechism; or, compendium of Christian doctrine
and practice. Boston, Lincoln & Edmands, 1817. 34 p.
NjPT. 40048

-- Christian baptism, as delivered to the churches, by
the evangelists and apostles, in the New Testament...
Utica, Pr. by William Williams, 1817. 36 p. NCH;
PMA; RPB. 40049

-- Missionary exertions encouraged. A sermon, delivered in Sansomstreet Baptist meeting-house, Philadelphia, May 4, 1817, before the "General missionary
convention of the Baptist denomination in the United
States, for foreign missions. Boston, Pr. by Lincoln
& Edmands [1817] 23 p. DLC; MB; MH-AH; MWA;
NRAB; PCC. 40050

Ballou, Hosea
A sermon, delivered at the dedication of the Universalist meeting-house at Shirley, Mass... Salem,

Mass., Pr. by Warwick Palfray, Jun., 1817. 23 p.
MHi; MMeT; MSaE; MWA.   40051

Baltimore (City)
    Ordinanaces of the corporation of the city of Balti-
more; passed at the extra session in May 1816, and at
the February session, 1817, to which is annexed a list
of the officers of the corporation.   Baltimore, Pr. by
William Warner, 1817.   45 p. MdBB; MdBE; MdHi.
                                              40052
Baltimore almanac for 1818.   Astron. by John Sharp.
Baltimore, William Warner [1817] DLC; MWA; MdBE.
                                              40053
The Baltimore city directory, 1817-1818.   Containing
the names, occupations, and residences of the inhabit-
ants... Baltimore, Pr. by James Kennedy, 1817. 234 p.
MdBB.   40054

Bancroft, Aaron, 1755-1839
    The duties enjoined by the fourth commandment...
Worcester, Mass., Pr. by William Manning, 1817. 39
p.   DLC; MDeeP; MWA; MeHi; NN; NjR.   40055

-- -- Ed. 2.   Worcester, Mass., Pr. by William Manning, 1817.   39 p. CSt; ICMe; MBAt; MH; MSaE; MWA;
MeHi; NN.   40056

-- A vindication of the result of the late mutual coun-
cil convened in Princeton [Mass.]   Worcester, Mass.,
Pr. by William Manning, June, 1817.   63 p. CBPac;
DLC; MAnP; MB; MLy; MWA; NIC.   40057

Bangs, Nathan
    An examination of the doctrine of predestination...
New York, Pr. by J.C. Totten, 1817.   179 p. CtY-D;
MA; MWA; N; OC; PPM.   40058

-- A vindication of some of the most essential doctrines
of the reformation: the errors of Hopkinsianism detected and refuted... Hudson,   N.Y., Pr. by Ashbel
Stoddard, 1817.   264 p. KWiU; MWA; NCH; NNMHi;
ViRut.   40059

Bank of the United States, 1816-1836
    An act to incorporate the subscribers to the Bank
of the United States. Washington city, Pr. by order of
the board of directors, 1817. 55 p. DLC; LU. 40060

-- General statement of the United States' Bank and its
branches, last of July, 1817. OCHP.   40061

-- Proceedings of the stockholders of the Bank of the
United States, on the twenty-eighth of October one
thousand eight hundred and sixteen, and the sixth of
January one thousand eight hundred and seventeen.
Philadelphia, Pub. by order of the stockholders, Willi-
am Fry, 1817. 10 p. NNP.   40062

-- Rules and regulations for the government of the offices of discount and deposit, established by the Bank
of the United States. [Philadelphia?] Pr. by order of
the board of directors, 1817. 14 p. DLC; MH; NNP.
                                                 40063
-- -- Washington City, Pr. by order of the board of
directors, 1817. 15 p. DLC.   40064

Bank of Vincennes
    A candid address to the stock-holders of the bank
of Vincennes...[1817] Broadside. In.   40065

The Baptist catechism; or, A brief instruction in the
principles of the Christian religion agreeable to the confession of faith &c which are added the proofs from
Scriptures. Philadelphia, 1817. 32 p. NjPT.   40066

The Baptist education society of the state of New-York.
    The Baptist education society of the state of New-
York, formed...September 25, 1817...[1817] MWA.
                                                 40067
Baptists. Connecticut. Groton Union Association.
    Minutes of the Groton Union Conference, held at
the Wickford Baptist meeting-house, with the church of
North-Kingston, June 18th & 19th, 1817, together with
their circular and corresponding letters. Norwich,
Conn., Pr. by Hubbard & Marvin, 1817. 8 p. MH-AH;
NRAB.   40068

-- -- Hartford association.
Minutes of the Hartford Baptist Association, convened at Wethersfield, [Conn.] first and second October, 1817. Hartford, Pr. by F. D. Bolles & Co., 1817. 12 p. CBB; Ct; MH-AH; MWA; NRAB.   40069

-- -- New London Association.
Minutes of the New-London Baptist Association, held at Waterford, October 21st and 22d, A. D. 1817. 8 p. PBa; NRAB.   40070

-- Delaware. Delaware Association.
Minutes of the Delaware Baptist Association [held in the meeting-house of the Baptist church, at Brynzion, May 31; June 1, & 2, 1817] 8 p. NRAB. 40071

-- Georgia. Savannah River Association.
Minutes...held at Newington Church, Scriven county, Geo. Commencing October 25th. Savannah, Ga., Pr. by Michael J. Kappel & co., 1817. 12 p. GU-De.
40072
-- Indiana. Blue River Association.
Minutes of the Blue River Association, held at Salem meeting-house, Harrison county, on the 4th Saturday of September, 1817. [Corydon, Ind., Pr. at the office of the Indiana Gazette, 1817] 4 p. InFrlC; NRAB.   40073

-- -- Wabash District Association.
The minutes of the Wabash District Association. Held at the Bethel meeting house. Posey county, Ia. From the 5th to the 7th day of October, 1817. [Vincennes, Ia., Pr. by S. Dillworth, 1817] 7 p. TxDaHi.
40074
-- Kentucky. Elkhorn Association.
Minutes of the Elkhorn Baptist Association, convened at Hillsborough meeting house, Woodford county, [Ky.] on the 9th of August, 1817. Georgetown, Ky., Pr. by John N. Lyle, 1817. 12 p. KyLoS; MoHi; NRAB.   40075

-- -- Gasper River Association.
Minutes of the sixth Gasper River Baptist Associa-

tion, holden at Smith's Grove Meeting-House, in War-
ren County, Kentucky, on Saturday preceding the fourth
Lord's day in Aug. 1817. Russellville, Ky., Pr. by
George B. Crutcher, 1817. 8 p. NRAB.   40076

-- -- Licking Association.
     Minutes of the Licking Association of Baptists,
held at the Town-Fork Meeting-House in Fayette County, Kentucky, the second Saturday in September and
the two following days, in the year of our Lord, 1817.
4 p. KyLoS; MoHi.   40077

-- -- Long Run Association.
     Minutes of the Long Run Association of Baptists,
held at Harrod's Creek Meeting House, Jefferson County, the first Friday and Saturday in September, 1817.
4 p. KyLoS.   40078

-- -- North District Association.
     Minutes of the North District Association of Bap-
tists, held at Bald Eagle Meeting House, in Bath county, state of Kentucky; on the 4th Saturday in July, in
the year of our Lord 1817. Lexington, Ky., Pr. by
Thomas T. Skillman, 1817. 8 p. KyLoS; NRAB. 40079

-- -- Russell's Creek Association.
     Minutes of the Russell's Creek Association of Bap-
tists held at Good-Hope Meeting-House, in Green County, on Saturday September 20th, [1817] and continued by
adjournment 'till Monday 22d. [Bardstown, [Ky.] Pr.
by J.P. Edrington, 1817] 4 p. (Henry S. Robinson's
Pri. Lib., Campbellsville, Ky.)   40080

-- -- Salem Association.
     Minutes of the Salem Association of Baptists, held
at Mill Creek Meeting-House, Nelson county, on the
4th Friday and Saturday in September 1817, being the
26th, and 27th of said month. [Bardstown, Ky., J.P.
Edrington, 1817] 4 p. ICU; KyLo; KyLoF.   40081

-- -- Tate's Creek Association.
     Minutes of the Tate's Creek Association of Bap-
tists, met at Bogg's Fork Meeting House, Fayette

County, Ky. on the 23d day of August, 1817. 4 p.
KyLoF.   40082

-- Maine. Bowdoinham Association.
    Minutes of the Bowdoinham Association, held in
Fayette, September 24th & 25th, 1817; together with
their circular and corresponding letters. Hallowell,
Me., Pr. by N. Cheever, 1817. 12 p. MH-AH; NRAB.
                                                 40083
-- -- Cumberland Association.
    Minutes of the Cumberland Association, holden in
Bath [Me.] October 1 and 2, 1817; with their circular
and corresponding letters. Hallowell, Me., Pr. by N.
Cheever, 1817. 12 p. MH-AH; NRAB.   40084

-- -- Lincoln Association.
    Minutes of the Lincoln Association, held at Blue-
hill, September 17 & 18, 1817. Hallowell, Me., Pr.
by E. Goodale, 1817. 8 p. MH-AH; MWA; NRAB.
                                                 40085
-- Massachusetts. Boston Association.
    Minutes of the Boston Baptist Association, held at
the Baptist Meeting House in Danvers, Sept. 17th &
18th, 1817. Boston, Pr. by Lincoln & Edmands, 1817.
19 p. MH-AH; MWA; MiD-B; NRAB.   40086

-- -- Sturbridge Association.
    Minutes of the Sturbridge Baptist Association, held
at Charlton, Worcester Co., Mass. August 27 & 28,
1817. Worcester, Mass., Pr. by William Manning,
1817. 12 p. MWA; NRAB.   40087

-- -- Union committee of the Sunday schools of the
three Baptist societieis in Boston.
    Report of the Union committee of the Sunday
schools of the three Baptist societies in Boston... Boston, Pr. by Farnham and Badger, 1817. 23 p. CSmH;
MWA; NNUT; PPL.   40088

-- -- Westfield Association.
    Minutes of the Westfield Baptist Association, held
in the Baptist meeting-house, in Russel, Mass., Wednesday, September 3, 1817. Springfield, Mass., Pr.

by Thomas Dickman, 1817. 8 p. MH-AH; NRAB. 40089

-- Mississippi. Baptist Missionary Soc.
Circular address of the Mississippi Society for
Baptist Missions...Natchez, M. T., Andrew Marschalk,
pr., 1817. 12 p. OCHP.   40090

-- New Hampshire. Meredith Association.
Minutes of the Meredith Baptist Association, holden
at Rumney, New Hampshire, Sept. 10 and 11, 1817.
With their circular and corresponding letters. Concord, N. H., Pr. by George Hough [1817?] 8 p. NRAB.
                                                40091
-- -- New Hampshire Association.
Minutes of the New-Hampshire Baptist Association,
held at the North meeting-house in Sanford [Me.] June
11th and 12th, 1817. Portland, Me., Pr. by F. Douglas, at the office of the Eastern Argus, 1817. 8 p.
MWA; NRAB.   40092

-- New York. Black River Association.
Minutes of the ...held...June 11th & 12th, 1817...
Sacketsharbor, Pr. by George Camp, for the Black-
River Baptist Association, 1817. 11 p. NRAB; NRCR.
                                                40093
-- -- Cayuga Baptist Association.
Minutes of the Cayuga Baptist Association, held
with the First Church in Camillus, September 18 and
19, 1817. Together with their circular, and corre-
sponding letter. Auburn, Pr. by H. C. Southwick,
1817. 8 p. NRAB.   40094

-- -- Hudson River Association.
Minutes...27th, 28th and 29th of August, 1817.
Troy, N. Y., Pr. by F. Adancourt, 1817. MWA. 40095

-- -- New York Association.
Minutes of the New-York Baptist Association, held
in the Meeting-House of the First Baptist Church in the
city of New-York, May 28th and 29th, 1817. [New-
York] Pr. by Van Winkle, Wiley & Co., 1817. 16 p.
NRAB.   40096

-- -- Ontario Association.

The minutes of the Ontario Baptist Association, holden at Palmyra, Sept. 24th & 25th, 1817, together with their circular and corresponding letter. Canandaigua, N. Y., Pr. at the Messenger Office, 1817. 11 p. NRAB; OClWHi.   40097

-- -- Otsego Association.

Minutes of the Otsego Baptist Association, held at Whitestown, County of Oneida, state of New-York, on the 3d and 4th of September, 1817. [Utica, N. Y., T. Walker, 1817] 8 p. MWA; NRAB; NRCR.   40098

-- -- Warwick Association.

Minutes of the Warwick Baptist Association, held in the Baptist Meeting House at Deer-Park, June 4th and 5th, 1817. 8 p. NRAB.   40099

-- North Carolina. Chowan Association.

Minutes of the North-Carolina Chowan Baptist Association; held at Potecasey meeting-house, Northampton County, May 10th, 11th, & 12th, 1817. Edenton, N. C., Pr. by James Wills, 1817. 14 p. NRAB. 40100

-- -- General Meeting.

The North-Carolina Baptist General Meeting of correspondence, convened according to appointment, at Grassy Creek meeting house, in Granville County, August 2, 1817. Raleigh, N. C., Pr. by J. Gales, 1817. 12 p. NRAB.   40101

-- -- Kohukee Association.

Minutes of the Kohukee Baptist Association, holden at the Falls of Tar River, Nash County, 1817. Raleigh, N. C., Pr. by T. Henderson, Jr., 1817. 12 p. NRAB.
40102

-- Ohio. East Fork of the Little Miami Association.

Minutes...holden at the Baptist meeting-house, on Ten Mile...on the 6th, 7th and 8th September, 1817. [Cincinnati, Williams and Mason, 1817] 4 p. NRAB.
40103

-- -- Miami Association.

Minutes...held at West Mill Creek...September 13th,

14th, 15th, 1817. [Cincinnati, Pr. by Williams & Mason, 1817] 4 p. OClWHi.   40104

-- -- Muskingum Association.
    Minutes...begun and held at Br. Joseph Denman's in Wayne Township, Knox Co., O.,...Aug. 21, 1817. Mount Vernon, O., at the office of the Ohio Register, by John P. M'Ardle [1817] 10 p. NRAB.   40105

-- -- Scioto Association.
    Minutes...at Pleasant Run meeting house Fairfield County (Ohio) on the 27th, 28th and 29th of Sept., 1817. Chillicothe, Pr. by John Bailhache, 1817. 8 p. OClWHi.   40106

-- Pennsylvania. Beaver Association.
    Minutes of the Beaver Baptist Association, held by appointment at Sharon, Mercer County, Pennsylvania, August 21st, 22d and 23d, 1817. 8 p. MoSM.   40107

-- -- Philadelphia Association.
    Minutes...October 7, 8, 9, 1817...[Philadelphia? 1817] MWA.   40108

-- Rhode Island. Warren Association.
    Constitution of the Education Society of the Warren Baptist Association; and circular letter to the ministers and churches on the importance of education to ministers of the Gospel. Boston, Pr. by James Loring, 1817. 8 p. MBC; MH; MWA; MiD-B; NRAB; OO; RPB.
                                                         40109
-- -- -- Minutes of the Warren Association, held at the First Baptist meeting-house in Boston, September 9 and 10, 1817. Boston, Pr. by James Loring, 1817. 15 p. CSmH; MH-AH; MWA; NRAB; RNHi.   40110

-- South Carolina. Broad River Association.
    Minutes of the Broad River Baptist Association convened at Mountain Sandy Run Meeting House, Rutherford County, North Carolina, October 18, 1816. Columbia, S.C., Pr. at the Telescope press, 1817. 5 p. NRAB.
                                                         40111

-- -- Charleston Association.
Minutes of the Charleston Baptist Association, convened at Hopewell, a branch of the Wateree-creek
church, on Saturday the 1st of November, 1817. 11 p.
NRAB.   40112

-- Tennessee.   Concord Association.
Minutes...August 2, 3, and 4, 1817...[Nashville,
Tenn., Pr. by Norvell & M'Lean, 1817] 8 p. MWA.
                                                     40113
-- -- Red River Association
Minutes of the Red River Baptist Association,
holden at Halfpone Meeting-House, in Robertson Coun-
ty, [Tenn.] on Saturday preceding second Lord's day in
August 1817.   Russellville, Ky., Pr. by George B.
Crutcher, 1817. 8 p. MoSM.   40114

-- U.S.
Proceedings of the General convention of the Baptist denomination in the United States, at their first
triennial meeting, held in Philadelphia, from the 7th to
the 14th of May, 1817: together with the third annual
report of the Baptist Board of Foreign Missions for the
United States.   Philadelphia, Pr. by Anderson & Meehan, by order of the convention, 1817.   180 p. DLC;
MH-AH; MeB; NRAB; OCHP.   40115

-- Vermont.   Barre Association.
Minutes of the Barre Association, holden at Wil-
liamstown, September 17 & 18, 1817; with their circular and corresponding letter.   Montpelier, Vt., Pr. by
E. P. Walton, 1817.   8 p. NRAB.   40116

-- -- Danville Association.
Articles of faith and practice; with the church cov-
enant, approved by the Danville Association, and
adopted by the churches.   Approved also by the Baptist
United Church at Guilford, Vt.   And recommended by
the publisher to other churches.   Brattleboro, Pr. by
Simeon Ide, for Jonathan Wilson, 1817. 8 p. MH-AH;
VtHi.   40117

-- -- -- Minutes of the Danville Association, holden at

Bethlehem, N. H. June 18th & 19th, 1817. Danville,
Pr. by Ebenezer Eaton, 1817. 8 p. NRAB.   40118

-- -- Fairfield Association.
    Minutes of the Fairfield Baptist Association, hold-
en at Georgia, August 27 and 28, A. D. 1817. Together with their circular and corresponding letter.
Burlington [Vt.] Pr. by Samuel Mills, 1817. 12 p.
NRAB.   40119

-- -- Shaftsbury Association.
    Minutes of the Shaftsbury Baptist Association,
held at Stephentown [N. Y.] the fourth and fifth of June,
1817. Together with their circular and corresponding
letters. Lansingburgh, N. Y., Pr. by Tracy & Bliss,
1817. 16 p. NRAB.   40120

-- -- Vermont Association.
    Minutes... October 1 & 2, 1817... Middlebury, Vt.,
Pr. by Frederick P. Allen, [1817] 11 p. MWA; NRAB.
                                               40121
-- -- Woodstock Association.
    Minutes... September 24 and 25, 1817. Windsor,
Vt., Pr. by A. & W. Spooner [1817] 12 p. MWA;
NRAB; VtHi.   40122

-- Virginia. Accomack Association.
    Minutes of the Accomack Baptist Association, held
at the Mesongo Baptist meeting-house, Accomack county, August 16th, 17th, and 18th, 1817. Norfolk, Va.,
Pr. by O'Connor & Broughton, 1817. 8 p. NRAB.40123

-- -- Dover Association.
    Minutes of the Dover Baptists Association held at
Upper King & Queen meeting-house in King and Queen
county, Virginia, October 11th, 12th, & 13th, 1817.
Richmond, Pr. by Ritchie, Trueheart & Du-Val, 1817.
14 p. DLC; NRAB; ViRU.   40124

-- -- General Association.
    Minutes of the Virginia Baptists General Meeting of
Correspondence, held at the Baptist Meeting House, in
the city of Richmond, June 7th, 8th, and 9th, 1817.

Richmond, Pr. by Ritchie, Trueheart & Du-Val, 1817.
8 p. NRAB; ViRU.   40125

-- -- Goshen Association.
Minutes of the Baptist association, in the district
of Goshen: held at Zion meeting-house, Orange county,
Virginia, beginning on the first Saturday in September,
1817. 12 p. NRAB; ViRU.   40126

-- -- Ketocton Association.
Minutes of the Ketocton Baptist Association held at
North-Fork meeting house Loudon County, Virginia, on
the 14th, 15th, 16th, and 17th days of August, 1817.
Winchester, Va., Pr. by J. Foster, for the Associa-
tion, 1817. 8 p. DLC; ViRU.   40127

-- -- Meherrin Association.
Minutes of the Meherrin Baptist Association, held
at Reedy Creek meeting house, Brunswick county, on
Saturday before the 4th Sunday in April, 1817. Peters-
burg, Va., Pr. by Lorrain & Dunnavant, 1817. 16 p.
NRAB; ViRU.   40128

-- -- Middle district association.
Minutes...October, 1817. Richmond, Va., Pr. by
Shepherd and Pollard, 1817. 8 p. MWA; NRAB. 40129

-- -- New River Association.
Minutes of two sessions, of the New River Associa-
tion, begun and held at Bartlett's meeting-house, in
Patrick County, Virginia on Saturday, the 8th day of
June, 1816. Richmond, Pr. by John Warrock, 1817.
8 p. NRAB.   40130

-- -- Portsmouth Association.
Minutes of the Virginia Portsmouth Baptists Association, held at Black Creek meeting house, Southamp-
ton County, May the twenty-fourth, twenty-fifth and
twenty-sixth, 1817. Richmond, Pr. by Shepherd &
Pollard, 1817. 11 p. NRAB.   40131

-- -- -- Minutes of two meetings of the Virginia Portsmouth Baptists Missionary Society, the one called and

held at Western Branch meeting house... April, 1817.
The other an annual meeting held at Black Creek meet-
ing house, on the 23 & 24, May, 1817. Richmond,
Pr. by Shepherd & Pollard [1817] 9 p. ViRU.   40132

-- -- Shiloh Association
    Minutes of the Shiloh Baptist Association, held at
Robinson River meeting-house, Madison County, September fifth and sixth, 1817. Fredericksburg, 1817.
12 p. NRAB; ViRU.   40133

-- -- Strawberry Association.
    Minutes of the Strawberry Baptist Associations.
Held at Liberty, County of Bedford, Oct. 23 & 24, 1816.
And at Webb's meeting house, Franklin county, May
24th, 25th & 26th, 1817. Lynchburg, Va., Pr. by
Haas & Bransford, 1817. 14 p. NRAB.   40134

-- -- Union Association.
    Minutes of the Union Baptist Association, held at
Coones Run meeting house, in Harrison County and
state of Virginia, August 29th, 30th & 31st, 1817.
[Clarksburg, Va., Pr. by G. Butler, 1817] 8 p.
NRAB.   40135

Barbauld, Mrs. Anna Letitia (Aikin)
    Hymns in prose for children... New Haven, Sidney's
press, 1817.   47 p. MB; MWA.   40136

Bard, Samuel
    A compendium of the theory and practice of mid-
wifery... Ed. 4.   New York, Collins and Co., 1817.
366 p. CtW; MWA; NNNAM; RPB.   40137

Barker, James Nelson
    How to try a lover; a comedy, in three acts...
New York, David Longworth, 1817. 67 p. DLC; MWA;
NNC; NjP; RPB.   40138

-- An oration, delivered at Philadelphia Vauxhall gar-
dens, on the forty-first anniversary of American independence... Philadelphia, Pr. by John Binns, 1817. 11 p.
DLC; MWA; NNS.   40139

Barlas, William
   A catalogue of scarce and valuable books, belonging to the estate of the late William Barlas, book-
seller...New York, 1817. 31 p. PPPrHi.   40140

Barrington, R. I., Congregational Church
   The articles of faith and the covenant of the Con-
gregational Church in Barrington, R. I.   Barrington,
R. I., 1817. 4 p. RHi.   40141

Barton, William Paul Crillon, 1786-1856
   A treatise containing a plan for the internal organization and government of marine hospitals, in the U-
nited States; together with observations on military and
flying hospitals and a scheme for amending and sys-
tematizing the Medical department of the navy...Ed. 2.
Philadelphia, Pr. for the author, 1817. 240 p. DLC;
KyLxT; MH; NNNAM; PPC; PPL; PU.   40142

-- Vegetable materia medica of the United States; or
Medical botany...Philadelphia, M. Carey & Son, 1817.
2 vols. CU-M; CtY-M; MB; MWA; NNC; NNNAM; PPC;
PU; ViRA; WaPS.   40143

Bascom, Ezekiel Lysander
   An address, delivered at Leicester, [Mass.] before
King Solomon's R. A. Chapter...Leicester, Mass., Pr.
by Hori Brown, 1817. MWA.   40144

Bates, Joshua
   Brief account of the happy death of Mary Ann Clap,
daughter of Mr. Jessie and Mrs. Betsey Clap, who
died July 15, 1816, in the eleventh year of her age;
...[Hartford, Pr. by Hudson & Co., for the Hartford
Evangelical Tract Society, 1817] 24 p. (Hartford Evan-
gelical Tract Society. Publications. no. 9a) CtHi.
                                               40145
-- A sermon, preached in Durham, at the ordination
of the Rev. Federal Burt...Dover, N. H., Pr. by John
Mann, 1817. 40 p. CSmH; CtY; MHi; MWA; NhU;
RPB.   40146

-- A sermon, preached, Feb. 26, 1817, at the ordina-

tion of the Rev. Rufus Hurlbut...Dedham, Mass., Pr.
by Abel D. Alleyne, 1817. 40 p. CSansS; CSt; CtSoP;
CtY; ICMe; MAnP; MB; MBAt; MH; MHa; MHi; MWA;
MiD-B; NjPT; RPB.   40147

Bates, Walter
    The mysterious stranger; or memoirs of Henry
More Smith; alias Henry Frederick Moon; alias William Newman; who is now confined in Simsbury Mines,
in Connecticut...New-Haven, Pr. by T. G. Woodward,
for Maltby, Goldsmith & Co., 1817. 108 p. Ct; CtHi;
DLC; ICU; MBAt; MH; MWA; NIC-L; NN; NNS.   40148

[Baudrand, Barthelemi, S. J.]
    The elevation of the soul to God, by means of
spiritual considerations and affections. Translated
from the French of the Abbe B. by R. P.   1st Amer.,
from the third London ed.   Philadelphia, Bernard Dornin, 1817.   364 p.   DGU; DLC; MdBLC; MdW; MoSU.
                                                    40149
Baxter, Richard, 1615-1691
    A call to the unconverted, to turn and live, and ac-
cept of mercy, while mercy may be had...Brookfield,
Mass., Pr. by E. Merriam & co., 1817. 262 p. CSt;
MBelc; MWA.   40150

-- The saints everlasting rest...New York, Pr. by
John C. Totten, for Joshua Soule and Thomas Mason,
for the Methodist Episcopal church in the United States,
1817.   312 p.   MWA; OClWHi; TxAbH; TxD-T.   40151

-- -- Philadelphia, Pr. by M'Carty and Davis, for
Jonathan Pounder, 1817.   310 p.   MWA; TxShA; ViU.
                                                    40152
[Baxter, Roger, S. J.]   1792-1827
    The Alexandria controversy: or A series of letters
between M. B. & Quaero, on the tenets of Catholicity,
which appeared in the Alexandria newspapers...George-
town, D. C., W. Duffy, 1817.   266 p.   CtW; DGU; DLC;
MH;   MWA; MdBLC; MdBS; MdW; PPL-R; ScU; ViU.
                                                    40153
Bayard, Lewis Pintand
    The trial of the spirits; a sermon delivered in...

Newark...at the institution of a church missionary society. New York, T. & J. Swords, Pr., 1817. 20 p.
MWA; N; NHi; NNG; NjN; NjPT. 40154

Bazman, J. L.
Sketches of the history of Maryland and three first years after its settlement. Baltimore, Coale, 1817.
KyLx. 40155

Bean, James
Christian minister's ...advice to a married couple.
New England Tract Society. No. 67. Andover, Mass.,
Flagg & Gould, 1817. MWA. 40156

Beauties of the New England primer. New York, S.
Wood & Sons, 1817. 29 p. MWA; RPB. 40157

Beaver Gazette. Beaver, Pa., A. Logan, Jan. 4,
1817, 1st issue with this title. A weekly continuation
of "The Crisis." MWA. 40158

Beck, John Brodhead
An inaugural dissertation on infanticide; submitted
to the examination of Samuel Bard, M.D., LL.D. President, and publickly defended , for the degree of Doctor of Medicine, on the 6th day of April, 1817...New
York, Pr. by J. Seymour, 1817. 95 p. DNLM; MBM;
MWA; N; NN; NNC; NNNAM; NjR; RNR. 40159

Becker, Christian Ludwig
Kurze entwurf der christlichen lehre...Dritte verbesserte auflage. Baltimore, Pr. by Schäffer &
Maund, 1817. 27 p. MWA; MdHi; PPLT. 40160

Beecher, Lyman
The Bible a code of laws. Andover, Mass., Flagg,
1817. 51 p. ICN. 40161

Beede, Thomas, d. 1848
The allegory of the olive tree, or The Abrahamic
covenant not disannulled. A discourse...Amherst
[N. H.] Pr. by R. Boylston, 1817. 27 p. CSmH;
CtSoP; MHi; MWA; NjPT. 40162

Beede, Thomas, d. 1840
A discourse delivered in Dublin, N.H., at the
consecration of Altemont lodge, and the installment of
its officers, September 18, 1816...Keene [N.H.] Pr.
by Brother John Prentiss, 1817. 16 p. CSmH; MBFM;
MWA; NAuT; NjPT.   40163

Beers, Andrew, 1749-1824
To the Episcopalians of Connecticut. [New Haven,
1817] Broadside. CtY.   40164

Beers' almanac for the year of our Lord, 1818...
Hartford, Pr. by George Goodwin & Sons [1817] [22] p.
MPiB; MWA; NCanHi; NN; WHi.   40165

Beers' almanack for 1818...New Haven, Steele & Gray,
[1817] [24] p. CtY; NHi.   40166

Beers' almanac for 1818. New Haven, T.G. Woodward, [1817] CtHi; MWA.   40167

Beer's calendar; or, Hosford's almanack, for the year
1818...Albany, E. & E. Hosford, 1817. 36 p. DLC;
MWA; NBLiHi; NHi; NN; N; NT; NWatt; NjR.   40168

Beers' Western calendar; or Southwick's almanack; for
...1818...By Andrew Beers. Auburn, N.Y., Pr. by
H.C. Southwick [1817] 36 p. NAuHi; NBuG; NBuHi;
PHi.   40169

Belfrage, Henry
Sacramental addresses and meditations...1st Amer.
ed. New York, Pr. by B.F. Lewis & Co., for James
Eastburn & Co., 1817. 360 p. MPiB; MWA; NbOP;
NjPT; PPiXT.   40170

Belknap, Jeremy
Sacred poetry consisting of psalms and hymns,
adapted to Christian devotion, in publick and private.
Selected from the best authors...A new edition; with additional hymns. Boston, Pr. by Lincoln & Edmands,
for Thomas Wells, 1817. 276 p. MB; MBC; MMeT;
MNoboroHi; MWA; MiU; MoSpD; NGH; NN; RPB. 40171

Bell, Benjamin
  A vindication of infant sprinkling...Oxford, N.Y.,
Pr. by Chauncey Morgan, 1817. 23 p. CtSoP; MWA.
                                                    40172
Bell, Sir Charles
  Engravings of the arteries, illustrating the second
volume of the anatomy of the human body, by J.
Bell; and serving as an introduction to the surgery of the
arteries. By Sir Charles Bell, and J. Bell. 1st Amer.
ed. Philadelphia, 1817. MBM.   40173

Bell, John, 1763-1820
  The anatomy and physiology of the human body...
3d Amer. ed. New York, Collins and Co., 1817. 3 v.
CtY; MWA; MoSW-M; NNNAM; TxU-M.   40174

-- Engravings of the bones, muscles and joints...1st
Amer. ed. from the 2d London ed. Philadelphia, Pr.
by William Fry, for Anthony Finley, 1816-17 [i.e.
1817-18] 2 v. DNLM; MBM; MdBJ-W; NNNAM;
PPiU-M.   40175

Bell, John, 1796-1872
  An inaugural dissertation on the liver: its influence
over the animal economy in health and disease...Phila-
delphia, Pr. by William Fry, for the author, 1817.
66 p. (Thesis - University of Pennsylvania) CtY-M;
DNLM; MBM; PPAmP; PPC.   40176

Bell, R.
  The veil withdrawn; or, Presbyterianism vindicated, and the character and intolerance of its enemies
exposed, in a letter to a rev'nd gentleman, by a minister of that church. Charleston, S.C., Office of the
Patriot, 1817. 38 p. NN.   40177

Bell, Shubail
  An account of the town of Boston written in 1817.
M.   40178

Benedict, David
  The history of baptism. Boston, Lincoln & Edmands, 1817. RHi.   40179

-- History of baptism. Boston, Lincoln & Gould,
1817. ODefC.   40180

-- The Pawtucket collection of conference hymns. Ed.
2, enl. Boston, Lincoln & Edmands, 1817. 124 p.
MB; RPB.   40181

The beneficial tendency of auctioneering and the danger
of restraining it. By a friend of trade. New York,
1817. 16 p. MB; N; NN.   40182

Benson, Egbert, 1746-1833
    Memoir, read before the Historical Society of the
state of New York, 31st December, 1816... New York,
Pr. by T. & W. Mercein, 1817. 72 p. CSmH; MB;
MBAt; NN; NNS; NjPT; NGlf; NSchU.   40183

[--] Vindication of the captors of Major André. New-
York, Pr. by T. & W. Mercein, for Kirk & Mercein,
1817. 99 p. DLC; KyU; MB; MWA; MeBa; NjR; ViU.
                                              40184
Benson, Joseph
    Sermons on various occasions... New York, Pr. by
A. Paul, for J. Soule and T. Mason... 1817. 434 p.
CtW; GEU-T; MWA; MnSH; TJaL; ViU.   40185

Bergen Express. Paterson, N.J., H. Jones, June,
1817, 1st issue. Weekly newspaper. NHi.   40186

Berkshire Bible Society
    A circular address, from the Berkshire Bible so-
ciety, with the constitution, list of officers, directors,
etc. Pittsfield, Mass., Pr. by Phineas Allen, 1817.
15 p. MPiB; MWiW.   40187

Berquin, Arnaud
    The history of Caroline: or, a lesson to cure van-
ity. New Haven, Sidney's press, 1817. [28] p. CtY;
PP.   40188

Berrian, Samuel
    An oration delivered at Tammany Hall, on the 31st
day of March, 1817... New-York, Pr. by E. Conrad,

1817.   20 p.   MiD-B; NN.   40189

[Bethune, Divie]
    Power of faith: exemplified in the life and writings
of the late Mrs. Isabella Graham.   Ed. 2.   New York,
Kirk & Mercein, 1817.   CtHC.   40190

Bertrand, Henri Gratien, 1773-1844
    Manuscript...from St. Helena.   New York, 1817.
MiD.   40191

Betty Brown, the St. Giles Orange girl...Philadelphia,
Pa., Pr. by D. Dickinson, for Benjamin Johnson,
1817.   24 p.   NjR.   40192

Bible
    A compendium of the religious doctrines, religious
and moral precepts, historical and descriptive beauties
of the Bible; with a separate moral selection from the
Apocrypha...Ed. 6.   By Rodolphus Dickinson...Deer-
field, Mass., Pr. by Newcomb & Wells, Pub. at the
compiler's office, 1817.   276 p.   ArCH; CSmH; CSt;
Ct; CtHT-W; DLC; IaHA; IaPeC; LNH; MBNHi; MH;
MHi; MWA; MiU-C; NN; NNQ; NNUT; NRivHi; NSyU;
OMC; VtBT; WEau; WHi.   40193

-- Stereotype ed.   The Holy Bible, containing the Old
and New Testaments...stereotype by B. & J. Collins
New York.   Albany, Pr. by Webster and Skinners,
1817.   792 p.   MWA; NIl; OHi.   40194

-- -- Boston, Pr. by W. Greenough, for Lincoln and
Edmands, and Collins & Co., New York, 1817.   DLC;
MB; MBev; MWA; MiD-B; NN; Nh.   40195

-- -- ...with original notes...by Thomas Scott...6th
Amer. (Armstrong's 2d) ed.   Boston, Samuel T. Arm-
strong, 1817-18.   6 v.   DLC; KWiU; MB; MCli; MMHHi;
MWA; NCaS; NWM.   40196

-- -- Holbrook's stereotype copy.   Ed. 4.   Brattleborough [Vt.] 1817.   930 p.   DLC.   40197

-- -- ...apocrypha...marginal notes and references...
Brown's concordance...embellish with plates. Collins
correct stereotype copy. Brattleborough, Vt., John
Holbrook, 1816. (2nd title page...Holy Bible...J.
Holbrook's stereotype copy. 9th ed. Brattleborough,
[Vt.] 1817) DLC; MWA.   40198

-- -- Hartford, Pr. by Hudson and co., 1817. 2 v. in
1. Ct; CtHi; CtY; MWA; NN.   40199

-- -- Stereotyped by D. & G. Bruce. New York, W.
E. Norman, 1817. 837 p. CSt; MWA; NN.   40200

-- -- Stereotyped for the American Bible Society by
D. & G. Bruce. New-York, 1817. 637-837 p. MWA.
                                                   40201
-- -- Stereotyped by E. & J. White. New York, The
American Bible Society, 1817. 1086 p. MWA; NN;
NSchHi.   40202

-- -- 2d Amer. ed. New York, Pr. by Abraham Paul,
for Daniel Hitt and Abraham Paul, 1817. GAGTh; ICN;
MWA.   40203

-- -- ...To which are added, an index. ...John
Brown's concordance...New York, Collins and co.,
1817. 988 p. CSmH; MnU; NN.   40204

-- -- ...marginal notes and references...Philadelphia,
M. Carey & Son...1817. 1080 p. CtHT; MWA;
PNazMHi; PP; WHi.   40205

-- -- ...marginal notes and references. An index; and
alphabetical table...John Brown's concordance... Trenton, N.J., D. & E. Fenton, 1817. 1152 p. MWA.
                                                   40206
-- The Holy Gospels of our Lord and Saviour Jesus
Christ, according to the four evangelists. Translated
out of the Latin Vulgate...Georgetown, D.C., Pr. by
W. Duffy, 1817. 234 p. MWA.   40207

-- Das kleine Davidische psalterspiel der kinder Zions,
von alten und neuen auserlesenen geistes gesangen...

Philadelphia, G. und D. Billmeyer, 1817. 594 p. MWA;
MiD-B; MiU-C.   40208

-- The New Testament of our Lord and Saviour Jesus
Christ, translated from the original Greek... 5th Amer.
(Armstrong's) ed.   Boston, Samuel T. Armstrong,
1817. 2 v. IaManc.   40209

-- -- 6th Amer. ed.   Boston, Samuel T. Armstrong,
1817. 2 v. MSherHi; MWeyHi; NCaS; WvH.   40210

-- -- Boston, Pr. by W. Greenough, for Lincoln and
Edmands... 1817. MWA; PLERC-Hi.   40211

-- -- Stereotype ed. Bridgeport, Conn., L. Lockwood,
1817. 240 p. CtB; DLC.   40212

-- -- Stereotyped by B. & J. Collins, New-York.
Bridgeport, Conn., L. Lockwood, 1817. 290 p. MWA.
                                                        40213
-- -- Cooperstown, N.Y., Pr. by H. & E. Phinney,
1817. MWA; N.   40214

-- -- ... Translated out of the Latin vulgate: diligently
compared with the original Greek: and first published
by the English college of Rhemes, anno. 1582...
Georgetown, D.C., Pr. by W. Duffy, 1817. 516 p.
DGU; DLC; MdBS; MWA; NN; NjR; PPL; ViRU.   40215

-- -- Hartford, Pr. by George Goodwin and sons, 1817.
330 p. NHem.   40216

-- -- The text carefully printed from the most correct
copies of the present authorized version... New York,
Abraham Paul, and Daniel Hitt, 1817-(1818) 2 v.
CtY-D.   40217

-- -- Stereotyped by E. & J. White. New-York, The
American Bible Society, 1817. 215 p. MWA.   40218

-- -- Wilmington, Del., Robert Porter, 1817. 276 p.
DeWI; NcC.   40219

-- El Nuevo Testamento de Nuestro Señor y Redentor
Jesu Christo. Nueva edicion. Cuidad osamente Cor-
regida. Año de 1817. 336 p. MWA.   40220

-- Psalms, carefully suited to the Christian worship in
the United States of America: being an improvement of
the old versions of the Psalms of David. ...A new ed.,
cor. New-York, Pr. by J. Seymour, for John Tiebout
and sons...1817. 596 p. MWA; N; PPPrHi.   40221

-- -- Philadelphia, Pr. by W. Hill Woodward, for
William W. Woodward, 1817. 389 p. DLC; MWA;
NNUT; PPPrHi.   40222

-- The Psalms of David, imitated in the language of
the New Testament, and applied to the Christian use
and worship. By I. Watts, D.D. A new ed. ...Ap-
proved and allowed by the General assembly of the
Presbyterian church in the United States of America.
Albany, Pr. by Websters and Skinners, 1817. 585 p.
Ct; DLC; ICN; ICP; MWA; NjR; RPB.   40223

-- -- Albany, Pr. by Packard & Van Benthuysen, for
Websters & Skinners, and Daniel Steele, 1817. 568 p.
MWA.   40224

-- -- ...At the request of the General association of
Connecticut...Hartford, George Goodwin and sons,
1817. 505 p. CtEhad; CtHi; DLC; MS; MWA; MeBaT;
NN; RPB.   40225

-- -- New ed. Hartford, Pr. by G. Goodwin & son,
for Silas Andrus and E. Peck & company, 1817. 505 p.
CtHi; MH; MWA; NN.   40226

-- The Psalms of David, imitated in the language of
the New Testament, and applied to the Christian state
and worship...Haverhill, [Mass.] Burrill and Tileston,
stereotyped by B. & J. Collins, 1817. 585 p. CLSU;
MB; MHa; MHaHi; MSaE; MWA.   40227

-- The Psalms of David, imitated in the language of
the New Testament, and applied to the Christian use

and worship... At the request of the General association of Connecticut... New-York, Pr. by J. Seymour,
for John L. Tiffany, 1817. 564 p. CSmH; DLC; LNT;
MWA; NN; NjMS.   40228

-- The whole book of Psalms, in metre; with hymns,
suited to the feasts and fasts of the church... Baltimore, Pr. by J. Robinson, for W. Warner, F. Lucas,
Jr. ... 1817. 192 p. DLC; MWA; MdBE; MdHi. 40229

-- -- Stereotype ed. New York, W. B. Gilley, 1817.
89 p. MWA.   40230

-- -- Stereotype ed. New York, W. B. Gilley, 1817.
242 p. DLC; MWA; MoInRC; NNG.   40231

-- -- Stereotyped by E. & J. White. New York, Pr.
by D. Fanshaw, for Robert & William A. Bartow, 1817.
105 p. MWA; N; OC; TxU.   40232

Bible Society in the County of Middlesex, Mass.
    First [second] report. Cambridge, Mass., Hilliard
& Metcalf, 1816-17. 2 v. MEab; MWiW; MiD-B.40233

Bible Society of Baltimore
    Report of the Board of managers of the Bible So-
ciety of Baltimore, presented at the seventh annual
meeting of the society, September 25, 1817. Baltimore, Pr. by Schaeffer & Maund [1817] 11 p. MdBE;
MdHi.   40234

-- The sixth annual report of the Bible society of Balti-
more. Presented at the anniversary meeting held in
the first Presbyterian Church, on the fourth Monday in
September, 1816. Baltimore, Pr. by Schaeffer &
Maund, by order of the society, 1817. 14 p. MWA;
MdHi; PPAmP.   40235

Bible Society of Delaware
    The second report of the Bible society of Delaware.
Wilmington, Del., Pr. by R. Porter, by order of the
society, 1817. 8 p. DeHi.   40236

Bible society of Massachusetts
Report of the executive committee of the Bible society of Massachusetts... Boston, Pr. by John Eliot...
1817. 15 p. ICT; MHi; MWA; MiD-B.   40237

Bible society of Rensselaer county, N. Y.
The second report... [Troy, N. Y.] Pr. by Francis
Adancourt, 1817. MWA.   40238

Bible society of Salem and vicinity, Mass.
Sixth report of the Bible society of Salem and vicinity, June 11, 1817. [5] p. MSaE.   40239

Bible society of Saratoga county, N. Y.
Extracts from the minutes... January 8th, 1817.
Ballston Spa, N. Y., Pr. by J. Comstock, 1817. MWA.
                                             40240
Bible society of the county of Middlesex, N. J.
Constitution... New Brunswick, N. J., Pr. by Deare
& Myer, [1817] MWA.   40241

Bickerstaffe, Isaac, d. 1812?
Love in a village. A comic opera... New York,
David Longworth, 1817. DLC; MH; MWA; NN; RPB.
                                             40242
-- The maid of the mill. A comic opera, in three
acts... New York, D. Longworth, 1817. 80 p. CSt;
DLC; MWA; NjR; RNR.   40243

Bickersteth, Edward
A scripture help, designed to assist in reading the
Bible profitably... Boston, Pr. by Monroe & Francis,
for S. H. Parker at the Union Circulating Library, 1817.
224 p. DLC; IAlS; MB; MBAt; MH; MMeT; MWA; NGH;
OC; OWoC.   40244

Biddle, Owen
The young carpenter's assistant... Philadelphia, Pr.
by William Dickson, for Benjamin Warner, 1817. 61 p.
MWA.   40245

Bigelow, Jacob, 1767-1879
An abstract... [New York, 1817] MH.   40246

-- American medical botany, being a collection of the native medicinal plants of the United States, containing their botanical history and chemical analysis, and properties and uses in medicine, diet and the arts... Boston, Cummings & Hilliard [etc.] 1817-1820. 3 v. CSfA; CSmH; CSt; CtHT; DLC; FU; ICF; ICJ; IEN-M; IaDaM; In; InNd; KyLxT; LNT-M; MB; MBAt; MBC; MBM; MH-M; MSaP; MWA; MWiW; MWCH; MdBM; MdBP; MeBat; MiU; MnS; NBLiHi; NBMS; NNA; NN; NNNAM; NNS; NRU; NcAS; NcD; NcU; Nh; NjP; OC; OO; OkU; PPA; PPAmP; PPC; PPF; PPL-R; PU; RPB; RPM; ScCMu; ScU; TNV; ViRMC; ViU; VtU; WU. 40247

-- Inaugural address, delivered in the Chapel of the University at Cambridge, December 11, 1816... Rumford professor in Harvard University. Boston, Pr. by Wells & Lilly, 1817. 24 p. DLC; DNLM; MBAt; MBC; MBM; MH-M; MHi; MSaE; MWA; MdBJ-W; MeHi; NBMS; NN; NjPT; P; PPAmP; PPL; RPB. 40248

-- A poem on professional life. Boston, 1817. 15 p. DNLM. 40249

Bingham, Caleb, 1757-1817
    The American preceptor... 10th New York ed. New York, Pr. by John C. Totten, for Evert Duyckinck, 1817. 228 p. DLC; MWA; MWiW; MdW; N; NN; NNC-T. 40250

-- The Columbian orator... Stereotype ed. Boston, Caleb Bingham and co., 1817. 300 p. CU; Ct; CtNl; CtSoP; CtY; DLC; KU; MB; MBAt; MBilHi; MH; MSaE; MStoc; MWA; MWo; MiD-B; MiU; NMto; NNUW; NRU; NSmB; NjPT; NjR; OClWHi; PPiU; RPB; TNP; TxU. 40251

Bingham, Thomas
    The sufficiency of the Holy Scriptures in the memoir of William Churchman, a poor cripple... Philadelphia, Religious tract society, 1817. 12 p. NjR. 40252

Binns, John
    Observations on the preface to, and report of, the trial of Edward Lyon, for subornation of perjury...

Philadelphia, Pr. at the office of the "Democratic
Press," 1817. DLC; MWA.   40253

Bioren's Pennsylvania pocket remembrancer, for 1818.
Philadelphia, John Bioren [1817] MWA.   40254

Bioren's town and country almanack, for the year of
our Lord 1818... Calculated by William Collom. Philadelphia, John Bioren, [1817] 48 p. MB; NCH; NjR;
PU.   40255

Birkbeck, Morris, 1764-1825
    Extracts from a supplementary letter... New York,
Wiley, 1817. DLC; MH; LNH.   40256

-- Notes on a journey in America, from the coast of
Virginia to the territory of Illinois. With proposals for
the establishment of a colony of English... Philadelphia,
Pr. by J.R.A. Skerrett, for Caleb Richardson, 1817.
189 p. DLC; GHi; MWA; MiU; NcWfC.   40257

Bishop, Sir Henry Rowley
    The slave; a musical drama in three acts. The
music by Mr. Bishop. New York, D. Longworth, 1817.
MB; MH; OS.   40258

Bisse, Thomas
    The beauty of Holiness in the Common prayer, as
set forth in four sermons, preached at the Rolls Chapel
in 1816... Baltimore, Smith & Colman, 1817. 101 p.
MdBD.   40259

Blackbeard, or the captive princess. A present for the
New-Year - 1817-. [1817?] MB; MWA; RPB.   40260

Blair, Hugh
    An abridgment of lectures on rhetoric. Haverhill,
Pr. by P.N. Green, for P.N. Green & Thomas Carey,
1817. 287 p. DGU; MB; MH; MHa; MHans; MNe; MWA;
MoSU; TxU-T.   40261

-- Advice to youth... Philadelphia, Benjamin Warner,
1817. 180 p. MWA.   40262

-- Lectures on rhetoric and belles letters. New York, Duyckinck, 1817. 466 p. DLC; MH; N; PPins.   40263

-- -- 7th Amer., from the last Edinburgh ed. New York, Pr. by G. Long, for Evert Duyckinck, 1817. 500 p. CtY; InUpT; MWA; N; NNUT; OCL; OO.   40264

-- -- 7th Amer., from the last Edinburgh ed. New-York, George Long, 1817. 500 p. MWA; NcD; NGoS; NNC; NdWah; OUrC; PU; VtMiS.   40265

-- -- 7th Amer., from the last Edinburgh ed. New York, Pr. by G. Long, for S. A. Burtus, 1817. 500 p. LU; MWA; MnHi; NElmC.   40266

Blair, Robert
    The grave, a poem. Brattleborough, Vt., Simeon Ide, 1817. (No known copies. Adv. in American Yeoman, April 15, 1817)   40267

-- -- Concord, N. H., Pr. by Isaac Hill, 1817. MWA.   40268
-- -- Pittsburgh, Pa., Butler & Lambdin, 1817. 31 p. PPiHi.   40269

Blanchard, Stephen
    A letter addressed to Ethan Smith... Concord, N. H., Pr. by Isaac Hill, 1817. MWA.   40270

Blatchford, Samuel, 1767-1828
    A sermon, delivered at the ordination of the Rev. Benjamin Franklin Stanton, in the city of Hudson, January 9, 1817... Hudson [N. Y.] Pr. by William L. Stone and Richard Corss, 1817. 31 p. CSmH; DLC; MB; NN; NcWfC.   40271

Blatchford, Thomas Windeatt
    An inaugural dissertation on feigned diseases... New York, Pr. by Forbes & Co., 1817. 76 p. CSansS; DLC; MBM; MH; MWA; MWiW; NN; NNNAM.   40272

Blatchley, C. C.
    Some causes of popular   poverty... [Philadelphia?

Eastwick & Stacy?, 1817] MWA.   40273

[Blocquerst, A. J.]
    Bureau de L'Abeille Américaine. [Philadelphia,
1817] MWA.   40274

Blumenbach, Johann Friedrich
    The institutions of physiology...Ed. 2. Philadel-
phia, Benjamin Warner, 1817. 426 p. KyLxT; MB;
MWA; NNNAM; PCC; PPAmP; PU; RPM.   40275

Blunt, Edmund March, 1770-1862
    The American coast pilot, containing the courses
and distances between the principal harbours, capes,
and headlands, from Passamaquoddy, through the Gulf
of Florida...Ed. 9. New-York, E. M. Blunt, 1817.
412 p. CtSoP; CtW; DLC; MNBedfHi; MSaP; MWA;
MsU; NN.   40276

-- Blunt's edition of the tariff, or rates of duty, with
the manner of transacting business at the custom-
house, including the act for regulating imposts and
tonnage, passed January 14, 1817. New York, Pr. at
the Quadrant [1817] 21 p. NCH.   40277

Blunt's stranger's guide to the city of New-York...To
which is prefixed, an historical sketch, general description, plan and extent of the city...New-York,
Edmund M. Blunt, 1817. 306 p. CtY; DLC; MHi; MW;
MiU-C; NNA; NNMer; NNS; RNR.   40278

Bodman, Manoah
    An oration on death...Williamsburgh, Mass., Pr.
by Ephraim Whitman, 1817. 300 p. CtH; DLC; MBelc;
MHad; MPiB; MWA; MnU; NNUT; NR; RPB.   40279

Boileau, Nathaniel B., 1762?-1850
    A private circular by the corresponding committee of
Montgomery County, appointed by the Harrisburg convention, to promote the election of William Findlay for
governor. A reply by N. B. Boileau, together with the
correspondence with the said committee...[Harrisburg,
1817] 16 p. DLC; PU.   40280

Bombastes Furioso: a tragic burlesque opera, in one
act. New York, David Longworth, 1817. 15 p. MB;
MH; OS.   40281

Bonaparte & Moreau. Baltimore, 1817. 19 p. MdBLC.
                                                    40282
Booth, Abraham
     The deity of Jesus Christ essential to the Chris-
tian religion: a treatise on the divinity of our Lord
Jesus Christ. A new ed. Charlestown, Mass., 1817.
290 p. MHi; MWA.   40283

[Bordelon, Laurent]
     The management of the tongue... Ed. 3. Boston,
Pr. by H. & W.H. Mann, for Isaiah Thomas, Jun.,
1817. MWA.   40284

Boston (City)
     Abstract of the bill of mortality for the town of
Boston, from the 31st December, 1815 to the 1st of
January, 1817. [Boston, 1817] Broadside. MH. 40285

-- ...An abstract of the by-laws of the town of Boston
and of the laws of the commonwealth enacted for the
special regulation of the town...[Boston,] 1817. 8 p.
DLC; MiD-B.   40286

-- Quarantine regulations...[Boston, 1817]   40287

Boston association of booksellers.
     Rules and regulations...[Boston, Pr. by Lincoln &
Edmunds [1817] MB; MWA.   40288

Boston dispensary.
     Institution of the Boston dispensary, for the medi-
cal relief of the poor. Incorporated 1801. Boston, Pr.
by J.T. Buckingham, 1817. 24 p. CtY-M; DLC;
DNLM; MBM; MWA; NHi.   40289

Boston Female Sabbath school society.
     Constitution of the Female Sabbath school society
of the Second Baptist church and congregation, in Boston. Boston, Farnham & Badger, 1817. 16 p. MB;

NNUT. 40290

Boston library society.
     Catalogue, no. 2, of books in the Boston library
...[Boston, 1817] MWA.   40291

Boston medical association.
     Rules and regulations... Boston, Pr. by John Eliot,
1817. 8 p. MWA.   40292

Boston Society for the Moral and Religious Instruction
of The Poor.
     Report of the Boston Society for the Moral and
Religious Instruction of the Poor. Presented at the
annual meeting, October 8, 1817. [1817?] 8 p. MB.
                                                    40293
Boston. Tabernacle Warren Avenue Baptist church.
Female Sabbath school society.
     Constitution... Boston, Pr. by Farnham & Badger,
1817. MWA.   40294

Bouilly, Jean Nicolas, 1763-1842
     Deaf and dumb: or, The orphan protected. An his-
torical drama, in five acts. Taken from the French
of M. Bouilly... New-York, D. Longworth, 1817. 67 p.
CtHT; DLC; MB; MH; MWA; MoKU.   40295

Bowditch, Nathaniel, 1773-1838
     The new American practical navigator; being an
epitome of navigation; containing all the tables necessary to be used with the nautical almanac, in determin-
ing the latitude; and the longitude by lunar observations;
and keeping a complete reckoning at sea... the whole
exemplified in a journal, kept from Boston to Madeira
... 1st stereotype (4th) ed. New York, E.M. Blunt,
1817. 597 p.   DLC; MBAt; MNBedf; MSaE;
MSaP; MWA; NN; OLima; PPL.   40296

Bowdoin College
     Catalogue of the officers and students of Bowdoin
College, Brunswick, October, 1817... Hallowell, Me.,
Pr. by E. Goodale, 1817. Broadside. MeB.   40297

-- Laws of Bowdoin College. Hallowell, Me., Pr. by
E. Goodale, 1817. 29 p. MeHi; MiD-B; NjR.   40298

-- Order of exercises for commencement, Sept. 8,
1817. Hallowell, Me., Pr. by Ezekiel Goodale, 1817.
4 p. MWA.   40299

[Bowman, Peter]
    Ein Zeugniss von der Taufe...Harrisonburg, Va.,
Pr. by Laurentz Wartmann, 1817. 98 p. MWA; PLDL.
                                              40300
Brackenridge, Henry Marie, 1786-1871
    An argument before the chancellor of Maryland, in
July 1816, on the extent of the chancellor's powers.
Baltimore, The author, 1817. 40 p. PHi; PPAmP.
                                              40301
-- History of the late war, between the United States
and Great-Britain, containing a minute account of the
various military and naval operations.   1st ed. Baltimore, 1817. (Amer. Art - Anderson (Dahlinger), January 1938, Cat. 4367, No. 60)   40302

-- -- Ed. 2, rev. and cor. Baltimore, J. Cushing,
1817. 363 p. CtU; DLC; IC; IaOskW; MB; MdBE;
MdBP; MWA; RHi.   40303

-- -- Ed. 3, rev. and cor. Baltimore, Cushing &
Jewett, 1817. 360 p. DLC; IC; MB; MdBE; MiU; NjR;
OClWHi; OFH; TNP; ViU.   40304

-- -- Ed. 4, rev. and cor. Baltimore, J. Cushing,
1817. 348 p. Mi.   40305

[--] South America; a letter on the present state of that
country, to James Monroe, president of the United
States.   By an American...Washington, Pr. and pub.at
the office of the National register...Oct. 15, 1817. 52 p.
DLC; MiGr.   40306

-- Views of Louisiana; containing geographical, statistical and historical notices of that vast and important
portion of America. Baltimore, Pr. by Schaeffer &
Maund [1817] 323 p. CtHT-W; DLC; IGK; M; MH; MWA;

MdBE; MdBP; MdHi; MiD; NN; NWM; OFH; RNR;
ViW.   40307

Bradford, Gamaliel
    No. XI. The seaman's friend. Published by
"The Boston Society for the Religious and Moral Improvement of seamen. " Boston, Pr. by John Eliot,
1817. 24 p. DLC.   40308

Bradford, John Melancthon, 1781-1826
    The word of life: a light held forth by the Bible
societies. A sermon, delivered in the new Presbyterian church in Chapel-street, Albany, ninth February,
1817... Albany, Pr. by Websters and Skinners, 1817.
48 p. CSmH; DLC; InID; MB; MBAt; MSaE; MWA;
MWiW; NA1; NIC; NjR.   40309

Bradford's Tennessee almanac for 1818.   Nashville,
T. G. Bradford, 1817. Advertised in the Clarion and
Tennessee State Gazette, Aug. 26, 1817.   40310

Braman, Isaac
    A sermon, preached at a parochial fast, in... Row-
ley, July 17, 1817... Haverhill, Mass., Pr. by Burrill
& Tileston, 1817. 16 p. MSaE; MWA; MeBat; NN.
                                             40311

[Branagan, Thomas] b. 1774
    A glimpse of the beauties of eternal truth... Phila-
delphia, Pr. and pub. for the author, 1817. MWA.
                                             40312

[--] The pleasures of contemplation, being a desultory
investigation of the harmonies, beauties, and benefits
of nature... Philadelphia, Eastwick & Stacy, 1817. 240
p. DLC; MH; MWA; RPB.   40313

Brera, Valeriano Luigi, 1772-1840
    A treatise on verminous diseases, preceded by the
natural history of intestinal worms, and their origin in
the human body... Boston, Cummings and Hilliard;
Cambridge, Hilliard and Metcalf, 1817. 367 p. CSt-L;
CtY; DA; DLC; GU-M; ICJ; InI; KyLxT; MB; MBM; MH-
M; MWA; MWiW; MdUM; MoSMed; NBMS; NNNAM; Nh;
OCGHM; OClM; ViU.   40314

Brewer, Lucy
    The female mariner or adventures of Miss Lucy
Brewer. Ed. 5. Boston, 1817. 90 p. MWA.   40315

Brice, James F.
    A familiar explanation of the laws of wills and
codicils, and of the laws of executors and administra-
tors... Annapolis, Pr. by Jonas Green, 1817. 152 p.
DLC; Md; MdBP; MdHi; MdBD; MdBE; MH-L; PPM.
                                                40316
A brief evangelical catechism, in three parts. New
York, Swords, 1817. 23 p. MH-AH.   40317

Brief remarks on the importance and practicability of
instituting a general theological seminary. By a member of the Protestant Episcopal Church. New York,
Clayton & Kingsland, 1817. 10 p. InID; MWA.   40318

Briggs, Isaac
    An address delivered before the Oneida Society for
the Promotion of American Manufactures, in their annual meeting in Whitesboro' on the 21st of October,
1817. Utica, N. Y., Pr. by William Williams, 1817.
8 p. DLC; MH; MdHi; NN.   40319

Bristol county, Mass.
    Rules and regulations of the bar... Taunton, Mass.,
Pr. by A. Danforth, 1817. MWA.   40320

British and foreign school society.
    Manual of the system of teaching reading, writing,
arithmetic, and needle-work, in the elementary schools
of the British and foreign school society. 1st Amer.
ed. Philadelphia, Pr. by B. Warner, for the Philadelphia society for the establishment and support of
charity schools, 1817. 90 p. DLC.   40321

British charitable society, Boston, Mass.
    The first annual report... Cambridge, Mass., Pr.
by Hilliard & Metcalf, 1817. MWA; WHi.   40322

Bronson, J.
    The domestic manufacturer's assistant, and family

directory, in the arts of weaving and dyeing...Utica,
Pr. by W. Williams, 1817, 204 p. CSmH; CtY; DLC;
LNH; MWA; N; NGH; NNS; PPPM; RP.   40323

Brooks, John
    Who is the hero of Saratoga...General Dearborn
or Brooks? Boston [1817] Broadside. MB.   40324

Broughton, John Cam Hobhouse, baron.
    A journey through Albania, and other provinces of
Turkey in Europe and Asia, to Constantinople, during
the years 1809 and 1810...Philadelphia, M. Carey &
Son, 1817. 3 v. ICMe; MMal; MWA; MdW; Ms; P.
                                                40325
[Brown, Bartholomew] compiler.
    Templi carmina. Songs of the temple, or, Bridge-
water collection of sacred music. Ed. 5, improved
and enlarged. Boston, West & Richardson, 1817. MH.
                                                40326
Brown, Erastus
    The trial of Cain, the first murderer, in poetry,
by rule of court. In which a Predestinarian, a Uni-
versalian, and an Arminian, argue as attornies at the
bar, the two former as the prisoner's counsel, the
latter as attorney general. Auburn, N.Y., Pr. for the
pedlars, 1817. 36 p. MH.   40327

-- -- Auburn, N.Y., A. Curtis, 1817? RPB.   40328

Brown, John
    A brief concordance to the Holy scriptures...
Hallowell, Me., E. Goodale, 1817. 286 p. MB;
MPeHi; MWA; MeHi.   40329

Brown, John, 1722-1787
    An essay towards an easy, plain, practical, and
extensive explication of the assembly's shorter catechism...From the latest Edinburgh ed. Pittsburgh,
Pa., Pr. by Butler & Lambdin, for Robert Patterson,
1817. 361 p. CtY; GDC; KyLx; MH-AH; MWA; OClWHi;
PPiHi.   40330

-- The mode and subjects of Christian baptism...

Cazenovia, N. Y. , Pr. by Oran E. Baker, 1817. 148 p.
MWA; NN; NRAB; NjPT.   40331

-- A short catechism, for young children... Morris-
town, N. J. , H. P. Russell, 1817. 24 p. NNG.   40332

-- Two short catechisms... Geneva, N. Y. , James Bogert, 1817. 72 p. N.   40333

Brown, Samuel R.
    The Western gazetteer; or, Emigrant's directory,
containing a geographical description of the western
states and territories, viz. The states of Kentucky, In-
diana, Louisiana, Ohio, Tennessee and Mississippi;
and the territories of Illinois, Missouri, Alabama,
Michigan, and North-Western... Auburn, N. Y. , H. C.
Southwick, 1817. 360 p. CSmH; CtHT-W; CtY; DLC;
DeGE; ICN; IHi; InU; MB; MBL; MBr; MWA; MoS;
NAuT; NBuG; NIC; NN; NNC; NRU; NjR; OClWHi; OCHP;
PPiU; TKL; WHi.   40334

Brown, Solyman
    An essay on American poetry, with several mis-
cellaneous pieces, sentimental, descriptive, moral and
patriotic... New Haven, Hezekiah Howe, 1817. 191 p.
Sabin 8559.   40335

[Brown, Thomas] 1778-1820
    The bower of spring, with other poems... Philadel-
phia, M. Thomas, 1817. 107 p. CU; ICU.   40336

[--] The paradise of coquettes. A poem, in nine
parts. 2d Amer. ed. Philadelphia, Abraham Small &
James Kennedy and son, Alexandria [Va. ?] 1817. 207 p.
DLC; ICU; MdBP.   40337

Brown, Thomas, of Troy.
    The ethereal physician: or, Medical electricity re-
vived... Albany, Pr. by G. J. Loomis & Co. , for the
author, 1817. 74 p. CtY; DLC; MA; MWA; NNNAM;
PP.   40338

-- Medical electricity, recommended as a remedy for

many diseases...Albany, E. & E. Hosford, 1817.
Broadside. DLC.   40339

Brown University
    Catalogue of the books in the library of the Phil-
ermenian society...Providence, Pr. by Miller and
Hutchens, 1817. MWA; RPB.   40340

-- Order of exercises and theses for commencement
...Sept. 3d, 1817. Providence, Pr. by William G.
Goddard, 1817. RPB.   40341

Bryant, William Cullen, 1794-1878
    Thanatopsis. Boston, Cummings and Hilliard,
1817. (Appeared in The North American Review and
Miscellaneous Journal. Vol. fifth. Boston, 1817.)
CSmH.   40342

Bunyan, John, 1628-1688
    The holy war, made by Shaddai upon Diabolus, for
the regaining of metropolis of the world...Boston, Pr.
by H. & W. Mann, for Isaiah Thomas, Jun., 1817.
290 p. DLC; IaGG; MAub; MH; MHi; MMeT-Hi;
MPeHi; MWA; OO.   40343

-- The pilgrim's progress...Boston, Pr. by E. Merriam & Co., for Isaiah Thomas, Jun., 1817. 300 p.
DGU; ICN; MWA; NN; NjP.   40344

-- -- Hallowell [Me.] N. Cheever, 1817. 346 p. DLC;
ICP; KyLxT; MBNMHi; MWA; NN.   40345

-- -- Philadelphia, Pr. by Griggs & Co., for David
Hogan, 1817. MWA.   40346

-- -- Philadelphia, Pr. by Griggs & Co., for Jonathan
Pounder and William W. Woodward, 1817. 328 p.
InFtwL; MWA.   40347

[Burder, George]
    Early piety...New York, T. & J. Swords, 1817.
MWA.   40348

[--] A new heart the child's best portion...[Philadel-
phia, Pr. by Lydia R. Bailey, 1817] (This is no. 28
of the Tracts of the Philadelphia female tract society)
MWA.   40349

[Burges, Bartholomew]
    A series of Indostan letters...New York, 1817.
147 p. In; MWA.   40350

Burk, John Daley
    Bunker-Hill; or, The death of General Warren: an
historic tragedy, in five acts. By J. Burk. New
York, D. Longworth, 1817. 44 p. MHi; MWA; NIC;
NjR; RPB; ViU.   40351

Burkitt, William
    Poor man's help, and young man's guide...Ed. 33.
Newburgh, N.Y., B.F. Lewis, 1817. 211 p. MWA; P.
                                                    40352
Burlingham, Marian Ann
    The mother-in-law, or memoirs of Madam De
Morville...Now first published. Boston, Pr. by Mun-
roe & Francis, for Cummings and Hillard, 1817. 190 p.
MB; MH; MWA; NCaS.   40353

Burney, Sarah Harriet, 1770?-1844
    Geraldine Fauconberg. Philadelphia, M. Carey &
son and Wells & Lilly, Boston, 1817. 2 v. PU. 40354

Burns, John, 1775-1850
    The principles of midwifery; including the diseases
of women and children...4th Amer., from 3d London
ed., greatly enl. Philadelphia, Pr. by J.R.A. Skerrett, for Benjamin Warner, Edward & Richard Parker
...1817. 2 v. DLC; MdBM; NNNAM.   40355

-- -- 4th Amer., from 3d London ed., greatly enl.
With improvements and notes, by Thomas C. James...
Philadelphia, Pr. by J.R.A. Skerrett, for Edward &
Richard Parker, 1817. 2 v. CLM; CU-M; CtY-M;
DNLM; ICJ; IEN-M; LNT-M; MBM; NNNAM; OClM;
PPC; PU.   40356

Burroughs, Charles, 1787-1868
    A sermon. Delivered at the institution of the
Rev. G.W. Olney, in the Protestant Episcopal church,
in Gardiner, Maine, Wednesday, November 19th,
1817... Hallowell, Me., Pr. by E. Goodale, 1817. 21
p. CSmH; MWA; Me; NjPT.   40357

Burroughs, Jeremiah
    The causes, evils, and cures of heart and church
divisions. Extracted from the works of Mr. Jeremiah
Burrough's and Mr. Richard Baxter... New York, Pr.
by J. C. Totten, for J. Soule and T. Mason, for the
Methodist Episcopal Church in the United States, 1817.
268 p. MBNMHi; MWA; NN; NcAS.   40358

Butler, Frederick, 1766?-1843
    A catechetical compend of general history, sacred
and profane; from the creation of the world, to the
year 1817, of the Christian era... Hartford, Pr. by P.
B. Gleason and Co., for Cooke & Hale, 1817. 212 p.
Ct; CtHi; CtHT-W; CtMW; CtY; DLC; ICU; IaHi; MH;
MWA; PIndt; PScrHi; TxU-T.   40359

Butler, John
    A sermon delivered April 28, 1817, before the as-
sociation for the suppression of intemperance, and the
promotion of morality in the town of Hanover, Massachusetts. Boston, Lincoln & Edmands, 1817. 16 p.
MHi; MWA.   40360

By-laws of encampment No. 1, held at Philadelphia.
Philadelphia, Pr. by S. Roberts, for Robert De Silver,
1817. 12 p. PPFM.   40361

Byron, George Gordon Noël Byron
    Childe Harold's pilgrimage. Canto the third...
Boston, Munroe & Francis, 1817. 72 p. MB; MSaE;
MWA.   40362

-- -- Boston, Munroe & Francis, 1817. 108 p. MWA.
                    40363
-- -- New York, Kirk, 1817. 2 v. (3 & 4) InThR.
                    40364

-- English bards and Scotch reviewers... a satire.
From the last London ed. New-York, A. T. Goodrich,
1817. 54 p. MH. 40365

-- The lament of Tasso. By Lord Byron. New-York,
Van Winkle & Wiley, 1817. 23 p. ("Unknown to Cole-
ridge. Probably 1st Amer. ed." Mathews cat.)
CSmH; MH; MWA; MdBJ. 40366

-- Manfred, a dramatic poem... (From the 1st London
ed. of June, 1817) New-York, D. Longworth, 1817.
70 p. DLC; MB; MH; MWA; NCH; NN. 40367

-- -- (From the 1st London ed. of June 1817) New-
York, D. Longworth, 1812 [i.e., 1817] 70 p. MH;
MWiW. 40368

-- -- New York, Van Winkle & Wiley, 1817. 70 p.
CtY; MWA. 40369

-- -- Philadelphia, M. Thomas, 1817. 72 p. MH.
40370
-- Pilgrimage to the Holy Land. Philadelphia, J. Maxwell, 1817. MWA. 40371

-- Poems. New York, Pr. by T. & W. Mercein, for
Thomas Kirk & Thomas R. Mercein... 1817. 143 p.
AzPh; DLC; DeGE; InFtwL; MB; MPem; MWA; MiD-B;
MsHaH; N; NPlaK; PPL-R; PHi. 40372

-- The prisoners of Chillon... Boston, Munroe & Francis, 1817. 36 p. MBC; MWA. 40373

C

C., R. C.
    The trial of episcopacy... Poughkeepsie, N. Y., Pr.
by P. & S. Potter, for P. Potter, 1817. MWA. 40374

The Cabin-boy and forecastle sailor's delight , being
Tim Magpie the Yankee's own native notions... A collection of choice songs, recommended by amateurs of the
highest commendation... New-York, Pr. by John Hard-

castle... 1817.   34 p.   MWA.   40375

The cabinet of nature, for the year; containing curious
particulars characteristic of each month.   Intended to
direct young people to the innocent and agreeable em-
ployment of observing nature... New York, Wood &
sons, 1817.   48 p.   MWA; RPB.   40376

-- New York, Samuel Wood & Sons, 1817. Varied covers.
MWA; RPB.   40377

Caesar, Caius Julius
    C. Julii Caesaris, quae extant, Interpretation et
Notis illustravit Johannes Godvinus... Ed. 2.   Philadel-
phia, Pr. by Griggs & Co., for M. Carey & Son;
Benjamin Warner... 1817.   410 p.   LNL; MWA; MdW;
NjP; P.   40378

Calcott, Wellins
    Calcott's masonry... Philadelphia, Pr. by J. Max-
well, for Robert Desilver, 1817.   208 p.   MWA; NUtHi;
PPFM.   40379

Caldwell, Joseph
    Sermon, Raleigh, November 10, 1816.   Raleigh,
N.C., 1817.   MBAt.   40380

Calhoun, John C.
    Speech of the Honorable John C. Calhoun, in the
House of Representatives, February 4th, 1817.   7 p.
MeHi; NN; NcD.   40381

Calvin, Jean
    A selection of the most celebrated sermons of
John Calvin... (never before published in the United
States) To which is prefixed a biographical history of
his life.   Philadelphia, Thomas Cowperthwait & Co.,
1817.   204 p.   KTW; WBeaHi.   40382

[Camden, William]
    Graecae grammaticae Westmonasteriensis instutio
compendiaria; J. Ross acc. Ed. 2.   Philadelphia,
1817.   MBAt.   40383

[Cameron, Mrs. Lucy Lyttleton (Butt)]
...The two lambs...[Hartford, Pr. by Hudson &
Co., 1817] MWA.   40384

[--] -- 2d Newburyport ed. [Newburyport, Mass., W.
& J. Gilman, 1817?] MWA.   40385

Campbell, Archibald
     Voyage round the world from 1806-1812, in which
Japan, Kamschatka, the Aleutian islands, and the Sand-
wich islands were visited, including a narrative of the
author's shipwreck...New York, Pr. by Van Winkle,
Wiley & co., 1817. 202 p. CtNl; MWA; NNMer; PPM;
WHi; WMMU.   40386

-- -- 2d Amer. ed. New York, Pr. by Broderick &
Ritter, 1817. 219 p. DLC; MdBE.   40387

Campbell, George
     The philosophy of rhetoric...A new ed. Boston,
Pr. by T.B. Wait & Co., for Thomas B. Wait & Co.,
1817. 517 p. MBrigStJ.   40388

Campbell, John
     Alfred and Galba; or, The history of two brothers
...Northampton, Mass., Pr. by J. Metcalf, for Simeon
Butler, 1817. 141 p. MH-AH; MNF; MWA.   40389

-- Walks of usefulness in London. Boston, 1817. 108
p. MWA.   40390

A candid appeal to the freemen of Maryland on the pro-
jected removal of their seat of government. By a
friend of the people. June 1817. 12 p. (Signed 'A
friend of the people' - attributed to John Mercer.) DLC.
                                                   40391
[Canfield, Russel]
     Letter addressed to a partialist...Hartford, 1817.
8 p. CtHi; MWA.   40392

Cannon, Josiah Weeks
     A sermon, delivered in Gill, Mass. August 6,
1817...Greenfield, Mass., Pr. by Denio and Phelps,

1817.   16 p. CtSoP; MDeeP; MWA; RPB.   40393

Carey, Henry, d. 1743
    The dragon of Wantley, a burlesque opera... New-
York, D. Longworth, 1817. 12 p. DLC; MB; NN.40394

Carey, Mathew, 1760-1839
    Appendix to the eighth edition of The olive branch
... Philadelphia, M. Carey and son, 1817. 48 p.
MWA; NNS; NjR; PPL-R.   40395

-- Columbian spelling and reading book. 15th imp. ed.
Philadelphia, M. Carey, 1817. MWA.   40396

-- Carey's general atlas, improved and enlarged, being a collection of maps of the world and quarters,
their principal empires, kingdoms, &c. Philadelphia,
M. Carey & Son, 1817. 58 maps. MH.   40397

-- The Olive Branch: or Faults on both sides, Federal
and Democratic. Ed. 8, enl. Philadelphia, M. Carey
and son, 1817. 508 p. KyU; MWA; WvC.   40398

-- -- Ed. 9. Winchester, Va., J. Foster, 1817. 458
p. ArU; CU; DLC; MWA; NcD; THi; Vi.   40399

-- Reflections on the present system of banking, in the
city of Philadelphia. With a plan to revive confidence,
trade, and commerce, and to facilitate the resumption
of specie payments. Philadelphia, The author, 1817.
30 p. DLC; DeGE.   40400

-- -- Philadelphia, The author, Jan. 30, 1817. 28 p.
MiD-B.   40401

-- -- Ed. 2, cor. Philadelphia, The author, 1817.
31 p. NNS.   40402

-- [Printed circular letter beginning:] Sir, I submit
the annexed preamble and resolution... Philadelphia,
1817. Single sheet printed on both sides. DeGE. 40403

Carlisle Patriot. Carlisle, Pa. , George Gangwehr,
1817, 1st issue. Newspaper. Brigham, p. 833. 40404

Carmichael, Richard, 1779-1849
    An essay on the venereal diseases which have
been confounded with syphilis and the symptoms which
exclusively arise from that poison. 1st Amer. ed.
Philadelphia, Pr. by William Fry, for Thomas Dobson,
1817. CtY; LNT-M; MdBM; NNNAM; OClM; ScCMe.
                                                40405
[Carroll, John] Abp.
    An address to the Roman Catholics of America.
By a Catholic clergyman. New York, 1817. 120 p.
MB; MWH; MdHi.   40406

[--] An address to the Roman Catholics of the United
States... New York, Pr. by Clayton & Kingsland, for
David Longworth, 1817. MWA.   40407

Carseer, G.
    Hymns for the nativity of our Saviour, Jesus
Christ. In four parts. Boston, Pr. by John Eliot,
1817. 24 p. MBAt; MH; MMeT; MWA; NNUT; PHi;
RPB.   40408

Carter, Abiel, 1791-1827
    A sermon on Free masonry, preached before the
Lodges, no. 45 and 113, of the city of Pittsburgh, on
Tuesday, June 24, 1817... Pittsburgh [Pa.] Pr. by John
Scull [1817?] 16 p. CSmH; MWA; NNG.   40409

Carver, James
    Facts of an epidemic disease among horses, oxen
and sheep. Philadelphia, 1817. PPL.   40410

-- Remarks and observations on the epidemic catarrh
[among horses] which prevailed in this city [Philadel-
phia] during the late winter of 1815 and 1816, and now
prevailing on the Lancaster line. [Philadelphia, 1817?]

16 p.   DNLM; PPAmP.   40411

-- Veterinary science, important to the physician, the
student, and the gentleman of Philadelphia; giving an
account of the Royal Veterinary College of London,
and a similar establishment in this city... [Philadelphia,]
Pr. by T.S. Manning, 1817. 49 p. CtY; DLC; DeGE;
DNLM.   40412

Case (in error) on the part of the appellant. David
Dunham vs. A. Dey. New York, 1817. MBAt.   40413

The Casket; or, The orphan's portion; together with
divine hymns. New Haven, Sydney's press, 1817. 46
p. OClWHi.   40414

Cassell, Alex G.
    Speech Senate January 22, 1807! on Bill to pro-
vide increased revenue from imports. Washington City,
1817. 16 p. OCHP.   40415

Catalogue...Roman and Greek coins for sale... First
part.   Coins of the Roman republic. New York, 1817.
PPL.   40416

A catechism for the instruction of children. Boston,
Pr. by John Eliot, 1817. 16 p. DLC; MH-AH; MHi.
                                                   40417
Catechismus oder kurzer Unterricht Christlicher Lehre.
3 verb. auflage. Baltimore, Schaeffer & Maund, 1817.
102 p. DLC; PA.   40418

Catholic Church
    (The decrees of the Synod of the Bishop of Balti-
more and his priests held in the year 1791 and the de-
crees of the informal meeting of the Archbishop of Baltimore and his suffragan bishops held in 1810, with an
introductory letter by Archbishop Marechal.) [1817] 34 p.
DGU; MdBS.   40419

-- A manual adapted for the use of children, containing
morning and evening prayers, prayers at Mass, rule of
life, principles of Roman Catholics, &c. Georgetown,

D.C., Pr. by W. Duffy, 1817. 107 p. DGU.   40420

-- Ordo divini officii recitandi missaeque celebrandae.
Ad usum diaecaesis [!] Baltimorensis. Baltimore,
[1817] MBAt.   40421

Catholic doctrine and Catholic principles explained...
New York, Pr. by A. Spooner, for William Higgins...
1817. 92 p. MWA.   40422

Catholic laity's directory for 1817. Sabin 11521. 40423

Cecil, Richard
    Remains of the Rev. Richard Cecil...Armstrong's
ed. Boston, Samuel T. Armstrong, 1817. 271 p. CSt;
GAT; MB; MBAt; MBNMHi; MH; MSerHi; MWA;
NBLiHi; NSchU; OO; TWcW; ViRUT.   40424

Celebrated trials of all countries and remarkable cases
of criminal jurisprudence; selected by a member of the
Philadelphia bar. Philadelphia, 1817. PU-L.   40425

Centlivre, Mrs. Susanne, 1667?-1723
    The busy-body. A comedy...New-York, David
Longworth, 1817. 83 p. CtY; DLC; MB.   40426

Certificate; we the subscribers inhabitants of the towns
of Brownville, Le Ray, and Wilna, Jefferson Co., N.Y.,
living on lands purchased of Mr. James Le Ray de
Chaumont, certify (that the lands are good for settlement) Watertown, 1817. MBAt.   40427

Chais de Sourcesol, Guillaume
    Summary, or general argument of the last mani-
festo of the last servant of Jesus Christ, to all the
churches of Christendom. Wilmington, Del., Porter,
1817. 184 p. (Alternate pages in French and English)
DeHi; DeWI; ICBB; ICN; MdBS; MWA; PHi; PPL-R.
                                                 40428
[Challoner, Richard]
    A caveat against the Methodists...Mount Vernon, O.,
Pr. by John P. M'Ardle, for the publishers, 1817. 47 p.
DGU.   40429

Chalmers, Thomas, 1780-1847
Discourses on the Christian revelation viewed in
connection with the modern astronomy. Andover,
Mass., 1817. InCW.   40430

-- The duty of giving an immediate diligence to the
business of the Christian life. New-York, Kirk and
Mercein, 1817. 52 p. MA; MB; MWA; MWiW; PPLT.
                                                     40431
-- The evidence and authority of the Christian revela-
tion... Philadelphia, Anthony Finley, 1817. 248 p. CtW;
MWA; NGeno; NcU; NjP; OClW.   40432

-- The influence of Bible societies on the temporal ne-
cessities of the poor. New York, Pr. [by J. & J.
Harper] for Kirk & Mercein, 1817. 35 p. MA; MWA;
MWiW; OClWHi.   40433

-- A series of discourses on the Christian revelation,
viewed in connexion with the modern astronomy... New
York, Kirk & Mercein, 1817. 218 p. CtY; MWA;
MWiW; MdW; ViRUT.   40434

-- -- [2d Amer. ed.] New York, Pr. [by J. & J.
Harper] for Kirk & Mercein, 1817. MWA; MWiW.
                                                     40435
-- A sermon preached in St. Andrew's church, Edinburgh, before the Society for the relief of the destitute
sick, on ... April 18, 1813... New York, Kirk and Mercein, 1817. 123 p. CU; DLC; MA; MWA; MWiW.40436

-- Thoughts on universal peace: a sermon, delivered
on Thursday, January 18, 1816, the day of national
thanksgiving for the restoration of peace... New-York,
Kirk and Mercein, 1817. 68 p. DLC; MWA; MWiW;
NN; OClWHi.   40437

[Chambers, Joseph G.]
Elements of orthography; or, An attempt to form a
complete system of letters... Philadelphia, Pr. by Den-
nis Heartt, for the author, and for M. Thomas, and J.
Bioren, 1817. 15 p. DLC.   40438

Chandler, Adoniram
    An oration, delivered before the New York Typo-
graphical Society, on their seventh anniversary, July 4,
1816...New York, Pr. by J. Seymour, for the Society,
1817. 15 p. DLC.   40439

Channing, Edward Tyrrel, 1790-1856
    An oration, delivered July 4, 1817...Boston, Pr.
by Joseph T. Buckingham [1817] 24 p. CSmH; CtY;
DLC; MBNEH; MH; MHi; MMal; MMeT; MWA; MeHi;
RHi; RPB.   40440

Channing, William Ellery, 1780-1840
    A letter to the Rev. Samuel C. Thacher, on the
aspersions contained in a late number of the Panoplist
on the ministers of Boston and the vicinity. Boston,
Wells and Lilly, 1817. 36 p. OClWHi.   40441

-- Sermon on war; delivered before convention of Congregational Ministers of Massachusetts, May 30, 1816.
Abridged.   Andover, Mass., 1817. 16 p. CtY; MB; OO.
                                                    40442
Chaplin, Calvin
    A sermon, delivered, 14th January, 1817, at the
funeral of the Rev. Timothy Dwight...New Haven, Pr.
by T. G. Woodward, for Maltby, Goldsmith & Co.,
1817. CSmH; CSt; CU; CtHi; CtY; DLC; MH; MWA;
MeHi; NNG; Nh-Hi; NjR; PHi; RPB.   40443

Chapman, Eunice (Hawley)
    An account of the conduct of the people called
Shakers; in the case of Eunice Chapman and her chil-
dren...Albany, Pr. for the authoress, 1817. 60 p. MB;
MHi; MWA; MWiW.   40444

Chapman, James
    The memorial of James Chapman...[Albany, 1817?]
MWA.   40445

-- Memorial, to the respectable legislature of the state
of New York, concerning his separation from Eunice
Chapman.   Albany, March 24, 1817. 8 p. MB.   40446

Chapman, Nathaniel
  Discourses on the elements of therapeutics and
materia medica...Philadelphia, Pr. by W. Brown, for
James Webster, 1817-19. 2 v. MBM; MWA; MdUM;
MoSW-M; NNNAM.   40447

Charitable education school for the county of Litchfield,
Conn.
  Constitution and laws...New Haven, Pr. by Nathan
Whiting, 1817. 16 p. MBC; MWA.   40448

Charles the Twelfth, or The battle of Pultowa; a military tragic piece in 4 acts. New York, 1817. 34 p.
MH; MPiB.   40449

Charless' Missouri-Illinois Magazine almanac, for 1818.
St. Louis, Charless, 1817. [62] p. MoHi.   40450

Charleston, S. C. (town)
  Board of health. Statement of deaths, with the
diseases and ages. In the city of Charleston, (S. C.)
from the 1st of October, 1816, to the 1st of October,
1817...[Charleston, S. C.? 1817] Broadside. MHi.
                                              40451
Charleston, S. C. First Presbyterian Church
  Documents relative to the controversy in the First
Presbyterian Church of the City of Charleston, (S. C.,)
which terminated in the resignation of the pastor.
Charleston, S. C., Pr. by A. E. Miller, 1817. DLC;
ScCC.   40452

[Charlestown, Mass.]
  Statement of the expenses and funds of the Charlestown Free Schools, for the year 1817. [Charlestown,
Mass., 1817] (Goodspeed's (Americana) Cat. 292, February 1938, No. 658)   40453

-- First Baptist Church
  A summary declaration of the faith and practice of
the First Baptist Church in Charlestown. Boston, Pr.
by C. Crocker, 1817. 8 p. MH.   40454

Charnock, Stephen
    A treatise of divine providence...1st Amer. ed.
Philadelphia, Pr. by A. Walker, for W.W. Woodward,
1817. 318 p. MWA; NB; NNUT; ViAl.   40455

Chase, Ebenezer
    A collection of hymns...Concord, N.H., Pr. by
George Hough, for the compiler, 1817. 70 p. MWA.
                                                 40456
Chautauque Gazette. Fredonia, N.Y., William A. Car-
penter, Jan. 7, 1817, 1st issue. MWA.   40457

Chazotte, Peter Stephen
    An essay on the best method of teaching foreign
languages...Philadelphia, Pr. by W. Fry, for Edward
Earle, 1817. 108 p. DHEW; MWA; PP; PPAmP; PPL-
R.   40458

Cheshire Agricultural Society
    An act establishing the Cheshire Agricultural So-
ciety. Together with the regulations and by-laws of the
Society, and a list of the officers for the present year.
Windsor, Pr. by Jesse Cochran, by order of the Society, 1817. 8 p. DLC.   40459

Chester, John
    The charge, delivered to the Rev. Benjamin Frank-
lin Stanton, at his ordination...[1817?] MWA. 40460

Chevallie, P.J.
    Claim of Beaumarchais' heir against the United
States, by P.J. Chevallie, her attorney. January,
1817. Washington, D.C., Pr. by J. Elliot [1817] 42 p.
DLC; ICJ; MBAt; MHi; N; PHi; WHi.   40461

Cheves, Langdon
    Opinions concerning the validity of the sessions of
the "Constitutional Court, " of South Carolina. Columbia, S.C., J. Seymour, 1817. 20 p. CSmH; MBS; NN.
                                                 40462

Chickering, Joseph
    A sermon, preached in Boston, before the Ameri-
can society for educating pious youth for the gospel min-

istry...Dedham, Mass., Pr. by Abel D. Alleyne, 1817. 44 p. CSt; Ct; GDC; ICN; ICP; MA; MBAt; MH; MSaE; MWA; MWo; MeB; MeBat; MeHi; NCH; NNUT; NjPT; TxH; VtMiM. 40463

Child, L. M.
    Flowers for children...New York, 1817. 184 p. DLC. 40464

Children in the wood.
    The affecting history of the children in the wood... New Haven, Sidney's press, 1817. 46 p. CtY; MWA. 40465

The child's battledoor. New York, Samuel Wood & sons, 1817. MWA. 40466

Chillicothe, O., citizens.
    Memorials to President and directors of the Bank of the United States...on behalf of...a branch...in Chillicothe. [1817] 26 p. OHi. 40467

Chinese philosophical and mathematical trangram. Ed. 2. [Philadelphia? 1817] MB. 40468

Chitty, Joseph
    A practical treatise on bills of exchange...New ed. Georgetown, D. C., Pr. by W. Fry, for George Richards, 1817. MWA. 40469

The Christian economy...Winchester, Va., J. Foster, 1817. 126 p. MWA; NcD; OCl; ViU; ViWin; WHi. 40470

A Christian exhortation to sailors...New York, Pr. by Samuel Wood & sons, 1817. MWA. 40471

Christian Journal and Literary Register. New York, T. & J. Swords, Jan. 22, 1817, 1st issue. GDC; MBD. 40472

The Christian messenger. v. 1. No. 1, Saturday, May 10, 1817 - (Vol. 1, No. 26, Saturday, November 1, 1817) Baltimore, Pr. by John D. Toy, for J. T. Russell, 1817- Weekly. MdBE; MdHi. 40473

Church music: selected by a Committee of the First
Ecclesiastical Society in Hartford... Hartford, Pr. by
Samuel Green, for George Goodwin & sons, 1817. 40 p.
CtHi; CtHT-W; MWA.   40474

Church of England
    Book of common prayer.   New York, 1817. MB.
                                                     40475
Citizen and farmer's almanac for 1818.   By David
Young.   Morris-Town, N.J., Jacob Mann [1817] [36] p.
DLC; MWA; NjMoW; NjHi; NjP; NjR.   40476

Citizens of Indiana, you will in a few days, be called
on to exercise one of the first privileges of freemen...
Indiana is in her infancy, just admitted into the union
...We want a man to represent us in the next Congress
...whose politics and character and patriotism are
firmly established; in our late governor Posey, we find
one every way qualified.   [1817] Broadside. In. 40477

City of Washington Gazette.   Washington, D.C., Jonathan Elliot, Oct. 27, 1817.   Daily and tri-weekly continuation of "Washington City Weekly Gazette." DLC;
MWA.   40478

Claim against Holland.   Opinion of John Woodward, esq.
of the city of New-York, in the case of the St. Michaels and Cargo, of Baltimore, vs. the King of Holland, (now styled the King of the Netherlands.) Involv-
ing a view of the legal effect of recent events upon the
continent of Europe, especially as they relate to the
rights and losses of neutral merchants, as connected
with the change of dynasties on that continent. [New
York, 1817] 32 p. N-L.   40479

Clark, Adam
    Observations on various passages of scripture,
placing them in a new light.   Charlestown, Mass., S.
Etheridge, Jr., 1817.   4 v. InSbNHi.   40480

Clark, Daniel Atkinson, 1779-1840
    The church safe: a sermon, preached before the
consociation at Watertown, Conn., June 25, 1817. ...

New Haven, Pr. by N. Whiting, 1817. 15 p. CSmH;
CU; CtHi; CtSoP; MWA; NN; NcD.   40481

Clark, G.
   General observations on the common mode of de-
fending the doctrine of the Trinity, and the union of the
two natures in Jesus Christ. Boston, Isaiah Thomas,
Jr., 1817. 12 p. ICMe; MB; MBAt; MH; MHi; MNe;
MWA.   40482

Clark, Peter I.
   An address, delivered at Flemington...4th July,
1817...New Brunswick, N.J., Pr. by William Myer,
1817. MWA.   40483

Clarke, Adam, 1760?-1832
   The doctrine of salvation by faith proved; or, An
answer to the important question, What must I do to be
saved? Philadelphia, Pr. by J.H. Cunningham, 1817.
32 p. CSmH; NjPT; NjR; OClWHi.   40484

Clarke, Edward Daniel
   Travels in the Holy Land...Philadelphia, Pr. by
A. Bowman, for David Brown, 1817. MWA; MdW.
                                             40485
-- Travels in various countries. Part I-II. 5th Amer.
ed. Hartford, Pr. by Hudson and Co., for John W.
Robbins, 1817. 2 v. CtHi; CtHT-W; CtMMHi; CtW;
MWA; MWiW; MiD-B.   40486

Clater, Francis
   Every man his own cattle doctor...Albany, 1817.
191 p. MWA.   40487

Clavijero, Francisco Javier, 1731-1787
   The history of Mexico. Collected from Spanish and
Mexican historians, from manuscripts, and ancient
paintings of the Indians...Philadelphia, T. Dobson, 1817.
3 v. DLC; MSaE; MWiW; Mi; RHi; RPB.   40488

Clavis Virgiliana... Philadelphia, A. Small, 1817.
(Bound in - Vergilius Maro, Publius. Opera...Philadel-
phia. A. Small. 1817) MWA.   40489

-- Philadelphia, M. Carey & son, 1817. (Bound in - Vergilius Maro, Publius. Opera... Philadelphia. A. Small, for M. Carey & son, 1817.) MWA.   40490

Clergyman's almanack for 1818. Boston, Parmenter & Norton [1817] ICMcHi; MWA; RNHi; RPB.   40491

Clergyman's minor almanack for 1818. Boston, Pr. by Parmenter & Norton, for the author [1817] MWA.40492

Clinton, Dewitt
    Memoir on the antiquities of the western parts of the state of New York. 1817. NIC; OMC.   40493

-- On certain phenomena of the Great Lakes of America. New York [1817?] 11 p. (Read before the Literary and Philosophical Society of New York. November 19, 1817) N.   40494

The close communion of the Baptists contrary to the word of God... Dedham, Mass., Pr. by Abel D. Alleyne, 1817. 12 p. MBC; MDedHi; MH; MWA; MiD-B; NjPT; PPM.   40495

Coalition et La France- Philadelphia, J. E. Hurtel, 1817. MWA.   40496

Cobb, Edward
    A few observations on some of the principles of the people called Quakers, in reply to some paragraphs in a pamphlet entitled Two sermons on Christian fellowship preached at Gorham, by Asa Rand. Portland, Me., Pr. by A. & J. Shirley, 1817. 30 p. MNBedf; MWA. 40497

[Cobbett, William] 1763-1835
    Our anti-neutral conduct reviewed. [New York? Pr. for the editor, 1817] 16 p. CtY; DLC; MB; MdHi.
                                                      40498
-- The pride of Britannia humbled... Cincinnati, Ohio, John R. Fletcher, William Poundsford and Williams and Mason, 1817. 216 p. Ct; DLC; ICU; MHi; NjR; OCHP; OClWHi; OO; PSC; WHi.   40499

-- -- Cincinnati, Ohio, Pr. by Williams and Mason,
for John R. Fletcher...1817. 216 p. DLC; MWA;
NHi; OCHP; OClWHi; NjR.   40500

Cock Robin
     The death and burial of Cock Robin. Boston, Pr.
by N. Coverly, 1817. MWA.   40501

Codman, John, 1782-1847
     A discourse, delivered before the Roxbury charit-
able society...Boston, Pr. by Munroe & Francis, 1817.
18 p. CtY; ICMe; MBAt; MBC; MBNEH; MH-AH; MSaE;
MWA; MeB; NjPT.   40502

-- A sermon delivered at the ordination of the Rev.
Leonard Withington...in Newbury, Oct. 31, 1816...
Newburyport, Pr. by W.B. Allen & co., 1817. MWA;
RPB.   40503

Coelebs deceived. By the author of ..."Cottage
Sketches"...New York, J. Seymour, 1817. 264 p. NjR.
                                                 40504
Coffin, Charles
     A discourse preached before the East Tennessee
Bible society at their annual meeting in Knoxville,
April 30th, 1817...Knoxville, Tenn., Pr. by Heiskell
& Brown, 1817. 35 p. CSmH; MH-AH; MSaE; NjPT;
T; TKL; TMaryC.   40505

Coffin, Robert Stevenson, 1797-1827
     The printer, and several other poems...Boston, Pr.
by Farnham and Badger, 1817. 84 p. CtY; DLC; MB;
MBAt; MH; MWA; NNC; RPB.   40506

Cohen, S.I.
     Elements of the Jewish faith...Richmond, Va., Pr.
by William W. Gray, for H. Cohen, 1817. 56 p. CSmH;
CtY; DLC; MH-AH; MWA; PHi; ScC; ScCC; Vi. 40507

Colden, Cadwallader David, 1769-1834
     The life of Robert Fulton, by his friend Cadwalla-
der D. Colden. Read before the Literary and philosophical society of New York. Comprising some account

of the invention, progress, and establishment of steam
boats... New-York, Kirk & Mercein, 1817. 371 p.
DLC; DeGE; MBat; MWA; NN; NSyHi; NjP.   40508

Cole, Samuel
    The Freemasons' library and general Ahiman Re-
zon; containing a delineation of the true principles of
freemasonry... Baltimore, Benjamin Edes, 1817. 452 p.
NjR.   40509

[Coleman, Eliphalet Beecher]
    Memoirs of Doctor Seth Coleman... New Haven, Pr.
by Flagg & Gray, 1817. 288 p. IEN-M; MB; MOra;
MWA; PSC-Hi.   40510

Coleman, Seth
    Memoirs of Doctor... of Amherst [Mass.] ... New-
Haven, Pr. by Flagg & Gray, at the Herald Office,
1817. 288 p. CSt; Ct; CtHi; CtY; ICJ; ICT; MB; MH;
MNF; MWA; MdBM; NBLiHi; NBuG; NNUT; NUt-Hi;
NcD; Nh; NjMD; NjP; OClWHi; OO; PSC-Hi; RHi;
VtMiS.   40511

Coleridge, Samuel Taylor
    Biographia literaria; or, biographical sketches of
my literary life and opinions... New York, Pr. by C.S.
Van Winkle, for Kirk & Mercien, 1817. 196 p. GAuY;
MWA; NbHi; WaT.   40512

-- -- New York, Pr. [by C.S. Van Winkle] for C.
Wiley & Co., 1817. 2 v. in 1. (Vol. 2 published by
Kirk and Mercein,) MWA.   40513

A collection of anecdotes, entertaining and interesting.
Lebanon, O., Pr. by Van Vleet & Cameron, 1817.
144 p. NbOM.   40514

A collection of hymns and spiritual songs, from various authors: for the use of the pious of all denominations. Wellsburgh, Va., Pr. by John Berry, 1817.
96 p. MWA; NjP.   40515

A collection of interesting tracts, explaining several

important points of scripture doctrine. New-York, Pr.
by T. and W. Mercein, by order of the General Conference, 1817. 359 p. MMeT-Hi; MWA; MeLewB.
                                                   40516
A collection of pieces for the pianoforte bound in one
volume. New York [1817] (Goodspeed's Book Shop
catalogue 168. 1927. No. 1153)   40517

A collection of sacred music, designed principally for
the use of churches which sing without a choir ...Al-
bany, E. F. Backus, 1817. RPB.   40518

Collection of sacred music, designed principally for the
use of churches which sing without a choir;...Albany,
E. F. Backus, Utica, Pr. typographically by William
Williams, 1817. 67 p. MWA; N; NUt; NNUT; NN.
                                                   40519
A collection of the most useful arithmetical tables, to
which is added a concise system of punctuation. Baltimore, J. Robinson, 1817. 16 p. MdBE.   40520

Collins & Co., New York
    A catalogue of books for sale by Collins & Co.
printers, booksellers, and stationers. No. 189, Pearl-
street, New-York: consisting of the last and most approved editions of books on history, biography, travels
and voyages, poetry, theology, arts and sciences; and
classical and school books in Greek, Latin, French,
and English...New-York, Pr. by Collins and Co., 1817.
56 p.   MWA.   40521

-- A catalogue of books; in medicine, surgery, anatomy,
physiology, the veterinary art, chemistry, mineralogy,
botany, and in other branches of natural history: for
sale by Collins & Co. No. 189, Pearl-street, New-
York, printers and importers of medical books to the
New-York College of Physicians and Surgeons, and to
the New York Hospital. New York, Collins & Co.,
1817. 40 p. MWA; NNNAM; PPiU.   40522

Colman, George, 1732-1794
    The clandestine marriage. A comedy...New York,
D. Longworth, 1817. 100 p. MH; MWA; TxU.   40523

-- The mountaineers; an opera in three acts...New York, D. Longworth, 1817. 68 p. CLU; MH; MWA; NCH.   40524

-- The review, or the wag of Windsor; a comic opera, in two acts. Ed. 3. New York, D. Longworth, 1817. 40 p. MH.   40525

Colman, Henry
    Catechisms for children and young persons. Boston, J. W. Burditt, 1817. 2 pt. MH; MWA.   40526

Columbia University. College of Physicians and Surgeons.
    Circular. (Dated Aug. 28th, 1817) [New York? 1817?] 2 p. MH   40527

Columbian almanac, for... 1818... Philadelphia, Pr. by David Dickinson [1817] [36] p. MWA.   40528

Columbian institute for the promotion of arts and sciences, Washington, D. C.
    Columbian institute for the promotion of arts and sciences. Washington, Pr. by Jonathan Elliot, 1817. 8 p. DLC; DNA.   40529

The Columbus almanac for... 1818... Columbus, O., Pr. by P. H. Olmsted, at the office of the Intelligencer, [1817] 100 p. (Lindley, Harlow - Columbus, O.) 40530

Columbus Gazette. Columbus, Ohio, P. H. Olmsted, Dec. 4, 1817, 1st issue with this title. A weekly continuation of the "Western Intelligencer." MWA. 40531

The Comet; or, He would be an astronomer. A farce, in two acts. Baltimore, J. Robinson, 1817. 31 p. MdHi; RPB.   40532

Comet. Perryopolis, Pa., Edward Humber & Co., May 22, 1817, 1st issue. Weekly newspaper. MWA.
                                                       40533
Commentator. Frankfort, Ky., Moses O. Bledsoe, Jan. 3, 1817, 1st issue. Weekly newspaper. DLC. 40534

Common things of divine service.   New York, 1817.
PPL.   40535

A companion to Dr. Thornton's lectures on botany.
Portland, Me., Pr. by Francis Douglas, 1817. 16 p.
MSaP.   40536

A compendious account of the most important battles of
the late war, to which is added the curious adventures
of Corporal Samuel Stubbs... Boston, Pr. by William
Walter, 1817. 24 p.   CSmH; CtHT-W; MBNEH; MWA;
NjP.   40537

Congregational Church Council.   Sandwich, Mass.
    Result of an Ecclesiastical Council, held at Sand-
wich, May 20, 1817. Boston, 1817. ICN.   40538

Congregational Churches in Connecticut.   General asso-
ciation.
    An address, to the emigrants from Connecticut...
Hartford, Pr. by Peter B. Gleason & Co., 1817.
MWA.   40539

-- -- Proceedings of the General Association of Connecticut June, 1817.   Hartford, Pr. by Peter B. Gleason & Co., 1817. 22 p. IEG; MiD-B; N; NcMHi.40540

Congregational Churches in Massachusetts.   General
Association.
    Extracts from the minutes of the General Associa-
tion of Massachusetts proper.   The General Association of Massachusetts convened at Belchertown, June
24, 1817...Boston, Pr. by Samuel T. Armstrong
[1817] 7 p.   MWA.   40541

Congregational Churches in Vermont.
    Articles of consociation, adopted by the Congrega-
tional churches in the western districts of Vermont,
and parts adjacent, A.D. 1798.   To which is annexed
A shorter confession of faith, with scripture proofs,
and a covenant for the use of the churches in receiving
members to their communion. Ed. 2.   Arlington, Vt.,
Pr. by E.G. Storer, 1817. 36 p. CSmH; CtY-D; MB;

MBC; MWA; NN; PPPrHi; VtHi; VtU-W.   40542

Congregational and Presbyterian ministers in Vermont
--General convention, 1817.
    Extracts from the minutes...September A.D. 1817.
Middlebury, Vt., Pr. by Francis Burnap [1817] 19 p.
MWA; NN.   40543

Connecticut (State)
    [Acts of the General court or assembly held May,
1817. Hartford, Hudson & Goodwin, 1817] 281-288 p.
CtSoP; OCLaw; Nb.   40544

-- [Acts of the General court or assembly held October,
1817. Hartford, Hudson & Goodwin, 1817] 289-298 p.
CtSoP; Nb; OCLaw.   40545

-- Report of the committee of the Connecticut Asylum
for the education and instruction of deaf and dumb persons. Hartford, Pr. by Hudson and Co., 1817. 15 p.
Ct; MB; MdFRED; MoS.   40546

-- Report of the committee on the claims of Connecticut against the United States. 1817. 8 p. Ct; CtHC;
NN.   40547

-- Report of the condition of the school fund...[Hart-
ford, 1817] WHi.   40548

-- Report of the controller of public accounts, to the
legislature of the state of Connecticut, May session,
1817. Hartford, Pr. by Goodwin & sons, 1817. 47 p.
DLC.   40549

-- Reports (Day's & others') of cases argued and de-
termined in the Supreme court of errors of the state of
Connecticut...Hartford, 1817-[69] v. 1-34. CStclU;
CtSoP; CSdCL; KyLoU; MLawL; MPiBL; MdBB; MoKU;
Ms; N-L; NNLI; NUtSC; NcWfC-L.   40550

-- ...Resolved by this assembly, that the Secretary of
this state be directed to transmit a copy of the statutes
of this state now in force ...to the executives of each of

the states in the Union...[1817] Broadside. DNA.
40551
Connecticut asylum for the education and instruction of
deaf and dumb persons.
Report. Hartford, 1817. NNNAM.   40552

Connecticut Bible society
Report of the Directing committee...May 8, 1817.
Hartford, Pr. by Hudson and Co., 1817. 24 p. A-Ar;
Ct; MBC; MWA; NN.   40553

Connecticut Register and United States Calendar for
1818. Astronomical calculations by Nathan Daboll.
New London, Samuel Green [1817] [176] p. Ct; CtHi;
CtNl; MWA.   40554

Connecticut Reserve Bible Society
An introductory address...and the 3d report of the
trustees...June 11, 1817. Canton, O., Pr. by John
Saxton, 1817. 17 p. MBC.   40555

Connecticut society for the encouragement of American
manufactures.
Address...Middletown, Conn., Pr. by T. Dunning,
1817. CtHi; CtMMHi; MB; MH; MWA; NNUT. 40556

...Consolation under convictions...[Philadelphia, Pr.
by Lydia R. Bailey...1817] (This is no. 31 of the
Tracts of the Philadelphia female tract society.) MWA.
40557
Constant de Rebecque, Henri Benjamin, 1767-1830
Adolphe: an anecdote found among the papers of an
unknown person...Philadelphia, M. Carey and son,
1817. 238 p. DLC; MWA.   40558

Constitution and proceedings of the Charitable Society,
formed in the western counties of the state of New-
York, for the education of indigent pious young men,
for the Gospel ministry. Rochester, N. Y., Pr. by A.
G. Dauby & Co., 1817. 8 p. MBC; NhD. 40559

The constitutions of all the United States...Declaration
of independence and the Federal constitution. Lexington,

Ky., Thomas T. Skillman, 1817.   ICU; IcHi; KyHi;
MWA; NcAS; RPL.   40560

Conversations of Emily.   Abridged from the French.
Doylestown, Pa., 1817.   200 p.   MWA.   40561

-- Philadelphia, 1817.   MWA.   40562

Conversion of a deist...[Philadelphia] 1817. MWA.
                                                     40563
Cook, Isaac P.
    History of Methodist Sabbath schools, Baltimore
...Baltimore, Cook, 1817.   52 p.   DLC; MB.   40564

Cook, Thomas
    The new and complete letter writer...New York,
Evert Duyckinck, 1817.   MWA.   40565

Cooke, Thomas Simpson
    The Lord's prayer, for four voices, with an ac-
companiment for the piano forte or organ, composed by
the celebrated Mr. Cooke of Dublin; also a funeral service and an anthem on the nativity, from the second
chapter of Luke.   Utica, N.Y., William Williams, 1817.
8 p.   N.   40566

Cooley, Timothy Mather
    A sermon, delivered in Springfield, before the Bible
society...Springfield, Mass., Pr. by Thomas Dickman,
1817.   20 p.   CSmH; IaDuU; M; MSaE; MWA; NjPT.
                                                     40567
Cooper, Daniel C.
    A short account of the conduct of Mr. James Welsh,
while a citizen of Dayton...[Dayton? 1817?] 22 p.
OCHP; WHi.   40568

Cooper, Edward
    Practical, familiar and doctrinal sermons...1st
Amer. ed.   Brookfield, Mass., Pr. by E. Merriam &
Co., 1817.   2 v.   CtY; ICMe; MH-AH; MWA; MWHi;
MoSpD; ViRUT; WvH.   40569

-- -- 1st Amer. ed.   Hartford, Pr. by B. & J. Rus-

sell, for Samuel G. Goodrich, 1817-18. 2 v. CSmH;
CtHC; CtHi; ICU; InCW; MA; MCW; MSherHi; MWA;
MeB; MoSpD; NSyU; NN; NjMD; NjR; OO; PLERC-Hi.
40570

Cordier, Mathurin, 1479-1564
Corderii Colloquiorum centuria selecta: or, A se-
lect century of the Colloquies of Corderius. With an
English translation... Baltimore, Pr. by J. Robinson,
1817. 142 p. DLC; MWA; MdHi; MiDSH; OCl; PHi;
PReaHi. 40571

[Corp, Harriet]
Coelebs deceived... Philadelphia, A. Small, 1817.
286 p. CtY; MWA. 40572

Cotton, Ward
Causes and effects of female regard to Christ, illustrated in a sermon, delivered before the Female Society in Boyleston, for the aid of foreign missions, at
their request, October 1, 1816. Worcester, Mass.,
William Manning, 1817. 19 p. ICMe; MWA; MWHi;
OClWHi; NjR. 40573

The country almanack, for the year 1818... containing
withal, a delineation and account of the spots on the
sun. Deerfield, Mass., John Wilson [1817] 46 p.
MDeeP; MWA; NjR. 40574

A country farmers' memorial, or An address to people
of all classes on the times. By a republican farmer in
the country. [Portsmouth, N.H.] Pr. for the author
[1817?] NN. 40575

County convention! At a meeting of Federal delegates
from the towns in the County of Essex, at Ipswich,
March 19, 1817. 8 p. MWA; MiD-B. 40576

The court of Neptune and The curse of liberty, with
other poems, on subjects connected with the late war...
New-York, Pr. by Van Winkle, Wiley & Co., 1817.
106 p. MWA; NN; NRU; PPL; RPB. 40577

Coustos, Jean
    Free-masonry persecuted! Unparalleled sufferings
of John Coustos who nine times undersent the most cruel tortures ever invented by man, and sentenced to the
gallies, four years, by command of the inquisitors of
Lisbon, in order to extort from him the secrets of
Free masonry. To which is added, a selection of Masonic songs. Boston, Pr. for the purchasers, 1817.
59 p. NjR; TxWFM.   40578

Cowper, William
    Memoir of the early life of William Cowper...1st
Amer. ed. Boston, James Loring, 1817. 120 p. CtY;
IEG; LN; MB; MBAt; MBC; MBL; MH; MHa; MS; MSaE;
MWA; MeB; NBLiHi.   40579

-- -- Newburgh, N.Y., Philo B. Pratt, 1817. 119 p.
MMeT; MWA.   40580

Cox, Francis Augustus, 1783-1853
    Female scripture biography: including an Essay on
what Christianity has done for women...New-York, Pr.
by Abraham Paul, for James Eastburn & co., 1817.
DLC; MWal; MdW.   40581

[Cox, Henry Hamilton] 1750-1821
    Metrical sketches...Philadelphia, Pr. by Joseph R.
A. Skerrett, for the author, 1817. 60 p. DLC. 40582

Coxe, John Redman
    The Philadelphia medical dictionary...Ed. 2. Phila-
delphia, Pr. by William Fry, for Thomas Dobson and
son, 1817. 433 p. CoCsE; KyLxT; MWA; MdBJ-W;
NNNAM; WU-M.   40583

[Coxe, Tench] 1755-1824
    A memoir of February, 1817, upon the subject of
the cotton wool cultivation, the cotton trade, and the
cotton manufactories of the United States of America.
[Philadelphia, 1817] 16 p. DLC; MH.   40584

Coxe, William
   A view of the cultivation of fruit trees... Philadelphia, Pr. by D. Allinson, for M. Carey and son, 1817.
253 p. CoFcS; DeGE; MWA; NIC-A; NcWfC; Nj; NjR;
OClW; PFal.   40585

Crafts, William
   An oration on the influence of moral causes on national character... Cambridge, Mass., Pr. by Hilliard
and Metcalf, at the University press, 1817. MWA.
                                                    40586
Craik, J.
   The past and present position of the church. Lexington, 1817. MB.   40587

Cramer, Johann Baptist, 1771-1858
   The brown Irish girl, arranged by J.B. Cramer,
Norfolk, Virginia, Pr. by G. Balls [1817?] 7 p.
CSmH.   40588

[Cramer, Zadok] 1773-1813
   The navigator... Ed. 9. Pittsburgh, Pa., Pr. by
Robert Ferguson & Co., for Cramer, Spear and Eich-
baum, 1817. MWA.   40589

-- The navigator, containing directions for navigating
the Monongahela, Allegheny, Ohio and Mississippi
rivers... Ed. 9. Pittsburgh, Pa., Pr. by Robert Ferguson & Co., for Spear and Eichbaum, 1817. CtHT;
CtY; DGU; ICU; In; KHi; MH; MNBedf; MWA; NNAIHi;
OCHP; OClWHi; OMC; PPF; PPL-R; PPi; PSeW; WaU.
                                                    40590
Cramer's Pittsburgh almanack, for the year of our
Lord 1818... Pittsburgh, Pa., Cramer and Spear [1817]
34 p. PSew; PWCHi.   40591

Cramer's Pittsburgh magazine almanack for... 1818...
calculated by the Rev. John Taylor... 15th number...
Pittsburgh, Pa., Cramer and Spear, [1817] 72 p.
MWA; OHi; PPi; PPiHi; WHi.   40592

The cries of London. Cooperstown, N.Y., H. & E.
Phinney, 1817. MWA.   40593

The crisis. Think twice ere you speak once: but when
you speak--speak the truth, without fear, favor or af-
fection...[Philadelphia, 1817?] 16 p. DLC; MWA.
40594

Cumming, Hooper, 1785-1825
Oration delivered July 4th, 1817...Albany, Pr. by
I.W. Clark, 1817. 15 p. DLC; MWA; PMA. 40595

-- The watchful servant. A discourse delivered in the
First Presbyterian Church, in the city of Schenectady,
January 5, 1817. Schenectady, N.Y., I. Riggs, 1817.
18 p. DLC; MBAt; MWA; NjR; N; PMA. 40596

Cummings, Jacob Abbot
An introduction to ancient and modern geography...
Ed. 4. Boston, Cummings and Hilliard; Cambridge,
Mass., Hilliard & Metcalf, 1817. 316 p. CtW; DLC;
LNMus; MBeHi; MH; MWA; NSyHi; OClWHi. 40597

-- -- Ed. 4. Boston, Cummings & Hilliard, 1817.
(Variant ed.) MWA. 40598

-- Questions on the historical parts of the New Testament...Boston, Cummings & Hilliard, 1817. 71 p.
CSt; MB; MBAt; MBC; MWA; MiD-B; NjPT. 40599

-- -- Ed. 2. Boston, Cummings & Hilliard, 1817.
CtSoP; ICU; MWA. 40600

-- School atlas to Cummings Ancient and modern geography. (T. Wightman, sc.) Ed. 4. Boston, 1817.
RPB. 40601

Cunningham, John William, 1780-1861
Sancho, or, The proverbialist...Boston, Wells &
Lilly, 1817. 188 p. CSmH; DLC; GSTA; ICP; ICU;
MB; MBL; MH; MWA; PPL-R; TNP. 40602

Cushing, John
A sermon, delivered at Ashburnham, Mar. 23,
1817, at the interment of George Wilker, jun. Andover,
Mass., Pr. by Flagg & Gould, 1817. 16 p. CSt; MBAt;
MSaE; MWA; MiD-B; NjPT. 40603

Cutbush, Edward
    An address, delivered before the Columbian insti-
tute, for the promotion of arts and sciences, at the
city of Washington, on the 11th January, 1817...Wash-
ington, Pr. by Gales and Seaton, 1817. 29 p. CtY;
DLC; DNA; KyLxT; MBBC; MWA; MnHi; NNNAM.40604

Cutting, John Browne, fl. 1795-1817
    Argument delivered before the judges of the Court
of Appeals, in Richmond, Virginia, in the case of
Carter's executors - appellants, against Cutting and
others -- appellees, by John Browne Cutting...chiefly
intended to demonstrate that by the operation of the
gaming statutes no gaming security can be rendered
valid by devise. Fredericksburg, 1817. 34 p. DLC;
MH-L.   40605

Cuyler, Cornelius C.
    The question answered. Whose children are en-
titled to baptism. Sermon preached, 6th June, 1816.
Raleigh, N.C., Pr. by Gales, 1817. PPPrHi.   40606

D

Daboll, Nathan
    Daboll's schoolmaster's assistant...Stereotype ed.
Albany, E. & E. Hosford, 1817. 240 p. InFtwL; MWA;
NRU-W.   40607

[Daggett, Leonard A.]
    Six numbers, (First inserted in the Columbian Reg-
ister of New Haven,) on banking and the shaving operations of directors; with general remarks, (never before
in print). New Haven, Pr. for the author, 1817. 24 p.
CtY; DLC; MB.   40608

Dalcho, Frederick
    A letter on public baptism, as established by "the
Protestant Episcopal Church in the United States of A-
merica." Charleston, (S.C.) E. Morford, 1817. 18 p.
NN.   40609

-- A sermon, preached in St. Michael's Church,

Charleston on the Festival of St. John the Evangelist,
Dec. 27th, 5817 before the Grand Lodge of Ancient
Free-Masons in South-Carolina... Charleston, S. C., Pr.
by A. E. Miller, 1817.   13 p.   IaCrM; MBFM; PPFM.
                                                      40610
Dame Trot and her comical cat.   Illustrated with 16
elegant engravings.   Philadelphia, Pr. by Wm. Charles,
1817.   [32] p.   CSmH; DLC; PP.   40611

Dana, Daniel, 1771-1859
    The connection between moral and intellectual im-
provement; an address delivered at the anniversary of
the New-Hampshire Alpha of the Phi Beta Kappa society, Dartmouth College, August 26th, 1817.   By Daniel
Dana... Exeter, N. H., Pr. by Charles Norris, for the
society, 1817.   20 p.   CSt; M; MA; MBAt; MReh; MWA;
MWiW; RPB.   40612

-- A sermon delivered at the ordination of the Rev.
Hervey Wilbur... Newburyport, Mass., Pr. by William
Brown Allen & Co., 1817.   23 p.   MNe; MWA; NN.
                                                      40613
-- A sermon preached in Boston, before the Massachusetts society for promoting Christian knowledge. May
28, 1817... Andover, Mass., Pr. by Flagg and Gould,
1817.   59 p.   CSt; MWA; NjPT.   40614

The danger of delay... Ed. 2.   Andover, Mass., Pr.
by Flagg & Gould, 1817.   12 p.   MMet.   40615

Darby, William, 1775-1854
    Emigrants' guide to the western and southwestern
states and territories.   New York, Kirk & Mercein,
[1817]   KyBgW-K.   40616

-- A geographical description of the state of Louisiana,
the southern part of the state of Mississippi, and territory of Alabama... Together with a map, from actual
survey and observation... of the state of Louisiana, and
adjacent countries.   Ed. 2, enl. and improved... New-
York, Pr. by J. Seymour, for James Olmstead, 1817.
356 p.   CSmH; CoD; DLC; LNH; LNT; NjR.   40617

Davidson, Ananias
    Kentucky harmony.   Harrisonburg, Va., 1817.
152 p. CtHT-W.   40618

Davidson, J., Ed.
    Selectae E Profanis Scriptoribus Historiae. Nova
Editio. Prioribus Longe Emendatior. Baltimore, Pr.
by J. Robinson, for J. & T. Vance, 1817. 299 p.
MNBedf.   40619

Davies, Samuel
    A minister's reflections on the death of one of his
people... [Boston, Munroe & Francis and Isaac Bowers,
1817] MWA.   40620

[Davis, Gustavus F.]
    Selection of the choicest metaphors, contained in
the second volume of Benjamin Keach, to which are
prefixed canons for expounding types and parables.
Norwich, Conn., Pr. by Hubbard & Marvin, 1817. 68 p.
CtHi.   40621

[Davis, John] 1774-1854
    Captain Smith and Princess Pocahontas, an Indian
tale. Philadelphia, Pr. by Wm. Greer, for Benjamin
Warner, 1817. 90 p. CSmH; DLC; MWA; ViW. 40622

Davis, William C.
    The millenium, or A short sketch on the rise and
fall of anti-Christ... Lexington, Ky., Repr. by J. Norvell & Co., 1817. 64 p. ICU.   40623

[Dauxion-Lavaysse, Jean François]
    Letters on the events of the revolutions in France:
by a French general officer. Addressed to his friends
in New York... New-York, J. Forbes & Co., 1817.
260 p. MH; NNS; ScU.   40624

Dawes, Edward
    The Philadelphia directory for 1817. 12 mo., half
morocco. Philadelphia, 1817. (Davis & Harvey cat.
no. 866. no. 30. Oct. 1901)   40625

Day, Jeremiah
     The mathematical principles of navigation and sur-
veying, with the mensuration of heights and distances.
Being the fourth part of a course of mathematics.
New Haven, Steele and Gray, 1817. 108 p. CU; Ct;
CtHi; MH; MWA; MA; MB; MeB; NWM; OClW; PU;
RNR.   40626

Day, Thomas, 1748-1789
     A concise historical account of the judiciary of
Connecticut. Hartford, Pr. by George Goodwin & Sons,
1817. 30 p. DLC; MH; MH-L; NHi; PHi; WHi. 40627

Dean, Henry
     Hocus pocus, or the whole art of legerdemain...
Ed. 18. Boston, 1817. 107 p. MB; MSaE.   40628

Dean, Paul
     Discourse before Grand Royal Arch Chapter of
Massachusetts at dedication of Adoniram Royal Arch
Chapter... Attleborough, June 24, A. L. 5817. Boston,
Munroe & Francis, 1817. 20 p. IaCrM; MBFM. 40629

Deane, Samuel
     A sermon, delivered before the Scituate Auxiliary
Society for the Suppression of Intemperance, at their
first annual meeting, in Scituate, May 26, 1817. Boston,
Pr. by John Eliot, 1817. 15 p. CtY; DLC; ICMe; MHi;
MWA; MeB; PHi.   40630

Dearborn Gazette. Lawrenceburg, Ind., Brown & Co.,
Dec. 1817, 1st issue. Weekly newspaper. MWA.40631

Deerfield, Mass.
     Regulations for the government of the schools in
the Town of Deerfield, reported April 7, 1817; accepted May 5, and published by vote of the town. Deerfield, Mass., Pr. by John Wilson, 1817. 8 p. MH;
MWA; NN.   40632

A defence of the distinguishing sentiments of the Baptists... Brattleborough, Vt., Pr. by S. Ide, for the author, 1817. 16 p. +   MWA.   40633

Defoe, Daniel
The true-born Englishman, a satire. By Daniel
Defoe. [Motto]...Bellows Falls, Vt., Pr. by Bill
Blake & Co., for the publisher, 1817. 36 p. VtHi.
40634

Delano, Amasa, 1763-1823
A narrative of voyages and travels in the northern
and southern hemispheres; comprising three voyages
round the world...Boston, Pr. by E.G. House, for the
author, 1817. 598 p. CLSM; CSmH; CU-B; CtW; DLC;
FOA; FWpR; ICJ; KyLx; MA; MB; MH; MHi; MNan;
MNS; MSaP; MWA; MWiW; MWal; MdBE; MeB; MeH;
MeLewB; MnU; MoSM; NBu; NNA; NNMer; NNS; NR;
NbO; NbU; NhD; NjR; OCl; PPAmP; PU; RPB; ScU.
40635

Delaware (State)
Journal of the House of Representatives of the
state of Delaware, Nov. 1816...Dover, Pr. by John
Robertson, 1817. 10 p. DLC; DeHi.   40636

-- Journal of the House of Representatives of the state
of Delaware, January 1817...Dover, Pr. by John Robertson, 1817. 288 p. DLC; DeHi.   40637

-- Journal of the Senate of the state of Delaware...
November 1816, Dover, Pr. by John Robertson, 1817.
11 p. DLC; DeHi.   40638

-- Journal of the Senate of the state of Delaware, January, 1817...Dover, Pr. by John Robertson, 1817.
135 p. DLC; DeHi.   40639

-- Laws of the state of Delaware, passed at a session
of the General assembly...7th day of January, 1817...
Dover, Pr. by J. Robertson, 1817. [201]-273, 17 p.
DLC; IaU; In-SC; MdBB; MiU-L; Nb; Nj; NN; O; R;
RPL; T; Wa-L.   40640

-- A report of the finances of the state of Delaware,
for the year 1816. [Dover, Pr. by John Robertson,
1817] 92 p. DLC; DeHi.   40641

Democrat. No. 1. Penn Yan, N.Y., 1817. See Amer.

Newspaper Reporter, N. Y., vol. 7, 1873, page 698.
(From NN imp. catal. but not in NN (1934)   40642

Democratic party. N. Y. (City)
    Address of the Republican General committee of
the city and county of New-York.   New-York, Pub. by
order of the Committee, 1817. 11 p. MWA; N.   40643

-- Pennsylvania.
    Democratic Republican convention.   [Harrisburg?
Pa., 1817] 8 p. DLC.   40644

[--] To the electors of the state of Pennsylvania.
[Philadelphia, Pr. by J. Binns, by order of the Com-
mittee of correspondence, for the city and county of
Philadelphia, 1817] 11 p. DLC.   40645

-- Pennsylvania.   Philadelphia.   Committee of Correspondence.
    ...Address of the Corresponding committee for the
district of the city and county of Philadelphia, to the
electors of the state of Pennsylvania.   Philadelphia,
1817. 16 p. PP.   40646

-- -- --.   ...Circular.   Philadelphia, July 18, 1817.
Philadelphia, Pr. by John Binns, 1817. Broadside. PP.
    40647

Dennie, Joseph
    The lay preacher...Philadelphia, Pr. by J. Max-
well, for Harrison Hall, 1817. 168 p. MB; MWA;
Nh-Hi; NjR; RPB.   40648

Depping, Georg Bernhard, 1784-1853
    Evening entertainments; or, Delineations of the
manners & customs of various nations, interspersed
with geographical notices...[Ed. 2] Philadelphia, Pr. by
D. Dickinson, for David Hogan, 1817. 384 p. CSt;
DLC; IP; MDeeP; MWA; MNBedf; PPL-R; PPM. 40649

Desault, Pierre Joseph
    A treatise on fractures...Ed. 3.   Philadelphia, Pr.
[By J. R. A. Skerrett] for Kimer & Sharpless, 1817.
398 p. CSt-L; KyLoJM; MBM; MWA; MoSW-M; NBMS;

NClsM; NNC-M; NNNAM; NbU-M; NcD; ScCMeS; RPB; WMAM.   40650

Description of the picture, Christ healing the sick in the temple, painted by Benjamin West... Philadelphia, Pr. by Clark & Raser, for James Webster, 1817. MWA; MWiW; N.   40651

-- ... Presented by the author to the Pennsylvania Hospital. Philadelphia, Pr. by William Brown, for the Pennsylvania Hospital, 1817. 13 p. MWA; N; PPM.
                                              40652
Destutt de Tracy, [Antoine Louis Claude] comte, 1754-1836.
    A treatise on political economy; to which is prefixed a supplement to a preceding work on the understanding; or Elements of ideology... Georgetown, D. C., J. Milligan, 1817. 344 p. CSmH; CtY; DLC; DeGE; MWA; NN; NjR; PU.   40653

Detroit Gazette. Detroit, Sheldon & Reed, July 25, 1817, 1st issue. Weekly newspaper. MWA; MiD.
                                              40654
The devout Christian's Vade Mecum; being a summary of select and necessary devotions... Philadelphia, M. Carey and son, 1817. 285 p. MWA.   40655

A dialogue between a clergyman and a layman, on the subject of Bible societies. By a churchman. New-York, Pub. for the author, 1817. DLC; MWA; NN.
                                              40656
A dialogue between a modern Calvinist... Bridgeport, Conn., Pr. by N. L. Skinner, for the author, 1817. 28 p. MBDiL.   40657

The diamond songster; containing the most approved, sentimental and lively, Scottish, Irish, and national songs. Baltimore, Pr. by Pomeroy & Toy, for Fielding Lucas, jun'r, 1817. 152 p. MdHi; NIC; NBuG; RPB.   40658

[Dibdin, Charles] 1745-1814
    The Quaker. A comic opera, in two acts... New-

York, David Longworth, 1817. 28 p. DLC; MH; MWA;
MiU-C; NN PU.   40659

-- The waterman; or, The first of August. A ballad
opera... Baltimore, J. Robinson, 1817. 35 p. DLC;
MB; MH; MdHi.   40660

Dickinson, David
    A sermon, delivered at Plainfield, New-Hampshire,
at the funeral of the Hon. Daniel Kimball... Hanover,
N. H., Pr. by Charles Spear, 1817. MWA.   40661

Dickinson, Rodolphus, 1787-1863
    A description of Deerfield, in Franklin County, in-
tended as an exhibition of the plan of a contemplated
gazetteer of Massachusetts proper... Deerfield, Mass.,
Pr. by G. J. Newcomb, for the author, 1817. 8 p.
DLC; MHi; MWA; NHi; NN.   40662

Dictionary of select and popular quotations which are in
daily use... Philadelphia, 1817. CSmH; DLC; MH.
                                                      40663
Dilworth, T.
    New guide to English tongue. Philadelphia, M.
Carey & son, 1817. MWA.   40664

[Dimond, William]
    The broken sword; a grand melo-drama, inter-
spersed with songs, choruses, &c. New-York, D.
Longworth, 1817. 39 p. MB; MH; MWA.   40665

-- The conquest of Taranto: or, St. Clara's eve...
Boston, Pr. by Russell, Cutler and Co., 1817. 48 p.
MB; MBB; MH; MHi; MWA.   40666

[--] -- New-York, D. Longworth, 1817. 62 p. ICU;
MH; MWA; NN.   40667

Directions for medicine chests, with a treatise of the
diseases most incident to seamen. Philadelphia, 1817.
27 p. DNLM.   40668

Directions for using the gold standard balances, in-

vented by Benjamin Dearborn, of Boston, Massachusetts...[Boston? 1817] MHi.   40669

The disfranchisement of the inhabitants of New-London,
New-Hampshire, March 11, 1817...[1817] MWA. 40670

Dissertations on the regenerate life...Philadelphia, Pr.
by Anderson & Meehan, 1817. MWA.   40671

Dixon, Joseph
    The African widow. Dedham, Mass., H. & W. H.
Mann, 1817. MWA; RPB.   40672

Dobson, Mrs. Susanna
    Life of Petrarch; collected from Memoirs pour la
vie de Petrarch. Philadelphia, S. A. Mitchell & Horace
Ames, 1817. 496 p. CtB; MoSM; NFred; OTU. 40673

Doctrines, (The) called Calvanism...Bath, Maine, 1817.
54 p. DLC.   40674

Documents, relating to the dissolution of the connexion
between the Rev. Mr. Forster, and the Independent or
Congregational church of Charleston, S. C. [Charles-
ton, S. C.] Pr. by Skrine & Duke, [1817] MWA. 40675

Documents relative to Indian affairs. [New York, Pr.
by Clayton & Kingsland, 1817] MWA.   40676

Doddridge, Joseph
    An oration delivered before the Masonic society, of
Wellsburgh and its vicinity, on St. Johns Day. June
24th, 1817...Wellsburgh, Va., Pr. by John Berry,
1817. 21 p. DSC; PPiU.   40677

[Doddridge, Philip]
    The principles of the Christian religion...Potsdam,
N. Y., Pr. by F. C. Powell, 1817. MWA.   40678

-- The rise and progress of religion in the soul...
Boston, James Loring, 1817. MWA.   40679

-- -- Ronald's 3d ed. New York, Pr. [by J. Oram] for

Thomas A. Ronalds, 1817. 368 p. MWA; NRU. 40680

-- A sermon, on the care of the soul...Boston, Repr.
by Thomas Rowe, 1817. 15 p. MWA; NAuT; NjPT.
40681
-- -- New York, Thomas A. Ronalds, 1817. MWA.
40682
-- Three discourses on the evidences of the Christian
religion; designed for the benefit of young persons.
Boston, Manning & Loring, 1817. 108 p. DLC; MB;
MWA; RPB.   40683

Dodge, Hosea
    A review of a sermon, entitled, The doctrine of
election illustrated and established: delivered by G.
Spring, A.M., pastor of the Brick Presbyterian Church
in the city of New-York: wherein his errors on that
subject are exposed and confuted...New York, Pr. by
J.H. Sherman, 1817. 56 p. NGH; NjPT; WHi. 40684

[Dodge, John]
    The first epistle of John, to the Rev. Walter Har-
ris...[Concord, N.H. ? Pr. by Th. Fillebrown, Jr.,
1817] MWA.   40685

Dodge, Peter, and others
    To the legislature of the state of New York.
[Watervliet, N.Y., March 20, 1817] 8 p. MB. 40686

Dodsley, Robert
    The economy of human life...Philadelphia, Pr. by
J. Maxwell, for Edward Earle, 1817. 99 p. CtY; MB;
MSaE; MWA; MoS.   40687

Dolbeare, Benjamin
    The poetical works of Doct. Benjamin Dolbeare;
consisting of his Art of Courtship and other pieces,
amatory and sentimental. Richmond, 1817. 36 p. RPB.
40688
[Dole, Benjamin]
    A humble attempt to refute "A refutation"...Salem,
Mass., Pr. by Thomas C. Cushing, 1817. 24 p. MSaE;
MWA.   40689

Domestic Missionary Society of Connecticut.
    Annual report.   Hartford, 1817.   8 p.   CSmH. 40690

Doresey, John Syng, 1783-1818
    Syllabus or heads of lectures on the materia medi-
ca, delivered in the University of Pennsylvania...
Philadelphia, Pr. by W. Fry, for the author, 1817.
48 p.   DLC; MB; MBM; MWA; NNNAM.   40691

Dow, Jabez
    A nosological arrangement of topical inflammations,
with their definitions and etymologies.   By Jabez Dow.
Dover, N.H., Pr. by John Mann, 1817.   12 p.   MBM;
Nh; Nh-Hi.   40692

[Dow, Lorenzo]
    Cosmopolite's thoughts, on the progress of light
and liberty... Philadelphia, Pr. for the author, 1817.
24 p.   MWA; PPL-R.   40693

[--] Lorenzo's thoughts, on the progress of light and
liberty... Philadelphia, Pr. for the author, 1817.   MWA.
                                                  40694
Ducachet, Henry William, 1796-1865
    An inaugural essay on the action of poisons... New-
York, Pr. by Van Winkle, Wiley & Co., 1817.   84 p.
DLC; MBM; MWA; NNNAM; NNS.   40695

Duer, William Alexander, 1780-1858
    A letter, addressed to Cadwallader D. Colden, es-
quire.   In answer to the strictures, contained in his
"Life of Robert Fulton," upon the report of the select
committee, to whom was referred a memorial relative
to steam navigation, presented to the Legislature of

New-York, at the session of 1814... Albany, E. and E. Hosford, 1817. 127 p. DLC; DeGE; MBAt; MWA; NWM; NjP.   40696

Dufief
  Dufief's nature displayed in her mode of teaching language to man; or, A new and infallible method of acquiring a language, in a shortest time possible. Adapted to the Spanish. By Don Manuel de Torres and L. Hargons. Philadelphia, 1817. 2 v. PPL-R.   40697

Dundas, Charles
  Stenography, or short-hand made easy. Boston, 1817. NN.   40698

Dunlap, William, 1766-1839
  The glory of Columbia her yeomanry! A play in five acts... New-York, David Longworth, 1817. 56 p. DLC; MWA; NIC; NjR; RPB.   40699

Duponceau, Peter Stephen, 1760-1844
  English phonology; or, An essay towards an analysis and description of the component sounds of the English language... Philadelphia, 1817. 55 p. ("Read as a memoir before the American philosophical society, and inserted in the first volume of their transactions, new series.') CtY; MBAt; NN; RPB.   40700

Durand, James R.
  The life and adventures of James R. Durand,... Bridgeport [Conn.]   Stiles Nichols & son, 1817. 83 p. CSmH; NN.   40701

Dutton, W. C.
  Frightened to death; a musical farce in two acts. By W. C. Dutton. The music composed and selected by T. Cooke. New-York, D. Longworth, 1817. MH.40702

Dwight, Henry
  A farewell sermon, to the First Utica Presbyterian society... Utica, N. Y., Pr. by William Williams, 1817. 26 p. CtY; MBAt; MBC; MWA; MWiW; MiD-B; NSy; NUt; NUtHi; NjPT; NjR.   40703

Dwight, Nathaniel
Short but comprehensive system of the geography
of the world...6th Albany ed., from the sixth Northampton ed., cor. and enl. Albany, Pr. by Websters
& Skinners, 1817. 215 p. NRU-W.   40704

-- A system of universal geography for common
schools, in which Europe is divided according to the
late act of the Congress of Vienna. Albany, Pr. by
Websters and Skinners, 1817. 210 p. MWA; NBuG;
NSyHi.   40705

-- -- Northampton [Mass.] Pr. by J. Metcalf, for
Simeon Butler, 1817. 216 p. Ct; MH; MNF; MWA;
NNC.   40706

Dwight, Timothy, 1752-1817
An address, to the emigrants from Connecticut,
and from New England generally, in the new settlements
in the United States. Hartford, 1817. 19 p. CtY.
                                                    40707
-- Hymns selected from Dr. Watts, Dr. Doddridge,
and various other writers. According to the recom-
mendation of the Joint committee of the General association of Connecticut, and the General assembly of the
Presbyterian church in America...New-York, Pr. by J.
Seymour, 1817. Ct; DLC; NjPT.   40708

Dyer, Samuel, 1804-1845
A new selection of sacred music, comprising a
great variety of approved psalm and hymn tunes, an-
thems, odes and chorusses...Baltimore, Pr. by Murphy and Milless, for F. Lucas, jr., and the author,
[1817] 225 p. CtY; MWA; MdBE.   40709

Dyster, Joseph Joshua
Five odes. Philadelphia, 1817. 14 p. PHi. 40710

E
Each for himself. A farce, in two acts...New-York,
David Longworth, 1817. 41 p. DLC; MWA; OC. 40711

Earle, Jabez
    The Christian's looking glass, or Sacramental ex-
ercises. By Jabez Earle. Ed. 3. Montpelier, Vt.,
Walton and Goss, 1817. 70 p. VtHi.   40712

Early piety, or memoirs of children eminently serious.
...New-York, T. & J. Swords, 1817. 85 p. MWA.
                                                40713
Eastburn, James & co., firm, booksellers, New York.
    A catalogue of books for 1817...1818; including
many rare and valuable articles in ancient and modern
literature, now on sale by James Eastburn & co. ...
New-York...New-York, Pr. by Abraham Paul, 1817.
101 p. DLC; MB; NNC.   40714

-- Plan of the literary rooms, instituted by James
Eastburn & Co., at the corner of Broadway and Pine-
Street, New-York. Ed. 2, cor. and enl. New-York,
Pr. by Abraham Paul, 1817. 15 p. MBAt; MH; MWA.
                                                40715
-- Prospectus for printing by subscription, by James
Eastburn & Co., at the Literary Rooms, corner of
Broadway and Pine-Street, New-York, limited editions
of scarce books, in the various branches of literature,
from the sixteenth century down to the present time...
New-York, Pr. by Abraham Paul, 1817. 16 p. MB;
MBAt.   40716

The Eastern Society, Maine
    ...Rules for the distribution of premiums...[1817]
Broadside. MB.   40717

Easton Centinel. Easton, Pa., Christian J. Hutter &
Son, July 11, 1817, 1st issue. Weekly newspaper.
PEa.   40718

Easton Gazette. Easton, Md., Alexander Graham,
Dec., 1817, 1st issue. Weekly newspaper. MdHi.
                                                40719
An easy introduction to the game of chess...A new ed.
Philadelphia, M. Carey and son, 1817. 282 p. MWA;
NjR.   40720

[Eaton, Amos] 1776-1842
A botanical dictionary, being a translation from the
French of Louis-Claude Richard...with additions from
Martyn, Smith, Milne, Wildenow, Acharius, &c. New-
Haven, Pr. by N. Whiting, for Hezekiah Howe, 1817.
[154] p. DLC; MWiW.   40721

[--] A manual of botany for the northern states; comprising generic descriptions of all phenogamous and
cryptogamous plants to the north of Virginia...by members of the botanical class of Williams College [Mass.]
...Albany, Pr. by Websters and Skinners, 1817. 164 p.
MWA; MWiW; MoSB; NNNBG; NTRPI.   40722

Eaton, John Henry, 1790-1856
The life of Andrew Jackson, major general in the
service of the United States: comprising a history of
the war in the South, from the commencement of the
Creek campaign, to the termination of hostilities before
New Orleans...Philadelphia, Pr. by Lydia R. Bailey,
for M. Carey & son, 1817. 425 p. DLC; GU-De; F; LU;
MB; MH; MWA; NN; NcD; NjP; TxU.   40723

Eddowes, Ralph
Sermons delivered before the First society of Uni-
tarian Christians, in...Philadelphia. Philadelphia,
Abraham Small, 1817. 230 p. CBPac; MBAt; MH; MWA.
                                                 40724

Edes, Henry
A sermon, delivered at Sherburne, Massachusetts,
July 2, 1817. At the ordination of the Reverend Sheer-
jashub Townsend...Providence, Pr. by Miller and
Hutchens, 1817. MWA.   40725

Edgeworth, Maria, 1767-1849
Comick dramas, in three acts...Boston, Wells and
Lilly, 1817. CSmH; MBL; MH; MWA; RNR; WHi.
                                                 40726

-- -- London Pr.; Philadelphia, Repr., T. Dobson and
son, 1817. 311 p. CtY; MH; PLFM.   40727

-- Frank. By Maria Edgeworth. Boston, Ezra Reed,
1817. 130 p. NGH.   40728

-- Harrington. New-York, Kirk & Mercein, 1817.
2 v. in 1. MWiW.   40729

-- Harrington, a tale; and Ormond...New York, Van
Winkle and Wiley, and James Eastburn & Co., 1817.
2 v. ICBB; ICMe; MWA.   40730

-- -- Philadelphia, 1817. 2 v. PPL-R.   40731

-- Rosamond...Boston, Ezra Reed. 1817. 72 p. MWA.
                                                    40732
Edwards, Jonathan, the Elder
    Account of Abigail Hutchinson, a young woman
hopefully converted at Northampton, Mass., 1734. Ed.
2. Andover, Mass., Flagg & Gould, 1817. 8 p. (New
England Tract Society, no. 78) MB.   40733

Edwards, Jonathan, 1745-1801
    The history of the work of redemption. By Jona-
than Edwards. Worcester, Mass., Thomas & Worcester, 1817. 355 p. NGH.   40734

-- Necessity of atonement and the consistency between
that and free grace, in forgiveness. Ed. 2. Portland,
Me., Pr. by John M'Kown, 1817. 107 p. OClW. 40735

Einfältige unterhaltungen mit Gott. Philadelphia, Pr. by
Conrad Zentler, 1817. MWA; NjP; PHi.   40736

Der 31ste October, 1817, zum feyerlichen Andenken...
Philadelphia, Pr. by Conrad Zentler, 1817. MWA.
                                                    40737
Elements and principles of the art of dancing, as used
in the polite and fashionable circles...Philadelphia, Pr.
by J. F. Hurtel, 1817. 93 p. DLC; PPiU.   40738

Eliot, John
    A sermon preached before the ancient and honorable
Artillery Co., in Boston June 2d, 1817...Boston, 1817.
25 p. MTa.   40739

Ellen O'Moore...1817. MWA.   40740

Ellingwood, John Wallace
Nothing too precious for Christ. A sermon de-
livered in Norridgewock, June 25, 1817; before the
Maine Missionary Society... Hallowell, Me., Pr. by N.
Cheever, 1817. 40 p. DLC; MWA; MeBat; MeHi; NjPT.
40741

Elliotson, John
The intitutions of physiology. From the Latin of
the third and last edition, and supplied with numerous
and extensive notes, by Elliotson. Ed. 2. Philadelphia, Benjamin Warner, 1817. 426 p. ILM; MB. 40742

Elliott, Benjamin
An oration, delivered in St. Philip's Church, be-
fore the inhabitants of Charleston, South-Carolina; on
Friday, the fourth of July, 1817... Charleston, S. C.,
Pr. by W. P. Young, 1817. 23 p. CSmH; DLC; ICN;
MB; MBAt; MBOS; MWA.   40743

-- A sermon delivered before the consociation of the
eastern district of New Haven county, in Meriden,
Sept. 30th, 1817. Hartford, 1817. 21 p. NjPT. 40744

[Elliott, Mrs. Mary (Belson)]
My brother... New York, Samuel Wood & Sons,
[1817]   MWA.   40745

[--] -- Philadelphia, Wm. Charles, 1817. MWA.
40746
-- My father, a poem for children. New York, Samuel
Wood & sons, 1817. MWA; PP.   40747

[--] -- Philadelphia, Wm. Charles, 1817. MWA. 40748

Elliott, Stephen
A sketch of the botany of South-Carolina and
Georgia... Charleston, S. C., Pr. by J. Hoff, 1817. 200
p. KyLoS.   40749

Elliott, William R.
Practical and comprehensive treatise on fruit and
floral culture and a few hints on landscape gardening.
By William R. Elliott. [Pittsburgh, Pa., Privately

printed, 1817] (William R. Elliott was a florist in
Pittsburgh where this book was probably published)
PPi.   40750

Emerson, Mrs. Eleanor [(Read)] 1777-1808
    Memoirs of the life, conversion, and happy death
of Mrs. Eleanor Emerson. New York, Pr. by C.
Dodge, 1817. 49 p. DLC; MWA; PHi.   40751

Emerson, Joseph
    The Evangelical primer, containing a minor doc-
trinal catechism, etc. Ed. 9. Boston, 1817. (The
Southern Library Service, List, 7, Nov., 1939. No.
241)   40752

Emerson, Ralph
    A sermon preached at Norfolk, Connecticut, May
16, 1816, the first Sabbath after his ordination...Hart-
ford, Pr. by George Goodwin & sons, 1817. 31 p. Ct;
CtHC; CtHi; CtY; CtSoP; MBC; MH-AH; MWA; MWiW;
N; NN; NjPT; OO.   40753

Emerson, Reuben
    Catechism exhibiting in a plain and concise manner,
the Scripture account of baptism...Boston, Pr. by
Armstrong, 1817. PPPrHi.   40754

Emigrant. St. Louis, Mo., Sergeant Hall, May 17,
1817, 1st issue. Weekly newspaper. In.   40755

Emmons, Nathanael
    A discourse, addressed to the Norfolk auxiliary so-
ciety for the education of pious youth for the gospel
ministry...Dedham, Mass., Pr. by Abel D. Alleyne,
1817. 39 p. CtY; ICMe; MAtt; MB; MBC; MH-AH;
MHolliHi; MSaE; MTa; MWA; MeB; MeBat; MiD-B; Nh;
NhD; VtMiM.   40756

Encyclopedia of wit...Philadelphia, M. Carey, 1817.
MWA.   40757

Engle, John Frederick
    Abschiede-Predigt, gehalten im October-Monat 1816

...Reading, Pa., Pr. by Heinrich B. Sage, 1817.
MWA; PHi.   40758

Enfield, William, 1741-1797
    The speaker: or, Miscellaneous pieces, selected
from the best English writers... Philadelphia, J. Bioren
and T. Desilver, 1817. 304 p. CSt; CtY; DLC; MWA;
NcWsHi; PPM.   40759

An enqiry into the doctrine of eternal punishment.
Baltimore, Pr. by Benjamin Edes, 1817. 13 p.
NNFMH; PPAmP.   40760

[Épinay, Louise Florence Pétronille de la Live d']
    The conversations of Emily... Philadelphia, Pr. [by
Asher Miner] for M. Carey & son, 1817. MB; MWA.
                                             40761
Episcopal Missionary Society of Philadelphia
    First annual report of the Board of Managers   of
the Episcopal Missionary society of Philadelphia. To
which is added the constitution and a list of officers
and members.   Philadelphia, John Brown, 1817. 20 p.
NcD; PHi.   40762

Ernste Uebersicht der Gewohnheit des Krieges.   Philadelphia, Pr. by Benj. & Thomas Kite, 1817. PHi.
                                             40763
The error of close communion in the Baptist churches
exposed.   And infant baptism, by sprinkling, vindicated;
in three letters from a layman, to a Baptist minister.
Second ed., cor. by the author.   New-Ipswich [N.H.]
Pr. by S. Wilder, 1817. 88 p. CSmH; MWA.   40764

[Erskine, Thomas Erskine]
    Armata... Ed. 2. New York, Pr. by E.G. Gould,
for James Eastburn & Co., 1817. 210 p. CSmH; MH;
MWA; RPB.   40765

Erskine, W.
    Harold the dauntless; a poem, in 6 cantos... New
York, 1817. PPL-R.   40766

An essay on the perseverance of the saints.   By one who

wishes to all, of whatever denomination, grace, mercy
and peace... Middletown, Conn., Pr. by T. Dunning,
1817. 36 p. CtHi; CtY; NjPT.   40767

Essex Patriot. Elizabethtown, N. Y., L. Person, Mar.
25, 1817, 1st issue. Weekly newspaper. MWA. 40768

-- Haverhill, Mass., P. N. Green, May 10, 1817, 1st
issue. Weekly newspaper. MBAt; MHa.   40769

Estill, Benjamin, 1780-1853
    To the electors of the congressional district com-
posed of the counties of Washington, Wythe, Grayson,
Tazewell, Russell, Scott and Lee... [Abingdon, Va. ?
1817?] 6 p. NcD.   40770

Evangelical association of North America
    Das geistliche saitenspiel, oder Eine sammlung
auserlessner, erbaulicher, geistreicher lieder... 1. aufl.
New-Berlin [Pa.] Pr. by S. Miller H. Niebel, for the
Evengelische gemischchaft, 1817. 436 p. DLC; MWA;
MiU-C; PReaAt; RPB.   40771

-- Glaubenslehre und kirchen-zucht-ordnung der Evange-
lischen gemeinschaft, nebst dem zweck ihrer vereinigung
mit Gott und untereinander. 2. und. verb. aufl. New-
Berlin, Pa., Pr. by S. Miller and H. Niebel, for the
Evangelische gemeinschaft, 1817. 144 p. DLC; MWA;
PReaAT.   40772

Evangelical Lutheran church.
    Die Augsburgische confession... York, Pa., Pr. by
C. T. Melsheimer, 1817. MWA; NcWsM; PPLT. 40773

-- A collection of hymns and liturgy for the use of
Evangelical Lutheran churches; to which are added
prayers for families and individuals. Philadelphia, G.
& D. Billmeyer, 1817. 483 p. GDC; IES; MWA; NRAB;
NNUT; OSW; P; PAtM; PPLT.   40774

-- North Carolina. Synod.
    Bericht der Verrichtungen... 1816. New-Market, Va.,
Pr. by S. Henkel's, 1817. 15 p. MWA; ViNmM; ViNmT;

ViU; ViW.   40775

Evans, E.
    An appeal to the people of New-Hampshire (rela-
tive to the claims of the representatives of Judge
Evans on the state of New Hampshire).   Exeter, N.H.,
1817. (BrMus. cat. 17. Estignard: 93)   40776

Evans, James
    David's companion, or, The Methodist standard:
being a choice selection of tunes adapted to the works
and measures in the large   hymn book... Ed. 2. New
York, Pr. by Abraham Paul, for the Wesleyan Sacred
Music Society of the city of New York, 1817. 162 p.
NNUT.   40777

Evans, Oliver, 1755-1819
    Oliver Evans to his counsel.   Philadelphia, 1817.
MH-BA; MWA.   40778

Evening amusement.   Maxims for the preservation of
health, and the prevention of diseases.   New York,
from Lee's patent & family medicine store, 1817. 35 p.
CtHi; MiD-B; PHi.   40779

The evil and natural consequences of idleness illustrated by examples... Boston, 1817. (BrMus. cat. 41)
                                         40780

Ewell, James
    The medical companion... with a dispensatory and
glossary... Ed. 3, greatly improved.   Philadelphia, Pr.
for the author, 1817. DLC; MWA; MdUM; NNNAM; PU.
                                         40781
Ewell, Thomas, 1785-1826
    Letters to the ladies, detailing important informa-
tion concerning themselves and infants... Philadelphia,
Pr. by W. Brown, 1817. 308 p. DLC; GU-M; MBM;
MWA; NNNAM.   40782

Examen du livre de M. Malthus sur le principe de pop-
ulation; auquel on a joint la truduction de quatre chapi-
tres... et une lettre a M. Say sur son Traite d'econo-

mique.   Philadelphia,   chez P. M. Lafourcade, 1817.
159 p. NjR.   40783

Ein Exempel- und Liederbüchlein für betende Kinder.
Philadelphia, Conrad Zentler, 1817. 144 p. MdBSHG;
PHi; PLERCHi; PPG; PPLT.   40784

Exhibition dialogues, being a selection of scenes, chiefly taken from the best English dramatists, and adapted
for exhibition in schools and academies... Boston, Pr.
by T. G. Bangs, for Caleb Bingham and Co., 1817.
228 p. MPlyA; MWA; MWHi; NjR; PMA.   40785

Exile. New York, Walter Cox, Jan. 4, 1817, 1st issue. Weekly newspaper. DLC; MWA.   40786

Experimental reflections, Nashville, Tenn., T. G.
Bradford, 1817. 147 p. LNH.   40787

                            F
Faber, George Stanley
    Sermons. Vol. I. Philadelphia, M. Carey & sons,
1817. 424 p. InID; MWiW; MeB; PLT.   40788

Falconer, W.
    The shipwreck. Ed. 8. Philadelphia, 1817. MB.
                                                       40789
False stories corrected. (With woodcuts) New-York,
S. Wood & Sons, 1817. 41 p. (BrMus. cat. 55. Sto.
41)   40790

...Familiar dialogues...[Philadelphia, Pr. by Lydia R.
Bailey...1817] (This is no. 18 of the Tracts of the
Philadelphia female tract society) MWA.   40791

Fansher, Sylvanus, fl. ca. 1817
    Rules to be attended to during vaccination. [Bos-
ton, 1817] 1 p. NNNAM.   40792

The farmer's almanac for the year of our Lord 1818...
Useful and entertaining matter by Father Abraham.
Astronomical clacalations by John Sharp. Baltimore,

William Warner [1817] 35 p. NNA; PPM.   40793

The farmer's almanack, calculated on a new and improved plan, for...1818...Boston, Hendee and co.,
[etc.] 1817. CU.   40794

Farmer's almanac...1818...Boston, T.W. White,
1817. MWA.   40795

-- Boston, T.W. White, 1817. (Varied ed.) MWA.
                                               40796
The farmer's almanack, calculated on a new and im-
proved plan, for the year of our Lord 1818, etc...by
Robert B. Thomas. Boston, West and Richardson
[1817] [48] p. CL; CoU; ICMeHi; MBNEH; MDedHi;
MHa; MMal; MMeT; MPeHi; MStouHi; MWA; MdHi;
MeBa; MiD-B; NjR; RBr; RWe.   40797

-- containing the usual astronomical calculations...by
David Young...Philadelphia, Pr. for every purchaser,
[1817] [36] p. NjR.   40798

-- by Andrew Beers. Poughkeepsie, N.Y., Pr. by P.
& S. Potter [1817] 24 p. N; NN; MWA; RPB.   40799

The farmers' calendar or Utica almanack for...1818,
by Andrew Beers...Utica, N.Y., Pr. by William Williams, 1817. [36] p. DLC; MWA; NHi; NN.   40800

The farmer's diary, or western almanack, for...1818,
by Andrew- Beers. Canandaigua, N.Y., J.D. Bemis
[1817] [36] p. NBuHi; NjR.   40801

Farquhar, George, 1677?-1707
     The beaux stratagem. A comedy...New York,
David Longworth, 1817. 84 p. DLC; MB; MWA; RPB;
RNR.   40802

Farrand, William P.
     Farrand's course of Latin studies; or classical se-
lections...Ed. 3, with notes for the use of American
schools. Philadelphia, Abraham Small, 1817. v. p.
ICMcHi; MWA; WMOSC.   40803

Farrar, Timothy
    Report of the case of the trustees of Dartmouth
college against William H. Woodward...By Timothy
Farrar.   Portsmouth, N. H. , Pr. by J. J. Williams,
for John H. Foster, 1817. 406 p. NjR.   40804

The Fathers, the reformers, and the public formularies
of the Church of England, in harmony with Calvin, and
against the bishop of Lincoln; to which is prefixed a
letter to the Archbishop of Canterbury, on the subject
of this controversary.   By A layman.   Philadelphia,
Philip H. Nicklin and A. Small, 1817.   203 p. MeBat;
PPL-R; PPLT; PPPrHi.   40805

Fay, Heman Allen, ed.
    Collection of the official accounts, in detail, of all
the battles fought by sea and land, between the navy
and army of the United States and the navy and army of
Great Britain, during the years 1812, 13, 14, & 15.
New York, Pr. by E. Conrad, 1817.   295 p. DLC;
MWA; Md; NIC; NWM; NjP.   40806

Federal party - Connecticut.
    Federal Republican nomination for council...[Hart-
ford, Conn. ? 1817?] MWA.   40807

-- Massachusetts.   Essex County.
    County convention!...[1817] MWA.   40808

The Federalist...A new ed.   Philadelphia, Pr. by William Greer, for Benjamin Warner, 1817. 477 p. MH;
MWA; MsG; MsJMC; OCHP; ScCoT; ViU.   40809

Female Association of Cincinnati for the benefit of Afri-
cans.
    Constitution of... Cincinnati, Morgan, Palmer and
Co. , 1817. 7 p. OCHP.   40810

Female auxiliary Bible society of Baltimore.
    Annual report.   Baltimore, 1817. PPAmP. 40811

Female Bible & charitable society of Nashville, Tenn.
    Constitution of the Female Bible and charitable so-

ciety of Nashville, 1817. [Nashville, Tenn., 1817] 1 p.
LNH.   40812

Female Bible and religious tract society of King's
County, L. I.
    Constitution and first report of the Female relig-
ious tract society of Flatbush and Flatlands: instituted
Oct. 26, 1815: and organization of the Female religious
tract society of Kings County (L. I.) Together with their
first report... New-York, Pr. by J. Seymour, 1817.
18 p. DLC; NN.   40813

Female Charitable Society of Cranbury (N. J.)
    Constitution... adopted Aug. 23, 1817. New Bruns-
wick, N. J., William Myer, 1817. 4 p. NjR.   40814

Female Domestic Missionary Society for the support of
the Gospel in the Almshouse, Philadelphia, Pa.
    Annual reports. 1817- Philadelphia, Pr. by
Scott [1817-] PPAmP; PPPrHi.   40815

Female Domestic missionary society of Philadelphia.
    The first annual report... Philadelphia, Pr. by J.
W. Scott [1817] MWA.   40816

The female marine, or Adventures of Miss Lucy
Brewer, a native of Plymouth County, Mass.... Boston,
Pr. for the purchaser, 1817. DLC.   40817

Female missionary society of New York City.
    New missionary field. A report of the Femal mis-
sionary society for the poor of the city of New-York
and its vicinity, at their quarterly prayer meeting,
March 1817. New-York, Pr. by Clayton & Kingsland,
1817. 55 p. MBC; NN; TxFwSB.   40818

Female Missionary Society of the Western District,
New York.
    The first annual report of the Trustees of the Fe-
male Missionary Society of the Western District, presented Sept. 2, 1817. Utica, N. Y., Pr. by William
Williams, for the Society, 1817. 48 p. NUtHi; PPPrHi.
                                                    40819

Female Sabbath School Society
    Constitution of the Female Sabbath School· Society
of the Second Baptist Church and congregation, in
Boston.   Boston, Pr. by Farnham and Badger, 1817.
16 p.   MWA.   40820

Ferguson, James, 1710-1776
    An easy introduction to astronomy for young gentle-
men and ladies... 3d Philadelphia ed.   Philadelphia, Pr.
by Wm. Dickson, for Benjamin Warner, 1817. 178 p.
In; KyU; MWA.   40821

-- Ferguson's astronomy explained upon Sir Isaac Newton's principles.   Philadelphia, A. Small, 1817. 2 v.
CtY; MB; MH; MWP; MWA; NTEW; P; TWcW; ViU.
                                                  40822
Ferguson, Richard
    Abaddon's steam engine, calumny, delineated, being
an attempt to stop its deleterious results on society,
the church and state.   By Richard Ferguson; to which is
subjoined, the infernal triumvirate... by a lover of
mercy rejoicing over judgment... Philadelphia, Pr. by
J. H. Cunningham, 1817.   228 p. CtW; MWA; NjMD; P;
PPL-R; PU; ScNC.   40823

Der Fertige Rechner... Philadelphia, Im verlag bey
Conrad Zentler und Georg W. Mentz, 1817. 144 p.
MWA; MiU-C; PNazMHi; PPESchw.   40824

A few hints on the subject of a theological seminary for
the Protestant Episcopal church... New-York, 1817. 1 p.
NNG.   40825

Field, David Dudley
    The reciprocal duties of ministers and people, a
sermon, preached... at the ordination of Rev. H. Tal-
cott.   Middletown, Conn., Pr. by T. Dunning, 1817.
22 p. CtHi; CtY; MWA.   40826

Fielding, Henry, 1707-1754
    Eurydice hissed; or, A word to the wise, a farce.
New York, D. Longworth, 1817. 12 p. OC; TxU. 40827

$50,000 [New Haven, 1817] Broadside. (Federalist campaign literature) CtY.   40828

Fisher, Abiel
    The existence of God...Worcester, Mass., Pr. by William Manning, 1817. 24 p. MDeeP; MWA; MiD-B.
                                                40829

Fisher, Jonathan
    A short essay on baptism...Boston, Pr. by Thomas G. Bangs, for Samuel T. Armstrong, 1817. 105 p. MB; MBNMHi; MH; MHi; MWA; MnHi; NBuG; NN; Nh; NjPT; NjR; RPB.   40830

-- The youth's primer...Boston, Samuel T. Armstrong, 1817. 108 p. MB; MH; NNC.   40831

Flagg, Joshua, 1773-1859
    Sermon delivered on the death of Miss Lydia Worth, of Hudson, who departed this life, June 23d, 1847. Hudson, N.Y., 1817. 24 p. MB.   40832

Flavel, John, 1630?-1691
    A saint indeed; or, The great work of a Christian, opened & pressed...Hartford, Pr. by B. & J. Russell, 1817. 245 p. Ct; CtHi; CtHT-W; MWA; NcG.   40833

[--] Seaman's compass - extracted and abridged from Flavel. No. 81. N.E. Tract Soc. Andover, Mass., Flagg & Gould, 1817. MWA.   40834

Fletcher, Mrs. Mary (Bosanquet)
    The life of Mrs. Mary Fletcher, consort and relict of the Rev. John Fletcher...[New York, 1817?] 458 p. MdBG.   40835

Florida
    Report of the Committee appointed to frame the plan of provisional government for the Republic of Florida...Fernandina, 1817. 7 p. FU.   40836

"The following observations were originally written in detached pieces. They are now thrown together and respectfully offered to the notice of the public." Richmond,

Pr. by John Warrock, 1817. ViW.   40837

Fonda, Jesse
    Confidence in God in a day of trouble. A vale-
dictory discourse... New Brunswick, N.J., Pr. by
David Fitz Randolph, 1817. 30 p. MWA; NjPT; NjR.
          40838
Forster, Anthony, 1785-1820
    Documents relating to the dissolution of the con-
nexion between the Rev. Mr. Forster and the Independent or Congregational Church of Charleston, S.C.
[Charleston] Skrine & Duke, 1817. 24 p. MWA. 40839

Foster, Festus
    The character of the churl and of the liberal man,
contrasted... Brookfield, Mass., Pr. by E. Merriam
& Co., 1817. 46 p. MWA; NjR.   40840

-- Documents, elucidating the nature and character of
the opposition made to the Rev. Mr. Foster. Brookfield, Mass., Pr. by E. Merriam & Co., 1817. 46 p.
CSt; DLC; MBC; MWA.   40841

Foster, John
    A sermon, preached 6 November, 1817... Cam-
bridge, Mass., Pr. by Hilliard and Metcalf, 1817.
MWA.   40842

Fothergill, Samuel
    Eleven discourses... Wilmington, Del., Coale &
Rumford, 1817. 263 p. DLC; DeHi; DeWI; GDC;
InRchE; KWi; MH; MWA; NcGuG; NjR; OClWHi; PHC;
PU; PHi; PPF; PPM; PSC.   40843

[Fox, Francis]
    A present, to accompany the Prayer book; being one
of the tracts, of the Society for Promoting Christian
Knowledge; accommmodated, to the use of the members
of the Protestant Episcopal Church, in the United States
of America... Albany, Pr. by E. & E. Hosford, for the
Society, 1817. 36 p. N.   40844

Fragment Society
    The act of incorporation and constitution of the
Fragment Society, with the subscribers' names. Instituted Oct. 1812, incorporated Dec. 1816. Boston, Pr.
by Munroe & Francis, 1817. 18 p. MH; MWA.   40845

Franklin, Benjamin, 1706-1790
    The life of Benjamin Franklin, written chiefly by
himself... A new ed., rev. and enl. by Mason L.
Weems. Philadelphia, M. Carey, 1817. 264 p. CSmH;
CtY; MMal; MWA.   40846

-- Some account of the Pennsylvania hospital; from its
first rise to the beginning of the fifth month, called
May, 1754. Philadelphia, Pr. at the office of the U-
nited States' gazette, 1817. 145 p. CtY; DLC; MWA;
MdBJ; MnU; NNNAM; NjR; PHi; PHC; PP; PPA;
PPPH; PU.   40847

-- Way to wealth. [Battleborough, Vt., Simeon Ide,
1817?] (No known copy. Adv. in American Yeoman,
April 15, 1817. May be unsold remainder of New Ipswich, N.H. ed. of 1816)   40848

-- -- New Ipswich, N.H., Simeon Ide, 1817. (Libbie
auction catal. June 19, 1919, item 1427)   40849

-- -- New York, S. Wood & Sons, 1817. 44 p. MWA.
                                                40850
Franklin Federalist. Greenfield, Mass., Russell Wells,
May 24, 1817, 1st issue. Weekly newspaper. MWA.
                                                40851
Franklin Republican. Chambersburg, Pa., John Sloan,
May, 1817, 1st issue. Weekly newspaper. P.   40852

Free-school society of New York.
    Twelfth annual report... [New York] Pr. by Collins
& Co., 1817. MWA.   40853

Freeman's Journal. Cooperstown, N.Y., J.H. Prentiss, 1817, 1st issue with this title. A weekly continuation of "Cooperstown Federalist." WHi.   40854

Freemasons. Delaware. Grand Lodge.
By-laws, rules and regulations for the government
of Lodge No. 5, held at Cantwell's Bridge, in the
state of Delaware, under the authority of the Right
Worshipful Grand Lodge of Delaware...[Dover, Del.,
Aug. M. Schee, 1817] 8 p. PPFM.   40855

-- Kentucky. Grand Lodge.
Proceedings of the Grand Lodge of Kentucky, held
at the Masons' Hall in the town of Lexington, August
A. L. 5817-A. D. 1817. Lexington [Ky.] Pr. by Worsley & Smith, 1817. 50 p. IaCrM; MBFM; NNFM.
                                                    40856
-- Maryland. Grand Lodge.
Extracts from the proceedings of the Grand lodge
of Maryland, at an annual communication, begun and
held in the city of Baltimore, on the fifth day of May,
5817. Baltimore, Pr. by I. Robinson, 1817. 30 p.
NNFM.   40857

-- -- -- The Freemasons' library and general Ahiman
rezon; containing a delineation of the true principles of
freemasonry...Baltimore, Benjamin Edes, 1817. 452 p.
CSmH; DLC; IaCrM; MdBE; NjR; OCM; PP; PPFM;
PU.   40858

-- -- Royal Arch Masons.
Proceedings of the Grand royal arch chapter of the
state of Maryland, and District of Columbia, Washington, Nov. 10, 1817. 7 p. NNFM; PPFM.   40859

-- Massachusetts.
Order of services at the dedication of the new
Masonick Hall in the Exchange coffee-house, Boston,
July 22, A. L. 5817. Boston, J. T. Buckingham [1817]
8 p. MH.   40860

-- New Hampshire. Grand Lodge.
Proceedings of Grand Lodge of masonic lodge in
New Hampshire; meeting held in 1816. Amherst [N. H.]
R. Boylston, 1816. 9 p. IaCrM.   40861

-- -- -- Summary of the proceedings of the Grand

Lodge of New-Hampshire, at their General Assembly in
Concord, begun June 11th, and continued by adjournment to June 12th, A.L. 5817.   Amherst, N.H., Pr.
by R. Boylston, 1817.   9 p.   PPFM.   40862

-- New York. Grand Lodge.
    Proceedings of the Grand lodge of the most ancient
and honorable fraternity of free and accepted Masons of
the state of New York, at its quarterly communication
and meetings of emergency, held between the 24th of
June, A.L. 5816, and the 24th of June A.L. 5817; New
York, Pr. by Brother David Longworth, 5817 [1817]
27 p. IaCrM; NNFM; PPFM.   40863

-- Ohio. Grand Lodge.
    Proceedings...[Jan. 6-8, 1817] Chillicothe, O., Pr.
by Brother Bailhache, 1817. 88 p. IaCrM; MBFM.
                                                      40864
-- -- -- Proceedings of the Grand Lodge of Ohio, held
in Chillicothe, Aug. 4, 1817... Chillicothe, John Bailhache [1817?] 76 p. IaCrM; MBFM; OCFM.   40865

-- Pennsylvania. Grand Lodge.
    Grand lodge of the most ancient and honourable
fraternity of free and accepted Masons of Pennsylvania
and masonic jurisdiction thereunto belonging, according
to the old institutions.   At a grand quarterly communication, held at their new hall in the city of Philadelphia,
on Monday the 1st December, Anno Domini 1817, Anno
Lucis 5817, in ample form, the Grand Lodge proceeded
to the election of Grand officers for the ensuing year...
Philadelphia, Pr. by T.S. Manning, 1817. PPFM.
                                                      40866
-- -- -- Grand lodge of the most ancienct and honorable fraternity of free and accepted Masons of Pennsylvania... in the city of Philadelphia, on Monday the 1st
December, anno Domino 1817, anno Lucis 5817. Phila-
delphia, Pr. by T.S. Manning, 1817. 16 p. NNFM.
                                                      40867
-- -- -- Statement: In answer to the Committee of
Carbon Lodge, of which Brother Lilly is the chairman.
The records show; that the City Brethren have, by spe-
cial contributions, paid the whole cost of the lot on

Chestnut Street, and the halls thereon, erected; and
that the Country Lodges have not been called upon to
pay one cent towards the same; and this is proved by
the following statement. 1817. 4 p. PPFM.   40868

-- South Carolina. Grand Lodge.
The proceedings and articles for the union of the
two Grand Lodges in South-Carolina, submitted to the
consideration of the subordinate lodges, under the jurisdiction of the Grand Lodge of South-Carolina Ancient-
York Masons. Charleston, S. C., Pr. by A. E. Miller,
1817. 26 p. PPFM.   40869

-- Tennessee. Grand Lodge.
Proceedings... at the grand annual communication
held in Nashville, Oct. 5, 5816. Nashville, Pr. by T.
G. Bradford, 1817. 9 p. NNFM.   40870

-- U.S. Knights templars. Grand encampment.
Constitution of the general Grand encampment of
Knights templars, and the appendant orders, for the
United States of America. Boston, Pr. by T.W. White,
1817. 12 p. IaCrM; N; PPFM.   40871

-- Vermont. Grand Lodge.
Grand Lodge of the most ancient and honorable society of free and accepted Masons of the state of Vermont. Attest, [!] Worshipful Jonathan Nye, Grand
Master. Brattleborough, Vt., Pr. by John Holbrook,
[1817] 36 p. MBFM; VtBFM.   40872

-- Virginia. Grand Lodge.
Proceedings of a grand annual communication...
held... the second Monday in December... Anno Domini,
1816... Richmond, Va., Pr. by John Warrock, 1817.
26 p. MBFM; MWA.   40873

-- -- Randolph Lodge No. 19.
By-laws for the government of the Richmond Randolph lodge, no. 19, passed at a meeting in August
A. L. 5894; the third edition altered and amended. Richmond, Pr. by Bro. Jon. Warrock, January A. L. 5817
[1817] 8 p. IaCrM; MBFM.   40874

Frey, Joseph Samuel Christian Frederick
    Narrative of the Rev. Joseph Samuel C. F. Frey
...New York, W. B. Gilley...1817. 480 p. MMal;
MMeT; MNowdHi; MWA; RP.   40875

-- A view of the principles upon which the Independent
...Society for public worship and the ministry of...
Mr. F., is established. New York, 1817. (BrMus.
Cat. 19. Free Agency: 237)   40876

Friendly gift for servants and apprentices...New York,
S. Wood & Sons, 1817. MiGr; WaSP.   40877

Frisbie, Levi
    Inaugural address, delivered in the chapel of the
University at Cambridge, November 5, 1817...Cam-
bridge, Mass., Pr. by Hilliard & Metcalf, at the University press, 1817. MWA.   40878

Frost, John
    Importance of the ministerial office. A sermon,
delivered at the ordination of the Reverend Henry Smith,
to the pastoral care of the church in Camden, October
8, 1817. Utica, N. Y., Pr. by William Williams, 1817.
32 p. CSmH; MBC; MHi; MWA; N.   40879

[Fuller, H. W.]
    A review of Warden's letters from St. Helena; con-
taining remarks on Bonaparte's massacres at Jaffa and
El Grish...Boston, 1817. 32 p. MHi.   40880

                        G
Gadsden, Christopher Edwards, bp.
    A discourse, preached and published by request of
the vestry and wardens of St. Michael's church...
death of Bishop Dehon...Charleston, S. C., Pr. by A.
E. Miller, 1817. DLC; ICU; MWA; NNG.   40881

Gaifer (pseud.)
    The conversion of a Mahometan, to the Christian
religion; described in a letter from Gaifer, in England,
to Aly-Ben-Hayton, his friend in Turkey. [Andover,

Mass., Flagg & Gould, 1817] 12 p. (New England
Tract Society. No. 82) ICN; MB; MWA.   40882

Gale, Edmund
    Epitome of book-keeping. Nantucket, A. G. Tan-
natt, 1817. MWA.   40883

Gales' North-Carolina almanack, for the year of our
Lord, 1818... By John Beasley. Raleigh, N. C., Pr.
by J. Gales... [1817] 34 p. NcD.   40884

Gallaudet, Thomas Hopkins, 1787-1851
    A sermon delivered at the opening of the Connecti-
cut asylum for the education and instruction of deaf and
dumb persons, at the request of the directors, on Sunday evening, April 20th, 1817, in the Brick church in
Hartford. Hartford, Pr. by Hudson and co., 1817.
15 p. CSt; CtHi; Ct; CtHC; CtSoP; CtY; IaU; MB;
MBC; MBD; MH-AH; MHi; MWA; MWiW; MeB; MiD-B;
N; NHi; NjPT; NcD; NjR; OCHP; PPAmP; PPPrHi;
RNHi; RPB.   40885

Ganz neuer westlicher, für die Staaten von Ohio, Kentucky und Indiana besonders eingerichteter Calender,
auf das Jahr... 1818... Lancaster, O., Johann Herman,
[1817] [34] p. (Lindley, Harlow - Columbus, O.)
        40886
Gardiner, John David, 1781-1849
    Preparation to meet God. A sermon, occasioned
by the death of Miss Mary Hill, who died of a consumption, January 19th, 1817, aged 26. ... Sag-Harbor,
N. Y., Pr. by Samuel A. Seabury, 1817. 24 p. DLC;
MWA; NEh; WGr.   40887

Gardiner, John Sylvester John
    A sermon preached at Trinity-church, March 30,
1817, being the Sunday after the interment of John
Gore. Boston, Munroe & Francis, 1817. 16 p. MH;
MHi.   40888

Gardiner Jan. 20, 1817. Fellow citizens... Congressional election... 5th Eastern district. ... John Hazeltine,
Wm. G. Warren, Zachariah Tarbox. [Gardiner, Me.,

1817] Broadside.   40889

Garnett, Robert Selden, 1789-1840
    To the freeholders of the Congressional district
composed of the counties of Caroline, Essex, King &
Queen and King William.   Fellow-citizens...March 20,
1817. [Fredericksburg? William F. Gray? 1817]
Broadside. ViU.   40890

Garrettson, Freeborn
    A letter to the Rev. Lyman Beecher containing
strictures and animadversions on a pamphlet: An address of the Charitable Society for the Education of Indigent Pious Young Men.   Boston, Repr. by Thomas
Rowe, 1817.   24 p.   MBAt; MBC; MBNMHi; MWA; Nh.
                                                    40891
Gaskill & Copper
    Patterns of rolls, stamps, scrolls and connecting
lines for ornamenting the covers of books.   Philadelphia, 1817.   PPF.   40892

[Gay de Vernon, Simon François, baron] 1760-1822
    A treatise on the science of war and fortification:
composed for the use of the Imperial polytechnick
school, and military schools; and translated for the War
department, for the use of the Military academy of the
United States...New-York, Pr. by J. Seymour, 1817.
2 v.   DLC; MBAt; MWA; MWiW; OkFlsFA; RP.   40893

No entry.   40894

Der gemeinnutzige landwirthschafts Calender.   Auf das
Jahr...1818.   Lancaster, Pa., 1817.   PHi.   40895

Das Gemeinschaftliche gesangbuch, zum gottesdienst-
lichen gebrauch der Lutherischen und Reformirten ge-
meinden in Nord-America...Ed. 2.   Baltimore, Schaffer & Maund, 1817.   370 p.   DLC; MWA; MdHi; NNUT;
NcD; PHi; PMA; PLT; RPB; ViU.   40896

General Sunday School Society
[The spelling book, or introduction to reading, of
the ...Society.   Chillicothe, 1817] (Amer. Imprint Inventory no. 17 (357))   40897

Genesee Farmer, Moscow, N. Y., H. Ripley, Feb.,
1817, 1st issue. Weekly newspaper. MWA.   40898

Genlis, Stéphanie Félicité Ducrest de St. Aubin,
comtesse de.
     Jane of France; an historical novel. Translated
from the French... Boston, Wells and Lilly, 1817. 2 v.
MH.   40899

-- A manual, containing the expressions most used in
travelling, and in the different circumstances in life.
By Madame De Genlis... Corrected and amended by an
instructor of languages.   Boston, Cummings and Hil-
liard... 1817.   145 p. CtY; LNT; MB; MH; MWA; NNC.
                                                    40900
-- Placide, a Spanish tale... New-York, Pr. by T. &
W. Mercein, for Kirk & Mercein, 1817. 2 v. in 1.
CSmH; DLC; GSTA; MWA; NjR.   40901

Genius of Liberty. Leesburg, Va., Samuel B. T. Caldwell, Jan. 11, 1817, 1st issue. Weekly newspaper.
MWA.   40902

The gentleman's amusement, containing a select collection of songs, marches, etc., for the flute, fife and
violin.   Norfolk, Va., Thos. Balls [1817?] 104 p. Vi.
                                                    40903
Georgia (State)
     Acts of the General assembly of the state of Geor-
gia, passed... November and December 1817... Milledgeville, Pr. by S. & F. Grantland, 1817. 169 p. DLC;
GU-De.   40904

-- Journal of the House of Representatives of the state
of Georgia, at an annual session... Nov. and Dec., 1817.
Milledgeville, Pr. by S. & F. Grantland [1817] 103 p.
DLC.   40905

-- Journal of the Senate of the state of Georgia, at an
annual session...Nov. and Dec., 1817. Milledgeville,
Pr. by S. & F. Grantland [1817] 74 p. DLC.   40906

-- The penal code of the state of Georgia; as enacted
December 19, 1816. With reflection on the same, and
on imprisonment for debt. Philadelphia, M. Carey &
son, 1817. 96 p. AB; C; GU-De; MH-L.   40907

Gerisher, Charles
Modern book-keeping, by double entry; adapted to
commission business, as it is conducted in the United
States of America; designed for mercantile young men.
New-York, Pr. by E. Conrad, 1817. MB; MWA;
NNMer.   40908

German society of Maryland.
Constitution of the German society of Maryland.
Baltimore, Pr. by Schaeffer & Maund, 1817. 21 p.
DLC; OClJC.   40909

Geschichte des americanischen kriegs, von 1812, vom
anfang bis zum endlichen schluss desselben, an dem
glorreichen achten januar, 1815, vor Neu-Orleans...
Reading, Pa., gedruckt und zu haben bey Johann Ritter
und comp. Herausgegeben und ebenfalls zu haben bey
William M'Carty, Philadelphia, 1817. 273 p. CSmH;
DLC; DeWI; MWA; NN; OClWHi.   40910

Gethsemane: or, thoughts on the sufferings of Christ...
1st Amer. ed. Philadelphia, Pr. by William Fry, for
Anthony Finley, 1817. 208 p. CtHC; MWA; MeBat;
NNS.   40911

Gilbert, Sylvester, and others.
Address to the people of the county of Tolland.
Hartford, 1817. MBAt; MWA.   40912

Gilchrist, James
Journal of a voyage. Salem, Mass., 1817. MSaE.
40913
Gildersleeve, Cyrus
Centurial jubilee. A sermon, preached...Oct. 31,

1817...a day of Thanksgiving. Newark, N.J., Pr. by Ward & Conover, 1817. 15 p. PPPrHi.   40914

Gill, John
    The antiquity of infant baptism...Utica, N.Y., Pr. by William Williams, 1817. 12 p. MWA; NN; NRAB; NUt.   40915

-- An exposition of the Old Testament...Philadelphia, Pr. by William W. Woodward, 1817-19. 6 v. ICU; LNB; MWA; MsCliM; ODaB; PPiXT.   40916

Gilleland, J.C.
    History of the late war, between the United States and Great Britain; containing an accurate account of the most important engagements by sea and land...Ed. 2. Baltimore, Schaeffer & Maund, 1817. 190 p. CSmH; CtY; DLC; KHi; MB; MH; MHi; MWA; MdBE; MdHi; NN; NNS; OCl; OClWHi.   40917

Gillet, Eliphalet
    Blessedness of the pious dead...interment of Mrs. Elizabeth Fillebrown...Hallowell, Me., Pr. by N. Cheever, 1817. 22 p. MWA; MeBat; MeHi.   40918

-- A sermon preached at the dedication of the new meeting house in Vassalboro', March 6, 1817...Hallowell, Me., Pr. by E. Goodale, 1817. 24 p. MBC; MMeT; MWA.   40919

Gillet, Wheeler
    The Virginia sacred minstrel, containing a collection of psalm and hymn tunes...public and family worship. Winchester, Va., Pr. by J. Foster, for the author, 1817. 124 p. MWA; RPB.   40920

Gilman vs. Brown & al.   The case in equity, tried in the Circuit of the United States for Massachusetts district at Boston, May term, 1817, before the Hon. Joseph Story, associate judge of the Supreme court, between Mary Gilman vs. Samuel Brown & al. [1817?] 38 p. Ct.   40921

[Gilpin, William] 1724-1804
The lives of John Trueman, and Richard Atkins;
to which is added a short account of Atkins' sister...
Philadelphia, James Webster, 1817. 111 p. DLC;
MWA; P.   40922

A glass from "the book," historical fact and ocular
demonstration; showing the mysteries of Swedenborg.
By a believer.   Philadelphia, 1817. 104 p. PHi. 40923

Gloucester Farmer.   Woodbury, N.J., John A. Crane,
Jan. 1, 1817, 1st issue.   Weekly newspaper.   MWA.
                                            40924
[Goffe, Joseph]
The result of an Ecclesiastical Council, published
at Princeton, March 7, 1817; and the protest of the
minority.   With remarks, notes and observations.   By
a member of the Council...Worcester, Mass., Pr. by
William Manning, 1817. 24 p.   CBPac; DLC; MBAt;
MBC; MH-AH; MWA; MiD-B; NNUT; NjR.   40925

[--] The result of council at Princeton incapable of
vindication; or, A review of Dr. Bancroft's vindication
of the result of the late mutual council convened in
Princeton, by a member of the council...Worcester,
Mass., Pr. by William Manning, 1817. 44 p.   C-S;
CSmH; CSt; CtHT-W; CtHC; CtSoP; CtY; DLC; ICMe;
M; MAuB; MBAt; MH; MWA; MWHi; NNUT; Nh; NjR;
OClWHi; WHi.   40926

Gold, Thomas
Address of Thomas Gold...before the Berkshire
association...Pittsfield, Mass., Pr. by Phinehas Allen,
[1817] 32 p.   MBAt; MBHo; MPiB; MWA; NHi; NN;
NNNBG.   40927

Goldsmith, Oliver
An abridgement of the history of England from the
invasion of Julius Caesar to the death of George II...
with interrogatories.   New York, Richard Scott, 1817.
397 p.   MH; MSan; MWA; TNP.   40928

-- The Grecian history from the earliest state to the

death of Alexander the Great.   5th Amer. ed Philadelphia, Abraham Small, 1817. 335 p. KyDC; MB;
MWA; MdBMSJ; NCoxhi; NcWfC; RPB.   40929

-- Goldsmith's natural history; abridged, for the use of
schools.   By Mrs. Pilkington.   Philadelphia, Benjamin
Warner, 1817. 304 p. MWA; TNP.   40930

-- Goldsmith's Roman history.   Abridged by himself.
For the use of schools.   6th Amer. ed.   New-York,
Richard Scott, 1817. 254 p. KyBC; MB; MWA; MdHi.
                                                   40931
-- -- Philadelphia, Ambrose Walker, 1817. 276 p.
MdHi; NR.   40932

-- -- Philadelphia, J. Maxwell, 1817. 240 p. DLC;
MWA; NSchU; VtWino.   40933

[Goodenow, John M.]
    Review of the question, etc.   Pittsburgh, Pa.,
1817. 44 p. OClWHi.   40934

Goodman, John & others.
    Circular letter.   Philadelphia, 1817. PPAmP. 40935

Goodrich, A. T. & Co.
    The new and fashionable Chinese puzzle...New
York, A. T. Goodrich & Co., 1817. [64] p. RPB.
                                                   40936
Goodrich, Charles Augustus, 1790-1862
    An address, delivered June 26, 1817, before the
Female reading and charitable society, of the First
parish in Worcester, Mass.   Worcester, Mass., Pr.
by William Manning, 1817. 20 p. CtY; DLC; M; MH;
MWA; MWHi; NN.   40937

-- History of the United States of America.   Boston,
Pr. by Holbrook & Fessenden, 1817. 352 p. MMeT.
                                                   40938
Goodridge, Elijah Putnam
    Report of the evidence at the trial of Levi and La-
ban Menniston before Hon. Samuel Putnam on an indictment for the robbery of Major Elijah P. Goodrich,

Dec. 19, 1817.   Salem, Mass., 1817. 32 p. MHi; VtU.
                                                    40939
Goodwin, William
    Fables ancient and modern.   Adapted for the use
of children.   By Edward Baldwin, pseud.   New-Haven,
Sidney's press, 1817. 47 p. MB.   40940

Gorham, John
    Inaugural address, delivered in the chapel of the
University at Cambridge, December 11, 1816...Boston,
Pr. by Wells and Lilly, 1817. 23 p.   CtY; DLC; ICMe;
MB; MBC; MH; MWA; MdBP; MeHi; N; NBMS; Nh;
NNNAM; PPAmP; RPB.   40941

An die Gottsuchende und Jesuliebende Seelen.   Lancaster, Pa., 1817.   PHi.   40942

[Gough, J.]
    A system of practical arithmetick, in four books,
agreeably to Telfair's edition of Gough's arithmetick...
(Ed. 2.) Baltimore, Pr. by William Warner, 1817.
342 p. MWA; MdToN; NNC; ScNc.   40943

Gould, William
    A sermon, delivered in Dracut, First parish, Oc-
tober 19, 1817...Haverhill, Mass., Pr. by Burrill &
Tileston, 1817. 28 p. DLC; MBAt; MHa; MHi; MNo;
MSaE; MWA; NjR.   40944

Graham, Mrs. Isabella (Marshall) 1742-1814
    The power of faith: exemplified in the life and
writings of the late Mrs. Isabella Graham, of New-
York. Ed. 2. New-York, Pr. by T. & W. Mercein,
for Kirk & Mercein, 1817. 428 p. MWA; NBuG;
NNMer; RPB; TU.   40945

Gram, Olaves Peter, b. 1779
    Letter to a friend, concerning the building of the
Capitol in the city of Washington...[Washington, 1817]
6 p. DLC.   40946

Grammatical exercises, on the moods, tenses and syntax of the Latin language; adapted to the method of Rud-

diman's rudiments. 1st Albany ed., from the Edinburgh stereotype ed. Albany, Pr. by Websters and
Skinners, 1817. 204 p. CoHi; CtNlC.   40947

Granger, Gideon
     Speech of Gideon Granger, Esq., delivered before
a convention of the people of Ontario County, N. Y.,
Jan. 8, 1817. on the subject of a canal from Lake Erie
to Hudson's River... Canandaigua, N. Y., Pr. by J. D.
Bemis, [1817] 24 p. DLC; MB; MH-BA; N; NN; NjPT;
PHi; PPF.   40948

Gray, Francis Calley
     An address to the Massachusetts Charitable Fire
Society, at their annual meeting, Oct. 10, 1817... Bos-
ton, Pr. by Chester Stebbins, 1817. 21 p. DLC; MB;
MBAt; MBB; MBC; MH-AH; MHi; MMeT; MSaE; MWA;
Nh.   40949

Gray, James
     Death's defence of his character against the slan-
ders of poets, orators, etc. Philadelphia, Pr. by W.
Brown, 1817. 12 p. NjR; PHi; PPPrHi; PPiXT. 40950

-- The fiend of the Reformation detected... Philadelphia,
Pr. by W. Brown, 1817. 141 p. MWA; OClWHi; OSW;
PLT; PPiW.   40951

Gray, Nicholas
     · Supplement to the Natchez Intelligencer. Natchez,
July 5, 1817. To the editor of the Natchez Intelligencer. [Natchez, 1817] Broadside. Ms-Ar.   40952

Gray & Cady, Fredericksburg, Va.
     A catalogue of books and stationery, for sale by
Gray & Cady, booksellers and stationers, Fredericksburg, Va. September, 1817. 56 p. DLC.   40953

Great Britain
     Reports of cases argued and determined in the
Court of King's bench, with tables of the names of the
cases and principal matters... Containing the cases in
the forty-first year of George III. 1800, 1801 [to the

fifty-second and fifty-third years of George III. 1812]
A new ed.   Philadelphia, M. Carey & son, 1817. 16 v.
CoU; DLC; ICLaw; IaDmD-L; LNT-L; M; MWA;
NNebgL; TChU; WaU.   40954

Gregory, John
    Lectures on the duties and qualifications of a
physician... Philadelphia, M. Carey & Son, 1817. 232 p.
KyLxT; MBM; MH-AH; MWA; NBMS; NNC-M; NNNAM.
                                                     40955
Griffin, Edward Dorr, 1770-1837
    A plea for Africa.   A sermon preached October 26,
1817, in the First Presbyterian church in the city of
New York, before the Synod of New-York and New-Jersey, at the request of the board of directors of the African school established by the synod... New-York, Pr.
by Gould, 1817. 76 p. DLC; MH; MNe; MWA; MWiW;
NjR.   40956

Griffin, John
    Early piety recommended... [Philadelphia, Pr. by
Lydia R. Bailey, 1817] (This is no. 19-20 of the
Tracts of the Philadelphia female tract society) MWA.
                                                     40957
Griswold, Alexander Viets, bp.
    Christ's warning to the churches.   A sermon de-
livered at the opening of the General Convention of the
Protestant-Episcopal Church in the United States of A-
merica, assembled in Trinity Church, in the city of
New York, May 21st, A. D. 1817... New York, Pr. by
T. & J. Swords, 1817. 30 p. InD; MWA; NIC; NGH;
NcD; NjR; OrPD; PPL; TJaU.   40958

[--] A sermon, on the blessedness of charitable giving
... Boston, R. P. and C. Williams, 1817. 24 p. MBAt;
MWA.   40959

[Grosvenor, Thomas Peabody] 1779-1817
    A sketch of the life, last sickness, and death of
Mrs. Mary Jane Grosvenor.   Left among the papers of
the late Hon. Thomas P. Grosvenor... Baltimore, Coale
and Maxwell, 1817. 82 p. DLC; MH; MdBE; PPL.
                                                     40960

-- -- Ed. 2. Baltimore, Pr. by Kennedy and Magauran, for Edward J. Coale, 1817. 86 p. CSt; CtY; MB; MWA; MdHi; MoS; PPL; PPPrHi. 40961

Das grosze ABC-Buch...Erste Aufl. Neu-Market, Va., S. Henkel, 1817. 92 p. DLC; MWA; MnU; NcWsS; PLDL; PPL-R. 40962

Grout, Jonathan
Preparation for the general judgment, an immediate duty...Northampton, Mass., Pr. by Thomas W. Shepard, & Co., 1817. 22 p. MDeeP; MNF; MW; MWA. 40963

Grove, Henry
The nature and design of the Lord's supper; with devotional exercises. Abridged from the treatise of Henry Grove. Andover, Mass., Pr. by Flagg and Gould, 1817. 44 p. (New England tract society. Vol. 4. Tract 84) MB; MWA; MiD-B; NjR; RPB. 40964

Guardian of Liberty. Cynthiana, Ky., John G. Keenan & Co., Jan. 4, 1817, 1st issue. Weekly newspaper. ICU. 40965

Guildersleeve, Cyrus
A sermon, preached at Bloomfield, N.J., Oct. 31, 1817...Newark, N.J., Ward & Conover, 1817. 15 p. NjR. 40966

Gummere, John, 1784-1845
A treatise on surveying, containing the theory and practice: to which is prefixed a perspicuous system of plane trigonemetry...Philadelphia, J. Richardson [etc] 1817. 206 p. DLC; PWW. 40967

-- -- Ed. 2. Philadelphia, J. Richardson, 1817. 358 p. MWA; NNC. 40968

Guthrie, Jessie
American schoolmaster's assistant, being a compendious system of vulgar and decimal arithmetic. Ed. 4, revised and cor. by the author. Paris, Ky., John Lyle [1817] ICU; KyBgW-K; KyU; MWA. 40969

Guy, Francis
    Letters addressed to Elizabeth Walker, minister of
the Society of friends in the state of New York. Baltimore, 1817. 18 p. PPM.   40970

Guy of Warwick
    The wonderful exploit of Guy, earl of Warwick...
Philadelphia, Wm. Charles, 1817. [16] p. DLC. 40971

                            H
[Haldane, James Alexander]
    Early instruction recommended... New Haven, Sid-
ney's press, 1817. 46 p. CtY; MWA.   40972

Hale, Sir Matthew
    A letter of advice to his grandchildren... Boston,
Wells and Lilly, 1817. 206 p. CSt; CtHT-W; CtY;
DLC; ICBB; MB; MBC; MBL; MS; MWA; NNS; NR;
NSchU; NhPoA; OClWHi; ScU.   40973

Hall, John
    Jacob's ladder... A new and improved ed. New
York, Pr. by A. Spooner, for A. & A. Tiebout, 1817.
MWA.   40974

-- Tracts on the constitutional law of the United States.
Selected from the Law journal, by J.E. Hall... Phila-
delphia, Pr. by J. Maxwell, for Harrison Hall, at the
Port Folio office, 1817. PU-L; TxU-L.   40975

Hall, Robert
    On terms of communion... 2d Amer. ed. Manlius,
N.Y., Pr. by Kellogg & Clark, 1817. CtHC; MWA.
                                                 40976
-- A sermon, occasioned by the death of her late Royal
Highness the Princess Charlotte of Wales... Boston,
James Loring, Cummings & Hilliard... [1817] 48 p.
ICMe; MBAt; MBDiL; MBNEH; MH-AH; MPlyP; MWA;
NjR.   40977

The Hallowell collection of sacred music; adapted to the
different subjects and metres, commonly used in

churches. Hallowell, Me., E. Goodale, 1817. 197 p.
MWA; MeHi; NN; RPB.   40978

Hamilton, Alexander, 1757-1804
    The soundness of the policy of protecting domestic
manufactures; fully established by Alexander Hamilton
in his report to Congress on the subject, and by Thomas Jefferson, in his letter to Benjamin Austin. To
which are added, extracts from the Address of the A-
merican society for promoting domestic manufactures
established in New York... Philadelphia, Pr. by J.R.A.
Skerrett, 1817. 24 p. CtY; MBAt; MMeT.   40979

Hamilton, Elizabeth
    A series of popular essays, illustrative of princi-
ples essentially connected with the improvement of the
understanding, the imagination, and the heart... Boston,
Wells and Lilly, 1817. 2 v. DeWI; KWiU; MA; MBev;
MLy; MWA; MoS; NNS; OMC; PPL-R; RBr.   40980

Hamilton, Ralph
    Elphi Bey: or, The Arab's faith. A musical drama,
in three acts... New-York, David Longworth, 1817. 53p.
DLC; MBr; MH; MWA; NIC.   40981

Hampshire charitable society.
    Report of the directors, at the second annual meet-
ing... at Whately, November 6th, 1816. Northampton,
Mass., E. Brooks, 1817. 10 p. Ct; MWA.   40982

Hampshire Register. Northampton, Mass., Elijah
Brooks, Jan. 8, 1817, 1st issue. Weekly newspaper.
MWA.   40983

Hand-book for drill & instruction of the companies attached to the field pieces. New York State Artillery.
New York, Van Winkle & Wiley, 1817. MWA.   40984

Handel, George Frederick
    The Messiah: an oratorio, for the voice, organ and
violin... from the London ed. Boston, [J. Loring, 1817]
[144] p. MiGr.   40985

Handel and Haydn society, Boston.
    Act of incorporation and bye-laws of the Handel
and Haydn society, instituted April, 1815, incorporated
February, 1816. Boston, Pr. by C. Stebbins, 1817.
16 p. DLC; MWA.   40986

-- Last oratoria by this society on December 18, 1817.
New York, 1817. 12 p. NjPT. (Sprague coll., vol.
367, no. 5)   40987

-- Oratorios, comprising the Messiah, by Handel and
the Creation, by Haydn, together with intermediate se-
lections; as performed at King's Chapel, Boston...
April 1, 3, 4, 1817, by the Handel and Haydn Society.
Boston, Pr. by C. Stebbins, 1817. 27 p. DLC; MB;
MBAt; MWA.   40988

-- Select oratorio, performed in Boston, the 5th July,
1817, in presence of James Monroe, president of the
United States. Order of performance. [1817] 4 p.
MBAt; MH.   40989

Handel Society, Salem, Mass.
    Articles of the Handel Society, instituted in Salem,
January, 1817. Salem, Mass., Pr. by W. Palfray,
Jr., 1817. 8 p. MSaE.   40990

Handelian charitable society, Baltimore.
    Constitution of the Handelian charitable society; as
revised by a committee appointed for that purpose.
Adopted Tuesday, February 11, 1817. Baltimore, Pr.
by J. Robinson, 1817. 8 p. MdHi.   40991

... The happy cottagers... [Philadelphia, Pr. by Lydia
R. Bailey, 1817] (This is no. 22 of the Tracts of the
Philadelphia female tract society) MWA.   40992

Happy poverty, or The story of poor blind Ellen. A
well authenticated narrative. [Hartford, Pr. by Hudson
& Co., for the Hartford Evangelical Tract Society] May,
1817. 12 p. CtHi. (Hartford Evangelical Tract Society.
Publications. no. 10)   40993

Hardie, James, 1750?-1826?
   The epistolary guide, containing models of juvenile
letters, on familiar subjects, with topics for the exercise of youth...New-York, Pr. by S. Marks, 1817.
287 p. DLC; ICU; MWA; NN.   40994

[--] Selectae e profanis scriptoribus historiae...Nova
editio...Baltimore, Pr. by Joseph Robinson, 1817.
MWA.   40995

[--] -- Nova ed...Baltimore, Pr. by J. Robinson, for
Fielding Lucas, jr., 1817. 305 p. MdHi.   40996

[--] -- New ed. rev. Baltimore, Cushing, 1817. 299 p.
NCH; OC.   40997

Hare, Robert
   A new theory of galvanism supported by some experiments and observations made by means of the cal-
orimotor...Philadelphia, 1817. 17 p. PHi.   40998

Harlem library, New York.
   Constitution of the Haerlem Library formed by a
convention of the inhabitants held in Haerlem, Oct., 1817.
New York, J. Seymour, 1817. NN. (Negative made 6
February-1925, from orig. in possession of E. F. Brown
of Harlem)   40999

Harold the dauntless. New York, 1817. MWA. 41000

The harp; or, Selected melodies: from authors eminent
for genius and taste. Dedicated to the lovers of music
and song...Greenfield, Mass., Denio & Phelps, 1817.
16 p. CSmH.   41001

[Harrington, Isaac R.]
   To Col. J.R. Mullany, Quarter-Master General of
the Northern Division of the United States Army. [Bur-
lington? 1817?] 15 p. CSmH.   41002

-- -- New York, 1817. DLC.   41003

Harris, Thaddeus Mason
     A valedictory sermon on leaving the old meeting-
house in the First parish in Dorchester... Boston, Pr.
by John Eliot, 1817. 36 p. ICMe; M; MB; MBAt; MBC;
MBFM; MH; MHi; MWA; MiU-C; NN; RPB.   41004

Harris, Walter
     Paul's determination how to preach, a sermon
preached at the ordination of the Rev. Enoch Corser,
to the pastoral care of the first Church in London, New
Hampshire, March 5, 1817... Concord, N. H., Pr. by
George Hough, 1817. 28 p. ICP; MWA.   41005

Harrisburg Guards
     Constitution of the Harrisburg Guards. Harrisburg,
Pa., Pr. by J. S. Wiestling, 1817. 10 p. P.   41006

Harrison, Ammi
     An oration, delivered before the Harmony Society,
in New Haven, on the 41st anniversary of American independence. New Haven, 1817. 16 p. CtY.   41007

Hart, Cyrus W.
     Two epistles addressed to the departed spirit of a
citizen, on deism and on universalism... Pittsfield,
Mass., 1817. MH-AH.   41008

Hart, W. J.
     Introduction to Study of chronology, Part 1. Phila-
delphia, M. Carey & Son, 1817. MWA.   41009

Hartford Auxiliary Bible Society
     First report... with an address delivered at their
annual meeting, by Horace Hooker. By Hartford Auxiliary Bible Society. Hartford, 1817. 15 p. NjPT.
      41010

Hartford County Agricultural Society
     Articles of association and by-laws of the... Hart-
ford, Pr. by George Goodwin & Sons, 1817. 8 p.
CtHi.   41011

Hartford Evangelical tract society.
     First report... January 1st, 1817... [Hartford, 1817]

MWA.   41012

Hartford.   First Ecclesiastical Society.
    Church music: selected by a committee of the First
Ecclesiastical Society in Hartford, and designed for the
use of that society, together with a few useful rules of
psalmody. Hartford, Pr. by S. Green, for G. Goodwin & Sons, 1817. 40 p. NRU; RPB.   41013

[Hartwell, Thomas?]
    Hints on the establishment and regulation of Sunday
schools, with forms of the books necessary for keeping
a methodical account of the scholars.   Copied from an
English publication.   [New York] New York Sunday
school union society, 1817. 19 p. MWA; NNUT; VtU;
WHi.   41014

Harvard university.
    The statutes of the University in Cambridge, relat-
ing to the degree of doctor in medicine.   Boston, Pr.
by Wells & Lilly, 1817. 8 p. DLC; MB.   41015

Harwood, Edward
    The life and character of Jesus Christ delineated
... Philadelphia, Pr. by T. H. Palmer, for Edward
Earle, 1817. 137 p. MWA; PPLT.   41016

Hascall, Daniel
    Caution against false philosophy... New York, Pr.
by John B. Johnson & son, 1817. 12 p. ICU.   41017

Haskel, Daniel
    The doctrine of predestination... Burlington, Vt.,
Pr. by Samuel Mills [1817] 24 p. MB; MBC; MWA;
MeB; NN; OO; VtHi; VtU-W.   41018

[--] Remarks on "some observations, taken in part
from an address..." [Brattleborough, Vt., Pr. by
Simeon Ide, 1817] 15 p. MB; MWA; OO; VtU-W. 41019

Hastings, Thomas
    Hasting's dissertation on musical taste by Thomas
Hastings. Utica, N. Y., William Williams, 1817. (Not

located; title from Williams, p. 77)   41020

[--] The musical reader, or Practical lessons for the
voice; consisting of phrases, sections, periods, and entire movements of melody in score...Utica, N.Y., Pr.
typographically by William Williams, 1817. 80 p.
CtHC; CtHT-W; MWA; N; NBuG; NCH; NNUT; NRHi;
NUtHi.   41021

[--] A new and choice collection of flute melodies;
consisting of duets, waltzes, cotillions, airs, marches,
etc., to which are prefixed the instructions for the
German flute and patent flagelet. Utica, N.Y., W.
Williams, 1817. 47 p. CtHT-W; N.   41022

Hawley, Daniel
    [The federal calculator, or American school-
master's assistant and young man's companion, which
is altered from Thomas Dilworth's arithmetic, and
adapted to the currency of the United States...By Daniel Hawley...5th stereotyped ed., rev. and cor., and
improved by William Stoddard. Troy, N.Y., 1817]
(Greenwood and Martin, p. 816)   41023

Hay, George, 1765-1830
    Speech, delivered in the Legislature of Virginia,
in the session of 1816-17, in support of a bill to repeal all the laws concerning usury...Richmond, Va.,
Shepherd & Pollard, 1817. 38 p. DLC; MBAt; NcD;
Vi; ViU; ViRut.   41024

Haynes, Lemuel
    Universal salvation, a very ancient doctrine...A
sermon, delivered at Rutland, West Parish in 1805.
Ed. 9. Kennebunk, Me., Pr. by James K. Remich,
1817. 12 p. MWA.   41025

-- -- Ed. 9. Providence, Pr. by Miller & Hutchens,
1817. MWA.   41026

Hays, Stephen
    The Bible the source of consolation and hope. An
address, delivered before the Newark Bible society; on

the last Sabbath in June, 1817, being its third anniversary meeting; in the First Presbyterian church in Newark...Newark, [N.J.] Pr. by John Tuttle & co., 1817.
16 p. CSmH; MWA; NBuDD; NjR.   41027

Heath, John
    Serious charges against Capt. Oliver H. Perry of
the United States Navy by John Heath, late Capt. of the
Marine Corps. Washington [1817] 24 p. OCHP; RHi.
                                                41028
Helmuth, Justus Christian Henry
    Der 31ste october, 1817, zum feyerlichen andenken
an den 31sten october, 1817, mit ruhrung begangen in
der St. Michaelis und Zions Gemeinde in Philadelphia.
Philadelphia, Pr. by Zentler, 1817. 80 p. PPLT.
                                                41029
-- Gedachtniss-predigt gehalten am 31sten October,
1817 als am dritten hundertjahrigen jubelfeste der Reformation Martin Luthers. Philadelphia, Pr. by G.
und D. Billmeyer, 1817. 22 p. MWA; PPLT.   41030

[Henkel, Ambrose] 1786-1870
    ABC-und Bilder-Buch. ABC and picture-book.
Neu-Market, Va., S. Henkel...1817. 22 p. CtHT-W;
NcD; PHi; PP; PPLT; Vi; ViNmT; ViU; ViW.   41031

-- Das grosse ABC-buch...1. aufl. Neu-Market,
Schenandoah caunty, Va., Pr. by S. Henkel, 1817.
92 p. DLC; MWA; MnU; NcWSc; PPL-R.   41032

-- Das kleine ABC-buch, oder erste anfangs-büchlein
...New-Market, Schenandoah county, Va., Pr. by S.
Henkel, 1817. 36 p. CtHT-W; ViHarHi.   41033

Henry, William
    The elements of experimental chemistry...4th
Amer. from 7th London ed. Philadelphia, Pr. by W.
Brown, for James Webster, 1817. 656 p. GU-M;
KyLxT; NbOM; PPC; PU.   41034

The hero; or, The adventures of a night; a romance.
Translated from the Arabic into Iroquese;...and from
French into English...Philadelphia, M. Carey & son,

1817. 2 v. in 1. MWA; NjR; PPL-R.   41035

Heustis, Jabez Wiggins, 1784-1841
    Physical observations, and medical tracts and re-
searches, on the topography and diseases of Louisiana.
New-York, Pr. by T. & J. Swords, 1817. 165 p. DLC;
MWA; MoSM; NNNAM; NjP; OC.   41036

[Heuzet, Jean] 1660-1728, comp.
    Selectae e profanis scriptoribus historiae. Quibus
admista sunt varia honeste vivendi praecepta, ex iisdem
scriptoribus deprompta. Novo editio prioribus longe
emendatior. Baltimore, F. Lucas, jr., 1817. 320 p.
DLC; MdBE; MdHi.   41037

-- -- Baltimore, Pr. by J. Robinson, for Joseph Cushing, 1817. 299 p. DLC; MdBE; MdHi; NN; PHi. 41038

Hey, William
    A treatise on the puerperal fever... Philadelphia,
M. Carey & son, 1817. 234 p. CSt-L; CSmH; MBM;
MWA; MdBT; NBuU-M; P.   41039

High, Thomas
    Narrative of a journey in Egypt and the country be-
yond the cataracts... Philadelphia, M. Thomas, 1817.
203 p. NcU.   41040

Hill, Sanford
    Sanford Hill, has just received a general... assort-
ment of goods... which he will dispose of at the lowest
Pittsburgh prices... Newlisbon, O., Pr. at the office of
the Ohio Patriot [1817] Broadside. DLC; OEalHi.
                                       41041
Hill, William
    "The doctrine of the New Jerusalem concerning the
Lord." Philadelphia, Lydia R. Bailey, 1817. 162 p.
MBNC.   41042

[Hiller, Margaret]
    Religion and philosophy united: or, An attempt to
shew, that philosophical principles from the foundation
of the New Jerusalem church, as developed to the world

in the mission of the Honourable Emanuel Swedenborg
...Boston, Pub. for the subscribers, 1817. 55 p.
DLC; MWA.   41043

Himes, Paul
    A selection of hymns from the best authors...
Greenfield, Mass., Pr. by Ansel Phelps, 1817. 324 p.
MWA; RPB.   41044

Hindmarsh, Robert
    A compendium of the chief doctrines of the true
Christian religion: as revealed in the writings of Emanuel Swedenborg...Philadelphia, William Schlatter, 1817.
176 p. MReh; OClWHi.   41045

Hippocrates
    The aphorisms of Hippocrates...by Elias Marks...
New York, Collins & Co., 1817. 169 p. CoDR; MB;
MBBCHS; MPiB; MStow; MWA; NNNAM; PPAN; ViU.
                                                 41046
Hiram beneficial society of the city and county of
Philadelphia.
    Constitution...Philadelphia, Pr. by Anderson and
Meehan, 1817. MWA.   41047

A historical sketch of opinions on the atonement interspersed with biographical notices of the leading doctors,
...Philadelphia, Pr. by W. Fry, for Edward Earle,
1817. 351 p. CSansS.   41048

...The history of a Bible...[Philadelphia, Pr. by
Lydia R. Bailey, 1817] (This is no. 17 of the Tracts
of the Philadelphia female tract society) MWA.   41049

History of Caroline: or, A lesson to cure vanity...
New-Haven, Sidney's press, 1817. 30 p. CtHi.   41050

History of Little Henry and his bearer. From 2d London ed. Andover, Mass., Flagg & Gould, 1817. MWA.
                                                 41051
-- 2d Amer., from 2d London ed. Hartford, Pr. by
Hudson and Co., 1817. 32 p. MWA; NIDHi.   41052

The history of Mrs. Wilkins; or, the happiness of having God for a friend, in time of trouble. [Philadelphia] 1817. MWA.   41053

The history of North and South America, from its discovery to the death of General Washington. Philadelphia, 1817. 2 v. in 1. NIC.   41054

History of Sinbad the Sailor - also...travels...of... Baron Munchausen. Chillicothe, O., Pr. for the publishers, 1817. 36 p. MWA.   41055

The history of Susan Ward. Philadelphia, Wm. Bradford, agent, 1817. MWA.   41056

...The history of William Black...[Philadelphia, Pr. by Lydia R. Bailey...1817] (This is no. 23 of the Tracts of the Philadelphia female tract society.) MWA.
                                                      41057
History of the American war of 1812, from the commencement, until the final termination thereof on the memorable eighth of January, 1815, at New Orleans... Ed. 3. Philadelphia, W. M'Carty, 1817. 252 p. CSmH; DLC; MB; MWA; PWgWHi.   41058

Hobart, James
    A confession of faith and covenant, adopted by the Church of Christ in Berlin...New London, Conn., Pr. by Samuel Green, 1817. 7 p. CSmH; MBC; MWA.
                                                      41059
Hobart, John Henry, bp.
    An address delivered before the New-York Protestant Episcopal missionary society of young men and others...New York, Pr. by T. & J. Swords, 1817. 16 p. MBAt; MWA; NHi; NNG.   41060

-- Companion for the festivals and fasts of the Protestant Episcopal Church in the United States of America ...Ed. 2. New York, T. & J. Swords, 1817. 337 p. MWA; NIC; NN; NcMHi; NjP; OC.   41061

[--] A sketch of the life and character of Dr. Poedagogus, the reformer...with remarks on his writings, by

Corrector...New York, The author, 1817. 71 p. NNG.
41062

Der Hochdeutsche Amerikanische Calender auf das Jahr
1816. Philadelphia, G. und D. Billmeyer, 1817. 47 p.
PPG; PReaHi.   41063

Hoffman, David
    A course of legal study...Baltimore, Pr. by Pom-
eroy and Toy, for Coale & Maxwell, 1817. 383 p.
ArU; CSmH; CSt; CLSU; IU; MBAt; MWA; MdBD;
MdBE; MdHi; NIC-L; NNC; OCLaw; PPL; PU-L; VtU;
WaU.   41064

Hofland, Mrs. Barbara (Wreaks) Hoole, 1770-1844
    The blind farmer, and his children...Albany, Pr.
by Websters & Skinners, 1817. 120 p. MWA.   41065

-- -- New York, Pr. by A. Paul, for William B. Gilley, 1817. MDeeP; MWA.   41066

-- The good grandmother and her offspring...New
York, Pr. by E. B. Gould, for James Eastburn & Co.,
1817. 170 p. MBAt; MPlyA; MWA.   41067

-- Matilda, or the Barbadoes girl, a tale for young
people...Philadelphia, M. Carey and son, 1817. 175 p.
PPL-R; ViU.   41068

Hoge, James, 1784-1863
    The law of love: a missionary sermon delivered in
Chillicothe, Oct. 5, 1817...Chillicothe, O., Pr. by
John Andrews, 1817. 15 p. OCHP; PPPrHi.   41069

Hoge, John Blair
    Ministerial usefulness: a sermon delivered at Rom-
ney, April 17, 1817, before the Presbytery of Winchester. Philadelphia, Pr. by W. Fry, 1817. 43 p.
MWA; NjPT; PLT.   41070

[Hogg, James] 1770-1835
    The poetic mirror; or, The living bards of Brit-
ain...Philadelphia, M. Carey and son, 1817. 188 p.
CtY; DLC; MB; MWA.   41071

Holcombe, Henry
    The funeral sermon of Joseph Moulder... Philadel-
phia, Pr. by John Bioren, 1817. 105 p. MWA; PHi;
PWW.   41072

[Holford, George Peter]
    The destruction of Jerusalem, an absolute and ir-
resistable proof of the divine origin of Christianity...
10th Amer. ed. Boston, T. W. White, 1817. MH.
                                              41073
Holman, Joseph George, 1764-1817
    Succinct account of the disturbance which occurred
at the Charleston theatre on the evening of the 12th of
March, 1817, with the addresses to the public by J. G.
Holman and J. H. Caldwell. Charleston [S. C.] A. E.
Miller, 1817. 39 p. NN; PU.   41074

Holman, Nathan
    A sermon, preached in Eaton, at the interment of
Mr. Isaac Lothrop, who died suddenly, in the field,
May 11, 1815... Boston, Pr. by Thomas Rowe, 1817.
12 p. MBC; MH; NN.   41075

Holmes, David
    By David Holmes, Gov. of Mississippi Territory,
a proclamation, May 9, 1817. Broadside. LNH. 41076

Holmes, John
    An address delivered at Dover, N. H. on the 23d
October, A. L. 5817, at the installation of Strafford
lodge... Dover, N. H., Pr. by John Mann, [1817] 16 p.
DLC; MWA; PPFM.   41077

Homer, Jonathan
    A sermon, delivered in Newton, Oct. 13, 1816, up-
on occasion of the decease of Mr. Samuel Hammond...
Dedham, Mass., Pr. by Abel D. Alleyne, 1817. 26 p.
CtY; MBC; MBr; MH; MHi; MW; MWA; MiD-B; Nh-Hi;
NjPT; VtMiM; WHi.   41078

Homespun, Barnabas, pseud.
    The modesty of the Democrats. [New Haven?
1817?] Broadside. (Anti-Democrat political broadside)

CtY.   41079

Homo, pseud.
    Homo's letters on a national currency, addressed
to the people of the United States. Washington, D. C.,
E. de Krafft, 1817. 37 p. DLC; MB; MWA; NN; NNC;
PPAmP; RPB.   41080

Hooper, Robert
    A new medical dictionary... Philadelphia, Pr. by
Griggs & Co., for Benjamin Warner, M. Carey &
son... 1817. 870 p. IEN-M; IU-M; MWA; MnSM;
MoKWD; NIC; NNMSCQ; NbU-M; OC; OClM; TNV.
                                               41081
Hort, W. Jillard
    An introduction to the Study of chronology, and
Universal history... Philadelphia, 1817. 193 p. MHi.
                                               41082
Houston, Samuel
    The essence of English grammar. Harrisonburg,
Pr. by Lawrence Wartmann, 1817. MWiW.   41083

How, Thomas Yardley
    An address delivered before the auxiliary New-
York Bible and common prayer book society, in St.
Paul's chapel, in the city of New-York, on Tuesday,
the 28th day of January, A. D. 1817... New-York, Pr.
by T. and J. Swords, 1817. 52 p. CSt; MHi; MWA;
NIC; NNG; NjR; OrPD.   41084

How to try a lover. A comedy. In three acts. New-
York, David Longworth, 1817. 67 p. MnU; NNC; PU;
RNR.   41085

Howe, Fisher
    The true site of Calvary, and suggestions relating
to the Resurrection, with an illustrative map of Jerusalem. New York [1817] 68 p. VtU.   41086

Howe, Nathanael
    A century sermon delivered in Hopkinton... Decem-
ber 24, 1815... Ed. 2, rev. and cor. Andover, Mass.,
Pr. by Flagg and Gould, 1817. 31 p. CSt; CtY; DLC;

M; MBD; MH-AH; MNe; MSbri; MWA; MWiW; MeHi;
MiD-B; NjR; RPB.   41087

Howe's genuine almanac for 1818. By Philo Astronomiae. Enfield, Mass. [1817] [24] p. MWA; WHi.
                                                   41088
...-- by Philo Astronomiae...Greenwich [Mass.] 1817.
MHi; MWA; WHi.   41089

Hubbard, John, 1759-1810
    The American reader: containing a selection of
narration, harangues, addresses, orations, dialogues,
odes, poems, &c...1st Bellows' Falls ed. Bellows'
Falls, Vt., Bill Blake, & Co., 1817. 215 p. CSmH;
Ct; MiU; NN; VtHi; MWA; VtU-W.   41090

[Huber, Marie] 1695-1753
    The state of souls, separated from their bodies:
being an epistolary treatise...Translated from the
French. 1st Amer., from the second London ed.
Cooperstown, N.Y., Pr. by I.W. Clark, for the pub-
lisher, 1817. 203 p. CSmH; MB; MH; MMeT-Hi;
MWA; NBuG; NCaS.   41091

Hughes, Joseph S.
    A discourse, delivered at Columbus, O., to Lodge
no. 30...Dec. 27th, A.L. 5816. Columbus, O., Pr.
by P.H. Olmsted & Co., 1817. 17 p. NjR; NjN. 41092

[Hughs, Mrs. Mary (Robson)]
    Aunt Mary's tales...for boys...1st Amer. ed.
New York, Pr. by Forbes & Co., for D. Bliss, 1817.
IEG; MWA.   41093

[--] Aunt Mary's tales, for...girls...New York, Pr. by
Forbes & Co., for D. Bliss, 1817. MH; MWA; NN.
                                                   41094
[--] The ornaments discovered...New York, Pr. by D.
Fanshaw, for W.B. Gilley, 1817. 180 p. MH; MWA;
NcD.   41095

[--] William's return...Ed. 2. Boston, Munroe &
Francis and Isaac Bowers, 1817. MWA.   41096

[Hulshoff, Maria Aletta] b. 1791, comp.
Peace-republicans' manual; or, The French constitution of 1793, and the Declaration of the rights of
man and of citizens, according to the Moniteur of June
27th, 1793; in the original French, together with a
translation in English... New-York, J. Tiebout & sons,
1817. 161 p. CtHT-W; DLC; MWA; MdBP.   41097

A humble attempt to refute "A refutation." Addressed
to "a layman." By layman, Jun. ... Salem, Mass.,
Pr. by Thomas C. Cushing, for the author, 1817. 24 p.
CSmH.   41098

Hume, David
Philosophical essays... 1st Amer. ed. Georgetown,
D. C., Pr. by W. Duffy, 1817. 2 v. DLC; MH; MWA;
MsSC; NcD; PHC; TxU.   41099

-- -- 1st Amer. ed.   Philadelphia, Edward Earle,
1817. 2 v. MB; MWA; MdBS; MdW; PHi; PPL-R; Vi;
ViRU.   41100

Hume, Jeremiah
The latest account of the glorious success of the
missionaries in the East... From the Union press, no.
2, 1817. MWA.   41101

Humphrey, H.
An address, to the emigrants from Connecticut, in
the new settlements of the United States. Hartford,
1817. 19 p. NjPT.   41102

Humphreys, David
Letters from the Hon. David Humphreys... New
York, Kirk & Mercein, 1817. 83 p. MWA.   41103

-- -- New York, Kirk & Mercein, 1817. 86 p. CtHi;
ICN; MH; MMeT; MWA.   41104

Hunt, Gilbert J.
The historical reader; containing "The late war between the United States and Great Britain, from June,
1812, to February, 1815... New-York, S. A. Burtus,

1817.   231 p.   MBNC; MdBE; OClWHi.   41105

Hunt, William Gibbs
    A Masonic oration, pronounced before the com-
panions of the Royal arch chapter and the brethren of
Lexington Lodge, no. 1, Paviess Lodge, no. 22 and
Murray Lodge, no. 35, at Lexington, Ky., on Dec.
27, A. L. 5816... Lexington, Ky., Thomas T. Skillman,
1817.   12 p.   CSmH; ICU; IaCrM; NNFM.   41106

Hunter, John
    A treatise on the blood... Philadelphia, Pr. by W.
Brown, for James Webster, 1817. 514 p.   MB; MWA;
MdUM; NIC-M; NNNAM.   41107

Huntington, Joshua
    Memoirs of the life of Mrs. Abigail Waters...
Boston, Pr. by Ezra Lincoln, for Samuel T. Arm-
strong... 1817.   180 p.   MBAt; MBB; MHi; MSaE;
MWA.   41108

-- -- Ed. 2.   Boston, Samuel T. Armstrong, 1817.
144 p.   CSt; DLC; ICBB; ICU; MA; MAub; MBC;
MBNEH; MH-AH; MHi; MNe; MSwe; MWA; MiOC;
MnHi; NGH; Nh-Hi; NjMD.   41109

Hurd, Bishop
    "Doctrines of the New Jerusalem Church, with
sketch of Life of Baron Swedenborg." New York,
Charles N. Baldwin, 1817. 20 p. MBNC.   41110

Hutchins improved: being an almanac and ephemeris...
1818 by John Nathan Hutchins, Philom. New York,
Alexander Ming, [1817] [36] p. CSmH; DLC; MWA; NN;
WHi.   41111

-- New York, G. Long, 1817. [32] p. MWA; N. 41112

Hutchinson, Samuel
    Practical holiness; or, The way of the cross. An
address to professors of religion of every denomination.
Kennebunk, Me., Pr. for the author, 1817. 80 p.
MiD-B.   41113

Hutton, Catherine
   The Welsh mountaineer... Philadelphia, M. Thomas, 1817. 2 v. MWA.   41114

Hutton, Charles, 1737-1823
   An astronomical dictionary, compiled from Hutton's mathematical and philosophical dictionary... New-Haven, Pr. by T. G. Woodward, for Hezekiah Howe, 1817. 207 p. DAU.   41115

Hyde, Alvan, 1768-1833
   The blessedness of those, who die in the Lord. Newburgh, N. Y., Pr. by U. C. Lewis, for Eldad Lewis, July 1817. 24 p. MPiB; MWiW; PLT.   41116

   -- The nature and danger of heresy. A sermon, preached before the convention of the clergy of Massachusetts, May 29, 1817... Boston, Samuel T. Armstrong, 1817. 22 p. CSt; Ct; DLC; LNH; MA; MAnP; MBAt; MBC; MH; MHi; MNe; MWA; N; NAuT; OClWHi; OO.   41117

Hymns for infant minds. By the author of original poems... Greenfield, Mass., Denio & Phelps, 1817. 72 p. MWA.   41118

   -- Ed. 5. Greenfield, Mass., [Lincoln & Edmands] 1817. MWA.   41119

Hymns for the use of society of United Christian friends professing the faith of universal salvation. New York, Seymour, 1817. 1024 p. ICP.   41120

Hymns for the use of the New Church, signified by the New Jerusalem in the Apocalypse... Philadelphia, Pr. by Lydia R. Bailey, for the use of the New Church, 1817. 148 p. MWA.   41121

I

Ide, Jacob
   Sermon... Boston, 1817. PPL.   41122

Illinois (Territory)

[Journal of the House of Representatives, of the
first session of the third General Assembly, of Illinois Territory, begun and held in the town of Kaskaskia, on Monday the second day of December, 1816.
Kaskaskia, Pr. by Cook & Blackwell, 1817] (No copy
known. Title in the above form assumed from the
titles of later journals. 250 copies were ordered to be
printed (MS copy of the journal of the Legislative Council of this session, preserved in the Illinois State Ar-
chives, p. 13). The order for printing is also mentioned in resolutions of the General Assembly (Laws of
1816/17, 1898 reprint edition, p. [57], 58). (Norton
1950 p. 670:1)   41123

-- [Journal of the Legislative Council, of the first
session of the third General Assembly, of Illinois Territory, begun and held in the town of Kaskaskia, on
Monday the second day of December, 1816. Kaskaskia,
Pr. by Cook & Blackwell, 1817] (No copy known; title
assumed. 250 copies were ordered to be printed (MS
copy of this journal preserved in the Illinois State Ar-
chives, p. 13). The order for printing is also mentioned in Resolutions of the General Assembly (Laws of
1816/17, 1898 reprint edition, p. [57], 58.) (Norton
1950 p. 670:1)   41124

-- Laws passed by the Legislative Council and House of
Representatives, of Illinois Territory, at thier [sic]
fifth session, held at Kaskaskia - 1816-'17. Kaskaskia,
I. T. Pr. by Cook & Blackwell, 1817. 60 p. I; ICHi;
IHi.   41125

-- -- Kaskaskia, I. T. , Pr. by Cook & Blackwell, 1817.
53 p. ICHi; ICN; IHi.   41126

An illustrated atlas of Carroll County, Md. Philadelphia, 1817. PPL.   41127

The importance of speaking the truth. [New York, Pr.
by D. Fanshaw, for the New-York Religious Tract Society, 1817.] (From NN imp. catal., but not in NN.)
(1930)   41128

The improved picture alphabet... Philadelphia, Wm.
Charles, 1817. 16 p. NNC.   41129

Independent Balance. Philadelphia, George Helmbold,
Apr. 16, 1817, 1st issue. Weekly newspaper. DLC.
                                                  41130
[Independent Republican party. Pennsylvania]
    Address of the Corresponding committee of the
county and city of Philadelphia: to the people of Pennsylvania. [Philadelphia, 1817] 8 p. DLC.   41131

Independent Republican Young Men of Philadelphia
    Address to their brethren throughout the state.
Philadelphia, 1817. 8 p. PHi.   41132

Index to the Bible, in which the various subjects which
occur in the Scriptures are alphabetically arranged,
with accurate references to all the books of the Old
and New Testaments... Philadelphia, James Webster,
1817. 343 p. CSmH; CSt; MWA.   41133

Indiana (Territory)
    A compend of acts of Indiana, from the year 1807
until 1814... by General W. Johnston... Vincennes, Pr.
by Elihu Stout, 1817. 198 p. In; N.   41134

Indiana (State)
    Journal of the House of Representatives of the
state of Indiana, at their first session at Corydon.
Corydon, Cox & Nelson, 1816 [!] [1817] 122 p. In; NN.
                                                  41135
-- Journal of the Senate of the state of Indiana, at
their first session at Corydon. Corydon, Pr. by Cox
& Nelson, 1816[!] [1817] 90 p. In.   41136

-- Laws of the state of Indiana, passed at the 1st session of the General assembly held at Corydon on the
1st Monday in Nov., 1816... Corydon, Cox & Nelson,
1817. 274 p. In; InHi; InU; N.   41137

Indiana Centinel. Vincennes, Samuel Dillworth and
Charles Keemle, Mar. 14, 1817, 1st issue. Weekly
newspaper. In; MWA.   41138

Indiana Republican. Madison, Samuel Pelham, Jan. 2,
1817, 1st issue. Weekly newspaper. In.   41139

The Indian's advocate: being, an answer to an objec-
tion against sending missionaries to the Indians; contained in a pamphlet entitled: "A plan for the more
successful management of domestic missions." Geneva, N.Y., Pr. by James Bogert, 1817. 50 p. N.
                                                   41140
The indictment, trial and punishment of the devil's
pedlars, post-riders, traders and receivers of slander.
By a lover of whole bones...Dover, Del., Pr. by J.
Robertson, 1817. 48 p. DLC.   41141

The infantry exercise of the United States army...Ed.
2. Poughkeepsie, N.Y., P. Potter and Sheldon Potter,
1817. CSmH; CtHT-W; MWA; N.   41142

An inquiry into the policy of forming an importing company in the city of Baltimore; shewing how such a
measure would promote the trade of the place...Balti-
more, Pr. by Schaeffer & Maund, for the author,
1817. 23 p. DLC; MdHi.   41143

An inquiry into the principles of the late act of the
Legislature, for incorporating the precincts with the
city of Baltimore. 1817. 35 p. MdHi.   41144

Installation. Order of singing. [Auburn, N.Y., 1817]
Broadside. (Five hymns printed on front of one sheet
of thin paper.) NAuT.   41145

... An interesting account of Elizabeth Allen...[Phila-
delphia, Pr. by Lydia R. Bailey, 1817] (This is tract
no. 27 of the Tracts of the Philadelphia female tract
society) MWA.   41146

The interesting life, travels, voyages, and daring en-
gagements, of that celebrated and justly renowned commander Paul Jones...Philadelphia, Robert Desilver,
1817. 64 p. DLC; MWA.   41147

The interpreter's house. From Pilgrim's progress.

Ed. 3.   Andover, Mass., Pr. by Flagg & Gould, 1817.
8 p. MMet.   41148

Ireland, William Matthews
    The Bather's assistant, or A guide to all those
who resort to the bathing rooms; with observations on
the beneficial and disadvantageous effects of cold bathing... New York, Pr. by A. Paul, for Edward A. Le
Breton, 1817. 22 p. DLC.   41149

-- Remarks on the medical properties of the stromoni-
um... New York, Pr. by A. Paul, for James Eastburn
& co., 1817. 24 p. CtHT-W; MBAt; NHi; NNNAM.
                                                    41150
The Irish emigrant: an historical tale founded on fact,
by an Hibernian... Winchester, Va., Pr. by J. Foster,
for John T. Sharrocks, 1817. 2 v. DLC; MB; MWA;
ViU.   41151

Irish Emigrant Association. New York.
    Observations... New York, 1817. 12 p. DLC.
                                                    41152
Isaiah Thomas, Junior's town & country almanack for
1818. Worcester, Mass., William Manning [1817]
[46] p. MBB; MDedHi; MHi; MWA; MWHi; MWeA;
NjR.   41153

                          J
Jackson, G. K.
    The choral companion, and elucidation of Dr. G. K.
Jackson's chants: the whole composed, arranged, and
published by him, for the use of the Episcopal churches.
Boston, Pr. by Ezra Lincoln [1817] 28 p. DLC; NRU.
                                                    41154
Jameson, Horatio Gates
    The American domestick medicine... Baltimore, Pr.
by J. Robinson, for F. Lucas, Jun., 1817. 675 p.
DLC; DNLM; MBM; MWA; MdBE; MdHi; MdBJ;
NNNAM.   41155

-- Lectures on fevers in general... Baltimore, Pr. by
John D. Toy, 1817. 24 p. MBM; MWA; MdBJ.   41156

Jefferson and Lewis Gazette. Watertown, N. Y.,
Dorephus Abbey and John H. Lord, Jr., 1817, 1st issue. Weekly newspaper. Brigham, p. 755.   41157

Jefferson County, New York.
    Certificate; we the subscribers... Watertown, N. Y.,
1817. Broadside. MBAt.   41158

Jenks, Benjamin
    Prayers and offices of devotion, for families...
5th Albany ed. Albany, Pr. by Websters and Skinners,
1817. 331 p. MBDil; MWA; NSct.   41159

Jenks, William
    A sermon, delivered in Woolwich, January 26,
1817, at the ordination of the Rev. Jonathan Adams...
Portland, Me., Pr. by A. & J. Shirley, 1817. 24 p.
MWA; MeB; MeBa; MeHi; RPB.   41160

Jess, Zachariah
    The American tutor's assistant, improved or, A
compendious system of decimal, practical arithmetic,
comprising the usual methods of calculation, with the
addition of federal money, & other decimals... Ed. 10.
Wilmington, Del., R. Porter, 1817. 204 p. CSmH;
Ct; TKL.   41161

Johnson, Samuel, 1709-1784
    Diary of a tour in North Wales, in the year 1774.
To which is added an essay on the corn laws... Phila-
delphia, Pr. by J. Maxwell, for Harrison Hall, at the
Port folio office, 1817. 148 p. CtY; DLC; MH-AH;
MWA; MdW; RNHS.   41162

-- ...Johnson's dictionary of the English language, in
miniature...1st New York, from the last English ed.
New York, G. Long, 1817. 295 p. MWA; N; NN; TxU.
                                              41163
-- -- Philadelphia, M. Carey, 1817. 295 p. CtHT-W;
MBarn; MH; NUtHi.   41164

Johnston, John
    An interesting correspondence between the Rev.

John Johnson [sic] ...and Miss Elizabeth Jones...New
York, Pr. by Charles N. Baldwin, for Riley & Adams,
1817. 43 p. CtY; MBAt; MHi; MWA; PBa; PPAmP;
PPPrHi.   41165

Jones, Thomas
    Dedication sermon, delivered at the New Brick
Meeting-House, of the Second Society of Universalists
in Boston, October 16th, 1817...Boston, Pr. by Thomas G. Bangs, 1817. 16 p. DLC; MBAt; MBAU; MH;
MWA; NjPT.   41166

Josephus, Flavius
    The works of Flavius Josephus, the learned and
authentic Jewish historian...New York, William Walker,
1817. 4 v. AzTeS; CoDI.   41167

A journal conducted by a number of physicians. Boston,
Wells and Lilly, 1817-19. LNOP.   41168

The journal of science and the arts. Ed. at the Royal
institution of Great Britain. Vols. 1-5; 1816-18. New
York, James Eastburn, 1817-18. MWiW.   41169

Joyce, Jeremiah, 1763-1816
    Scientific dialogues. A new ed. Philadelphia, M.
Carey & Son, [etc.] 1817. 3 v. CtY; MBC; MWA;
MWiW; ViU.   41170

Judson, Adoniram, 1788-1850
    Christian baptism. A sermon, preached in the
Lal bazar chapel, Calcutta, on Lord's-day, September
27, 1812...Boston, Repr. and pub. by Lincoln & Ed-
mands, 1817. 71 p. DLC; LNB; MB; MH-AH; MMeT;
MWA; NAuT; NNUT; NRAB; NSy; NjR; PPPrHi; WHi.
                                                       41171
-- -- 2d Amer. ed. Boston, Pr. by Farnham &
Badger, for Lincoln & Edmands, 1817. 40 p. CBPSR;
CSt; MB; MH-AH; MWA; MeHi; NRAB.   41172

-- -- Hamilton, N.Y., Repr. and pub. by John B.
Johnson, 1817. 72 p. MiD-B.   41173

Junior fire society of Exeter, N. H.
    Constitution... Exeter, N. H., Pr. by C. Norris &
Co. [1817?] MWA.   41174

Justinian?
    Reflection on the later proceedings of the legisla-
ture, addressed to the people of Maryland. Baltimore,
1817. (Anderson catal. 119, 1909, no. 437)   41175

Juvenile poems, or, the alphabet in verse... New Haven,
Sidney's press, 1817. 28 p. CtHi; MWA.   41176

Juvenile sketches of natural history of birds. New-
York, Samuel Wood & sons, 1817. 68 p. CtY; N N.
                                              41177
The juvenile story teller, a collection of original moral
tales. New-Haven, Sidney's press, 1817. 31 p.
CSmH; MWA.   41178

K

Kanawha County, [West] Virginia
    At a meeting of the Standing Committee of Kanawha
County, for the promotion of Internal improvements, by
opening the James and Great Kanawha Rivers to the
highest points of navigation, and connecting the same by
an artificial road, held in the town of Charlestown, on
Wednesday the 3d September, 1817... Broadside. O-Ar.
                                              41179
Keene, N. H. Congregational church.
    A remonstrance, of the Congregational church of
Christ, in Keene, N. H. ... Bellows Falls, Vt., Pr. by
Bill Blake & Co., 1817. 12 p. CtHT; MH; MH-AH;
MWA.   41180

Kelly, James
    An improved method of education... Philadelphia,
1817. MWA.   41181

Kemble, Charles
    The point of honor; a play in three acts taken from
the French. New-York, D. Longworth, 1817. 46+ p.
MH; MWA; N.   41182

Kemp, James, bp., 1764-1827
A sermon on the Christian warfare; preached at
the funeral of the Right Rev. Dr. Claggett, late bishop
of the Protestant Episcopal Church in Maryland... Baltimore, J. Robinson, 1817. 24 p. MdBD; MdBE; MdHi;
TJaU.   41183

Kennedy, Thomas
Songs of love and liberty... Washington, D. C., Pr.
by Daniel Rapine, 1817. 98 p. CSmH; ICU; MB; MWA;
RPB.   41184

Kenney, James, 1780-1849
The touchstone; or, The world as it goes. A comedy, in four acts... New-York, David Longworth, 1817.
77 p. DLC; MWA; N; OC.   41185

Kenrick, John, 1755-1833
Horrors of slavery, in two parts, Part I containing
observations, facts, and arguments, extracts from
speeches of Wilberforce, Grenville, Pitt, Burke, Fox,
Martin, Whitehead and other distinguished members of
the British Parliament. Part II, containing extracts
chiefly American, compiled from authentic sources,
demonstrating that slavery is impolitic, anti- republican, unchristian, and highly criminal, and proposing
measures for its complete abolition throughout the U-
nited States. Cambridge, Mass., Pr. by Hilliard and
Metcalf, 1817. 59 p. MWA; ViHaI.   41186

[Kenrick, William]
The whole duty of woman... Philadelphia, Pr. by J.
Maxwell, for Edward Earle, 1817. 80 p. CtHT-W;
CtY; MWA.   41187

Kentucky (State)
An act to amend the act, entitled An act to reduce
into one the several acts respecting the militia. [Frank-
fort] Pr. by Gerard and Kendall, 1817. 9 p. MB; MHi.
                                                           41188
-- Acts passed at the first session of the twenty-fifth
General Assembly, for the Commonwealth of Kentucky,
begun and held in the town of Frankfort, on Monday...

the second day of December, one thousand eight hundred and sixteen... Frankfort, Ky., Gerard & Kendall,
1817. 296 p. CSfLaw; DLC; IaU-L; KyU; MHi; Mi-L;
NN; OCLaw; Wa-L.   41189

-- Journal of the House of Representatives of the Com-
monwealth of Kentucky... Dec., 1816... Frankfort, Ky.,
Gerard & Kendall, 1816! [1817] 291 p. DLC; ICU; Ky;
KyLoF; KyU.   41190

-- Journal of the Senate of the Commonwealth of Ken-
tucky, begun and held in the town of Frankfort, on
Monday the second day of December, 1816, and of the
Commonwealth the twenty-fifth. Frankfort, Ky., Ger-
ard & Kendall, 1816! [1817] 242 p. DLC; ICU; Ky;
KyLxT; KyU-L; MWA.   41191

-- Resolutions proposing an article of amendment to
the constitution of the United States. Resolved, by the
General assembly of the commonwealth of Kentucky,
that the. following amendment be proposed to the constitution of the United States, to-wit; that no law varying
... [Frankfort, 1817] Broadside. DLC.   41192

Kentucky Agricultural Society
    Cattle. A collection of papers, giving an account
of the English cattle in Kentucky... Lexington, Ky., Pr.
by J. Norvell & Co., 1817. 44 p. ICU.   41193

The Kentucky almanac, for the year of our Lord 1818
... Lexington, Ky., Pr. by John Norvell & Co., at the
office of the Kentucky Gazette [1817] [36] p. KyLo;
MWA; MoHi; NCH; WHi.   41194

Kentucky Auxiliary Bible Society
    First report of the managers... 3d day of April,
1817. Lexington, Ky., Pr. by Thomas T. Skillman,
1817. 12 p. Cadmus Book Shop.   41195

The Kentucky farmer's almanac, for the year 1818...
by T. Henderson. Georgetown, Ky., Pr. by John N.
Lyle, for William Sebree, [1817] [36] p. ICU; WHi.
                                                    41196

Kentucky Herald. Louisville, Ky., H. Deming, Nov.
1817, 1st issue. Weekly newspaper. OHi.   41197

No entry   41198

Keyser, C.
    Arithmetic rules.   Philadelphia, J. Rakestraw,
1817. MWA.   41199

Kilbourn, John, 1787-1831
    The Ohio gazetteer; or, Topographical dictionary,
containing a description of the several counties, towns
[etc.]...in the state of Ohio; alphabetically arranged...
Ed. 3, improved. Albany, Pr. by G.J. Loomis & Co.,
for Joshua Fish, 1817. 180 p.   CtY; DLC; MWA;
NUtHi; OClWHi; OHi; WHi.   41200

Kilbourn, John
    The Ohio gazetteer...Ed. 3, improved. Columbus,
O., Pr. by P.H. Olmsted at the office of the Intelli-
gencer and Gazette, for J. Kilbourn, 1817. 74 p. CtY;
DLC; ICN; MWA; N; NN; NNA; NNS; NjPT; OClWHi;
OHi; PHi; PPiHi; PPiU; WHi.   41201

King, Thomas A.
    Explanation to the public.   In the course of human
affairs, it not unfrequently happens, that the character
of a man may suffer by a partial representation of
some facts...Thomas A. King, Vincennes, Aug. 1,
1817. Broadside. In.   41202

-- To the public.   My fellow citizens will recollect
that on the 1st of August last, I presented to them an
explanatory statement of the mercantile transactions between myself and H. B. & H. Marrick which then was
and yet remains a subject of litigation...Sept. 27th,
1817. In.   41203

[Kingsley, James Luce]
Remarks on the present situation of Yale College
for the consideration of its friends and patrons [New
Haven, 1817] 16 p. CtHi.   41204

Kingston, John
The life of General George Washington... Baltimore,
J. Kingston, 1817. 228 p. (This is Condie's Life with
a new title-page only)   Sabin 37899.   41205

Kinloch, Francis
Letters from Geneva and France, written during a
residence of between two and three years, in different
parts of those countries, and addressed to a lady in
Virginia. By her father. Boston, Pr. by Wells, 1817.
319 p. PPM.   41206

Die kleine Harfe gestimmet von unterschiedlichen lieb-
lichen Liedern... Vierte Auflage.   Philadelphia, Pr. by
G. & D. Billmeyer, 1817. PHi.   41207

[Knapp, Samuel Lorenzo] 1783-1838
Extracts from the journal of Marshal Soult [pseud.]
addressed to a friend: how obtained, and by whom
translated is not a subject of enquiry... Newburyport,
W. B. Allen & co., 1817. 143 p. DLC; MWA.   41208

Kneeland, Abner, 1774-1844
Remarks on pamphlet entitled A review, of an
anonymous publication styled strictures, on a pamphlet
entitled "A religious tract, " ... Manlius [N. Y.] Pr. by
Kellog & Clark, for the Genesee missionary society,
1817. 16 p. CSmH; MWA.   41209

Knox, Vicesimus
Elegant extracts, a copious selection of instructive,
moral, and entertaining passages from the most eminent poets.   New York, Kirk & Mercein, 1817. 12 v.
MdBS.   41210

[Kohlmann, Anthony] 1771-1836
Centurial jubilee, to be celebrated by all the Reformed churches throughout the United States... dedi-

cated to the Lutheran synods of New York, Pennsylvania, Maryland and adjoining states...[Baltimore]
Pr. for the author, 1817. 72 p. DGU; MH; MWA;
MdW; MiU; PPL.   41211

Kollmann, August Friedrich Christoph, 1756-1829
    An essay on musical harmony, according to the
nature of that science, and the principles of the greatest musical authors...1st Amer. ed., with notes...
Utica, N.Y., Seward and Williams, 1817. 289 p.
CtHT-W; CtY; DLC; GU; LNH; MAnP; MBAt; MBNEC;
MPiB; MdBJ; NN; NNF; NPV; NUt; NUtHi; PP; PPL.
                                                  41212
Koster, Henry
    Travels in Brazil...In the years from 1809, to
1815...Philadelphia, M. Carey & son, 1817. 2 v.
CoU; DLC; MBL; MWA; ViAl.   41213

Kotzebue, August Friedrich Ferdinand von.
    The stranger, a drama in five acts...New York,
David Longworth, 1817. 65 p. ICU; MB; MH; MWA.
                                                  41214
Eine kurzegefastze Geschichte der Reformation...Philadelphia, Pr. by Conrad Zentler, 1817. MWA; PPG.
                                                  41215

                         L
LaBaume, Eugene, 1783-1849
    Circumstantial narrative of the campaign in Russia,
embellished with plans of the battles of the Moskwa and
Mals-Jaroslavitz...By Eugene LaBaume...translated
from the French. Hartford, Pr. by Hamlen & Newton,
for Silas Andrus, 1817. 356 p. C-S; CLO; CSmH; Ct;
CtHi; GEU; ICartC; ICP; IU; IaDaP; InCW; KU; KyDC;
KyLoN; KyMaY; LN; LNH; MAbD; MH; MNowd; MWA;
MoSW; MdRo; MoSU; NAlbi; NCH; NCanHi; NGH; NN;
NRHi; NRMA; NRU; NWars; NcWaS; OCn; OCo; OCY;
ODa; OFH; OSW; OT; PLFM; PMA; PNT.   41216

-- -- Hartford, Silas Andrus and E. Peck & Co.,
Rochester, N.Y., 1817. MWA.   41217

Lacey, Henry
  Principal events in the life of Moses... Philadelphia,
Benjamin Johnson, 1817. 84 p. MnHi.   41218

The ladies' and gentlemen's diary, and almanack; with
an ephemeris, for the year of Creation, according to
sacred writ, 5780, and of the Christian era, 1818...
By Asa Houghton. Bellows Falls, Vt., Bill Blake &
Co., [1817] 48 p. MWA; NN.   41219

Ladies' weekly museum. New York, James Oram,
May 3, 1817, 1st issue with this title. A weekly con-
tinuation of the "New-York Weekly Museum." DLC;
MWA; NHi.   41220

The lady of the lake; a melo-dramatic romance in three
acts. New York, 1817. 48 p. MH.   41221

Lafoy, John B. M. D.
  The complete coiffeur; or, An essay on the art of
adorning natural, and of creating artificial, beauty...
New-York, Stereotyped for the proprietors, and sold by
all the principal booksellers, 1817. 2 v. in 1. DLC;
MH; NNS; RPB.   41222

The Laity's directory to the church services, for the
year of our Lord, 1817... To which are added, an obit-
uary, biography, and an account of the Catholic
churches, colleges, seminaries, benevolent institutions,
&c, &c. in the United States and Canada. Also, a
New Year's gift, and a variety of edifying and interesting information. With an almanac exclusive of all use-
less matter. New York, N. Field, 1817. 68 p. DGU.
                                               41223

Lambert, William
  Abstracts of calculations, to ascertain the longitude of the capitol... Washington, D. C., Pr. by Edward De Krafft, 1817. 20 p. LNH; MBAt; MH; MWA;
NNC; NWM; O.   41224

Lancastrian Institution, Richmond, Va.
  The fundamental rule & regulation of the Lancastrian institution within this city. Richmond, Pr. by

Ritchie, Trueheart & Duval, 1817. 8 p. DLC; Vi.
41225

Langsdorff, Georg Heinrich, Freiherr Von
Voyages and travels in various parts of the world,
during the years, 1803, 1804, and 1807... Carlisle
[Pa.] Pr. by G. Philips, for M. Carey and son, 1817.
617 p. MWA; MWH; OAU; PPL-R.   41226

Lansing, Dirck Cornelius
A sermon, preached March 6, 1817, at the dedication of the new Presbyterian church, in the village of
Auburn... Auburn, N. Y., Pr. by H. C. Southwick, 1817.
16 p. MWA; NAuT; NCH.   41227

[Las Cases, Emmanuel, comte de] 1766-1842, supposed author.
Letters from the cape of Good Hope, in reply to
Mr. Warden; with extracts from the great work now
compiling for publication under the inspection of Napoleon. New-York, C. Wiley & co., 1817. 186 p.
DLC; LN; N; NCH.   41228

The last resource of Democracy. [New Haven, 1817]
(Federalist campaign literature.) Broadside. CtY.
41229

[Lathrop, John]
A compendious account of the most important battles of the late war... Boston, Pr. by William Walter,
1817. MB; MWA.   41230

Latour, T.
Latour's favorite waltz. New York, W. Dubois
[1817] [2] p. CSmH.   41231

Lavater, Johann Caspar
The pocket Lavater... New York, Van Winkle &
Wiley, 1817. 140 p. DNLM; MWA; NNS.   41232

Learned, Erastus
The call, work, trials and encouragements of the
gospel minister considered in a sermon delivered at
Southbridge, Mass. December 18, 1816 at the ordination of Rev. Jason Park. Worcester, Mass., William

Maning, 1817. 32 p. M; MBAt; MH-AH; MWA; MWHi.
41233
Leavitt's genuine, improved New-England Farmer's almanack, 1818...Exeter, N.H., Pr. by H.A. Ranlet,
for Nath'l Boardman [1817] [24] p. MWA; Nh-Hi.41234

Lee, Chauncey
    A sermon delivered at the funeral of Mr. Cyrus
Babcock...Hartford, Pr. by George Goodwin and sons
...1817. 16 p. CtSoP; CtY; MH-AH; MB; MWA; NjPT.
41235
Lee's patent & family medicine store. Evening amusement. Maxims for the preservation of health, and the
prevention of diseases...New York, from Lee's patent
& family medicine store, 1817. 33 p. PPL.   41236

Legh, Thomas
    Narrative of a journey in Egypt and the country
beyond the cataracts...Philadelphia, Pr. by James
Maxwell, for M. Thomas, 1817. 203 p. DLC; DeGE;
GU-M; MWA; MWiW; MiD; NPtW; NjR; ViAl.   41237

Lehigh Centinel. Allentown, Pa., Charles L. Hütter,
June, 1817, 1st issue. Weekly newspaper. Brigham
p. 824.   41238

Leonard, Lewis
    Plain truth, concerning infant baptism...Poughkeep-
sie, N.Y., Pr. by Barnum & Nelson, 1817. 31 p.
MH-AH; MWA; NRAB.   41239

Leonard, Seth
    The key to etymology and syntax...Middlebury, Vt.,
Pr. by Frederick P. Allen, 1817. 32 p. VtMiS. 41240

Le Pappe de Trévern, Jean François Marie, 1754-1842
    An amicable discussion of the Church of England,
and on the reformation, dedicated to all Protestant
clergy; translated by Rev. William Richmond. Baltimore, Pr. by J. Robinson, for Fielding Lucas, Jr.,
[1817?] 2 v. IaDmDC; KyLoP.   41241

Lescallier, D.
    The enchanted throne; an Indian story translated
from the Persian language. By Baron D. Lescallier,
member of several societies of sciences and academies
in Europe, an honorary member of the Philosophical
and Literary Society of New-York, and of the anti-
quarian American Society of Boston, &c. New-York,
Pr. by Joseph Desnoues, 1817. 14 p. MBAt; NNS.
                                                      41242
Letter addressed to the members of the Legislature of
Pennsylvania. By a meeting of Pennsylvania freeholders, held at Philadelphia, March 15, 1817. 8 p.
MBAt; PHi.   41243

A letter from a minister to a man on a sick bed.
[Boston, Munroe & Francis...and Isaac Bowers, 1817]
12 p. MMeT; MPeHi; MWA.   41244

A letter to Cadwallader D. Colden, in answer to the
strictures, in his "Life of Fulton, " on the report of
the select committee (on) steam navigation, 1814; with
an appendix, containing laws, petitions, reports, etc.
Albany, 1817. 127 p. NIC.   41245

Letters addressed to a friend on the following subjects;
1. Is God the author of sin? ...Knoxville, Tenn., Pr.
by Heiskell & Brown, 1817. 52 p. LNH; PPPrHi;
TMaryC.   41246

Letters from the South written during an excursion in
the summer of 1816. By the author of John Bull and
Brother Jonathan...New York, Pr. by Abraham Paul,
for James Eastburn & Co., 1817. 2 v. CtHT; Ia; NIC;
NNUT.   41247

Letters critical and pathological. (A criticism on Dr.
Chas. Caldwell's preliminary discourse to Cullen's
practice.) Baltimore, Cushing & Jewett, 1817. 19 p.
DNLM; MdBM; PU.   41248

The letters of the British spy. Ed. 6, with the last
corrections of the author. Baltimore, Pr. by J. Robinson, for Fielding Lucas, Jr., 1817. 186 p.

NUtHi.   41249

Letters on the events of the revolution in France by a
French General officer addressed to his friends in New
York...New York, Forbes & Co., 1817. 260 p. CtY;
NWM.   41250

Letters to a friend, on the marriage of a deceased
wife's sister...New York, Pr. by Forbes & co., 1817.
149 p. NNUT; PPPrHi.   41251

[Levy, Aaron]
    Hand book for the drill and instruction of the com-
panies attached to the field pieces...New York, Pr. by
Van Winkle, Wiley & Co.,[1817] MWA.   41252

[Lewis, Mrs. Hannah]
    Narrative of the captivity and sufferings of Mrs.
Hannah Lewis, and her three children, who were taken
prisoners by the Indians, near St. Louis, on the 25th
May, 1815...Ed. 2. Boston, Pr. by H. Trumbull,
1817. 24 p. CSmH; DLC; ICN; MH; MWA; MnHi;
MoSHi; WHi.   41253

Lewis, Isaac, 1745-1840
    A sermon, delivered in New-Haven, at the ordina-
tion of the Rev. Jeremiah Day, A.M., president of
Yale-college, July 23, 1817...New-Haven, Pr. at the
Journal office, 1817. 27 p. CtHi; CtSoP; CtY; DLC;
MH-AH; MWA; MWiW; MnSM; NCH; NHi; NjPT; NjR;
OClWHi.   41254

[Lewis, Winslow]
    Description of the light houses, on the coast of the
United States. Boston, Pr. by Thomas G. Bangs
[1817] 16 p. MH; MHi; MMal; MSaE; MWA; NN.41255

Lewis's diary, or Newburgh almanack for 1818. By
Andrew Beers. Hudson, N.Y., Ashbel Stoddard, for
B.F. Lewis [1817] MWA.   41256

Lexington Library
    Addition to the catalogue of the Lexington library.

Lexington [Ky.] Pr. by F. Bradford, Jr., 1817. 26 p.
ICU.   41257

Lexington Library Company
    Addition to the catalogue... Lexington, Ky., Pr.
by F. Bradford, Jr., 1817. 16 p. (Rusk's Mid. West.
Frontier, 1925, vol. 2, p. 86.)   41258

(Circular) Lexington, November 10, 1817... Broadside.
(Report of Committee of Correspondence to encourage
domestic manufacturers.) O-Archives.   41259

L'Homond, A.
    Epitome Historiae Sacrae, New ed.   New York,
E. Duyckinck, 1817. MWA.   41260

L'Homond, C. F.
    Epitome historiae sacrae, ed. G. Ironside.   New
York, Pr. by G. Long, for J. Eastburn, 1817. MWA.
                                                  41261
Lhomond, Charles François
    Epitome historiae sacrae   ad usum Tyronum lin-
guae latinae... Editio nova.   Quam... adornavit Georgius
Ironside.   Editio tertia.   Novi Eboraci: James East-
burn & Soc., 1817. 167 p.   MB; MWA; N; NjR.41262

-- De viris illustribus Romae a Romulo ad Augustum
...to which is added a dictionary of all the words
which occur in the book... by James Hardie.   New-
York, E. Duyckinck, 1817.   MH; MWA; PPL; PPM.
                                                  41263
-- Pious lectures explanatory of the principles, obliga-
tions and resources of the Catholic religion.   Translated from La Doctrine Chretienne par Lhomond.   By
the Rev. James Appleton.   1st Amer., from 8th English ed.   Philadelphia, Bernard Dornin, 1817. 388 p.
MWA; MdBLC; MdW.   41264

The life and confession of John Tuhi, an Indian of the
Brothertown tribe, while under sentence of death, for
the murder of his brother, Joseph Tuhi, as taken from
his own mouth, in prison at Whitestown, Oneida County, state of New-York, a few days previous to his exe-

cution which took place at Utica, July 25th, 1817...
[1817] Broadside. MWA; NHi; PHi.   41265

The life and death of two young ladies, contrasted.
Pittsburgh, Pa., Pr. by Butler & Lambdin, 1817.
MWA.   41266

The life of Henry Phillips, now under sentence of
death...With the particulars of the murder. Boston,
Pr. for the purchasers, 1817. 12 p. NNCoCi.   41267

...Life of Henry Phillips, sentenced to be executed at Boston, Mar. 13, 1817, for the murder of Gaspard Denegri.
[Boston, Russell, Cutler & co., 1817] 8 p. DLC.   41268

The life of John Engelbrecht...translated out of the
German original...Hallowell, Me., Pr. by E. Goodale,
1817.   108 p. MeU.   41269

The life of the Pilgrim, Joseph Thomas, containing an
accurate account of his trials, travels and gospel labours, up to the present date. Winchester, Va., Pr.
by J. Foster, 1817. 372 p. NcElon; ViU.   41270

The life of William Kelley. (An authentic narrative)
[Andover, Mass., Pr. by Flagg and Gould, for the New
England Tract Society, 1817] 16 p. MWA; MiD-B.
                                                41271
Linnaean society of New England, Boston.
    Report of a committee of the Linnaean society of
New England, relative to a large marine animal, sup-
posed to be a serpent, seen near Cape Ann, Massachu-
setts, in August 1817. Boston, Cummings and Hilliard,
1817. 52 p. CtHT-W; DLC; DCU; ICT; MBAt; MH-AH;
MLow; MNBedf; MSaP; MWA; MeB; MiD-B; MoSM;
NjN; PBL; ScC.   41272

Litchfield County Charitable Education School
    Constitution and laws. New Haven, 1817. 16 p. MBC.
                                                41273
Littell, William
    Directions to the Sheriffs of the different counties in
the state of Kentucky. Louisville, Ky., Pr. by Butler

& Hughes, 1817. 7 p. OCHP.   41274

Little, William
    The easy instructor: or, a new method of teaching
sacred harmony... (The music types used in printing
this book are secured to the proprietor by patent right)
Albany, Websters, Skinners and Daniel Steele (proprietor)... Pr. by Packard-Van Benthuysen [1817] 120
p. MWA.   41275

Little Charles, Margaret, and other stories... New-
Haven, Sidney's press, 1817. 30 p. CtHi.   41276

The Little Christian; a novel, founded on fact, written
by himself. Brookfield, Pr. for the author, 1817.
MWA.   41277

Little sins, a dialogue... To be had of Benjamin &
Thomas Kite... Philadelphia, Pr. [by Joseph R. A.
Skerrett] for Solomon W. Conrad, Kimber & Sharpless
... 1817. 12 p. MH; MWA; PSC-Hi.   41278

The lives of Dr. John Donne: Sir Henry Wotton and
others... Edition 3. New York, 1817. 2 v. (Anderson
cat. no. 2250. March 1920. title no. 870)   41279

The lives of Sir Walter Raleigh and Capt. John Smith;
with an account of the Governors of Virginia, to the
year 1781. By a Virginian. Shepherd's-Town, Va.,
Pr. by Maxwell & Harper, 1817. 121 p. NcD; WHi.
                                          41280
The lives of John Trueman and Richard Atkins, to
which is added a short account of Atkins' sister. Also
the life of William Baker and a sermon at his funeral.
Philadelphia, 1817. 111 p. MWA.   41281

Livingston, Mrs. Ann Hume (Shippen)
    Sacred records abridged in verse... Philadelphia,
T. S. Manning, 1817. MWA; RPB.   41282

Livingston, William, 1723-1790
    An English grammar; calculated in conjunction with
the syntactical atlas, to render the study of grammar

easy and pleasing to the scholar. Middlebury, Vt.,
Pr. by Francis Burnap, 1817. 84 p. MWA; VtHi.
41283
-- The syntactical atlas... Middlebury [Vt.] Pr. by
Copeland and Allen, [1817?] (Copy right secured)
Broadside. (McCorison list)   41284

Long Island Bible & Common Prayer Book Society.
    Annual report of the board of managers... Brook-
lyn, N.Y., A. Spooner, Pr., 1817. 12 p. NBLiHi.
41285
Long Island Bible society.
    The second annual report of the Long Island Bible
society, read and adopted at the meeting of the society
at Jamaica, the 17th day of September, 1817. New-
York, Pr. by J. Seymour, 1817. 20 p. MBAt; N;
NSmB.   41286

Loring, E.H.
    A brief history of facts relative to the unfortunate
misunderstanding between the town of Sudbury and Timothy Hilliard, as taken down on the several occasions
and meetings on the subject. Concord, Mass., Pr.
for the author, 1817. 16 p. MH.   41287

The lottery. Philadelphia, Pr. by D. Dickinson, for
Benjamin Johnson, 1817. 23 p. MnHi.   41288

Louisiana (State)
    Acts passed at the 1st session of the 3d Legisla-
ture of the state of Louisiana, begun ... 18th day of
November, 1816 ... New-Orleans, Pr. by J.C. de St.
Romes, 1817. 223 p. DLC; IU; LNH; LU.   41289

-- Journal de la chambre des representans durant la
premiere session de la troisieme legislature... Nouvelle
Orleans, J.C. de St. Romes, 1817. 83 p. L.   41290

-- Journal du senat durant la premiere session de la
troisieme legislature... Nouvelle Orleans, J.C. de St.
Romes, 1817. 67 p. L.   41291

-- Journal of the House of Representatives during the

first session of the third legislature... New Orleans,
Pr. by J. C. de St. Romes, 1817. 82 p. LNH; N.
41292

-- Journal of the Senate during the 1st session of the
3d legislature... New-Orleans, Pr. by J. C. de St.
Romes, 1817. 66 p. LNH; LU.   41293

Louisiana Rambler. Alexandria, La., Hugh Chain,
1817. 1st issue. Weekly newspaper. MWA.   41294

Loveland, Samuel C.
    An elegy on Mrs. Rhoda Caryl, wife of Mr. John
Caryl, of Stockbridge, who departed this life, April
23d, 1817... [1817?] 8 p. MiD-B.   41295

Lowell, Charles
    A discourse delivered March 16, 1817 the Sabbath
after the execution of Henry Phillips Stonehewer Davis
for the murder of Gaspard Denegri... Boston, Pr. by
John Eliot, 1817. 16 p. M; MBev; MBrof; MH; MWA;
MeLewB; NjR; PHi; RPB.   41296

-- -- Ed. 2. Boston, Pr. by John Eliot, 1817. 16 p.
ICN; MBB; MBNEH; MH; MMeT; MWA; MWHi; VtMiM.
41297
[Lowell, John]
    A review of Warden's letters from St. Helena con-
taining remarks on Bonaparte's massacres at Jaffa and
El Arish; with observations on the North American Review. Boston, 1817. 32 p. MHi.   41298

Low's almanack, and astronomical and agricultural reg-
ister; for the year... 1818. Boston, Pr. by Munroe &
Francis [1817] [36] p. MDedHi; MHi; MMhHi; MWA;
MeHi; NCH; NjR; WHi.   41299

Lucinda, the orphan... Philadelphia, Wm. Charles,
1817. MWA.   41300

Ludlow, Maxfield
    To the public. I presume you will have seen be-
fore this comes to hand, an address by Thomas Freeman... Town of Washington... Oct. 24, 1817. [Natchez,

1817] Broadside.   (Streeter collection)   41301

[Lullin de Châteauvieux, Frédéric] 1772-1841
    Manuscript transmitted from St. Helena, by an un-
known channel.   Translated from the French.   New-
York, Van Winkle and Wiley, 1817.   204 p.   DLC;
IaMP; MWA.   41302

Luther, Martin
    Der Kleine catechismus des sel. D. Martin Lu-
thers; nebst den gewoehnlichen morgen-abend-und tisch-
gebeten... Philadelphia, Pr. by Mentz, 1817. 143 p.
PU.   41303

Lyceum of natural history. (New York)
    The constitution of the... New York, The society,
1817. 8 p. NNNAM.   41304

Lyman, Elijah
    A sermon, delivered at Brookfield... July 21, 1811
at the interment of Mrs. Sarah Pratt... Boston, Pr. by
Thomas Rowe, 1817. 16 p. MBC; MH; NN.   41305

                            M
[M., Y.]
    Mary the milk-maid... [Philadelphia, Pr. by Lydia
R. Bailey, 1817] (This is no. 26 of the tracts of the
Philadelphia female tract society) MWA.   41306

M'Carty, William
    Geschichte des americanischen kriegs, von 1812,
vom anfang bis zum eadlichen schluss desselben, an
dem glorreichen achten January, 1815, vor Neu-Orleans... Aus dem englischen übersetzt. Reading, J.
Ritter und comp; Philadelphia, W. M'Carty, 1817. 273
p. OClWHi.   41307

-- History of the American war of 1812, from the commencement, until the final termination thereof, on the
memorable 8th of January, 1815, at New Orleans.
Philadelphia, McCarty, 1817. 252 p. LNH; NcWfC.
                                                    41308

McChord, James
A plea "for the hope of Israel," - for the hope of all the world: delivered...before the General synod of the Associate-Reformed Church. Philadelphia, Port Folio office, 1817. 85 p. MBC; NjPT; NjR.   41309

McClure, George, 1771-1851
Causes of the destruction of the American towns on the Niagara frontier, and failure of the campaign of the fall of 1813... Bath, N.Y., Pr. by Benjamin Smead, 1817. 72 p. MB; N; NN; NRMA; OClWHi; WM.
41310
McClure, John
To the public. Having been unwarrantably assailed, it is a duty I owe myself and my friends, to vindicate my character...as I have become a candidate to represent the people of Knox, Daviss [sic] and Sullivan, counties, in the next legislature... Liverpool, July 24, 1817. Broadside. In.   41311

McConaughy, David
The duties and dangers of prosperity: A sermon, delivered in the Presbyterian church in Gettysburgh, on Nov. 20, 1817... Gettysburg, Pa., Robert G. Harper, 1817. 18 p. MWA; NbOP; P; PPPrHi.   41312

McCulloh, James Haines, 1793?-1870
Researches on America; being an attempt to settle some points relative to the aborigines of America, &c. [Ed. 2] Baltimore, Joseph Robinson, 1817. 220 p. CU; CtHT; DLC; ICN; MBAt; MWA; MdBJ; MdHi; MdUM; NNA; NNG; OC; PPAN.   41313

Macdonnel, D.E.
A dictionary of select and popular quotations...2d Amer. ed. Philadelphia, A. Finley, 1817. 315 p. CSmH; MWA; NjR; PP.   41314

McEwen, Abel
Sermon preached at the anniversary election, Hartford, May 8, 1817. Hartford, George Goodwin, 1817. 22 p. Ct; CtHC; CtHi; CtHT; CtNL; CtY; NjPT. 41315

Mac-Intosh, A.
Address, interment of Sylvanus Bourne. Harlem,
N. Y., John Euschede & sons, 1817. 16 p. RPB.   41316

McKean, Joseph
A sermon, preached at Dorchester, June 25, 1817,
on the occasion of organizing the Third Church, in that
town...Dedham, Mass., Pr. by Abel D. Alleyne, 1817.
38 p. DLC; ICMe; MAnP; MB; MBAU; MBC; MBNEH;
MDHi; MH; MHi; MSaE; MWA; MeBat; MiU-C; NN;
NjR; RPB; VtMiM.   41317

McKendree, William
The substance of a sermon, preached...the 6th of
June, 1817...New York, Pr. by J. & J. Harper, for
J. Soule and T. Mason, 1817. 24 p. IEG; MWA; MoS.
                                               41318
M'Kenney, Frederic
(A complete key to) the new system of practical
arithmetic; (compiled by Titus Bennett;) in which the
operation of all the examples necessary for the learner,
are exhibited at large...Philadelphia, Pr. by Griggs &
Co., for Bennett & Walton, 1817. 208 p. P.   41319

-- A key to the American tutor's assistant revised; in
which all the examples necessary for a learner are
wrought at large; and also solutions given of all the
questions for exercise in the various rules. Designed
principally to facilitate the labour of teachers, and assist such as have not the opportunity of a tutor's aid.
By Frederic McKenney...Philadelphia, Joseph Cruk-
shank, 1817. 182 p. DLC; MH; MWA; NjR.   41320

MacKnight, James
An essay on justification. Boston, Pr. by Munroe
and Francis, 1817. 72 p. ICMe; ICU; MB; MH-AH;
MSaE.   41321

M'Leod, Alexander
The life and power of true Godliness...New-York,
A. Paul, 1817. 424 p. PPiXT.   41322

-- -- New York, James Eastman, 1817. KyDC. 41323

Macleod, Malcolm
    Mcleod's history of witches... New York, 1817.
MWA.   41324

Maclure, William, 1763-1840
    Observations on the geology of the United States of
America; with some remarks on the effect produced on
the nature and fertility of soils, by the decomposition
of the different classes of rocks... Philadelphia, Pr. by
A. Small, for the author, 1817. 127 p. DI-GS; DLC;
LNH; MWA; NIC-L; NjP; NjR.   41325

[M'Quin, A. D.]
    Description of the picture, Christ healing the sick
in the Temple... Philadelphia, S.W. Conrad, 1817. 14
p.   ScCC.   41326

Maddock, Henry, d. 1824
    A treatise on the principles and practice of the
High court of chancery... New-York, Pr. by Clayton &
Kingsland for, Gould, Banks, and Gould, and William
Gould and co., 1817. 2 v. DLC; MWA; MWiW; N-L;
OMC; PPB.   41327

Madison Gazette.   Hamilton, N.Y., John B. Johnson
& Son, 1817, 1st issue. Weekly newspaper. Brigham,
p. 579.   41328

Madox, D. T.
    Late account of the Missouri Territory, compiled
from notes taken during a tour through that country in
1815, and a translation of letters from a distinguished
emigrant, written in 1817... Paris, Ky., Pr. by John
Lyle, for the author, 1817. 65 p. CSmH; PPiU; WHi.
                                                  41329

Maginness, James
    The family clerk and students' assistant, contain-
ing a neat, concise, and plain method of book-keeping,
by single entry; and a variety of useful forms... Harrisburg, Pa., Pr. by Wm. Greer, for the author,
1817.   194 p.   DLC; MB; MWA; NN; NNC; OAU; PHar;
PHi.   41330

Maine Charitable Mechanic Association.
Constitution of the Maine Charitable Mechanic Association...Portland, Me., Pr. by Francis Douglas,
1817. 16 p. MeHi.   41331

Maine missionary society.
(Annual sermons, reports, etc.) 1810- Hallowell,
Me., N. Cheever, 1817. RPB.   41332

Maine Peace Society
Portland, Me., 1817. Broadside.   41333

Mair, John
An introduction to Latin syntax...A new ed., rev.
by James Hardie. Baltimore, Pr. by J. Robinson, for
Fielding Lucas, Jr., 1817. 299 p. MH; MWA; MdBE;
NPot.   41334

-- -- A new ed. rev. and cor. by T.S. Joy. New
York, Pr. by J. and J. Harper, for Evert Duyckinck,
1817. 311 p. IaHi; MWA; MoSpD; TxD-T.   41335

Male Adult School Association of Philadelphia
Constitution and by-laws of the Male Adult School
Association of Philadelphia. Instituted June 8, 1816.
Philadelphia, Pr. by Anderson & Meehan, for the Insti-
tution, 1817. 12 p. DLC.   41336

Mallory, Rollin Carlos
Oration at Whitehall, N.Y., July 4, 1817...Rut-
land, Vt., Pr. by Fay, Davison & Burt [1817] 16 p.
MWA; N.   41337

The management of the tongue...Ed. 3. Boston, Pr.
by H. & W.H. Mann, for Isaiah Thomas, Jr., 1817.
252 p. CSmH; DLC; MAtt; MBC; MBoy; MDedHi;
MWeyHi; NN.   41338

Managers of Roman Catholic Sunday school society.
Philadelphia, May 27, [1817]   MWA.   41339

Manchester, Phebe
A journey to the westward...Providence, Pr. by

H. H. Brown, 1817. MWA.   41340

Mannock, John
    Poor man's controversy... Georgetown, D. C., Pr.
by Wm. Duffy... 1817. 105 p. CtHi; DLC; MWA;
MdBS.   41341

Manvill, Mrs. P. D.
    Lucinda; or the mountain mourner. Being recent
facts, in a series of letters, from Mrs. Manvill, in
the state of New York, to her sister in Pennsylvania.
Ed. 3, with additions. Ballston Spa, N. Y., Pr. by J.
Comstock, for R. Sears, 1817. 180 p. CSmH; DLC;
MWA; RPB.   41342

Marblehead union moral society, Mass.
    The constitution and by-laws... Salem, Mass., Pr.
by T. C. Cushing, 1817. 16 p. MMhHi; MSaE; MWA.
                                            41343
-- An abstract from sundry laws of the commonwealth,
for the use of the Marblehead Union Moral Society.
Salem, Mass., Pr. by Thomas C. Cushing, 1817. 20 p.
MH-AH; MSaE.   41344

[Marcet, Mrs. Jane (Haldimand)]
    Conversations on political economy... Philadelphia,
Pr. by J. Maxwell, for Moses Thomas, 1817. DeGE;
GHi; IGK; MB; MWA; NGeno; NcU; NhD; PHC; PHi;
PPA; PPAmP; PMA; PPL-R; PU.   41345

Marine Bible Society of New York
    Constitution... of the society... auxiliary to the
American Bible Society; together with an address to
merchants and masters of vessels and an address to
seamen. New York, J. Seymour, 1817. 16 p. DLC;
MBC; MWA; NN; NIC-L; NjPT.   41346

-- Constitution. Ed. 2. New-York, J. Seymour, 1817.
MWiW.   41347

-- Report of the Marine Bible Society of New York, at
their first anniversary meeting April 21, 1817. New-
York, Pr. by J. Seymour, 1817. DLC; MBC; MWA;

MWiW; NNUT; NjPT.   41348

[Marius, pseud.]
    To the Democratic electors of the state of Penn-
sylvania...[Philadelphia, Pr. by John Binns, at the office of The Democratic press, 1817] MWA.   41349

Marshall, John, 1755-1835
    Opinion of Judge Marshall, in relation to the Po-
tomac company; and agreement by the Potomac company with General Henry Lee, relative to the use of
the surplus water at Great Falls of Potomac.   Georgetown, D. C., Pr. by W. A. Rind and co., 1817. 4 p.
DLC; DWP.   41350

Marshall's sale. By virtue and in pursuance of two
warrants from the Honorable the Secretary of the
Treasury of the United States, to me directed, will be
sold, at public auction, for cash, on Friday, the 16th
day of January, 1818, at 11 o'clock, A. M. at the
Court House, in Charles County, state of Maryland,
the following valuable property, to wit: First...A tract
of land, called the Grange, whereon Col. Francis Newman lately lived...Paul Bentalou, Marshall Dist. Md.
District of Maryland, Charles County, 22 December,
1817.   Pr. at the Baltimore Patriot Office.   Broadside.
NHi.   41351

Mary Gilman vs. Samuel Brown.   Case in equity, tried
at Boston, May term, 1817.   Boston, 1817. MWA.
                                    41352

Maryland (State)
    Laws made and passed by the General Assembly of
the state of Maryland, at a session begun and held at
the city of Annapolis, on Monday the second day of December, eighteen hundred and sixteen.   Annapolis, Pr.
by Jonas Green, 1817. 246 p. DLC; MdBB; MdHi;
Wa-L.   41353

-- -- Annapolis, Pr. by Jonas Green, 1817. 254 p.
IaU-L; MdBB; MdHi; Mo; Nb; Nc-SC; Nj; Nr; TxU-L;
Wa-L.   41354

-- Laws made and passed by the General assembly of
the state of Maryland... Annapolis, Pr. by Jehu
Chandler, 1817. 266 p. Nv.   41355

-- The state of Maryland, against the Vestry of St.
Peter's church; in which, a portion of the members of
the church prayed for a mandamus, to be directed to
the vestry, "commanding them to report the vacancy in
the rectorship of St. Peter's church to the bishop;...
Baltimore, Joseph Robinson, 1817. 80 p. MH; MdBD;
MdBE; MdHi.   41356

-- Votes and proceedings of the House of Delegates of
the state of Maryland, Dec. session, 1816. Annapolis,
Pr. by Jonas Green, 1817. 141 p. DLC; MdBB; MdBE;
MdBJ; MdHi.   41357

-- Votes and proceedings of the Senate of Maryland,
December session, 1816... Annapolis, Pr. by Jonas
Green, 1817. 61 p. DLC; MdBE; MdBJ; MdHi.   41358

Maryland Auxiliary Society for Colonizing the Free
People of Color in the United States.
     Constitution for the government of the Maryland
Auxiliary Colonizing the Free people of Color in the
United States. [Baltimore, 1817?] Broadside. MdHi.
                                                    41359
Maryland Volunteers
     By-laws of the Columbian volunteers... Baltimore,
1817. (The Anderson Galleries, Sale no. 1912, Janu-
ary 1925. no. 421)   41360

Massachusetts
     Act of incorporation... an act to incorporate the
master, wardens and members of the Grand lodge of
Massachusetts... [Boston, 1817] 16 p. MWA; PPFM.
                                                    41361
-- ... The commissioners appointed to inquire into the
mode of governing the penitentiary of Pennsylvania,
submit the following... [Boston] 1817. 30 p. MB; MH;
MWA.   41362

-- The laws of the Commonwealth of Massachusetts,

from February 28, 1807 to December 14, 1816, including the political years 1807, 1808, 1809, 1810,
1811, 1812, 1813, 1814, 1815 & 1816. Vol. IV to
Royal edition, or Vol. V to Dewy ed. Boston, Pr.
by Ezra Lincoln, for Thomas and Andrews, 1817. 699
p. C; MA; MH; MLowDC.   41363

-- Laws of the Commonwealth of Massachusetts,
passed by the General Court at their session, which
commenced on Wednesday the 28th day of May and
ended on the 18th of June 1817... Boston, Pr. by Russell, Cutler & Co., for Benjamin Russell, 1817. 387-
466 p. CSfLaw; DLC; IaU-L; MDi; MKiTH; MPiBL;
MeWebr; MdBB; Nc-S; Nj; R; TxU-L.   41364

-- List of members of the House of Representatives,
1817. Hon. Timothy Bigelow, Speaker. Benjamin Pollard, Clerk. Rev. Daniel Sharp, Chaplain. [Boston?
1817] Broadside. MHi.   41365

-- A proclamation, for a day of public fasting, humili-
ation and prayer. Given at the Council Chamber in
Boston, [March 4, 1817]... Broadside. MHi; NbO. 41366

-- A proclamation for a day of Thanksgiving and
prayer to be observed Dec. 4, 1817. Boston, Pr. by
Russell, Cutler & Co., 1817. Broadside. MAtt; MBB.
                                                41367
-- Report of the directors of the Massachusetts state
prison. Boston, 1817. MB; PPL-R.   41368

-- Resolves of the general court of the Commonwealth
of Massachusetts, passed at their session which commenced on Wednesday, the 28th day of May, and ended
on the 18th of June, 1817... Boston, Pr. by Russell,
Cutler & Co., for Benjamin Russell, 1817. 383-466 p.
C; DLC; MKiTH; MHam-BA; MMeT; MeHi; R.   41369

-- Rules and orders to be observed in the Senate of the
Commonwealth of Massachusetts, for the year 1817.
Boston, Pr. by Russell, Cutler and Co., 1817. 31 p.
MeHi.   41370

-- A system of artillery discipline; to which is prefixed, the soldier's drill, containing the facings, wheel-
ings, marchings, manual exercise, firings, formations,
etc.   Published according to a resolve of the legislature of Massachusetts. Boston, Munroe and Francis,
1817. 60 p. M; MH; MWA.   41371

-- Tax for the year 1817... [Boston, 1817]   41372

-- A true abstract of the statements from the Presi-
dents and Directors of the different banks, rendered
January and June, 1817. Made in conformity to a law
of this Commonwealth. Printed by order of the Honorable House of Representatives. Attest, Benjamin Pollard, Clerk of the House. [1817] Broadside. MHi.
                                                  41373
Massachusetts election! First Monday in April next.
American nomination. Major-General Henry Dearborn,
for governor. Hon. William King, for lieut. governor.
[Boston, Pr. at the office of the Yankee, 1817] 24 p.
CSmH; Ct; DLC; ICN; MiD-B; NN; PBL.   41374

Massachusetts peace society.
    Circular letter in behalf of the Massachusetts
peace society, to the friends of peace of all denominations. Boston, Pr. by J. Eliot, 1817. 8 p. DLC;
ICMe; ICT; MH; MWA; MeB; MeHi.   41375

The Massachusetts Register and United States calendar;
for the year of our Lord, 1818. Boston, James Loring
and West & Richardson [1817] CtHT; DLC; MMal;
MNF; MPeHi.   41376

-- Boston, West & Richardson and James Loring [1817]
304 p. CSmH; MS; MWo; MeBat.   41377

Massachusetts society for promoting Christian knowledge.
    Extracts from the annual report of the directors of
the Massachusetts society for promoting Christian knowledge. [Boston, 1817] [19]-50 p. CSt.   41378

[Matignon, F. A. ?]
    Rules of the Confraternity, or Association of the

Holy Cross, established at Boston, with the approba-
tion of the Right Rev. Bishop. [Boston, 1817?] 8 p.
DGU.   41379

Matteson, Isaiah
     A discourse on believer's baptism, delivered at
Bennington...1816, being a reply to the Rev. Daniel
Marsh on infant baptism... Bennington, Vt., Darius
Clark, 1817. 40 p. MH-AH; MiD-B; NNUT; NRAB;
OO; PPPrHi.   41380

Maturin, Charles Robert, 1780-1824
     Bertram, or The castle of St. Aldob...(?) a trage-
dy in five acts. 2d Amer., from the London ed. of
1816. New York, D. Longworth, 1817. 68 p. ICU;
MH.   41381

-- Manuel; a tragedy, in five acts... Baltimore, J.
Robinson, 1817. 68 p. MH; MWA; NN; OAlM. 41382

-- -- New-York, David Longworth, 1817. 64 p. DLC;
MWA.   41383

-- -- Philadelphia, Thomas, 1817. 90 p. PU. 41384

Mavor, William Fordyce
     Catechism of botany... New York, Samuel Wood &
Sons, 1817. 70 p. CtHi; MBHo; MWA; RJa.   41385

Maxcy, Jonathan
     An introductory lecture, to a course on the philo-
sophical principles of rhetorick an criticism; designed
for the senior class of the South-Carolina College; and
delivered in the publick chapel on Wednesday, April 8th,
1817... Columbia, S. C., Pr. by Daniel & J. J. Faust
[1817] DLC; MWA.   41386

Maxims for the preservation of health... Lee's patent
medicine. New York, 1817. PPL.   41387

Mayer, Lewis, 1783-1849
     The gifts of God. A discourse... 4th day of July,
1817... Shepherd's-Town, Va., Pr. by John N. Snider,

1817. 14 p. Stutler.   41388

Mead, Samuel Barlow
    Oration delivered in Amesbury, July 4, 1817.
Newburyport, Mass., 1817. MSaE.   41389

Meade, Richard Worsam, 1778-1828
    The case of Richard W. Meade, esq., a citizen
of Pennsylvania, U. S. A., seized and imprisoned, 2d
of May, 1816, by the government of Spain, and still
detained. Cadiz, November 27th, 1817. [Washington?
1817?] 25 p. DLC; MWA.   41390

Meade, William
    An experimental enquiry into the chemical proper-
ties...of the principal mineral waters of Ballston and
Saratoga...Philadelphia, Pr. by William Fry, for Harrison Hall, 1817. 195 p. DLC; MH; MWA; MnHi;
NNNAM; PPA; PPAmP; PPAN; PPC; PPF; PPL-R.
                                                41391
Mease, James, 1771-1846
    An address on the progress of agriculture, with
hints for its improvement in the United States. Delivered before the Philadelphia Society for Promoting
Agriculture, at their annual meeting, January 14th,
1817...[Philadelphia?] Pub. by order of the Society,
1817. 45 p. DeGE; MB.   41392

Medical Society of Orange County [New York]
    An act to incorporate medical societies for the
purpose of regulating the practice of physic and surgery
in this state. Passed April 10, 1813. Together with
the bye-laws of the Medical Society of the state of New
York, and of the County of Orange. Goshen, D. Mac-
Duffee, 1817. 20 p. NNNAM.   41393

Medical Society of South Carolina
    Report, on the failures attributed to the vaccine in
Charleston, in destroying the susceptibility to small
pox. Also, on secondary small pox...[Charleston,
1817] 8 p. NNNAM.   41394

Medical Society of the state of New York
    By-laws. [Cooperstown, N. Y. , 1817] MBM. 41395

-- Transactions of the Medical society of the state of
New-York... together with the annual address, by Jos-
eph White, M. D. ... Cooperstown, N. Y. , Pr. by J. H.
Prentiss, 1817. 39 p. NNNAM; NjR.   41396

Meditations, resolutions, & prayers, preparatory to
confirmation: by a father to a beloved daughter. Baltimore, J. Robinson, 1817. 8 p. MdBD.   41397

Medway, Mass. West Parish Library
    Constitution of the library, with a catalogue of the
books. Dedham, Mass., 1817. 8 p. MBC.   41398

Meikle, James
    Solitude sweetened... 5th Amer. ed. Brattleborough,
Vt., John Holbrook, 1817. 312 p. CSmH; CSt; MH;
MWA; NjPT; OClWHi; Vt; VtBratt; VtHi; VtMiM; VtVe.
                                                 41399

Melincourt. By the author of Headlong Hall. In two
volumes. Philadelphia, Pr. by William Fry, for
Moses Thomas, 1817. 2 v. ViAl.   41400

Melish, John
    Map of Indiana... The surveys furnished by Burr
Bradley. Philadelphia, John Melish and Samuel Harrison, 1817. 16 x 12 in. In.   41401

Memoirs of the life and gospel labors of the late Daniel Wheeler, a minister of the Society of Friends...
Philadelphia, 1817. 600 p. NjR.   41402

Memorial, intended to make an appeal to the Supreme
Judicial Court, for the county of Norfolk, on a judgment issued by the Inferior Court in September, 1817.
[1817?] 15 p. MH.   41403

Memorial of the citizens of Missouri Territory. To
the Honourable the Senate and the House of Representatives, of the United States... St. Louis, Pr. by S. Hall,
1817. Broadside. MoHi.   41404

Memorial of the inhabitants residing on the Niagara frontier, respectfully addressed to the Senate and House of representatives of the United States of America. City of Washington, Pr. by Jonathan Elliot, 1817. 56 p. DLC; MHi; MWA.   41405

Mennonites
    Extract of the twenty-one doctrinal articles of the Augustan or Augsburg Confession, for the use of the Brethren's congregations, and in particular of the children. Philadelphia, Pr. by Conrad Zentler, 1817. 22 p. PNazMHi.   41406

-- Die täglichen Loosungen und Lehrtexte der Brüdergemeine für das Jahr 1818. Philadelphia, Pr. by Conrad Zentler, 1817. 126 p. PNazMHi.   41407

Mercantile advertiser, and daily vehicle, Feb. 17, 1817. Petersburg, Va., 1817. (Newspapers) MBAt.
                                                        41408
Mercantile Manual, or Accountant's guide... Rogersville, Tenn., Repr. by Patrick Carey, 1817. 28 p. MWA.   41409

The mermaid, or Nautical songster; being a selection of favorite sea songs. New-York, R. & A. Tiebout, 1817. 69 p. MWA.   41410

Merrick, James Lyman, 1803-66
    The life and religion of Mohammed, as contained in the Sheeah traditions of the Hyat-Ul-Kuloob, translated from the Persian. Boston, Phillips, Sampson & Co., 1817. 483 p. ScU.   41411

Merrick, Pliny
    An oration, delivered in Worcester, July 4, 1817 .... Worcester, Mass., Pr. by Henry Rogers, 1817. 16 p. CSt; MB; MBAt; MBC; MDeeP; MW; MWA; MiD-B; NNC.   41412

Merrill, Daniel
    The kingdom of God. A discourse delivered at Concord, before His Excellency the Governor... June 5,

1817... Concord, N. H., Pr. by Isaac Hill, 1817. 44 p.
NjR.   41413

Merrill, Eliphalet
    A gazetteer of the state of New Hampshire...
Exeter, N. H., Pr. by C. Norris & Co., for the author, 1817. 281 p. MHi; MWey; NRU.   41414

Merriman, Samuel
    A dissertation on retroversion of the womb...
Philadelphia, Pr. by William Fry, for Thomas Dobson
and son, 1817. 80 p. MB; MWA; NNNAM; RPM.
                                                    41415
A mess of messes, or Salmagundi outwitted for the
laughing philosophers; consisting of the most admired
anecdotes, and song of songs. Compiled by Smell-
fungus and Mundungus, descendants of the risible die-
ties... Philadelphia, pub. for the subscribers, 1817.
144 p. CSmH.   41416

A mess of salmagundi... Philadelphia, pub. for the subscribers, 1817. MWA.   41417

A method of increasing the quantity of circulating-
money; upon a new and solid principle. Now first published. 1817. no. XXI. 31 p. In.   41418

[Methodist Episcopal church]
    A collection of interesting tracts... New York, Pr.
by T. & W. Mercein, for J. Soule and T. Mason,
1817. 359 p. CSmH; MWA; NN; NcD.   41419

-- The doctrines and discipline... Ed. 19. New York,
Pr. by John C. Totten, for J. Soule and T. Mason,
1817. 216 p. CoDI; IEG; MWA; NIC; TNMPH. 41420

-- Minutes taken at the several annual conferences of
the Methodist Episcopal Church in the United States of
America, for the year 1817. New York, Pr. by J. C.
Totten, for Joshua Soule; Thomas Mason, and for the
Methodist Episcopal Church in the United States of A-
merica, 1817. 48 p. IEG; MWA; NSmB; PPM. 41421

The Methodist Pocket Hymn-Book, revised and improved... Ed. 43. New-York, Pr. by Abraham Paul, for J. Soule and T. Mason, 1817. 304 p. MWA. 41422

Methodist Protestant Church
Constitutions and discipline of the Methodist Protestant Church. Ed. 2. Baltimore, 1817. 178 p. (The Green Bookman list, 17, Nov. 1933)   41423

Methodist Sunday School Library, Portland, Me.
Rules of the Methodist Sunday-School library, Portland. Portland, Me., 1817. IEG.   41424

Miami Herald. Hamilton, Ohio, W. & J. Camron & Co., Sept. 12, 1817, 1st issue. Weekly newspaper. MWA.   41425

Michaux, François Andre
The North American sylva; or, a description of the forest trees of the United States, Canada, etc., added, the European forest trees; (tr. by A. L. Hillhouse). Philadelphia, Thomas Dobson, 1817-19. 3 v. MBAt; OCN; PPC.   41426

Middlebrook's almanack for 1818... Bridgeport, Conn., Nathl. Skinner, and Sherman Baldwin & co. [1817] [24] p. MWA.   41427

-- New Haven, Pr. by T. G. Woodward [1817] [24] p. CtY; MWA.   41428

Middlebury College. Middlebury, Vt.
Catalogue of the officers and students of Middlebury College, October, 1817. Rev. Joshua Bates, A. M. President, elect. ... Middlebury, Vt., Pr. by Frederick P. Allen, 1817. Broadside. MH.   41429

-- Catalogus Senatus Academici, et eorum, qui munera et officia academica gesserunt, quique alicujus gradus laurea exornati fuerunt, in Collegio Middleburiensi, in Republica Viridimontana, ab anno 1802 ad annum 1817. Medioburgi, Typis Frederici P. Allen, 1817. 10 p. CSmH; VtMiM; MH.   41430

The Middlebury college charitable society.
A concise account...Middlebury, Vt., T. C. Strong,
1817. 16 p. CtHC; MWA; MiD-B; N; VtMiM.   41431

Middlesex Canal
Report to the board of directors of Middlesex Canal.
By a committee. April, 1817. Boston, Pr. by John Eliot,
[1817?] 20 p. MLow; MWo.   41432

Middletown, Conn. -- Citizens
To the president and directors of the Bank of the
United States...[Middletown, Conn., 1817] MWA. 41433

Mifflin Eagle. Mifflintown, Pa., Andrew N. Gallaher,
July 5, 1817, 1st issue. Weekly newspaper. Brigham,
p. 880.   41434

[Milledoler, Philip]
An account of the origin and formation of the American society for evangelizing the Jews; with its constitution, and an address to the public. New York, The
society, 1817. 15 p. CtW.   41435

Miller, Wm.
Report on the claim of lands in the Province of
Louisiana. Washington, 1817. (Aldine Book Co. Cat.
Louisiana Historical Library, Jan. 1917, no. 962)
                                                41436
Miller's planters' & merchants' almanac for 1818.
Astronomical calculations by Andrew Beers. Charleston,
S. C., A. E. Miller [1817] 48 p. MWA.   41437

Mills, Alfred, 1776-1833
Costumes of different nations in miniature from
drawings, by Alfred Mills, with descriptions. New
York, S. Wood, 1817. 190 p. OC.   41438

-- Pictures of English history in miniature, designed
by Alfred Mills, with descriptions. vol. I. New-York,
S. Wood & son, 1817. 192 p. DLC.   41439

Mills, Henry
Narrative of the life and dying confession of Henry

Mills of Galesboro' Pennsylvania, who on the night of
the 29th January last, inhumanly murdered his wife
and five children...written by himself, since his con-
finement in Galesboro' prison...Boston, Pr. by H.
Trumbull, 1817. 24 p. MBS; MWA.   41440

-- Narrative of the pious death of the penitent Henry
Mills, who was executed in Galesboro (Penn.) on the
15th July last for the murder of his wife and five children! To which is annexed, his serious and solemn
address to youth...Boston, H. Trumbull, 1817. 24 p.
DLC; MBNEH; MMeT; MWA.   41441

Miln, William, 1761-1801
     The Comet; or, He would be an astronomer. A
farce. In two acts...Baltimore, J. Robinson, 1817.
31 p. CSmH; CtY; DLC; MH; MWA; MdBE; MdHi; NN;
PU; RPB.   41442

[--] -- Baltimore, J. Robinson, 1817. MWA; RPB.
                                             41443
Milner, Joseph
     An abridgment of Milner's Church history of the
use of schools and private families. By Rebecca Eaton.
Andover, Mass., Flagg & Gould, 1817. 324 p. CtY;
MB; MH; MBC; MNowdHi; MWA.   41444

Milnor, James
     Address delivered before the superintendents,
teachers, and pupils, of the Sunday schools attached to
St. George's church...New-York... New York, Pr. by
John C. Totten, 1817. 30 p. InID; MWA; NIC. 41445

-- -- New York, Pr. by G. F. Bunce, Re-pub. by
Robert and Wm. A. Bartow, 1817. 28 p. MWA; NjR;
TxDaM.   41446

-- A sermon preached in St. George's church...New-
York, on Thursday the thirteenth day of November,
1817, being a public day of thanksgiving...New York,
Pr. by John C. Totten, for Robert and Wm. A. Bartow, 1817. 28 p. MWA.   41447

Miner's agricultural and miscellaneous almanac for
1818. By William Collom. Doylestown, Pa., Asher
Miner [1817] DLC; MWA.   41448

A miniature almanack, for the year of our Lord, 1818
...Boston, Pr. by C. Crocker, for Charles Ewer,
[1817] 25 p. MSha.   41449

-- Boston, Charles Ewer and Henry Bowen [1817]
MWA.   41450

Minter, Jeremiah
    A brief account of the religious experience, travels,
preaching, persecutions from evil men, and God's special helps in the faith and life, &c. of Jerem. Minter
...Washington City, Pr. for the author, 1817. PHi;
ViRut.   41451

Mirror for the parlor window, worthy a single perusal
and due reflection being a descriptive journal down the
North River. By a gentleman who lost his property by
the ravages of war and sold by him for the benefit of
his family. Utica, N.Y., Pr. for the author, 1817.
22 p. OClWHi.   41452

Missionary society of Connecticut.
    Eighteenth annual narrative...Hartford, Pr. by
Peter B. Gleason & Co., 1817. MWA; N; NCH; OCHP.
                                               41453

Mississippi (State)
    Constitution and form of government for the state
of Mississippi. Natchez, Pr. by Andrew Marschalk,
1817. 30 p. MWA; Ms-Ar; NN.   41454

-- -- Natchez, Pr. by P. Isler, 1817. 41 p. DNA;
Nh-Hi.   41455

Mississippi (Ter.)
    Ballot list, constitutional convention of 1817, July
& August, beginning thus: "Ayes." Mr. President,
Barnes, Burnet (of Claiborne) Balch..." and ending:
"...Williams, Wilkinson, West," a total of 47 names.
Printed as broadsides on strips varying in width from

8 to 10 cm. and 41 cm. long.   No internal indication
of printer nor of exact date.   MsJS.   41456

-- By David Holmes, Governor... A proclamation...
Washington, May 9, 1817.   [Natchez, 1817] Broadside.
LNH; Ms-Ar.   41457

The Mississippi and Louisiana almanac for 1818... cal-
culated for the meridian of Natchez... by the Rev. John
Taylor, of Pittsburgh... Natchez, Andrew Marschalk
and William Snodgrass [1817] 44 p. Ms-Ar; MsJS; ViU.
                                                     41458
Missouri (Ter.)
    Acts passed by the General Assembly of the Terri-
tory of Missouri, in December 1816... St. Louis, (M.
T.) Pr. by Joseph Charless, 1817. 143 p. DLC;
MoHi; MoSHi; MH-L.   41459

The Modern messenger.   Newark, N.J., P. Couderer,
1st issue October 10, 1817. Weekly. Hill, no. 97.
                                                     41460
Moffat, John S.
    The lives of Robert & Mary Moffat by their son
John S. Moffat with portraits and illustrations.   New
ed., with preface and supplementary chapter.   New
York, A.C. Armstrong & son,1817. 484 p. ViRut.41461

Monitor.   Franklin, Tenn., Henry Van Pelt, 1817,
1st issue. Newspaper. Brigham, p. 1057.   41462

Monstrous sea serpent; (description of the sea serpent
reported to have been seen in Gloucester Harbor, Aug.
1817) Boston, [1817] Broadside. MBAt.   41463

Montgomery, James
    A new and complete edition of the works of James
Montgomery... Morristown, N.J., Pr. by Dodd and
Stevenson, for Peter A. Johnson, 1817. 2 v. InRchE;
KyDC; MB; MWA; NN; RBr; TNP.   41464

-- Verses to the memory of the late Richard Reynolds
... New York, Pr. by T. & W. Mercein, for Thomas
Kirk and Thomas R. Mercein, 1817. 44 p. MB; MH;

MWA.   41465

-- The wanderer of Switzerland... Philadelphia, Pr. by
W. Brown, for Mitchell & Ames, 1817. 292 p. MWA;
NCH.   41466

-- -- Salem, N. Y. , Pr. by Dodd & Stevenson, 1817.
120 p. CSmH; MWA; NGH; NjR.   41467

-- The world before the flood... Salem, N. Y. , Dodd &
Stevenson, 1817. MWA; NT.   41468

Moore, Edward
    The Gamester: A tragedy, in five acts. New
York, David Longworth, 1817. 72 p. CLU; CSmH;
MWA.   41469

Moore, Martin
    A sermon, delivered Jan. 5, 1817, containing a
history of Natick (R. I.) Cambridge, Pr. by Hilliard
and Metcalf, 1817. MWiW.   41470

Moore, Nathaniel L.
    The restoration of Sodom, Samaria and Judah; or,
the return of the Jews, to their former estate... Hamilton, Pr. by John B. Johnson, 1817. 15 p. NjR. 41471

Moore, Thomas
    Irish melodies... Salem, N. Y. , Pr. by T. Hoskins,
for J. P. Reynolds, 1817. 144 p. CSmH; MWA; NNF.
                                                 41472
-- Lalla Rookh... New York, Kirk and Mercein, 1817.
MWA.   41473

-- --... an oriental romance. New York, Leavitt &
Allen, [1817] 346 p. NIC.   41474

-- -- New York, Van Winkle and Wiley, 1817. 284 p.
CtW; MWA; NcRSM.   41475

-- -- Philadelphia, Pr. by J. Maxwell, for M. Thomas,
1817. 288 p. MWA; NNUT; NjR.   41476

-- The poetical works of Thomas Moore, including his
melodies, ballads, etc. Complete in one volume.
Philadelphia, Cowperthwait & co., 1817. 431 p. LAlP.
41477

Moral and political observations, addressed to the en-
lightened citizens of Virginia. By E. B. [Richmond,
1817] 8 p. CtY.   41478

Mordente, John Emmanuel
    A new, easy, and complete grammar of the Span-
ish language, commercial and military... 1st Amer.,
from the last London ed. New-York, Pr. by George
Long, for Daniel D. Arden, 1817. 356 p. CSmH; MH;
MWA; MiD-B.   41479

[More, Hannah]
    The history of Mr. Fantom... Philadelphia, Benja-
min Johnson, 1817. MWA.   41480

-- Poems from the London edition. Boston, Wells &
Lilly, 1817. 294 p. CtHC; MB; MiToC; RBr; RPB.
41481
-- The shepherd of Salisbury-Plain... Boston, Lincoln
& Edmands, 1817. 52 p. MB; MWA; RPB; ViFTBE.
41482
[--] The thunderstorm... Philadelphia, Wm. Bradford,
agent, 1817. MWA.   41483

-- 'Tis all for the best. Entertaining, moral, and religious... Boston, Pr. by Lincoln & Edmands, [1817]
15 p. MWA.   41484

-- -- [Philadelphia, Pr. by Lydia R. Bailey, 1817]
(This is no. 16 of the tracts of the Philadelphia female
tract society.) MWA.   41485

-- The works of Hannah More, with a sketch of her
life. Complete in two volumes. Boston, S. G. Goodrich, 1817. 2 v. ViRVal.   41486

Morgan, Sydney (Owenson), lady.
    France... New York, Pr. by E. & E. Hosford, for
James Eastburn & Co., 1817. 2 v. MSaE; MWA; MdAS;

NCH; NNS; NcWsS; PMA; ViPet; ViU; VtU.   41487

-- -- With an English translation of the French words
and phrases. Philadelphia, M. Thomas, 1817. 193 p.
DLC; LNMus.   41488

-- -- 3d Amer. ed. Philadelphia, Pr. by James Maxwell, for M. Thomas, 1817. 370 p. DeGE; MA; MWA;
MWiW; RNR; ViU.   41489

Morning Chronicle. Savannah, Ga., Samuel Ker, 1817,
1st issue. Daily and tri-weekly newspaper. MWA.
                                                 41490
Morris, Jacob, 1755-1844
    Address of Gen. Jacob Morris, president of the
Otsego county agricultural society, delivered before
said association established for the promotion of agriculture and manufactures, at Cooperstown, Oct. 14,
1817... Cooperstown [N. Y.] Pr. by H. and E. Phinney,
1817. 16 p. DLC; ICMcHi; MB; MH; MWA; MiD-B.
                                                 41491
Morrison, William
    A sermon, delivered in the West parish of London-
derry, May 5, 1817. Occasioned by the death of John
Pinkerton... Concord, N. H., Pr. by George Hough,
1817. MWA.   41492

Morse, Jedidiah
    The Christian ambassador. A sermon delivered at
the ordination of... E. Phelps, etc. Brookfield, Mass.,
Pr. by E. Merriam & Co., 1817. 24 p. CSmH; MBC;
MWA.   41493

Morton, Thomas
    The slave, a musical drama in three acts... New
York, D. Longworth, 1817. MB; MWA; RPB. 41494

The most important public meetings of the people in
Great Britain, that have taken place in their counties,
cities, etc. on the distresses of the country, from
August 1st, 1816, to the latest accounts from England,
with the speeches and resolutions agreed to be presented to the Prince Regent and both Houses of Parlia-

ment, in the ensuing sessions... New York, Pr. by
Clayton and Kingsland, for Cobbett and Oldfield, 1817.
99 p. DGU.   41495

[Mott, Richard]
A short account of the last sickness and death of
Maria Mott... New York, Samuel Wood & sons, 1817.
MWA.   41496

Mount Carmel, Ill. (City)
Articles of association... Chillicothe, Ohio, Pr. by
John Bailhache, 1817. 22 p. ICHi; WHi.   41497

[Mower, Arthur]
The white cottage, a tale... Philadelphia, Mathew
Carey and son, 1817. 216 p. LU.   41498

Muckarsi, John
The children's catechism... new ed. West Union,
Ohio, Pr. by James Finley, 1817. 33 p. PPPrHi.
                                                     41499
Muhlenberg, Henry i.e. Gotthilf Henry Ernest, 1753-
1815.
Descriptio uberior graminum et plantarum calama-
riarum Americae Septentrionalis indigenarum et cicur-
um. Philadelphiae, S.W. Conrad, 1817. 295 p. CSfA;
DLC; KyLxT; MBHo; MWA; NIC; NTR; NjP; RPB. 41500

Multum in parvo; being a system of divinity in this...
two paradoxes... New York, 1817. 24 p. NjR.   41501

Munchausen
Lustige Aufschneidery... 1817. MWA.   41502

Munsell, Hezekiah, Jr.
English grammar, made easy by the means of a
new and improved grammatical chart... Bennington, Vt.,
Pr. by Darius Clark, 1817. Broadside. MH; NN;
VtHi.   41503

Murphy, Arthur, 1727-1805
All in the wrong. A comedy... New York, D. Longworth, 1817. 95 p. MH; MWA; PU; TxU.   41504

-- Three weeks after marriage. A farce in two acts
...New York, David Longworth, 1817. 32 p. MH;
MWA; MWo; NN.   41505

-- The way to keep him. A comedy...New York,
David Longworth, 1817. 112 p. MH; MWA.   41506

Murray, Lindley, 1745-1826
    Abridgement of Murray's English grammar. 9th
Boston ed. Boston, J. Loring, 1817. MWA.   41507

-- -- Ed. 10. Boston, J. Loring, 1817. CtHT-W; MB;
MWA.   41508

-- A compendium of religious faith and practice. De-
signed for young persons of the Society of Friends...
New-York, Samuel Wood & sons, 1817. 88 p. DLC;
MH; MWA; NNUT.   41509

-- The duty and benefit of a daily perusal of the Holy
Scriptures, in families...New York, Pr. by J. T. Mur-
dock, for. C. Wiley & Co., 1817. 35 p. NNG.   41510

-- English exercises, adapted to Murray's English gram-
mar...7th Boston, from the 20th English ed. Boston,
Pr. by J. Loring, 1817. 213 p. DLC; MWA; ViU.
                                                41511
-- -- From the 20th English ed. New York, Collins
& Co., 1817. 192 p. MWA.   41512

-- English grammar, adapted to the different classes
of learners...Stereotyped by B. and J. Collins, from
the last English ed. New-York, Collins and Co., 1817.
312 p. MWA; MoSM; NjR; OC; RKi.   41513

-- An English grammar: comprehending the principles
and rules of the language...3d Amer. ed. New York,
Collins & co., 1817. 2 v. CSmH; MWA.   41514

-- -- Ed. 3. Philadelphia, D. Hogan, 1817. MWA.
                                                41515
-- The English reader: or, Pieces in prose and poetry.
Baltimore, Fielding Lucas, Jr., and Coale and Max-

well, 1817. 263 p. (Mrs. R. F. Waugh, 112 S. High
St., Belleville)   41516

-- -- From the 10th English ed. Baltimore, Pr. by
Burrill and Tileston, for J. Cushing, 1817. 264 p.
MdBE; TNT.   41517

-- -- Boston ed. Boston, Lincoln & Edmands, 1817.
MWA.   41518

-- -- Burlington, Vt., Samuel Mills, 1817. 288 p.
MH; MWA; VtMiM; VtMiS; VtU-W.   41519

-- -- Second Hallowell ed. Hallowell, Me., N.
Cheever, 1817. MWA; MeP.   41520

-- -- From the 10th English ed. Haverhill, Mass.,
Burrill and Tileston, 1817. 264 p. DLC; MHa; MWA;
WMOSC.   41521

-- -- From the 10th English ed. Keene, N. H., Pr.
by Burrill & Tileston, for John Prentiss, 1817. 264 p.
CSt; DLC; MH; MWA; Nh.   41522

-- -- New York, Pr. by Collins and Co., 1817. 316 p.
NN; WM.   41523

-- -- Philadelphia, G. W. Mentz, 1817. 263 p. MWA;
OO.   41524

-- -- Philadelphia, Pr. by McCarty & Davis, 1817.
263 p. CSt.   41525

-- -- 3d Pittsburgh ed. Pittsburgh, Pa., Pr. by Butler & Lambdin, for Robert Patterson, 1817. 275 p.
CtHT-W; KyDC; MH; MWA.   41526

-- --...With a key...by M. R. Bartlett. 4th Utica ed.
Utica, N. Y., William Williams, 1817. 288 p. MWA;
NUt.   41527

-- English spelling-book. From last English ed. New
York, Collins & Co., 1817. MH.   41528

-- Exercises, adapted to Murray's English grammar
... Philadelphia, Pr. by M'Carty and Davis, for Benjamin Warner, 1817. 168 p. MiDSH.   41529

-- Grammatical questions adapted to... grammar.
Salem, Mass., T. C. Cushing, 1817. MH; MWA. 41530

-- Introduction to the English reader... From the 7th
English ed., improved by the author. Burlington, Vt.,
Samuel Mills, 1817. 192 p. MWA; VtU-W.   41531

-- Key to the exercises adapted to Murray's English
grammar... From the 12th London ed. New York,
Collins & co., 1817. 171 p. MHi; MWA; ViU. 41532

-- Sequel to the English reader... From the 3d English
ed., enl. and imp. Baltimore, Pr. by William Warner,
1817. 366 p. InNd.   41533

-- -- From the 4th English ed., enl. and improved.
New-York, Collins & co., 1817. 372 p. N.   41534

Musical monitor; or New-York collection of devotion
church music... Utica, N. Y., Pr. by William Williams,
1817. 119 p. MWA.   41535

The musical reader, or practical lessons for the
voice... to which are prefixed the Rudiments of music
... Utica, N. Y., Pr. typographically by William Williams, 1817. 80 p. MWA.   41536

My brother. A poem for children. New York, Samuel Wood & Sons, 1817. MWA.   41537

-- Illustrated with engravings. Philadelphia, Wm.
Charles, 1817. 12 p. NNC.   41538

My grandfather; a poem. Illustrated with engravings.
Philadelphia, Wm. Charles, 1817. 10 p. NNC. 41539

My grandmother, a poem... Philadelphia, Wm. Charles,
1817. MWA; RPB.   41540

My Tippoo. A poem illustrated with engravings.
Philadelphia, Wm. Charles, 1817. [12] p. PP.   41541

                        N

Nancarrow, J.
    Letter, addressed to Elias Hicks, minister of the
Society of Friends in the state of New York. Baltimore, 1817. 18 p. DLC; PHC; PPL.   41542

[Nancrede, Paul Joseph Guerard de]
    The forum orator, or the American public speaker.
Consisting of examples and models of eloquence...
Stereotype ed. Boston, Bingham & Co., 1817. MB.
                                             41543
Nantucket Weekly magazine. Nantucket, Mass., A. G.
Tannatt, June 28, 1817, 1st issue. MB.   41544

Napoleon I.
    Napoleon's own memoirs printed from a manu-
script transmitted from Saint Helena through an unknown channel. Translated from the French. Pittsburgh, Pa., Pr. by Butler and Lambdin, for Robert
Patterson... 1817. 176 p. Bowe.   41545

Narden, N.
    Letters written on board the Northumberland.
Philadelphia, 1817. MB.   41546

Narrative of the life of James Lane, who was executed at Gallipolis (Ohio) Sept. 9, 1817, for the murder
of William Dowell... Chillicothe, O., Pr. by John Bailhache, 1817. 20 p. CSmH; OClWHi.   41547

A narrative of the state of religion, within the bounds
of the General assembly, of the Presbyterian Church,
and of the general associations of Connecticut: of New
Hampshire and of Massachusetts proper. Philadelphia,
Thomas and William Bradford, 1817. 62 p. PMA.
                                             41548
A narrative of the travels of John Vandeluer, on the
Western continent. Containing an account of the con-
version of an Indian chief and his family to Christian-

ity. Hallowell [Me.] Pr. by E. Goodale, 1817. 87 p.
CSmH; DLC; MWA.   41549

National Messenger. Georgetown, D.C., James C.
Dunn & Co., Oct. 27, 1817, 1st issue. Tri-weekly
continuation of "The Messenger." DLC.   41550

Nature and danger of heresy; sermon. Boston, 1817.
MH-AH.   41551

Nature and efficacy of Cross of Christ. Philadelphia,
Kite, 1817. PSC-Hi.   41552

[Neal, John] 1793-1876
    Keep cool, a novel. Written in hot weather...
Baltimore, J. Cushing, 1817. 2 v. CtY; DLC; IU; MH;
MdHi; NN; NNS; PPL; PU.   41553

Neal, William
    A lunatic. Philadelphia, 1817. PPL.   41554

Negro servant. Religious tract society. Philadelphia,
William Bradford, 1817. MWA; PPPrHi.   41555

Neill, William
    The benignity of the creator... Philadelphia, Pr. by
John W. Scott [1817] MWA.   41556

Neue Americanische Landwirthschafts Calender, 1818.
Reading, Pa., Johann Ritter und comp. [1817] MWA;
P; PHi.   41557

Der Neue Baltimore Stadt und Land Calender. Auf das
Jahr 1818. Baltimore, Pr. by William Warner, 1817.
Seidensticker p. 200.   41558

Neue, Gemeinnützige Landwirthschafts Calender, 1818.
Lancaster, Pa., Anton Albrecht [1817] MWA; PHi.
                                                   41559
The new American songster; being a collection of naval,
martial, patriotic songs... Philadelphia, 1817. RPB.
                                                   41560
A new and highly improved violin preceptor, containing

in addition to the rudiments a choice and extensive
selection of the most approved cotillions, dances,
waltzes, songs, airs, &c. &c. Utica [N. Y.] William
Williams, 1817. 47 p. OCHP.   41561

Nevius, John W.
    New Brunswick collection of sacred music. By
John W. Nevius et al. New Brunswick, N. J., Pr. by
W. Meyer, 1817. 72 p. MWA; NjR; PPPrHi.   41562

New American primer containing short and easy lessons...Ed. 9. Boston, 1817. (Charles F. Heartman,
Sale no. 294, March, 1940. no. 130)   41563

A new and elegant general atlas containing maps of
each of the United States. Baltimore, F. Lucas
[1817] MB; MdBE.   41564

A new collection of family prayers, and offices of devotion... carefully selected from those pious authors,
Jenks, Ven, and Palmer, and from the new manual of
private devotions... Greenfield, Mass., Pr. by Denio
and Phelps, 1817. 180 p. CSt; MWA; NcD.   41565

New collection of hymns, and spiritual songs. Portsmouth, N. H., 1817. 48 p. Nh-Hi.   41566

New England almanack for 1818. Boston, Parmenter
& Norton [1817] MWA.   41567

No entry.   41568

The New-England almanack for the year of our Lord
1818, by S. Capen. Boston, Pr. by Parmenter & Norton, for C. Ewer [1817] MBev-F; MHi.   41569

The New-England almanack, for the year of our Lord
Christ, 1818... The astronomical calculations performed by Nathan Daboll... New-London, Samuel Green
[1817] [32] p. CtHi; CtHT-W; CtNl; MWA; NjR. 41570

New-England farmer's diary and almanac for 1818.

Weathersfield, Vt., 1817. NhHi.   41571

The New-England Farmer's diary, and almanac, from
the year of the creation, according to sacred writ,
5780, and the Christian era, 1818... By Truman Abel.
Windsor [Vt.] Jesse Cochran, [1817] [48] p. MBC;
MWA.   41572

New-England Galaxy. Boston, Joseph T. Buckingham,
Oct. 10, 1817, 1st issue. Weekly newspaper. MWA;
NIC.   41573

The New-England primer, improved... Middletown
[Conn.] Frederick Spencer, 1817. [72] p. CSmH;
CtHi; CtY; MWA.   41574

New England Tract Society
    The hermit. Ed. 2. Andover, Mass., 1817. Nh.
                                                   41575
New Hampshire (State)
    Journal of the Honorable Senate of the state of
New Hampshire, at their session... Nov.... 1816...
Concord, Pr. by Isaac Hill, 1817. 159 p. DLC. 41576

-- Journal of the Honorable Senate of the state of New
Hampshire, at their session, June... 1817... Concord,
Pr. by Isaac Hill, 1817. 218 p. DLC.   41577

-- Journal of the House of Representatives of the state
of New Hampshire, at their session, November 1816...
Concord, Pr. by Isaac Hill, 1817. 271 p. DLC. 41578

-- Journal of the House of Representatives of the state
of New Hampshire at their session, June... 1817... Concord, Pr. by Isaac Hill, 1817. 280 p. DLC.   41579

-- Laws of the state of New Hampshire, November session, 1816. [Exeter? Norris? 1817?] [67]-100 p. DLC.
                                                   41580
-- Laws of the state of New Hampshire, June session,
1817. [Exeter? Norris? 1817?] [101]-128 p. DLC.
                                                   41581
-- Message of the Governor, June session, 1817.

[1817] MWA.   41582

[New Hampshire missionary society]
    Report on the concerns of the New-Hampshire cent
institution...Concord, N.H., Pr. by George Hough,
1817. MWA.   41583

-- The sixteenth report of the board of trustees...Sep-
tember 19, 1817...Concord, N.H., Pr. by George
Hough, 1817. MWA.   41584

The New-Hampshire Register, and United States Calendar, for...1818...Concord, Isaac Hill [1817] 108 p.
MWA; Nh-Hi.   41585

New Haven. Citizens.
    [Resolutions passed by a meeting of the citizens of
New Haven, Nov. 8, 1816, and petition, with accompanying documents, for a change of the location of a
branch of the Bank of the United States from Middletown to New Haven] [New Haven? 1817] 44 p. DLC;
MWA; RPB.   41586

A new introduction to reading: or, A collection of easy
lessons arranged on an approved plan...Washington city,
D. Rapine, 1817. 165 p. DLC; MWA; NcD.   41587

New Jersey (State)
    Journal of the proceedings of the Legislative Coun-
cil of the state of New Jersey...October, 1817...1st
sitting of the 42d session. Elizabeth-town, N.J., Pr.
by Shepard Kollock, 1817. [2081]-2108 p. Nj; NjHi;
N; NjR.   41588

-- Journal of the proceedings of the Legislative Council
of the state of New Jersey...Jan., 1817...2d sitting of
the 41st session. Elizabeth-town, N.J., Pr. by Shepard Kollock, 1816[!] [1817] [1957]-2078, [351]-374 p.
Nj; NjHi.   41589

-- Private and temporary acts. Acts of the 41st General Assembly of the state of New Jersey...Oct., 1816
...1st sitting. Trenton, Pr. by Justice & Cox, 1817.

9 p. DLC; NjR.   41590

-- -- Acts of the 41st General Assembly of the state of
New-Jersey...Jan., 1817...2d sitting. Trenton, Pr. by
Justice & Cox, 1817. [11]-86 p. DLC; NjR.   41591

-- Public acts. Acts of the 41st General Assembly of the
state of New-Jersey...Oct., 1816...1st & 2d sittings.
Trenton, Pr. by Justice & Cox, 1817. 39 p. DLC; NjR.
                                                  41592
-- Report of the Commissioner's appointed by an act of
the Legislature, 1816. New Brunswick, N.J., 1817.
NN.   41593

-- Report of the commissioners, appointed by an act of
the Legislature of the state of New Jersey, for ascer-
taining the most eligible route for, and the probable expense of, a canal to connect the tide waters of the Delaware with those of the Raritan. Passed February 13,
1816. New-York, Pr. by Van Winkle, Wiley & co.,
1817. 40 p. DBRE.   41594

-- -- Trenton, Pr. by James J. Wilson, 1817. 31 p.
DeGE; NjR.   41595

-- Report of the commissioners, appointed...for set-
tling certain differences between this state and...Penn-
sylvania. Trenton, N.J., Pr. by James J. Wilson,
1817. 34 p. MWA; NjR.   41596

-- Rules and orders, of the Court of Chancery...
[Trenton? 1817] 11 p. NjR.   41597

-- Votes and proceedings of the 41st General Assembly
of the state of New-Jersey...Oct., 1816...1st sitting.
Bridgeton, Pr. by Peter Hay, 1817. 76 p. Nj; NjR.
                                                  41598
-- -- 2d sitting. Bridgeton, Pr. by Peter Hay, 1817.
[77]-264 p. Nj; NjR.   41599

The New-Jersey and Pennsylvania almanac, for...1818.
By Joshua Sharp...Trenton, N.J., George Sherman
[1817] [40] p. DLC; MWA; N; NjR.   41600

New Jersey Bible Society
Seventh report of the Board of Managers of the
New Jersey Bible Society... held at New Brunswick.
New Brunswick, N.J., Pr. by William Myer, 1817.
28 p. N; NjR.   41601

New manual of private devotions, in three parts.   3d
Amer. ed. New-York, T. & J. Swords, 1817. 371 p.
NBuDD.   41602

New Orleans (City)
Ordinances ordained and established by the mayor
and City council, of the city of New Orleans. [New
Orleans] Pr. by J. C. de St. Romes, 1817. 341 p.
MdBJ.   41603

New St. Tammany almanac, for 1818.   Philadelphia,
George W. Mentz [1817] MWA.   41604

New spiritual songs, for those who wish to praise God.
[Text]... Montpelier, Vt., Pr. by Cyrus Hill, 1817.
24 p.   McCorison List.   41605

New York (City)
By Jacob Radcliff mayor, and Richard Riker re-
corder, of the city of New-York, it is hereby certified,
that pursuant to the statute... we have this day examined (one) certain (male) negro slave named (George)
the property of (John Delancy) which slave (is) about to
be manumitted... we have granted this certificate, this
(twenty-fourth) day of (April) ... one thousand eight hundred and (seventeen).   Broadside. (Facsimile reprint.
Printed from... with blank spaces filled in) NN. 41606

-- The constitution and by-laws of the fire-department
of the city of New-York... New York, Pr. by Samuel
Wood & sons, 1817. MWA.   41607

-- Laws and ordinances ordained and established by the
mayor, aldermen, and commonalty of the City of New-
York, in Common Council convened, during the mayor-
alty of Jacob Radcliff, passed the fifth day of May,
1817... New-York, T. and J. Swords, 1817. 172 p.

MH-L; NN; NNLI. 41608

-- Report of deaths...In the city and county of New-York, for the year 1816. Published by order of the common council. New-York, Pr. by Thomas P. Low, 1817. 11 p. NNNAM. 41609

-- Report of the Comptroller, with the accounts of the corporations; May 12, 1817. New York, 1817. 7 p. PHi. 41610

New York (State)
An act for establishing the New York vaccine institution. [Albany, 1817] 31 p. NN. 41611

-- An act for giving relief in cases of insolvency; passed...April 12, 1813...New-York, Pr. by Jansen & Cleves, for Thomas B. Jansen, 1817. 16 p. CSmH. 41612
-- An act, for the assessment and collection of taxes. Passed Apr. 5, 1813. [Albany, 1817] 20 p. N. 41613

-- An act to incorporate medical societies, for the purpose of regulating the practice of physic and surgery in this state. Passed April 10, 1813. Together with the bye-laws of the medical society of New York, and of the county of Orange...Goshen, N.Y., Pr. by D. Mac-Duffee, for the society, 1817. 20 p. NNNAM. 41614

-- Act to incorporate the members of the religious society of Roman Catholics belonging to the congregation of St. Patrick's cathedral, in the city of New York, passed April 14, 1817. New York, 1817. 11 p. NNC. 41615
-- An act to incorporate the Village of Utica. Passed April 7, 1817. Utica, N.Y., Pr. by T. Walker, 1817. 24 p. NUt; NUtHi. 41616

-- In the court for the trial of impeachments and the correction of errors. George W. Mancius and James Brown, respondents, ads Archibald McIntyre, George A. M'Leish, Daniel Creighton, and John M'Intyre, appellants. Case on the part of the respondents. Albany, Pr.

by Websters and Skinners, 1817. 8 p. N.   41617

-- Journal of the Assembly of the State of New-York, 40th session - second meeting. [Albany, Pr. by J. Buel, 1817] [53]-869 p. DLC; (Caption title)   41618

-- Journal of the Assembly of the state of New York: at their fortieth session, begun and held at the Capitol, in the city of Albany, the fifth day of November, 1816. Albany, Pr. by J. Buel, 1816! [1817] 867 p. DLC; NNLI.   41619

-- Journal of the Senate of the state of New-York. 40th session - second meeting. [Albany, Pr. by J. Buel, 1817] [37]-375 p. DLC. (Caption title)   41620

-- Journal of the Senate of the state of New York: at their fortieth session, begun and held at the Capitol, in the city of Albany, the fifth day of November, 1816. Albany, Pr. by J. Buel, 1816! [1817] 375 p. DLC; NNLI.   41621

-- Laws of the state of New-York, passed at the fortieth session of the Legislature, begun and held at the city of Albany, the fifth day of November, 1816. Albany, Pr. by J. Buel, 1817. 352 p. CU; In-SC; MH-L; N-L; NNLI; NNebgL; Nj; NjR; OClWHi; W.   41622

-- Laws of the state of New-York, relating to the City of Schenectady, and the laws and ordinances of the Common Council of the city of Schenectady, and of the First and Second Wards of the said City. Schenectady, Pr. by I. Riggs, 1817. 72 p. MH-L; MWA; N; NSchHi.
          41623
-- Laws relative to slaves and servants, passed by the Legislature of New-York, March 31st, 1817. Together with extracts from the laws of the United States, respecting slaves. New-York, Pr. by Samuel Wood & sons, 1817. 38 p. MWA; NNG.   41624

-- Laws of the state of New-York, respecting navigable communications between the Great Western and Northern Lakes and the Atlantic ocean. New-York, Pr. by T. &

W. Mercein, 1817. 14 p. NbU.   41625

-- The militia act of the state of New-York; to which
are added all the Acts amending the same, including
the Act passed on the 15th of April, 1817.   With a
copious index.   Albany, Pr. by Websters and Skinners,
1817. 42 p. N.   41626

-- The new revised twenty-five dollar act; added, the
decisions of the Supreme Court explanatory of the duties of justices and the rights of parties; also, a complete set of forms for justices.   Albany, 1817. 36 p.
NIC.   41627

-- The official reports of the Canal commissioners of
the state of New York, and the acts of the Legislature
respecting navigable communications between the great
western and northern lakes and the Atlantic ocean; with
perspicuous maps and profiles.   Published at the request of the Board of canal commissioners.   New-York,
Pr. by T. & W. Mercein, 1817. 186 p. DLC. 41628

-- -- Newburgh, N. Y. , B. F. Lewis, and Shelton &
Kensett, 1817. 112 p. CSmH; DLC; ICJ; NN; NNE;
NRAL; NjR; PPF.   41629

-- Report of the commissioners of the state of New
York, on the canals from Lake Erie to the Hudson riv-
er, and from Lake Champlain to the same.   Presented
to the legislature, 17th Feb. 1817.   Albany, Pr. by J.
Buel, 1817. 90 p. CSmH; In; MH-BA; NN; NUtHi.
                                                  41630
-- Report of the joint committee of the Legislature of
New York, on the subject of canals from Lake Erie to
the Hudson river, and from Lake Champlain to the
same, in Assembly, March 19, 1817.   Albany, Pr. by
Webster and Skinners, 1817. 24 p. MH-BA; N; WHi.
                                                  41631
New York academy of sciences.
     The constitution of the Lyceum of natural history.
New York, Pr. by George Forman, for the Society,
1817. 15 p. DLC; MHi; MWA; MWiW.   41632

New-York Advertiser. New York, John W. Walker,
Mar. 26, 1817, 1st issue. Semi-weekly newspaper.
MWA; N.   41633

New York Baptist missionary society.
    Report...1817. [New York, 1817] MWA.   41634

New-York Daily Advertiser. New York, John W.
Walker, Apr. 9, 1817, 1st issue. Daily newspaper.
NHi.   41635

The New York directory. New York, David Longworth,
1817. 464 p. MWA.   41636

New York Evangelical Missionary Society of Young Men
    A brief view of facts, which gave rise to the New-
York Evangelical Missionary Society of Young Men, together with the constitution. Published by direction of
the Society. New-York, Day & Turner, 1817. 19 p.
GDC; MB; MWA; MWiW; NRAB; OClWHi.   41637

-- Proceedings of the first anniversary. New-York,
Pr. by J. C. Totten, 1817. MWA; MWiW.   41638

New-York farmer's almanac, for 1818. By David Young.
New-York, Charles N. Baldwin [1817] [36] p. MWA;
NHi; NjR.   41639

New York Female Association
    The annual report of the Female Association of the
city of New York. New York, Pr. by Collins & Co.,
1817. 7 p. DLC.   41640

New York female union society for the promotion of
Sabbath schools.
    The first report...New York, Pr. by J. Seymour,
1817. 32 p. MWA; MiD-B.   41641

New York hospital.
    Annual reports. New York, 1817. PPC.   41642

New York Irish Emigrant Association
    Constitution of the New York Irish Emigrant Asso-

ciation. Instituted December 5, 1817. New York,
1817. 12 p. NHi.   41643

New York Literary & Philosophical Society
Memoir, on the antiquities of the western parts of
the state. New York, [1817] 16 p. MWA.   41644

New York missionary society
Report... April 2, 1817. New York, Pr. by J.
Seymour, 1817. MWA.   41645

New York public sale report. New York, Eldredge &
Wood, 1817. 1 no.   (weekly) Ct.   41646

The New York reader, no. 2, being selection of prose
and poetry for the use of schools. New York, 1817.
215 p. MWA; OCHP.   41647

The New York reader no. 3. Being selections in prose
and poetry from the best writers... New York, Samuel
Wood & sons, 1817. 238 p. CoGrS; MWA; TxU-T.
                                               41648
New York religious tract society.
    The fifth and sixth annual reports... New York, J.
Seymour, 1817. 48 p. MiD-B.   41649

New York. St. George's church. Society for the cultivation of sacred music.
    Constitution of the Society of St. George's church,
for the cultivation of sacred music, formed 12th of February, 1817. New-York, the Society, 1817. 7 p. DLC.
                                               41650
New York. St. Paul's Church.
    Solemnization of the third centurial jubilee, com-
memorative of the blessed reformation commenced by
Dr. Martin Luther, on the 31st Oct. 1817. New York,
1817. PPPrHi.   41651

New York Stock Exchange
    Constitution of the New York stock exchange board.
New York, Chambers & co, 1817. (Facsimile copy)
13 p. MH-BA.   41652

New York Sunday school union society.
    First report...New York, Pr. by J. Seymour,
1817. 44 p. CtY-D; MWA.   41653

New York Tract Association No. 3.
    Christian exhortation to sailors.   New York, 1817.
PSC-Hi.   41654

Newark church missionary society, N. J.
    Constitution...Newark, N. J., Pr. by John Tuttle
& Co., 7 p. MWA; NjR.   41655

Newark female Bible and common prayer book society.
    The first annual report...Newark, N. J., Pr. by
John Tuttle & Co. [1817] MWA.   41656

Newark Messenger.   Newark, N. J., Peter Conover,
Oct. 10, 1817, 1st issue. Weekly newspaper. NjHi.
                                                  41657
[Newbery, John] 1713-1767
    The history of Tommy Trip, and his dog Jowler.
And of birds and beasts...New-Haven, Sidney's press,
1817.   30 p.   DLC.   41658

Newcastle, Me., Church of Christ
    Confession of faith and covenant.   Portland, Me.,
1817.   8 p.   MBC.   41659

Newton, John
    An account of Eliza Cunningham.   An abridgment.
Ed. 1.   Andover, Mass., Pr. by Flagg & Gould, 1817.
8 p.   MMeT; MWA.   41660

Nichols, Ammi, 1781-1873
    A discourse, delivered at the ordination of the Rev.
Jeremiah Flint, to the pastoral charge of the church in
Danville, July 31, 1817.   By Ammi Nichols, Pastor of
the Congregational Church in Braintree.   Danville, Vt.,
Pr. by Ebenezer Eaton, 1817.   20 p. CSmH; MWA; NN;
RPB.   41661

Nikelsburger, Jacob
    Koul Jacob in defence of the Jewish religion: con-

taining the arguments of the Rev. C. F. Frey, one of
the committee of the London Society for the conversion
of the Jews and answers thereto. Liverpool, pr.; Boston, repr. 1817. 56 p. DLC; MB; MHi; MiD-B;
PPAmP.   41662

Noah, Mordecai Manuel, 1785-1851
    Oration, delivered by appointment, before Tammany
society of Columbian order, Hibernian provident society, Columbian society, Union society of shipwrights and
caulkers, Tailors', House carpenters', and Masons' benevolent societies. United to celebrate the 41st anniversary of American independence... New-York, Pr. by
J.H. Sherman, 1817. 24 p. DLC; MWA.   41663

North, Selah
    An oration, delivered at Goshen, July 4, 1817...
Hartford, F.D. Bolles & Co., 1817. 14 p. NN. 41664

The North-American calendar; or, the Columbian almanac for the year 1818. Calculated for the meridian
of the middle states. Wilmington, Del., Pr. by Robert
Porter, 1817. [36] p. NCH; PHi.   41665

North Carolina (State)
    Journal of the House of Commons. At a General
assembly, begun... 18th day of November, 1816.
[1817?] 56 p. N.   41666

-- Journal of the Senate... At a General Assembly, begun and held at the city of Raleigh, on Monday the 18th
day of November, in the year of our Lord one thousand
eight hundred and sixteen... [Raleigh? Thomas Henderson, 1817?] 58 p. N; Nc-SC.   41667

-- Laws of North-Carolina, enacted by a General Assembly begun and held at Raleigh on 18th day of November in the year of our Lord 1816, and in 41st year of
the Independence of the said state. [1817?] 54 p.
MdBB; Nc-SC; OCLaw.   41668

-- Laws of the state of North-Carolina, enacted in the
year 1816... Raleigh, Pr. by Thomas Henderson, 1817.

55 p. MdBB; NcU; RPL; T.   41669

-- Report on education, made to the General Assembly
of North Carolina, at its session of 1816. Raleigh,
Pr. by Tho. Henderson, Jr., 1817. 8 p. NN; NcD;
NcU.   41670

North Carolina University
    A catalogue of books. Belonging to the Dialectic
Society, at Chapel Hill, May 1817. [1817?] Broadside.
NcU.   41671

-- Catalogus Universitatis Carolinae septentrionalis.
Raleigh, Typis, J. Gales, 1817. 16 p. NcD; NcGW;
NcU; TKL; TxU.   41672

Northcote, James, 1746-1831
    Memoirs of Sir Joshua Reynolds... Philadelphia, M.
Carey & Son, 1817. 503 p. DLC; MB; MMe; MS;
MWA; NNC; NjP; NjR; RNR; Vi.   41673

Northern Missionary Society
    Report of the directors... September 3d, 1817...
Albany, Pr. by Websters and Skinners, 1817. 14 p.
NN.   41674

[Norton, Jacob] 1764-1858
    A candid and conciliatory review of the late corre-
spondence of the Reverend Dr. Worcester with the Reverend William E. Channing, on the subject of Unitarianism. By a serious inquirer... Boston, Pr. by Lincoln
& Edmands, for the author, 1817. 88 p. CBPac; CSt;
DLC; MB; MBC; MH-AH; MMeT-Hi; MWA; NN; NNUT;
RPB.   41675

Nott, Samuel
    A sermon, on the idolatry of the Hindoos, delivered
Nov. 29, 1816, at the annual meeting of the female foreign mission society, of Franklin, Connecticut... Norwich, Conn., Pr. by Hubbard & Marvin, 1817. 95 p.
CSfCW; CtHi; MH; MHi; MeB; MiD-B; MWA; MWiW.
                                                41676

Noyes, Thomas
A sermon, preached at Barrington, R. I. January
28, 1817, at the installation of the Rev. Luther Wright
...Providence, Pr. by Miller & Hutchens, 1817. 32 p.
MBC; MWA.   41677

Nugent, Thomas
The new pocket dictionary of the French and English languages, in two parts. I. French and English...
II. English and French...2d Amer., from the last
London ed. New York, James Eastburn and co., 1817.
519 p. MB; MWA; MWHi; NbOC.   41678

-- -- 2d Amer. ed. New York, E. Duyckinck, 1817.
MWA.   41679

-- -- 2d Amer. ed. New York, S. A. Burtus, 1817.
MWA.   41680

Nye, Arius
A concise alphabetical index to the Laws of Ohio.
Zanesville, Pr. by E. Putnam & Co., 1817. 32 p.
OCLaw; OClWHi; OMC.   41681

O

O'Connor, Thomas, 1770-1855
An impartial and correct history of the war between the United States of America, and Great Britain;
comprising a particular detail of the naval and military
operations, and a faithful record of the events produced
during the contest. From its commencement, June 18,
1812, to the treaty of peace, ratified at the city of
Washington, February 17, 1815...4th ed., rev. and cor.
New-York, John Low, 1817. 336 p. DLC; MWA; MiD;
OCY; RP; RPB.   41682

Ogilvie, J. G.
Religious doctrines and sects explained; viz. Atheism; Deism, Catholicism; Arianism...Independency,
and Bibleism. New-York, Pr. by T. & W. Mercein,
1817. 113 p. N; NNG; PPPrHi.   41683

Ohio (State)
     Acts passed at the 1st session of the 15th General
Assembly of the state of Ohio...Dec. 2, 1816...Vol.
XV...Columbus, Pr. by P. H. Olmsted & Co., 1817
269 p. C-L; Ct; CtY; DLC; ICLaw; In-SC; M; MH-L;
MdBB; Mi-L; NN; NNB; NNC; OCLaw; OCHP; OClWHi;
PPB; RPL; WHi; WaU-L.   41684

-- Catalog of books in the Library of Ohio. Columbus,
O., P. H. Olmsted, 1817. 11 p. OCHP.   41685

-- Journal of the House of Representatives of the state
of Ohio, being the 15th General Assembly, begun...2d
day of Dec., 1816...Chillicothe, Pr. at the office of
the Supporter, by Geo. Nashee, 1816! [1817] 334 p.
DLC; MH; NN; O; OClWHi; OHi; O-LR.   41686

-- Journal of the Senate of the state of Ohio, being the
15th General Assembly, begun...2d day of December,
1816...Chillicothe, Pr. at the office of the Supporter,
by Geo. Nashee, 1816[!] [1817] 339 p. DLC; MH; MHi;
NN; O; O-LR; OClWHi; OHi.   41687

Ohio Bible Society
     Extracts from the 5th annual report...Zanesville,
O., Pr. at the express office, 1817. 16 p. CSmH; NN;
OClWHi; RNR.   41688

Ohio register, and western calendar...for 1818...by
William Lusk, no. 2. Columbus, O., P. H. Olmsted
[1817] 96 p. DLC; MWA; OCHP; OClWHi; OHi. 41689

Ohio Spectator. Wooster, Ohio, Cox & Hickcox, June
6, 1817, 1st issue. Weekly newspaper. MWA. 41690

Old Colony musical society in Plymouth County
     Old Colony collection of anthems, selected and pub-
lished under the particular patronage and direction of
the Old Colony musical society in Plymouth county and
the Handel and Hayden society in Boston. Ed. 2. Boston, Loring [1817-18] 2 v. CtHT; MWA.   41691

Old grand-papa, and other poems, for the amusement of

children. By a young lady. Embellished with wood en-
graving. Philadelphia, B. Warner, 1817. 48 p. RPB;
TxU.   41692

The olio... Trenton, N. J., Pr. by Deare & Myer, for
D. & E. Fenton, and Deare & Myer, New-Brunswick,
1817. 120 p. MWA; NjR.   41693

Olive Branch. Circleville, Ohio, James Foster, Aug.
10, 1817, 1st issue. Weekly newspaper. DLC; MWA.
                                                       41694
[O'Meara, Barry Edward]
    Letters from the Cape of Good Hope... New York,
Pr. [by C. S. Van Winkle] for C. Wiley & Co., 1817.
MWA.   41695

On the Lord's supper... Annapolis, Md., Pr. by J.
Green, 1817. MWA.   41696

On the nature and efficacy of the cross of Christ.
Philadelphia, Pr. [by J. R. A. Skerrett] for Benjamin &
Thomas Kite, 1817. 24 p. MWA; NbU; PSC-Hi. 41697

On the neglect of Confirmation and the Lord's supper.
Annapolis, Md., Pr. by J. Green, 1817. 20 p. LNB;
MWA; MdBD.   41698

[Onis, Luis de] 1769-1830
    Observations on the existing differences between the
government of Spain and the United States. By Verus.
No. III. Philadelphia, 1817. 52 p. MBAt; MdHi; N;
NN; NHi; PPAmP.   41699

Oracle of New-Hampshire. Portsmouth, Samuel Whid-
den, May 22, 1817, 1st issue. Weekly newspaper.
NhHi.   41700

Orations for the use of schools. Philadelphia, D. Allinson, for I. Riley, 1817. MWA.   41701

-- Selected from Ch. J. Marshall, Pinkney, Wirt, Fox,
Phillips, &c. Philadelphia, I. Riley, 1817. MH; MWA.
                                                       41702

Oratorio, as performed at Windsor, July 4th, 1817.
Order of performance. First part... Forenoon. ...Second part... Afternoon... Windsor, 1817. Broadside. (Selections from Chapple, Handel, Hayden, Hubbard and
Leach. Printed in three columns. (McCorison List)
41703
Order, discipline, and management of a school, intended
for the religious education of youth. Hartford, Cooke
& Hale, 1817. 3 p. MBeHi.   41704

Order of exercises at the ordination of the Rev. Sereno
E. Dwight, and several missionaries to the heathen, on
the 3d of September, 1817, at the Park Street Church,
Boston. [Boston? 1717] Broadside. MHi.   41705

O'Reily, Burnard
    Greenland the adjacent seas. New York, Eastburn,
1817. KyLx.   41706

Orfila, Mathieu Joseph Bonaventure
    A general system of toxicology... Philadelphia, M.
Carey & son, 1817. 465 p. KU; KyLxT;. MWA;
NNNAM; PPAmP; PPC; PPPH; PPM.   41707

Ornaments discovered. New York, D. Fanshaw, 1817.
MWA.   41708

Orphan society of Philadelphia
    Second report... Jan. 7, 1817... Philadelphia, Pr.
by William Fry, 1817. MWA.   41709

The orphans, or Honesty rewarded. Together with select hymns. New Haven, Sidney's press, 1817. 46 p.
CtHi.   41710

Oson, Jacob
    A search for truth; or, an inquiry for the origin of
the African nation: an address, delivered at New-Haven
in March, and at New York in April, 1817. By Jacob
Oson, a descendant of Africa. Published for, and by
the request of Christopher Rush, a descendant of Africa.
New York, Pr. for the proprietor, 1817. 12 p. MB;
ScCC.   41711

Oswego Gazette.   Oswego, N. Y. , S. A. Abbey & Bro. ,
1817. Weekly newspaper. Brigham, p. 714.   41712

Otsego County Bible Society
    The fifth annual report of the Board of Managers of
the Otsego Co. Bible Society, June 12, 1817, with a
list of subscribers and donors.   Cooperstown, N. Y. ,
Pr. by J. H. Prentiss, for the Society, 1817. 48 p.
NFred.   41713

Oulton, Walley Chamberlain, 1770?-1820?
    Frightened to death; a musical farce in two acts...
New York, D. Longworth, 1817. 35 p. MH; MWA; N.
                                               41714
-- My landlady's gown.   A farce... Baltimore, J. Rob-
inson, 1817. 47 p. DeGE; ICU; MBr; MH.   41715

Ovid Gazette.   Ovid, N. Y. , Michael Hayes, 1817. A
newspaper. Brigham, p. 714.   41716

Ovidius Naso, Publius
    Publii Ovidii Nasonis Metamorphoseon Libri XV.
Novi-Eboraci,   Impensis J. Eastburn et Soc. , 1817.
MBC; MWA; MdW.   41717

Owen, John, 1766-1822
    The history of the origin and first ten years of the
British and foreign Bible society... New-York, Pr. by
A. Paul, for James Eastburn & co. , 1817. 634 p.
CtHT; MA; MWA; RPB.   41718

                          P
Paine, Thomas
    Examination of the passages in the New Testament,
quoted from the Old, and called Prophecies concerning
Jesus Christ... Boston, 1817, 60 p. PPDrop.   41719

[Palacio Fajardo, Manuel] 1784-1819
    Outline of the revolution in Spanish America; or,
An account of the origin, progress, and actual state of
the war carried on between Spain and Spanish America;
New-York, J. Eastburn & Co. , 1817. 219 p. DLC; MB;

MH.   41720

Paley, William
   A grammar of moral philosophy natural theology;
... From the works of Dr. Paley. To which are sub-
joined, questions and tables, adapted to the study of
sacred scriptures. By the Rev. J.W. Baker... New
York, Pr. by J. Forbes and co., 1817. 248 p. MA;
MBC.   41721

-- A view of the evidences of Christianity... New York,
Pr. by E. & E. Hosford, for James Eastburn & Co.,
1817. 310 p. CtW; DLC; MMeT; MWA; MiPh; NCoxhi;
NElmC; ScCoT.   41722

Palladium of knowledge... for the year 1818... Charles-
ton, S.C., Pr. by W.P. Young, [1817] 52 p. ScC.
                                                       41723
Palladium of Liberty. Warrenton, Va., J. Caldwell,
Mar. 1817, 1st issue. Weekly newspaper. DLC. 41724

Palmyra Register. Palmyra, N.Y., Timothy C. Strong,
Nov. 26, 1817, 1st issue. Weekly newspaper. N. 41725

Parker, Daniel
   New Year's discourse, before the Literary Institu-
tion in Greenville, Greene County, N.Y. Catskill,
N.Y., M. Croswell & Co. [1817] MWA; N.   41726

Parkinson, William
   A selection of hymns and spiritual songs in two
parts... designed for the use of congregations... New
York, Pr. by J. Tiebout, 1817. 560 p. DLC; MWA;
NRAB; NjP.   41727

Parkman, George, 1790-1849
   Management of lunatics, with illustrations of in-
sanity... Boston, Pr. by John Eliot, 1817. 36 p. CSt;
MB; MH; MWA; NAuT; NBMS; NNNAM.   41728

The Parlour companion. v. 1- Philadelphia, 1817-
Weekly. Superseded the Juvenile port-folio and literary
miscellany. DLC; MMeT; NjR.   41729

A particular account of a monstrous sea-serpent, the
largest ever seen in America. Which has lately made
its appearance in Glouster Harbor, Cape Ann, (Mass.)
...Published at the Brattleboro' Book Store, 1817. 24
p. N.   41730

Particulars of the late horrid murder, of the accom-
plished--but unfortunate Miss Maria Pattan...Added, A
dreadful murder committed on board Capt. Cochran's
brig, the Earl of Sandwich.   New York, 1817.
CtHT-W.   41731

Pasquin of Mobton; or the Baltimore satirist.   Baltimore, 1817. No. 1, 2. PPL.   41732

Patterson, John
    Journal of the travels & religious experience of
John Patterson...Harrisburg, Pa., Pr. for the author,
1817. RPB.   41733

Patterson, Robert
    John Brown...Pittsburgh, Pa., 1817. 361 p. PPiHi.
                                                          41733a
Patterson, Samuel
    Narrative of the adventures and sufferings of Sam-
uel Patterson...Palmer, Mass., Pr. [by Ezekiel Terry]
from the press in Palmer, 1817. 144 p. DLC; MBNEH;
MWA; MoSM; NbHi; OrP; RHi.   41734

Patterson's Ohio almanac for 1818. No. 1. By John
Armstrong. Pittsburgh, Pa., R. Patterson [1817]
MWA.   41735

Patterson's Ohio magazine almanac for 1818. No. 1.
By John Armstrong. Pittsburgh, Pa., R. Patterson,
Pr. by S. Engles, [1817] MBAt; MWA.   41736

Patterson's Pittsburgh town & country almanac for 1818.
By John Armstrong. Pittsburgh, Pa., R. Patterson
[1817] [56] p. CSmH; MWA.   41737

[Paulding, James Kirke] 1778-1860
    Letters from the South, written during an excursion

in the summer of 1816. By the author of John Bull
and Brother Jonathan...New-York, Pr. by Abraham
Paul, for James Eastburn & co., 1817. 2 v. CSmH;
DLC; MWA; MWiW; N; NcWfC; NjR; OMC.   41738

Payne, John, fl. 1800
A new and complete history of America from the
earliest ages, down to the present time; describing its
subdivisions of republics, states, empires, and kingdoms...appearance of the country, curiosities of nature and art...1st Amer. ed., from the last English ed.
New York, 1817. 525 p. WHi.   41739

Peace-republicans' manual; or, The French constitution
of 1793, and the declaration of the rights of man and
of citizens, according to the Moniteur of June 27th,
1793; in the original French, together with a translation in English...New-York, J. Tiebout & sons, 1817.
161 p. MNBedf; NNS.   41740

Peace Society. At a meeting of a number of gentlemen who had signed proposals for establishing a peace
society, holden at the meeting-house of the first Parish
in Portland, on Friday the 31st day of January, A.D.
1817, the Rev. Jesse Appleton was chosen Chairman,
and Mr. Edward H. Cobb, Clerk...Broadside. MeHi.
          41741

[Peacock, Thomas Love] 1785-1866
Melincourt. By the author of Headlong hall...
Philadelphia, Pr. by J. Maxwell, for Moses Thomas,
1817. 2 v. in 1. DLC; DeGE; MH; MWA.   41742

Pearson, Hugh
Memoirs of the life and writings of the Rev. Claud-
ius Buchanan, D.D. Philadelphia, Pr. by J. Rakestraw, for Benjamin & Thomas Kite, 1817. 537 p.
KyLx; NcWsS; WNaE.   41743

Pearson, Jane
Sketches of piety in the life and religious experi-
ences extracted from her own memorandums. New
York, 1817. 119 p. PHC.   41744

Peck, John
    Description of the last judgment... Palmer, Mass.,
from E. Terry's press, 1817. 34 p. CSmH; CtHi;
MWA; RPB.   41745

Peck, Phinehas, fl. 1812-19
    A discourse, delivered on the day of general elec-
tion, at Montpelier, October 9, 1817, before his excellency Jonas Galusha, Esq. Governor; his honor Paul
Brigham, Esq. Lieut. Governor; the honorable Council,
and House of Representatives of the state of Vermont
...Windsor, Vt., Jesse Cochran, state printer, 1817.
23 p. DLC; IaCresco; MWA; MiD-B; OCHP; Vt; VtHi;
VtMiS; VtU-W.   41746

Pedder, James
    The yellow shoe-strings: or, The good effects of
obedience to parents. Philadelphia, A. Bowman, for
Benj. Warner, 1817. [48] p. PP.   41747

Pennsylvania (State)
    Acts of the General Assembly of the Commonwealth
of Pennsylvania, passed at a session...Dec., 1816...
Harrisburg, Pr. by C. Gleim, 1817. 334 p. DLC; Ia;
IaU-L; MdBB; RPL.   41748

-- Bills of the Senate members which they proposed
and read before the Senate. Harrisburg, Pr. by John
Wyeth, 1817-18. P.   41749

-- Copy of the record of the Court of Common Pleas of
Lancaster county, in the case of Robert W. Houston,
against General John Dicks and others. (Furnished to
the House of Representatives, by John Passmore, Esquire, prothonotary of the Court in conformity with a
resolution adopted on the eighteenth of February, 1817.
Harrisburg, William Green, 1817. 39 p. DLC; MWA;
P.   41750

-- A digest of select British statutes, comprising those
which, according to the report of the judges of the Supreme court, made to the legislature, appear to be in
force, in Pennsylvania: with some others... Pittsburgh,

Pa., Pr. by Robert Ferguson & Co., 1817. 442 p.
C; DLC; LNB; MWA; MnU; Nj; Nv; OCHP; PPT; PPB;
PU; PPM; PPL-R; PU-L; RNR; RPL; WaU.   41751

-- Governor's message. To the Senate and House of
Representatives of the Commonwealth of Pennsylvania
...Simon Snyder, Harrisburg, Pr. by James Peacock,
December 5th, 1817. 6 p. DNA.   41752

-- Journal of the 27th House of Representatives of the
Commonwealth of Pennsylvania, commenced...3d of
December...1816...Harrisburg, Pr. by James Pea-
cock, 1816-17. 754, lii p. DLC; KyLxT; RPB. 41753

-- Journal of the Senate of the Commonwealth of Pennsylvania, which commenced...3d day of December,
1816...Vol. XXVII. Harrisburg, Pr. by Christian
Gleim, 1816[!] [1817] 463, 38, 16 p. CSmH; DLC;
ICBB; RPB.   41754

-- Letter of the Auditor general...1817. MWA. 41755

-- The opinion of the Court of Common Pleas of Lan-
caster County in the case of Robert W. Houston against
Gen. John Dicks...Lancaster, William Dickson, 1817.
MWA.   41756

-- Receipts and expenditures in the treasury of Pennsylvania, from the first day of December, 1816, to
the thirtieth day of November, 1817...Harrisburg, Pr.
by James Peacock, 1817. 299 p. CSmH; DLC; P.
        41757
-- Report of the auditor general, in conformity with a
resolution of the House of representatives, adopted January 15th, 1817. Harrisburg, Pr. by J. Peacock
[1817] 13 p. CSmH; MiD-B.   41758

-- Report of the secretary of the Commonwealth of the
names of all persons holding office under this Commonwealth, by appointment of the governor, to which sala-
ries or emoluments are attached...Harrisburg, J. Peacock, 1817. 69 p. P; PHi.   41759

-- Report of the sitting of the court of impeachment against Walter Franklin, Jacob Hibshman and Thomas Clark... Harrisburg, Pr. by Christian Gleim, 1817. 12 p. Andres, 139.   41760

-- Report on the finances of the Commonwealth of Pennsylvania, for the year 1817... Harrisburg, Pr. by James Peacock, 1817. 23, v p. DLC; P.   41761

-- Reports of cases adjudged in the Supreme court of Pennsylvania; with some select cases at nisi prius, and in the circuit courts. By the honorable Jasper Yeates,... Philadelphia, John Bioren, 1817. 4 v. Az; CLCL; Ia; In-SC; KyLxFL; KyU-L; MBU-L; MTaB; Me-LR; Mi-L; MoSPCa; Ms; Nj; Nv; OCLaw; P; PLL; PP; PPT-L; PPiAL; PU-L; PWWL; W.   41762

-- Tagebuch des sieben und zwanzigsten Hauses der Representanten der Republik Pennsylvanien. Lancaster, Pr. by B. Grimler, 1816! [1817] Seidensticker p. 197.   41763

-- Tagebuch des Senate der Republik Pennsylvanien 1816-17. Harrisburg? Pr. by Charles Greer, 1817. Seidensticker p. 201.   41764

-- William Findlay's inaugural address to the legislature, December 1817. Broadside. DLC.   41765

Pennsylvania Gazette. Lancaster, Pa., Hugh Maxwell, Aug. 12, 1817, 1st issue. Weekly newspaper. PHi.   41766

Pennsylvania Society for the Promotion of Public Economy.
     Report of the Committee on Domestic Economy to the Pennsylvania Society for the Promotion of Public Economy, read at its meeting, on November 10, 1817. Philadelphia, Pr. for the Society, 1817. 27 p. DeGE.   41767

-- Report of the Committee on public schools to the Pennsylvania society, for the promotion of public economy, read at its meeting, on November 10, 1817. Philadelphia, Pr. by S. Merritt, for the Society, 1817. 13 p. DHEW; PPL-R; PPM; PHi; NjR.   41768

-- Report of the Library Committee of the Pennsylvania society for the promotion of public economy, containing a summary of the information communicated by sundry citizens, in reply to the circular letter of the committee of superintendence of Feb. 21, 1817. Philadelphia, Pr. by Merritt, 1817. 53 p. DeGE; MWA; WHi. 41769

People's Advocate. Northumberland, Pa., James Forrest, 1817. Newspaper. Brigham, p. 886. 41770

Perkins, Nathan
	A funeral sermon, delivered in Amherst, Sept. 12, 1815, at the interment of Doctor Seth Coleman...New Haven, Pr. by Flagg & Gray, 1817. 16 p. CtHC; CtHi; DLC; MWA; RPB; TxH. 41771

-- Memoirs of Doctor Seth Coleman, A.M. of Amherst, (Mass.) ...New Haven, Pr. by Flagg & Gray, at the Herald office, 1817. 288 p. NUtHi. 41772

-- A sermon delivered at the interment of the Rev. Nathan Strong...Hartford, Pr. by George Goodwin and Sons, 1817. 27 p. CBPSR; CSmH; Ct; CtHC; CtHi; MWA; MnSM; NcD; NjR; OO; PPPrHi; RPB; WHi.41773

Perrin, Jean Baptiste, fl. 1786
	Entertaining and instructive exercises with the rules of the French syntax. Ed. 11, carefully rev. and cor. by a competent person. New York, Pr. by George Long, for Duyckinck and T.A. Ronalds, 1817. 334 p. MB; MWA; MH; MoCgSV. 41774

-- Fables ammusantes, avec une table des mots et de leur signification in Anglois, selon l'ardre des fables. Carefully rev. and cor. New York, Duyckinck, 1817. MSaE; MBr; MiD-B. 41775

-- Grammar of the French tongue, grounded upon the decisions of the French Academy...From the 11th London ed., rev. by M. Tocquot. New York, R. Scott, 1817. 304 p. CtMW; MH; MWA; MeHi; PHi. 41776

Perrine, Matthew La Rue
Women have a work to do in the House of God. A
discourse delivered at the first annual meeting of the
female missionary society for the poor... New-York,
Pr. by Edward W. Thomson, 1817. 32 p. MWA;
NNMuCN; NjR.   41777

Perry, William
The only sure guide to the English tongue, or new
pronouncing spelling book. 22d improved ed. Worcester, Mass., Isaiah Thomas, Jun., 1817. 180 p.
MCanHi; MWA; SdMit.   41778

Peters, Samuel
The Rev. Samuel Peters, LL.D. General history
of Connecticut... causes of the rebellion in America...
1781... additions... by Samuel J. McCormick. New
York, 1817. PPL.   41779

Philadelphia (City)
Manual for the guardians of the poor of the city of
Philadelphia, the district of Southwark, and township
of the Northern Liberties. Philadelphia, U.S. Gazette,
1817. 16 p. PHi; PPAmP.   41780

-- Report of the Joint committee appointed by the Select and Common councils on the subject of steamboats.
[Philadelphia, 1817] 13 p. DLC; PHi; PPF; PPL; RP.
                                                41781
-- Report of the Watering committee to the select and
common councils. Read January 23, 1817. Published
by order of the councils. Philadelphia, Pr. by William
Fry, 1817. 18 p. THi.   41782

Philadelphia athenaeum
Charter and by-laws of the Athenaeum of Philadelphia: to which are added, a list of the directors, stockholders, and annual visiters, and of persons who have
presented to, or deposited at the Athenaeum, books,
maps, minerals, &c. belonging to the institution. Philadelphia, Pr. by W. Fry, 1817. 35 p. DLC; MH; NHi;
MiD-B.   41783

The Philadelphia directory, for 1817, containing the names, trades, and residence of the inhabitants of the City, Northern Liberties, Southwark and precincts. With other useful information. By Edward Dawes. Pr. for the proprietor and pub. at 13 S. Sixth St. [1817] DLC; MWA; PPC; PPL. 41784

Philadelphia dispensary
Rules of the Philadelphia dispensary for the medical relief of the poor. With a list of contributors, managers, and officers, and the annual report for 1816. [Philadelphia? 1817] 12 p. MH. 41785

Philadelphia Female Tract Society
The second annual report...for the year 1817... Philadelphia, Pr. by Lydia R. Bailey, 1817. 16 p. (Contains tracts no. 16-31, v.p., as appendix) MWA; NjR. 41786

Philadelphia medical society.
The act of incorporation and laws...published by order of the Society, February, 1817. Philadelphia, Bradford, 1817. 20 p. MdBM; PU. 41787

Philadelphia. New Jerusalem Church.
The repository. V. 1, No. 1: Jan. 1817...Philadelphia, 1817. PHi. 41788

Philadelphia saving fund society.
Articles of association of the Saving fund society, with an explanation of the principles of the institution, and its objects: together with tables, showing the accumulations produced by deposits with the society. Philadelphia, Pr. for the Society, 1817. 18 p. DLC; DeGE; MWA; PHi; PPL-R. 41789

Philadelphia society for alleviating the miseries of public prisons.
A statistical view of the operations of the penal code of Pennsylvania...Philadelphia, 1817. 14 p. MH-L; MWA; NNS; PHi. 41790

Philadelphia society for the promotion of American
manufactures.
(Circular) Sir, The committee appointed on the
part...to report a plan in aid of the internal industry
...[Philadelphia? 1817] 1 p. DeGE.   41791

Philadelphia society for the promotion of national manufactures.
The soundness of the policy of protecting domestic
manufactures, fully established by Alexander Hamilton
in his report to Congress on the subject, and by Thomas Jefferson in his letter to Benjamin Austin. To
which are added extracts from the address of the American society for promoting domestic manufactures, established in New York. Philadelphia, Pr. by J. R. A.
Skerrett, for the society, 1817. 36 p. CSmH; MH.
41792

Philanthropist. Mount Pleasant, Ohio, Charles Osborn,
Aug. 29, 1817, 1st issue. Weekly newspaper. InU.
41793

Philidor, François André Dunican, called
An easy introduction to the game of chess to which
are added, Caissa: a poem by Sir W. Jones; the mor-
als of chess by Dr. Franklin chess and whist compared; anecdotes respecting chess and chess-players.
Philadelphia, 1817. PPL-R.   41794

Phillips, Charles
Speeches...Baltimore, Pr. by James Kennedy,
1817. 306 p. CSmH; MWA; MdBE; MdHi; MnHi; WHi.
41795
-- The speeches of Charles Phillips...New York, Pr.
by T. & W. Mercein, for Kirk & Mercein, 1817. 205 p.
MBBC; MWA.   41796

-- -- 2d Amer. ed. New York, Pr. by J. & J. Harper, for Kirk & Mercein, 1817. 228 p. FTa; MBS;
MWA; OT.   41797

Phillips, Ebenezer, 1786-1834
A charge, delivered at Smithtown, October 23,
1817, to the united congregations, of Smithtown and
Fresh-pond, at the ordination of the Rev. Henry Fuller

...Brooklyn, Pr. by Alden Spooner, 1817. 16 p. DLC;
MWA; NBLiHi; NSmB. 41798

Phillips, Richard, 1758-1816
Concise remarks on watchfulness and silence.
Baltimore, Pr. by Pomeroy & Toy, 1817. 16 p.
PSC-Hi. 41799

[Phillips, Sir Richard] 1767-1840
An easy grammar of geography, intended as a com-
panion and introduction to the "Geography on a popular
plan, for schools, and young persons," by the Rev. J.
Goldsmith [pseud.] a new ed... Philadelphia, Benjamin
Warner; Griggs & co., 1817. 179 p. DLC; OCHP;
ViU; ViW. 41800

[--] An easy grammar of natural and experimental philosophy. For the use of schools... Ed. 3. Philadelphia, Pr. by Joseph Rakestraw, for S.W. Conrad,
1817. 160 p. MHi; MWA; RPB. 41801

[--] Five hundred questions on the New Testament...
1st Amer. ed. New Haven, Nathan Whiting, 1817.
MWA. 41802

[--] A general view of the manners, customs and curiosities of nations. Philadelphia, B. Warner, 1817. 2 v.
DLC; MWiW; MdBS; NcD; NcU; OSW. 41803

[--] A grammar of chemistry, wherein the principles
of the science are familiarized by a variety of easy
and entertaining experiments... Ed. 2. Philadelphia,
D. Hogan, 1817. 180 p. CSt; DLC; DeGE; ICU; KyBC;
MWA; NcU. 41804

[--] The universal preceptor; a general grammar of
arts, science, and useful knowledge... 1st Amer., from
8th London ed., with additions and improvements.
Philadelphia, E. & R. Parker, 1817. 316 p. DLC;
ICU; MH; MWA; MWHi; MeBa; P. 41805

[--] -- 2d Amer. ed. Philadelphia, J.R.A. Skerrett,
for E. & R. Parker, 1817. MWA. 41806

Phillips Academy, Andover, Mass.
     Catalogue. 1817. MBC.   41807

-- The constitution of Phillips academy in Andover.
Andover, Mass., Pr. by Flagg & Gould, 1817. 13 p.
DLC; MAnP; MNe; RPB.   41808

Philom's address to the people of New-England, with
remarks on the plans to establish Kingcraft and priest-
craft in these United States, as exhibited by the charitable society, in their address, and vigorous attempts
to beg money to educate indigent young men for the
ministry of the gospel...[1817] MWA.   41809

Phinney's calendar, or, Western almanack for 1818.
By Andrew Beers. Cooperstown, N.Y., H. & E. Phinney [1817] [36] p. DLC; MWA; NjR; OClWHi; WHi.
                                              41810

Phoebus, William, 1754-1831
     An essay on the doctrine and order of the evangel-
ical church of America; as constituted at Baltimore in
1784, under the patronage of the Rev. John Wesley,
A.M., Rev. Thomas Coke, LL.D., Rev. W.F. Oter-
bine, D.D...Rev. F. Asbury, V.D.M., Rev. Martin
Boehm, a bishop of the Menonists, two presbyters
from the British conference, and sixty itinerant
preachers, raised in the United States...New York, Pr.
by A. Paul, for the author, 1817. 143 p. CtMW; MWA;
MdBAHi.   41811

Physico-Medical society of New-York.
     Constitution and by-laws of the Physico-Medical So-
ciety of New-York. New York, Pr. by Collins & Co.,
1817. 14 p. NNC; NNNAM.   41812

-- Transactions of the Physico-medical society, of New-
York. v. 1... New York, Collins & Co., 1817. 466 p.
DLC; MWA; PPA; PU.   41813

Picket, Albert
     Geographical grammar. Combining the interroga-
tive mode of instruction, with concise definitions, the
use of maps, and the terrestrial globe. Ed. 2. New

York, D.D. Smith, 1817. 72 p. LNL; NN; NcD.41814

-- The juvenile penman...New York, Smith & Forman,
1817. 3 v. NN.   41815

-- Juvenile spelling book. Stereo. ed. Exeter, N.H.,
E. Little & Co., 1817. MWA.   41816

Pierce, Deborah
    A scriptural vindication of female preaching,
prophesying or exhortation. Auburn, N.Y., Pr. for
the publisher, 1817. 26 p. NAuHi.   41817

Pierce, John
    Brookline, Church in, Centennial discourse, Nov.
9, 1817. Boston, Pr. by John Eliot, 1817. 32 p.
MBC.   41818

-- A discourse, delivered at Princeton, June 18, 1817,
at the ordination of the Rev. Samuel Clark...Worces-
ter, Mass., Pr. by William Manning, 1817. 36 p.
CBPac; ICMe; MBNEH; MSaE; MWA; MiD-B; NCH;
Nh-Hi; NjR.   41819

-- A discourse, delivered at the dedication of the
Brick meeting-house, erected by the First Congrega-
tional society, in Burlington, Vermont...Burlington,
Vt., 1817. 20 p. MBC; MBAt; MHi; MWA; MH; MeB;
RPB; Vt; VtU-W.   41820

[Pierce, Thomas]
    A poetical gift to the patrons of the "Western Spy,"
on the commencement of the year 1818...Cincinnati
[1817] 23 p. OCHP.   41821

Pierpont, John, 1785-1866
    Airs of Palestine; a poem...Ed. 2. Boston, Wells
and Lilly, 1817. 58 p. CBPac; CSmH; CU; DLC; MB;
MH; MMeT; MNe; MSaE; MShM; MWA; MdBE; RPB;
TxU.   41822

-- -- Ed. 3. Boston, Wells and Lilly, 1817. 66 p.
ICN; MH-AH; MMeT; MWA; MdHi; NBuG; NN; NjP;

PPM; RPB; TxU.   41823

Pike, Stephen
   The teacher's assistant; or, system of practical
arithmetic... Philadelphia, stereotyped by B. & J. Collins, for Benjamin Warner, 1817. 191 p. MWA; PIndt.
                                          41824
-- -- Ed. 3, with improvements. Philadelphia, stereotyped by B. & J. Collins, for Benjamin Warner, 1817.
198 p. MH; PCDHi.   41825

Pilkington, Mrs. [Mary]
   Confidence in parents, the only security for happi-
ness: or the misery that is certain to attend deceit.
New-Haven, Sidney's press, 1817. 46 p. CtHi. 41826

The pious guide to prayer and devotion... Ed. 4. Georgetown, D. C., Pr. by William Duffy, 1817. 376 p. MWA.
                                          41827
The pious parent's present... New York, Samuel Wood
& sons, 1817. MWA.   41828

Pious resolutions. The following resolutions must have
been written by a man who had made great progress in
Christian life... Ed. 3. Andover, Mass., Flagg &
Gould, 1817. 4 p. MMeT.   41829

Pirates-brief account of horrid massacre- July 1816.
Boston, H. Trumbull, 1817. MWA.   41830

Pitkin, Timothy, 1766-1847
   Statistical view of the commerce of the United
States... Ed. 2. New Haven, Durrie and Peck, 1817.
445 p. MnM.   41831

-- -- Ed. 2. New York, Pr. by Hamlin & Newton, for
James Eastburn & Co., 1817. 445 p. CSt; Ct; CtW;
DLC; GU; DeGE; MB; MBAt; MH; MWA; MWborHi;
MWiW; MnM; MoSW; NBuG; NIC-L; NWM; NcD; NjR.
                                          41832
Pittsburgh citizens.
   Petition to the president and directors of the United
States Bank, from the citizens of Pittsburgh for a

branch at that place.   Pittsburgh, Pa., 1817. PPi.
41833
Pittsburgh, Pa.   Manufactures
     Report of the committee appointed by the citizens
of Pittsburgh, at a meeting held at the court house on
the 21st of December, 1816, to inquire into the state of
the manufactures in the city and its immediate vicinity.
Pittsburgh, Pa., 1817. 16 p. MB; NHi; PPi; WHi.
41834
Pius VII, Pope
     Homily directed to the people... in the Cisalpine
Republick... 1797.   Translated... into Spanish by a citizen of Venezuela in South America, who publishes it in
replication to a letter of the same Pope in the behalf of
Ferdinand VII against the insurgents of the cidevant
Spanish colonies.   Philadelphia, 1817. MdBP.   41835

-- Homily of the Cardinal Chiarmonti... Philadelphia,
Pr. by J. F. Hurtel, 1817. MWA.   41836

Pius VII assists the cause of liberty in 1797.   Pius VII
assists Ferdinand VII against the patriots of South America and Mexico in 1816.   Philadelphia, 1817. 73 p.
MBC.   41837

Plagiarism; or, a hint at the case.   By a layman...
Albany, April, 1817. 12 p. MB; N.   41838

A plain statement of the proceedings respecting the Ken-
sington burying ground... Philadelphia, 1817. MWA.
41839
The planters' and merchants' almanac, for... 1818...
for the states of South Carolina and Georgia.   Charleston, A. E. Miller [1817] 48 p. MWA.   41840

Playfair, John
     Dissertation second: exhibiting a general view of
the progress of mathematical and physical science,
since the revival of letters in Europe.   Boston, Wells
and Lilly, 1817. 197 p. MMeT; MSaP; MWA; MtBu;
NR; NhD; PPAmP; PPL-R.   41841

Pleasing toy.   New York, 1817. (Woodcuts) (Goodspeed's cat. 292, (1938) No. 448.)   41842

The pleasures of contemplation, being a desultory investigation of the harmonies, beauties, and benefits of
nature: including a justification of the ways of God to
man, and a glimpse of his sovereign beauty... Philadelphia, Eastwick & Stacy, [1817] 240 p. KyLxT; MiDSH.
                                                       41843
[Plinth, Octavius]
      A memorial...[1817?] MWA.   41844

The pocket chronological directory or compend of gen-
eral history, in the form of questions and answers.
Hartford, Pr. by Peter B. Gleason & Co., 1817. 176 p.
CtY; IaDL; LU; MDedHi; MH; MWA.   41845

The pocket Lavater, or, The science of physiognomy;
...New York, Van Winkle & Wiley, 1817. 140 p.
MWA; NcWsS.   41846

Poehls, Meno
      A compend of German grammar. Cambridge,
Mass., Pr. by Hilliard and Metcalf, at the University
press, 1817. MWA; MWiW.   41847

Poems for children. New York, S. Wood & sons, 1817.
44 p. MWA.   41848

Pond, Enoch, 1791-1882
      An apology for religious conferences...Worcester,
Mass., Pr. by William Manning, 1817. 32 p. CSt;
CtY-D; MH-AH; MBC; MWA; MWHi; MeBat; MiD-B;
NCH; PMA.   41849

-- Review of Dr. Bancroft's appendix...Worcester,
Mass., Pr. by William Manning, 1817. MWA. 41850

Poor Robin's almanac, for 1818. Philadelphia, David
Hogan [1817] MWA.   41851

Poor Will's almanac...1818...Philadelphia, Joseph
Rakestraw [1817] [36] p. NjR; WHi.   41852

Pope, Alexander
    An essay on man...Canandaigua, N.Y., H. Under-
hill, stereotyped by H. Simmons & Co. [1817?] 54 p.
NCanHi.   41853

-- -- Concord, N.H., Isaac Hill, 1817. MWA; Nh-Hi.
                                                          41854

-- -- Haverhill, Mass., Pr. by Burrill and Tileston,
1817. 49 p. CSt; MH; MSaP; MWA.   41855

-- -- Keene, N.H., John Prentiss, 1817. 46 p.
MFiHi; MH; MWA; Nh-Hi.   41856

-- -- To which are added, the Universal prayer, and
other valuable pieces selected from his works. New
York, E. Duyckinck, 1817. MH; NN.   41857

-- -- New York, Forbes & Co., 1817. MWA.   41858

No entry   41859

Porter, Anna Maria
    The knight of St. John...New York, Pr. by Abra-
ham Paul, (Vol. 2, Pr. by J. & J. Harper), for
James Eastburn & Co., 1817. 2 v. MH; MWA; MWalp;
NBuU.   41860

-- -- Philadelphia, Pr. by J. Maxwell, for M. Thomas,
1817. 2 v. MWA.   41861

Porter, Jane
    The pastor's fire-side, a novel...New York, Pr.
by Van Winkle, Wiley & Co., for W.B. Gilley, 1817.
2 v. CtHT; MFai; MWalp.   41862

-- The Scottish chiefs...New York, Pr. by J.C. Totten,
for Evert Duyckinck, 1817. MWA. (v. 1)   41863

-- Thaddeus of Warsaw. New-York, S. Marks, 1817.
4 v. in 2. NBuU; NPlaK.   41864

-- -- 3d Amer. ed.   Philadelphia, Pr. by Thomas H.
Palmer, for B. Warner, Cushing & Jewett...1817. 4 v.
in 2.   KyU; NcWsM.   41865

Porteus, Beilby, bp. of London, 1731-1808
    A summary of the principal evidences for the truth
and divine origin of the Christian revelation.   A new
ed.   Hartford, Sheldon & Goodrich, 1817.   CSt; Ct; CtHi;
CtSoP; DLC; MWA; MsWP; RPB.   41866

Portland, Maine
    The by-laws of the town of Portland in the county
of Cumberland.   Portland, Me., Pr. by A. & J. Shirley, 1817.   21 p.   MH.   41867

Portsmouth, N.H.
    Correct list of taxes, assessed on the persons and
property in the town of Portsmouth, for the year 1817.
Portsmouth, N.H., 1817-18.   44 p.   Nh-Hi.   41868

Portsmouth society for the suppression of vice, N.H.
    Extracts from a report...Portsmouth, N.H., Pr.
by Charles Turell, 1817.   17 p.   MH; MWA; MiD-B;
Nh-Hi.   41869

Potter, Nathaniel, 1770-1843
    A memoir on contagion, more especially as it re-
spects the yellow fever: read in convention of the medical and chirugical faculty of Maryland, on the 3d of
June, 1817.   Baltimore, Pr. by B. Edes, for E.J.
Coale, 1817.   117 p.   MdBE.   41870

Potter, William
    Essays, moral and religious...Philadelphia, Pr. by
W. Frey, 1817.   MWA; TxAuPT.   41871

-- -- Savannah, S.C. and J. Schenck, 1817.   234 p.
GU-De.   41872

The power of grace...[Philadelphia] William Bradford,
agent, 1817.   MWA.   41873

Prentiss, William
     Reading room, continued on an improved plan...
William Prentiss. Washington City, March 4, 1817.
1 p. DLC.   41874

Presbyterian Church in the U.S.A.
     Extracts from the minutes of the General Assembly
of the Presbyterian Church, in the United States of
America, A.D. 1817. Philadelphia, Pr. by Thomas
and William Bradford, 1817. 62 p. GDC; KyLoP;
MMonsA; NcMHI; PLT; ViRUT.   41875

-- -- ...From A.D. 1812, to A.D. 1816, inclusive.
With a copious index...Vol. III. Philadelphia, extracts
pr. by Jane Aitken, and index by J.W. Scott, 1817.
44 p. NcMHi.   41876

-- A narrative of the state of religion...Philadelphia,
Thomas and William Bradford, 1817. MWA.   41877

-- A pastoral letter...Philadelphia, Thomas and William Bradford, 1817. MWA.   41878

-- Sketch of the rise, progress [and] present state of
the Theological Seminary of...To which is subjoined,
a copy of the constitution. Elizabeth-town, N.J.,
Shepard Kollock, 1817. 19 p. PPPrHi; NjR.   41879

-- Synod of Ohio.
     Proceedings of the board of missions of the Synod
of Ohio. [Chillicothe?1817] 8 p. PPPrHi.   41880

-- West Lexington Presbytery.
     Extracts from the minutes...Paris, Ky., Pr. by
John R. and Abraham I. Lyle, 1817. 24 p. PPPrHi.
                                                41881
[Prescott, Mrs. Margaret (Hiller)]
     Religion and philosophy united; or, an attempt to
show, that philosophical principles form a foundation of
the New Jerusalem Church as developed to the world in
the mission of the Hon. Emanuel Swedenborg...Boston,
Pub. for the subscribers, 1817. 55 p. DLC; MB; MBAU;
MCNC; MH; MWA; PBa.   41882

...A present for Sunday-school children...Boston, Pr. by Ezra Lincoln, 1817. MWA.   41883

Preston, John
    Every man his own teacher; or, Lancaster's theory of education, practically displayed...Albany, Pr. by E. & E. Hosford, for the author, 1817. 520 p. DLC; MWA; MiU; NNC; Vi.   41884

The prices for the Kingsbridge marble, 1817. [New York,] Pr. by George Long [1817] MWA.   41885

Prime, Nathaniel Scudder
    Divine truth, the established means of sanctification...Salem, N. Y., Pr. by Dodd and Stevenson, 1817. 32 p.   MBC; MWA; VtMiS.   41886

The primer improved; or The child's companion. Embracing the usual variety in a primer: Likewise, a minor catechism for young children; Dr. Watts' catechism for children; The Westminster Assembly's shorter catechism; and a Selection of hymns. Designed to impress upon the tender minds of children the importance of early piety. Middlebury, Vt., Pr. by T. C. Strong, for the Ver. Miss. Society, sold by their Gen. Agent, W. G. Hooker, 1817. 48 p.   CSmH; MH; MWA; PP; VtStJ; VtHi; VtMiS.   41887

Princeton university.
    Catalogus Collegii Neo-Caesariensis...Trenton, N. J., Pr. by George Sherman, 1817. MWA.   41888

[--] To the friends of the college of New Jersey. (Statement regarding student disturbances made by the president in behalf of the Faculty. [Princeton] 1817. [4] p.   MH.   41889

The prize: or, The lace makers of Missenden; a tale. Philadelphia, M. Carey & son, 1817. MH.   41890

The progress of society: a poem...New-York, Pr. by Clayton & Kingsland, for D. Longworth, 1817. 62 p. DLC; MWA; RPB.   41891

Protestant Episcopal Church in the U. S. A.
　The Book of Common Prayer, and administration of
the sacraments, and other rites and ceremonies of the
Church...Baltimore, Pr. by J. Robinson, for W. War-
ner, F. Lucas, 1817. 428 p. DLC; MWA; MdBS;
MdHi; NBuG; WHi; WW. 41892

-- -- ...Together with the Psalter, or Psalms of
David. Baltimore, Joseph N. Lewis, [1817?] 360 p.
MWA; N; NLC. 41893

-- -- Stereotyped by E. and J. White. New-York, Pr.
by D. Fanshaw, for Robert and William A. Bartow,
1817. 465 p. MWA; OC. 41894

-- -- Stereotype ed. by B. and J. Collins. New York,
W. B. Gilley, 1817. 377 p. MWA; MoInRC. 41895

-- Canons for the government of the Protestant Episco-
pal church in the United States...Newburyport, Mass.,
William B. Allen & Co., 1817. 44 p. MH; MSaE;
MWA. 41896

-- Catechism of the Protestant Episcopal church in the
United States of America. To which is annexed a catechism, designed as an explanation and enlargement of
the church catechism. New Haven, from Sidney's press,
1817. 43 p. CtHi. 41897

-- -- New-Haven, From Sidney's press, 1817. 48 p.
CtHi; MWA. 41898

-- Journal of the proceedings of the Bishops, clergy,
and laity of the Protestant Episcopal Church in the
United States of America, in a General convention, held
in Trinity Church, in the City of New York, from the
20th to the 27th day of May inclusive. A. D. 1817. New
York, Pr. by T. and J. Swords, 1817. 59 p. MBD;
MWA. 41899

-- Journals of the general conventions of the Protestant
Episcopal Church, in the United States of America,
from the year 1784, to the year 1814, inclusive. Also

first appendix, containing the constitution and canons.
And second appendix, containing three pastoral letters.
Philadelphia, John Bioren, 1817. 381 p. MA; MBD;
MsJPED; OCHP; RPB;WNaE.   41900

-- A pastoral letter to the members of the Protestant
Episcopal Church in the United States of America from
the house of Bishops of said church, assembled in Gen-
eral Convention, in Trinity Church, in the city of New
York, May, A. D. 1817. New York, Pr. by T. and J.
Swords, 1817. 19 p. InID; MWA; NGH.   41900a

-- Protestant Episcopal theological seminary.
       Address to Episcopalians. New York, Pr. by T.
and J. Swords, 1817. MWA.   41900b

-- Connecticut (Diocese)
       Journal of the proceedings... in convention: from
Aug. 3, 1813, to Oct. 16, 1816, inclusive. New Haven,
Pr. by Steele & Gray, 1817. 46 p. Ct; DGU; PPL.
                                                41900c
-- Maryland (Diocese)
       An address to the members of the Protestant Epis-
copal Church in Maryland. By French Tilghman, Esq.
Annapolis, Pr. by J. Green, 1817. 18 p. CSmH; InID;
MWA; MdBD; PHi.   41900d

-- -- Journal of a convention of the Protestant Episco-
pal Church in Maryland, held in All Saint's Church,
Frederick-town, June 4th, 5th & 6th, 1817. Annapolis,
Pr. by Jonas Green, 1817. 23 p. DLC; InID; MB;
MBD; MWA; MdBD; MdHi; NBuDD; NN.   41900e

-- Massachusetts (Diocese)
       Constitution and canons of the Protestant Episcopal
Church in the Commonwealth of Massachusetts. Boston,
R. P. and C. Williams, 1817. 8 p. MB; MBDil; MSaE;
MWA; NBuU-M.   41900f
 -- New Jersey (Diocese)
       Journal of the proceedings of the Annual Convention
of the Protestant Episcopal Church, in the state of
New-Jersey. New-Brunswick, Pr. by W. Myer, 1817.
38 p. MBD; NjR; PPL-R.   41900g

-- New York (Diocese)
    ...A catechism designed as an explanation...Ed. 7.
New York, T. & J. Swords, 1817. 72 p. NNG.   41900h

-- -- Journal of the proceedings of the annual conven-
tion of the Protestant Episcopal church in the state of
New-York: held in Trinity Church, in the city of New-
York, on the 21st and 22nd days of October, A.D. 1817.
New-York, Pr. by T. and J. Swords, 1817. 48 p.
CtHT; InID; MWA; NjR; WHi.   41900i

-- Pennsylvania (Diocese)
    Journal of the thirty-third convention of the Protes-
tant Episcopal Church in the state of Pennsylvania...
Philadelphia, Pr. by John Bioren, 1817. 20 p. MBD.
                                              41901
-- South Carolina (Diocese)
    Journal of the proceedings of the annual convention
of the Protestant Episcopal Church in the state of South
Carolina; held in St. Michael's Church, Charleston, on
the 18th and 20th February 1817.   Charleston, S. C.,
J. Hoff, 1817. 6 p. NNG.   41902

-- Virginia (Diocese)
    Journal of the proceedings...the 6th of May, 1817.
Richmond, Va., Pr. by Ritchie, Trueheart & Du Val,
1817. 21 p. DLC; MWA; OCHP.   41903

Protestant Episcopal Society for the advancement of
Christianity in South Carolina.
    Report...Charleston, 1817. PPAmP.   41904

Protestant Episcopal Sunday School Society of N. Y.
    ...Annual report of the Board of managers of the
New York Protestant Episcopal Sunday school society.
[New York, 1817-28] 11 v. in 1. NNG.   41905

-- Constitution...New York, 1817. 7 p. MHi. 41906

Proudfit, Alexander Moncrief
    The extent of the missionary field...Middlebury,
Vt., Pr. by Frederick P. Allen, 1817. 32 p. CSmH;
M; MH; MWA; N; NN; Vt; VtHi; VtMiM; VtMis;

VtU-W.   41907

Providence female tract society, Providence, R. I.
The second annual report... Providence, R. I., Pr.
[by William G. Goddard] at the Rhode-Island American
office, 1817. MWA.   41908

Provident association of clerks, Washington, D. C.
Articles of the Provident-association of clerks, em-
ployed in the civil department of the government of the
United States, within the District of Columbia; adopted
March 1, 1817. [Washington? 1817?] 7 p. DLC.
                                              41909
Provident Institution for Savings, Boston.
The Provident Institution for Savings in the town of
Boston. Its office is established at a room in the Old
Court House, in Court Street. It will be open only
every Wednesday from 9 to 2 o'clock... Boston? [1817?]
Broadside. MHi.   41910

-- [Report of the trustees made at the meeting held the
31st of December, 1816. Also by by-laws and act of
incorporation. Boston, 1817] 15 p. MH.   41911

Public auction on Wednesday, April 23rd, 1817, at 10
o'clock A. M. S. M'Lellan & T. Fletcher, auctioneers,
at the Bank room of the Portland Bank, will be sold
the real estate described as follows, belonging to said
Bank, viz... Broadside. MeHi.   41912

Public sale. By order of Montgomery County court,
the subscribers, commissioners to divide the real estate of Lewis Bealmear... parts of two tracts of land,
called Valentine Garden, enlarged, and the two Broth-
ers, containing in the whole about two hundred and
forty acres,... December 11, 1817. Pr. at the office
of the Rockville Journal and Montgomery Advertiser.
Broadside. NHi.   41913

[Putnam, Israel]
Universal death in Adam, and life in Christ. Containing a refutation of the doctrine of total depravity
and endless mercy. By a layman. Salem, Mass., Pr.

for the author, 1817. 16 p. MSaE; MWA.   41914

Pyke, Alexander
    An oration, delivered on the 17th March, 1817, be-
fore the Shamrock friendly association... New York, Pr.
by Van Pelt and Riley, 1817. MWA.   41915

Pyron du Marte, Antoine
    Syllabaire françois; or A French spelling book...
also, an introduction to French grammar, by way of
question and answer... By Mr. Porney [pseud.]... New
York, Pr. [by J. Desnoues] for David Longworth, 1817.
151 p. MWA; NcAS; ViU.   41916

                              Q
The Quarterly Theological review; conducted by the Rev.
Ezra Stiles Ely, A. M. Philadelphia, Anthony Finley,
1818 [1817] 1 v. CSmH.   41917

Quincy, John
    Lexicon-medicum: a new medical dictionary; con-
taining an explanation of the terms... comp. from the
best authors by Robert Hooper. Philadelphia, Parker,
1817. 870 p. MdBM; NNNAM.   41918

-- Quincy's Lexicon medicum. A new medical dictionary; containing an explanation of the terms of anatomy,
physiology, practice of physic, materia medica, chemistry, pharmacy, surgery, midwifery, and the various
branches of natural philosophy connected with medicine.
Selected, arranged, and compiled from the best authors.
By Robert Hooper. Philadelphia, Carey, 1817. 800 p.
MBM.   41919

Quitman, Frederick Henry, 1760-1832
    Three sermons; the first preached before the Evan-
gelical Lutheran synod... the second and third on the
reformation of Doctor Martin Luther... Hudson, N. Y.,
William E. Norman, 1817. 42 p. MWA; N; NjR; WHi.
                                                41920

R

Raffles, Thomas
The Sabbath school teacher's monitor: being the
substance of two addresses delivered to the teachers of
Great George street Sunday school, Liverpool, England... Philadelphia, John W. Scott, pub. at the office
of the Religious Remembrancer, 1817. 76 p. KLindB.
41921
-- Sunday school teacher's monitor... New York, Pr. by
J. Seymour, 1817. MB; MWA.   41922

Rahauser, Jonathan
Ein kurzer auszug aus dem Heidelberger Catechis-
mus, in frag und antwort. von Jonathan Rahauser...
Hagerstaun, Md., Pr. by Gruber und May, 1817. 107 p.
(In German and English) MdBE; MdHi; MoWgT; PPLT;
PPPrHi.   41923

Ramsay, Alexander, 1754?-1824
Dr. Ramsay, formerly lecturer on anatomy and
physiology in Surgeon's Square, Edinburgh, and in several of the colleges and cities of North-America... will
commence his course of anatomical and physiological instructions in Fryburg, District of Maine, on the beginning of December next... New-York, November 8, 1817.
[New-York, 1817] Broadside. PPL.   41924

-- Eight lectures, on the animal and intellectual economy of human nature... [Announcement] Charleston,
1817. 1 p. NNNAM.   41925

Rand, Asa
Two sermons on Christian fellowship... Portland,
Me., Pr. by A. & J. Shirley, 1817. 35 p. MWA;
MeB; MeHi.   41926

Randall, Ephraim
Discourse in Ashby (Mass.) April 3, 1817. Concord,
Mass., Pr. by J. T. Pitters, 1817. 20 p. RPB. 41927

Ravenscroft, John Stark, bp.
Sermon preached... at Speed's church, in Mecklen-

burg county... Fredericksburg, Va., William F. Gray,
1817. 15 p. MWA; MdBD; NNG; ViU.   41928

[Raymond, Mrs. Jane (Osborn)]
    The loving invitation of Christ... Exeter, N. H.,
Pr. by C. Norris & Co., 1817. MWA.   41929

Rayner, Menzies
    Observations on the Rev. Mr. Tyler's sermon on
The doctrine of the saints' perseverance... New Haven,
Pr. by Flagg & Gray, 1817. 23 p. CtHi; CtHT; CtY;
MBAt; MBD; MF; MWA; NN; NNUT; NjR.   41930

-- A review of the Rev. Mr. Taylor's sermon on re-
generation, preached and published at New-Haven, 1816.
New-Haven, Pr. by Steele & Gray, 1817. 40 p. CtHT;
CtHi; MBC; MBDil; MBD; MF; MWA; MWiW; NNC;
NNUT; NjR; RPB.   41931

Read, Alexander
    An address, delivered before the New-Bedford
auxiliary society for the suppression of intemperance...
New Bedford, Mass., Pr. by Benjamin Lindsey, 1817.
27 p. DNLM; MB; MWA.   41932

Read, Nathan Sherman
    An astronomical dictionary... New Haven, Pr. by
T. G. Woodward, for Hezekiah Howe, 1817. 207 p.
CtHT-W; CtHi; MWA; VtU.   41933

Read, William Thompson
    Oration delivered at New-Castle (Del.) on the anni-
versary of St. John the Evangelist. December 27th,
A. D. 1816... Wilmington, Del., Pr. by R. Porter,
1817. 15 p. DeHi; DeWI; MBFM; MWA; PHi; PPFM;
PPPrHi.   41934

The ready reckoner, or traders' assistant, in dollars
and cents... Philadelphia, Pr. [by Conrad Zentler] for
George W. Mentz and Conrad Zentler, 1817. MWA.
                                                  41935
Reed, Ephraim, comp.
    Musical monitor; or New-York collection of devo-

tional church music... Utica, N. Y., Pr. by William
Williams, 1817. 119 p. MPiB; NNUT; WHi.   41936

Reed, John
    A sermon preached before the Plymouth Association
of Ministers, in the third congregational society in
Middleborough, Sept. 25, 1810. Boston, W. Wells,
1817. MdBLC.   41937

Reformed Church in America
    The acts and proceedings of the General synod of
the Reformed Dutch Church, in North America, at Albany, June, 1817. Albany, Pr. by Websters and Skinners, 1817. 53 p. DLC; NSchHi; NjR.   41938

-- The acts and proceedings of the General synod of
the Reformed Dutch Church, in North America, at
Kingston, October, 1817. Albany, Pr. by Websters &
Skinners, 1817. 22 p. MiD-B; NSchHi; NjR.   41939

-- Pastoral letter. The General Synod of the Reformed Dutch Church, convened in the city of Albany,
June 1817. [Albany, 1817] 8 p. NjR.   41940

-- Albany Synod.
    The acts and proceedings of the particular synod of
Albany, of the Reformed Dutch Church, in North America, at Albany, 8th Oct., 1817. Albany, Pr. by Websters and Skinners, 1817. 26 p. NSchHi.   41941

The Reflector. Milledgeville, Ga., J.B. Hines, Nov.
12, 1817, 1st issue. Weekly newspaper. DLC. 41942

Refutation of the doctrine of total depravity. Salem,
Mass., 1817. 16 p. MB.   41943

The Register. Windham, Conn., Samuel Webb, Mar.
6, 1817, 1st issue. Weekly newspaper. MWA.   41944

Reid, John, 1776-1822
    Essays on hypochondriacal and other nervous affec-
tions... Philadelphia, M. Carey & son, 1817. 209 p.
DLC; InU; MBM; MWA; MoSW-M; NNC-M; NNNAM;

ScCMeS.   41945

Religious tract society of Baltimore
    First annual report of the Religious tract society of
Baltimore... Baltimore, Pr. by Richard J. Matchett,
1817. 12 p. MdHi.   41946

Remarks on children's play. New York, S. Wood &
sons, 1817. MWA.   41947

Remarks on, The doctrine of the influence of the Holy
Spirit. Philadelphia, Pr. by J.R.A. Skerrett, for
Benjamin & Thomas Kite, 1817. 12 p. MH; NcGu;
PSC-Hi.   41948

A reply to an address to the Roman Catholics of the
United States of America. By the author of a letter to
the Roman Catholics of the city of Worcester. New
York, Pr. by Clayton & Kingsland, for David Longworth,
1817. 96 p. InID.   41949

Reply to Mr. Abbot's statement of proceedings in the
First Society in Coventry, Conn. Tolland County, Conn.
Hartford, 1817. 48 p. MHi.   41950

Reply to the author of the letter on South America and
Mexico, by an American, addressed to Mr. James
Munroe [!] president of the United States, printed at
Washington, in this present year, 1817. Philadelphia,
Pr. by J.F. Hurtel, 1817. 16 p. DLC; MBAt; MWA;
PPAmP.   41951

Reply to "The crisis." Harrisburg [Pa.] Pr. by James
Peacock, [1817] 14 p. DLC; MB; MWA; PHi.   41952

A report of the case of Hunter against Martin; decided
in the Supreme Court of Appeals of Virginia. With the
speeches, at length, of Leigh, Williams, Wirt, Nicholas, and Hay; and the opinions of all the Judges. Together with the resolutions of the Supreme Court of the
United States on a writ of error in the same case.
Philadelphia, Pr. by J. Maxwell, for Harrison Hall,
1817. 148 p. CSfLaw; NIC; NcD.   41953

Report of the evidence and arguments of counsel at the
trial of Levi & Laban Kenniston, before the Supreme
judicial court, on an indictment for the robbery of Major Elijah Putnam Goodridge, on the evening of the
19th of December, 1816... Boston, J. T. Buckingham,
1817. 63 p. CSmH; Ct; CtY; DLC; Ia; MB; MBAt;
MH-L; MMeT; MSaE; MWA; MeBa; N; NN; NjR; RPL.
41954

Report of the evidence at the trial of Levi & Laban
Kenniston, before Hon. Samuel Putnam, on an indictment for the robbery of Major Elijah P. Goodridge,
Dec. 19, 1816. Salem, Mass., Pr. by T. C. Cushing,
1817. 32 p. MeBa; NjR.   41955

Report of the trial of Henry Phillips for (the murder of)
Gaspard Dennegri, heard and determined in the Supreme
judicial court of Massachusetts, at Boston, on the 9th
and 10th Jan. 1817... Boston, Russell Cutler & Co.,
1817. 55 p. MH; MHi; MoU; PHi; PP.   41956

Report of the trial of John Quay, vs. The Eagle Fire
Company of New-York; before the Honourable William
W. Van Ness, one of the Justices of the Supreme
Court of Judicature of the State of New-York, at the
City-Hall of the City of New-York; commencing on Fri-
day, the sixth day and ending on Tuesday, the tenth
day of December, 1816... New-York, Pr. by J. Sey-
mour, 1817. 51 p. MBS; MWA; NIC-L; NNS.   41957

Report of the trials of Stephen Murphy and John Doyle
before the Supreme judicial court, at Dedham, Oct. 23,
1817. For the rape of Rebecca Day, Jun., on the 10th
Aug. 1817. By a gentleman of the Norfolk bar. Boston, Pr. by Chester Stebbins, 1817. 33 p. DLC;
MBAt; MH; MHi.   41958

Report on the failures attributed to the vaccine in
Charleston, in destroying the susceptibility to small pox.
Also in secondary small pox, and in the prevalence of
small pox and chicken pox as they occurred in the last
year. Read before the Medical Society, at a meeting
held 1st January, 1817. [Charleston, 1817] 8 p.
NNNAM.   41959

Republican Chronicle. New York, Charles N. Baldwin
and Abraham Asten, Apr. 2, 1817, 1st issue. Semi-
weekly and daily. MWA; NjR.   41960

The result of council at Princeton incapable of vindication: or, a review of Dr. Bancrofts vindication of the
result of the late mutual council convened at Princeton
...Worcester, Mass., Pr. by William Manning, 1817.
44 p. NjR.   41961

The return of the Jews, and the second advent of our
Lord, proved to be a Scripture doctrine, by a citizen
of Baltimore. Baltimore, Pr. by Richard J. Matchett,
1817. 60 p. MdHi.   41962

The returned captive. A poem. Founded on a late fact.
Hudson, N. Y., Pr. by Ashbel Stoddards, 1817. 60 p.
CSmH.   41963

Retz, Jean François Paul de Gondi de.
    Memoirs of the Cardinal de Retz...Philadelphia,
Pr. by T. H. Palmer, for Edward Earle, 1817. 3 v.
ArL; KAStB; MWA; MWiW; NIC; NNS; NYStJ; PLT;
RNR; RP; Vi.   41964

Review [extracted from the Panoplist] of Dr. Bancroft's
discourse, against conferences. Boston, Samuel T.
Armstrong, 1817. 16 p. CSt; MAuG; MH-AH; MWA;
MWey; NjR.   41965

Review of the late correspondence of the Reverend Dr.
Worcester with the Reverend William E. Channing on
the subject of Unitarianism, by a serious inquirer.
Boston, Lincoln & Edmands, for the author, 1817. 88 p.
MH-AH.   41966

A review of the scriptures on internal depravity...
Danville, Vt., Pr. by Ebenezer Eaton, 1817. 48 p.
CSmH; MWA; VtHi.   41967

A review of Warden's letters from St. Helena, containing remarks on Bonaparte's massacres at Jappa and El
Arish...Boston, Pr. by John Eliot, 1817. DLC; MH;

MWA.   41968

Reynolds, Frederic, 1764-1841
    The dramatist; or, Stop him who can! A comedy
in five acts...Baltimore, J. Robinson, 1817. 72 p.
MdBE; NN.   41969

Rhode Island (State)
    At the General Assembly of the state of Rhode-Is-
land...by adjournment...third Monday of February,
1817. [Providence, Pr. by Hugh H. Brown, 1817] 40 p.
DLC.   41970

-- --...First Wednesday of May, 1817. [Providence,
Pr. by Hugh H. Brown, 1817] 24 p. DLC.   41971

-- --...By adjournment...second Monday of June, 1817.
[Providence, Pr. by Hugh H. Brown, 1817] 56 p. DLC.
                                                       41972
-- -- ...Begun...last Monday of October, 1817. [Provi-
dence, Pr. by Hugh H. Brown, 1817] 55 p. DLC.
                                                       41973
The Rhode-Island almanack for 1818. By Isaac Bicker-
staff. Providence, Hugh H. Brown [1817] [24] p.
MWA; NjR; RHi; RPB.   41974

[Rhodes, William Barnes]
    Bombastes Furioso...New York, David Longworth,
1817. MWA.   41975

Rice, John Holt
    The importance of the gospel ministry...Richmond,
Va., Pr. by Shepherd and Pollard, 1817. 19 p. CSmH;
DLC; IEG; MWA; NcU; PHi; PLT; PPPrHi; ViU. 41976

Richard, Louis Claude Marie
    A botanical dictionary...New Haven, Pr. by N.
Whiting, for Hezekiah Howe, 1817. 154 p. CtHT-W;
CtY; CtHi; DLC; DNLM; ICJ; IEN-M; IGK; InCW; MA;
MB; MBM; MBC; MBP; MH; MNF; MSaP; MWA; MdBD;
MiKC; NR; NTR; OClW; OHi; PPAmP; PPL-R; PPM;
PPPH; PWcT; RPB.   41977

[Richards, George Hallam]
    The politics of Connecticut...Hartford, Pr. [by
Frederick D. Bolles and John M. Niles] at the Times
office, 1817. 36 p. CSmH; Ct; CtHi; CtSoP; CtW; DLC;
LNH; MWA.   41978

Richardson, Joseph
    An address, in celebration of the nativity of St.
John the Baptist, pronounced before the brethren of
Washington Lodge in Roxbury, on the 24th of June,
A. L. 5817...Dedham, Mass., Pr. by Abel D. Alleyne,
1817. 14 p. MBFM; MDedHi; MWA; PPFM.   41979

Richardson, Samuel, 1689-1761
    History of Pamela; or, Virtue rewarded.   Abridged
from the works of Samuel Richardson, Esq. Wilmington, Del., Porter, 1817. 106 p. DeWi.   41980

Richmond, Edward
    A sermon, delivered November 29, 1816, at the
ordination of the Reverend Luther Bailey...Dedham,
Mass., Pr. by Abel D. Alleyne, 1817. 23 p. DLC;
MB; MBAt; MBC; MH-AH; MHi; MSaE; MWA; MiD-B;
RPB.   41981

[Richmond, Legh]
    The negro servant...Philadelphia, Wm. Bradford,
agent, 1817. MWA.   41982

[--] The orphan...[Philadelphia, Pr. by Lydia R.
Bailey, 1817] (This is no. 29 of the Tracts of the
Philadelphia female tract society) MWA.   41983

-- The young cottager. An authentic narrative ...And-
over, Mass., Pr. by Flagg and Gould, for the New
England Tract Society, 1817. DLC; MB; MWA. 41984

-- -- New York, Pr. by J. Seymour, 1817. MWA.
                                                   41985
Richmond. Virginia Museum.
    The building for the Virginia Museum, in this city
is now nearly completed, and the establishment will, we
flatter ourselves, be opened early the ensuing summer.

Richmond, Virginia, 4th March 1817. [Richmond, 1817]
Broadside. NHi.   41986

Richmond county society for charitable and religious
purposes.
    The first annual report of the board of directors
of the Richmond county society for charitable and religious purposes, presented December 1, 1817; with a
discourse on Christian charity by the Rev. P. I. Van-
pelt... New-York, Pr. by J. Seymour, 1817. 37 p. N.
                                                   41987
Riley, James, 1777-1840
    An authentic narrative of the loss of the American
brig Commerce... [Hartford, Pub. by the author, 1817]
460 p. CtHi; NjR; RPB.   41988

-- -- New-York, T. & W. Mercein, 1817. 554 p.
CSmH; CSt; CU-B; CtHC; CtHi; DLC; InCW; MH; MSa;
MWA; MWiW; MnHi; NjR; TJoS.   41989

Ripley, Samuel
    The mutual influence of religion and free masonry
upon the knowledge, virtue and happiness of mankind;
illustrated in a discourse, delivered before Meridian
Lodge, Newton, on the anniversary of St. John Baptist,
June 24, A. L. 5817. Cambridge, Mass., Pr. by
Hilliard and Metcalf, 1817. 20 p. MHi; MWA.   41990

... The robber's daughter... [Philadelphia, Pr. by Lydia
R. Bailey, 1817] (This is no. 30 of the Tracts of the
Philadelphia female tract society) MWA.   41991

Robbins, Archibald
    A journal comprising an account of the loss of the
brig Commerce, of Hartford (Conn.) James Riley,
Master, upon the western coast of Africa, August 28th,
1815... Hartford, F. D. Bolles & Co., 1817. 268 p.
CSmH; Ct; CtHi; CtHT-W; CtSoP; CtNLC; MS; MDeeP;
MWA; MWborHi; MnHi; NIC.   41992

Robbins, Thomas
    A sermon, preached at Orford, at the funeral of
Mrs. Esther Hills Cook... Hartford, Pr. by Peter B.

Gleason & Co., 1817. 19 p. CtHC; CtHi; CtSoP;
MH-AH; MWA; MWiW; N; RPB. 41993

Robert, Thomas
The modern practice of physic, exhibiting the characters, causes, symptoms, prognostics, morbid ap-
pearances, and improved method of treating the diseases of all climates. Abridged from the 5th and last
London edition by Wm. Currie and David F. Condie.
Philadelphia, 1817. 518 p. RPM. 41994

Roberts, Samuel
A digest of select British statutes... Pittsburgh, Pa.,
Pr. by Robert Ferguson & Co., 1817. MWA. 41995

Roberts, Sylvester
Robert's second edition of the secret "customs,"
and revenue of the Sheriff's office. "The Customs of
the Office" 'are true as the existence of time, and certain as perpetual duration.' Philadelphia, Sylvester
Roberts, 1817. 29 p. Sabin 62196. 41996

Robin, Claude C. b. 1750
Florula ludoviciana; or, A flora of the state of
Louisiana. Tr., rev. and improved from the French
of C. C. Robin, by C. S. Rafinesque... New-York, C.
Wiley & co., 1817. 178 p. DLC; LNH; LU; MSaP;
MWA; NIC. 41997

Robinson, Isaac
Angels rejoicing over the repenting sinner. A ser-
mon, preached at Stoddard, February 2, 1817. Keene,
N. H., Pr. by John Prentiss, 1817. DLC. 41998

Robinson, James
Abstract of bill of mortality for Boston, 1817. M.
41999
Robinson, Robert
The history of baptism... Boston, From the press
of Lincoln & Edmands, 1817. 566 p. CBB; CSmH; CSt;
CtSoP; GDC; GMM; IaIS; IEG; KyLoS; LNB; MA; MB;
MH; MHi; MWA; MeLewB; NN; NNUT; NcRSH; OCo;
OkEnS; PCC; PPM; PPiXT; RHi; RPB; ScCoT; ViLC;

ViU.   42000

Robinson's original annual directory. Ed. 14. Philadelphia, Pr. at White-Hall, and may be had at Mc-
Mahon's store, N. G. Dufief's; J. Pounder's and D. Ho-
gans [1817] 524 p. MWA; P.   42001

Robinson's town & country almanac for 1818. Baltimore, [1817] MWA.   42002

Roche, Regina Maria
    The children of the Abbey. A tale, in four vol-
umes. 8th Amer. ed. Philadelphia, D. Dickinson,
1817. 4 v. PHi.   42003

Rockingham charitable society, N. H.
    Constitution of the Rockingham charitable society,
in New-Hampshire. With an address. Portsmouth
[N. H.] Pr. by Charles Turell, 1817. 10 p. CSmH; ICN;
NN; Nh-Hi.   42004

Rogers, Daniel
    Reports of the most interesting trials and deci-
sions which have arisen in the various Courts of judicature, from the trial of jury cases in the Hall during
(those) years, 1816-1822, by Daniel Rogers. New York,
Charles N. Baldwin, 1817-1822. 6 v. Nj.   42005

Rogers, John, 1648-1721
    The Book of the Revelation of Jesus Christ, which
God gave unto Him...[First printed in Boston, 1720]
2d New-London ed. ¡[New-London] Pr. by Samuel
Green, for Henry Waterous and Alexander Rogers,
1817. 248 p. CSmH; CtHi; CtNLC; DLC; MWA. 42006

Rogniat, Joseph, vicomte
    An abstract of the Baron de Rogniat's considerations
on the art of war...By S. Swett...Boston, Cummings
and Hilliard...University press...Hilliard & Metcalf,
1817. 24 p. MWA; WHi.   42007

Rohlwes, Johann Nicolaus
    Vollatändiges Gäuls-Doctor-Buch...Reading, Pa.,

Heinrich B. Sage, 1817. 108 p. MWA; PP. 42008

Roman Catholic Sunday school society.
The managers of the Roman Catholic Sunday school
society, request... Philadelphia, 1817. 4 p. MWA.
42009

Root, Erastus, 1773-1846
An inaugural dissertation on the chemical and medicinal properties of the mineral spring in Guilford.
Read before the Second Medical Society of the state of
Vermont, on the 8th day of January, 1817. Brattleborough, Vt., Pr. by Simeon Ide, 1817. 15 p. NNNBG.
42010

[Roscio, Juan Germán] 1769-1821
El triunfo de la libertad sobre el despotismo, en
la confesion de un pecador arrepentido de sus errores
politicos... Filadelfia, En la imprenta de Thomas H.
Palmer, 1817. 406 p. DLC; LU; MB; MBAt; MWA;
NN; PPL-R. 42011

Roscoe, William
To the memory of Richard Reynolds of Bristol...
New York, 1817. MDeeP. 42012

Ross, Mrs. of New York.
· The balance of comfort; or, The old maid and married woman. A novel. New York, C. Wiley & co.,
1817. 2 v. DLC; MB; MWA. 42013

Ross, James, 1744-1827, ed.
Graecae grammaticae westmonasteriensis institutio
compendiaria in usum juventutis civitatibus americanis
studiosae... Editio secunda. Philadelphia, impressa
typis Gulielmi Fry, sumptibus auctoris, 1817. 100 p.
CSmH; DLC; MH; MdBD; NjR. 42014

Rowson, Mrs. Susanna (Haswell) Mrs. W. Rowson
A spelling dictionary. Boston, 1817. MH. 42015

Roy, William
The key of David, to open the door of revelations:
being a critical and scriptural comment, on the Book of
Revelations... Albany, Pr. by E. & E. Hosford, for the

author, 1817. 320 p. MWA; NBuG; NCH; NT. 42016

Royalty of federalism! Read, try, decide, on the charge of Washington, that leading Federalists are to monarchy devoted. [Boston, Pr. at the Yankee office, 1817] 16 p. CSmH; DLC; MB; MBAt; MH; MHi; MWA; MiU-C. 42017

Ruddiman, Thomas
  The rudiments of the Latin tongue...27th genuine ed. Baltimore, Pr. by J. Robinson, for Joseph Cushing, 1817. 148 p. MWA; WyU. 42018

Rules and directions in art of penmanship. Hartford, Cooke & Hale, 1817. MWA. 42019

Rumrille, J.L.
  The drummer's instructor...Albany, Pr. by Packard and Van Benthuysen, 1817. 40 p. MWA; N. 42020

Rundall, M.A.
  An easy grammar of sacred history. 1st Amer. ed. Philadelphia, M. Carey, 1817. MWA. 42021

[Rundell, Mrs. Maria Eliza (Ketelby)] 1745-1828
  A new system of domestic cookery, formed upon principles of economy; and adapted to the use of private families, throughout the United States. Ed. 3. New-York, Pr. by Forbes & Co., for Robert M'Dermut, 1817. 317 p. DLC. 42022

Rush, Benjamin
  An inquiry into the effects of ardent spirits... Ed. 8. Springfield, Mass., Pr. by Thomas Dickman, 1817. 36 p. MWA. 42023

Ryley, Samuel William
  The itinerant; or, memoirs of an actor. Part II... Philadelphia, M. Carey & Son, 1817. 3 v. MWA. 42024

S

[S., R.]
  Jachin and Boaz...1817. MWA.   42025

[--] -- London, Pr.; Boston Repr. for the purchaser,
1817. 168 p. PPFM.   42026

Sacket's Harbor Gazette. Sacket's Harbor, N.Y.,
George Camp, Mar. 18, 1817, 1st issue. Weekly news-
paper. Jefferson Co. Historical Soc., Watertown,
N.Y.   42027

Saco and Biddeford fire society, Me.
  Rules and regulations...Portland, Me., Pr. by
Francis Douglas, 1817. MWA.   42028

[Sade, Jacques François Paul Aldonce de]
  The life of Petrarch. Philadelphia, Pr. by W.
Brown, for Samuel A. Mitchell & Horace Ames, 1817.
496 p. LNT; MMeT; MWA; MWiW; OT; PV. 42029

St. Andrews parish, West Virginia. Benevolent society.
  First annual report...Shepherd's-Town, West Va.,
Pr. by John N. Snider, 1817. MWA. 42030

St. Andrew's Society of the city of Charleston, Charles-
ton, S.C.
  Rules of the Saint Andrew's Society of the city of
Charleston, in South Carolina, established in the year
of our Lord one thousand seven hundred and twenty-
nine. Charleston, A.S. Willlington, 1817. 8 p. ScC.
              42031
Salem, Mass.
  Expences of the town of Salem for the year ending
March 10, 1817...David Cummins, Town clerk. Salem,
Mass., 1817. Broadside. MSaE.   42032

Salem Charitable Mechanic Association
  Constitution of the Salem Charitable Mechanic Association, instituted Oct. 1, 1817. Salem, Mass., Pr.
by W. Palfray, Jr., 1817. 23 p. MSaE; MWA. 42033

Salem Gazette
    Carriers' New Year address.   Salem, Mass., 1817.
Broadside. MSaE.   42034

Salem, Mass.   Hamilton Fire Club
    Names and places of residence of the members of
the Hamilton Fire Club.   Salem, Mass., 1817. Broadside. MSaE.   42035

Salem Independent Cadets
    Rules and regulations of the Company of Salem In-
dependent Cadets; instituted December 6, 1786; revised
and adopted by a vote of the Company, Nov. 1816.
Salem, Mass., Pr. by W. Palfray, Jr., for the Company, 1817. 20 p. MSaE.   42036

Sallustius Crispus, Caius
    Belli Catilinarii et Jugurthini Historiae... Novi-
Eboraci: Impensis James Eastburn et Soc.   Typis E. &
E. Hosford, Albania, 1817. 196 p. CtSoP; MB; MMal;
MWA; NSyU; OMC.   42037

[Salvandry, Narcisse Achille, comte de]
    La coalition et La France... Philadelphia, Reimpri-
mé... par Jean F. Hurtel, 1817. MWA.   42038

Sampson, John Philpot Curran
    A valedictory delivered at the Forum on the
eleventh day of April, 1817... New York, Pr. by Van
Winkle, Wiley & Co., 1817. 23 p. DLC; MWA; N;
NUtHi; PHi; PPAmP; PPL; Vi.   42039

Sampson, William
    Memoirs of William Sampson... Ed. 2.   Leesburg,
Va., Samuel B. T. Caldwell, 1817. 432 p. CSmH; MH;
MWA; NPtw.   42040

Sampson [sic] against the Philistines, designing to im-
prove the administration of the laws, to render the at-
tainment of justice easy... By a gentleman of Pennsylvania. Knoxville, Tenn., Pr. by Heiskell & Brown,
1817. 104 p. MB; TKL.   42041

Samson, Hollis
   A masonic discourse delivered at Wilmington, Vt.,
June 24, 1817. Brattleborough, Vt., Pr. by Simeon
Ide, at the American Yeoman office, 1817. 14 p.
MBFM; MWA.   42042

-- A sermon, delivered at Wilmington, Vt., January
16, 1817, at the funeral of Mr. George Reynolds...
Springfield, Mass., Pr. by Thomas Dickman, 1817.
16 p. MWA; RPB.   42043

Sanders, Daniel Clarke, 1768-1850
   A sermon preached before the Ancient and Honourable Artillery Company in Boston, June 2d, 1817, being the 180th anniversary of their election of officers
...Boston, Pr. by John Eliot, for Benjamin Loring,
1817. 25 p. M; MBAt; MBC; MH; MHi; MMedHi;
MMeT; MSaE; MWA; MeB; NCH; NNC; NjR; PHi. 42044

-- A sermon, preached in Medfield, 5th January, 1817
...Dedham, Mass., Pr. by Abel D. Alleyne, 1817.
27 p. CSmH; DLC; ICMe; ICN; M; MB; MBAt; MBC;
MBNEH; MH; MHi; MMedHi; MWA; NNUT; NjR; RPB.
                                                  42045
-- A sermon, preached in Roxbury, before Washington
lodge, 24th June, 1817...Dedham, Mass., Pr. by Abel
D. Alleyne, 1817. 18 p. CSt; MBFM; MWA; PPFM.
                                                  42046
-- A sermon, preached 20th November, 1816, at the
dedication of the new house of worship for the use of
the First church and Christian society in Medway...
Dedham, Mass., Pr. by A.D. Alleyne, 1817. 20 p.
DLC; ICMe; MBC; MMedHi; MSaE; MWA; MeB; MiD-B;
OClWHi; RPB; VtU.   42047

[Sands, Benjamin]
   Metamorphosis; or, a transformation of pictures...
New York, Pr. by J. Rakestraw, for Samuel Wood and
sons, 1817. MWA.   42048

Sands, Robert C.
   An address delivered June 13, 1817, before the
Columbian Peitho-logian Society of Columbia College, on

the occasion of the death of their fellow-member James
S. Watkins, M.D. New-York, Pr. by Abraham Paul,
for the society, 1817. 11 p. NNC.   42049

[--] The bridal of Vaumond; a metrical romance...New-
York, Pr. by Abraham Paul, for James Eastburn and
co., 1817. 186 p. DLC; MWA; NIC; RPB.   42050

Sandwich, Mass. Ecclesiastical Council
    Result of an ecclesiastical council, held May 20,
1817. Boston, Samuel T. Armstrong, 1817. 7 p. ICN;
MBC; MeB; NN.   42051

Sansom, Joseph, 1765, or 6-1826.
    Sketches of lower Canada, historical and descrip-
tive...New-York, Kirk & Mercein, 1817. 301 p. DLC;
MBBC; MLaw; MMedHi.   42052

[Sargent, Charles Lenox]
    A system of general signals for night and day,
whereby merchant vessels may communicate at a distance by means of the common colours of the ship, and
with four lanterns by night, without going out of their
course. Boston, Wells and Lilly, 1817. 64 p. M;
MBAt; MH; PPAmP.   42053

Sass, Henry
    Journey to Rome and Naples, 1817. New York,
1817. 282 p. MWA.   42054

Savage, George
    Remarks on "American Unitarianism"...Boston,
1817. 36 p. MH.   42055

Savannah Gazette. Savannah, Ga., Michael J. Keppel,
Jan. 14, 1817, 1st issue. Tri-weekly newspaper. GHi;
MWA.   42056

Say, Jean Baptiste, 1767-1832
    Catechism of political economy; or, Familiar con-
versations on the manner in which wealth is produced,
distributed, and consumed in society...Philadelphia,
M. Carey & son, 1817. 144 p. DLC; MB; MBL; MWA;

MdBLC; NSyU; NjR.   42057

Say, Thomas
    American entomology... Philadelphia, Pr. by W.
Brown, for Mitchell & Ames, 1817. MWA.   42058

Schaeffer, Frederick Christian
    "The blessed reformation"... New York, Pr. by T.
& W. Mercein, for Kirk & Mercein, 1817. 56 p. MWA;
NN; WHi.   42059

Schaeffer und Maund, calendar auf das jahr 1818... zum
zweyten mal herausgegeben. Baltimore, Schaeffer und
Maund [1817] 42 p. (Cover: Volksfreund und Baltimore
calendar) MWA; PPAmP.   42060

Schaffer, George
    A collection of cotillions and contra dances... Bos-
ton, Elisha Bellamy, 1817. MWA.   42061

Schermerhorn, John Freeman
    A sermon, delivered before the Schoharie Bible so-
ciety... Albany, Pr. by Websters and Skinners, 1817.
20 p. MWA; N.   42062

Schmucker, John George
    The prophetic history of the Christian religion ex-
plained... Baltimore, Schaeffer and Maund, 1817-21.
2 v. DLC; GDC; ICBB; MWA; NbOP; OSW; PPL; PPLT;
PWW; ViRuT.   42063

Schoharie Budget. Schoharie, N.Y., D. Van Veghten,
June, 1817, 1st issue. Weekly newspaper. PPiU.
                                               42064
Schoharie County, N.Y.
    Address of the committee of Schoharie, to the con-
vention of delegates, of the state of New-York, April,
1817. Albany, 1817. 16 p. N.   42065

Schuylkill Navigation Company
    Address of the President and Managers of the
Schuylkill Navigation Company, to the stockholders, and
to the publick in general. Philadelphia, Pr. at the of-

fice of the United States' gazette, 1817. 8 p. DeGE.
                                                    42066

Scituate auxiliary society for the suppression of intemperance, Mass.
    The constitution...Boston, Pr. by John Eliot, 1817.
8 p. MWA; MeB.   42067

Scott, Job
    The baptism of Christ...Wilmington, Ohio, Pr. by
Rice Gaddis for John Hunt, 1817. 138 p. MWA; OClWHi.
                                                    42068

Scott, John
    An inquiry into the effect of baptism...New York,
Pr. by Abraham Paul, for James Eastburn and Co.,
1817. 299 p. CtW; MWA.   42069

Scott, Jonathan M.
    Blue lights, or, The convention. A poem, in four
cantos. New York, Charles N. Baldwin, 1817. 150 p.
CtHT-W; CtHi; CtSoP; DLC; MWA; NIC; RPB.   42070

-- The sorceress, or Salem delivered; a poem. New
York, Charles N. Baldwin, 1817. 120 p. MBAt;
MSaE; MWA; RPB.   42071

Scott, Thomas
    The force of truth...Hartford, Peter B. Gleason &
Co., 1817. 165 p. CtHi; MB; MH; MWA.   42072

-- Remarks on a Refutation of Calvinism, by George
Tomline...Philadelphia, Pr. [by M'Carty & Davis] for
W.W. Woodward, 1817. 2 v. ICBB; MWA; MWiW; NcC;
ODaB; PPPrHi; ScCliP; TWcW.   42073

-- Treatises on various theological subjects, published
at different times, and now collected into volumes...
From the Philadelphia ed. Middletown, Conn., Clark
& Lyman, 1817. 6 v. CtHi. (Vols. 2, 4, 5 were published in 1816)   42074

-- Two essays, on the deity of Jesus Christ; and on
the doctrine of Christ's deity shown to be essential to
Christianity: and some objections to the doctrine briefly

answered... Charleston, S. C., Repr. April, 1817. 44 p.
NN; ScHi.   42075

[Scott, Sir Walter, bart.] 1771-1832
    Harold the Dauntless; a poem, in six cantos. By
the author of "The bridal of Triermain." New-York,
Pr. by Van Winkle, Wiley & Co., for James Eastburn
& Co., 1817. 143 p. DLC; MWA; NIC.   42076

-- ...Rob Roy... from the last rev. ed. containing the
author's final corrections, notes &c. Parker's ed.
Boston, Bazin & Ellsworth, 1817. 2 v. PV.   42077

[--] Tales of my landlord... Philadelphia, Pr. by J.
Maxwell, for M. Thomas, 1817. 2 v. in 1. MWA;
NjR; PPL-R.   42078

[--] -- 2d Amer. ed. New York, Pr. by E. & E.
Hosford, for James Eastburn & Co., 1817. 4 v. in 2.
KyDC; MWA; NjR; PHi; ViAl.   42079

Scott, William
    Lessons in elocution.   From 4th ed.   Concord,
I. Hill, 1817. MWA.   42080

-- -- Leicester, H. Brown, 1817. MWA; RPB.   42081

-- --...Or a selection of pieces in prose and verse.
Worcester, Mass., 1817. MBC.   42082

Scripture instruction; or, Christian doctrine and prac-
tice, set forth in the words of scripture. Abridged
from Bishop Gastrell's Christian institutes. New York,
Pr. by T. and J. Swords, for the use of the New York
Protestant Episcopal Sunday school society, 1817. 64 p.
MPiB; NjR; WHi.   42083

The seaman's friend... Boston, Pr. by John Eliot, for
the Boston society for the religious and moral improvement of seamen, 1817. (Tracts), no. 11. MWA. 42084

Secor, Joshua, comp.
    Treatise on internal navigation... to which is an-

nexed the report of Albert Gallatin on roads and canals.
Ballston Spa, Doubleday, 1817. 279 p. MCM.   42085

Select fables, in prose and verse...New York, Samuel
Wood & sons, 1817. MWA.   42086

Select harmony: 4th part of Christian psalmody. Boston, 1817. MBC.   42087

A selection of hymns, for the use of social religious
meetings and for private devotions. Brooklyn, N. Y.,
A. Spooner, 1817. 207 p. ICN; NBLiHi; TxU.   42088

A selection of hymns, from various authors, designed
as a supplement to the Methodist pocket hymn book...
Ed. 9. New York, Pr. by Abraham Paul, for J. Soule,
1817. 282 p. CtY-D; MWA.   42089

Seneca, Lucius Annaeus
    Seneca's morals by way of abstract. 5th Amer. ed.
New-York, Pr. by J. & J. Harper, for Evert Duyckinck,
1817. CSmH; CtW; MNBedf; MWA; MWiW; N.   42090

Seneca Patriot. Fayette, N. Y., J. G. Hathaway, 1817,
1st issue at Fayette. A newspaper formerly published
at Ovid, N. Y. Brigham, p. 570.   42091

A series of Indostan letters...New York, 1817. 147 p.
ScCC.   42092

Sermon, on the blessedness of charitable giving;
preached before the Prayer-Book and Tract Association, in Trinity church, Boston, Jan. 23, 1817. Boston, R. P. and C. Williams, 1817. 24 p. CtHT;
MiD-B; NN.   42093

A sermon written by a lover of truth, and a friend to
its promotion...Middlebury [Vt.] Pr. by Frederick P.
Allen, 1817. 16 p. (Written by Rev. Mr. Meeker ?)
McCorison list.   42094

[Seton, Elizabeth A.]
    Memoirs of Mrs. S---, written by herself. 1st ed.

Elizabeth-town, N. J., I. A. Kollock, 1817. 88 p.
DGU; NHi.   42095

Sewall, Samuel
    The Christian's triumph; substance of a discourse,
Edgcomb, December 25, 1815, interment of (Mrs.)
Sarah Parsons. Portland, Me., Pr. by Francis Doug-
las, 1817. 8 p. MeBat; RPB.   42096

Shakers
    Memorial of the Shakers of Watervliet to the Leg-
islature, respecting the case of James Chapman. Albany, 1817. N; OCL; WHi.   42097

-- To the Legislature of the state of New-York. Albany, 1817. 8 p. MWA; N.   42098

Shakespeare, William
    The dramatic works of William Shakespeare...New
York, Henry Durell, 1817-18. 10 v. KyU; MWA.
                                                            42099
-- The merry wives of Windsor...New York, David
Longworth, 1817. 75 p. DLC; MH; MWA; NN.   42100

Shallus, Francis
    Chronological tables, for every day in the year.
Compiled from the most authentic documents...Phila-
delphia, Pr. by Merritt, for A. P. Shallus's circulating
library, 1817. 2 v. CtW; DLC; IaGG; MWA; PPAmP;
PPF; PReaAT; RP.   42101

Sharp, Daniel
    Report of the union committee of the Sunday schools
of three Baptist societies in Boston...Boston, Pr. by
Farnham and Badger, 1817. 23 p. MBAt; MWA; MiD-
B; NAuT; OClWHi.   42102

Shaw, Benjamin
    Brief exposition of the principles and details of the
Lancasterian system of education...[Philadelphia, pref.
1817] 20 p. DHEW; MB.   42103

Shaw, Charles, 1782-1828
A topographical and historical description of Boston,
from the first settlement of the town to the present per-
iod; with some account of its environs... Boston, Oliver
Spear, 1817. 311 p. CSt; CtSoP; CtW; DLC; FWpR;
IaU; LNT; MA; MAnP; MB; MBB; MBC; MBeHi;
MDedHi; MDeeP; MH; MHa; MHi; MLy; MNBedf; MS;
MSaE; MWA; MeLewB; MiD-B; MnHi; MnU; NjR;
OClWHi; P; PP; PPA; PPM; RNHi; RPB; T.   42104

Shaw, Elijah
A collection of songs, for pilgrims and strangers
... Auburn, N. Y., Pr. for the compiler, 1817. RPB.
                                                42105

Shecut, John Linnaeus Edward Whitridge
An essay on the prevailing, or yellow-fever, of 1817 together with preliminary observations, and an enquiry into
the causes which produced it... Charleston, S. C., Pr. by
A. E. Miller, 1817. 34 p. DLC; DSG; MB; MBM; NNNAM.
                                                42106

Sheil, Richard
The Apostate; a tragedy... New-York, D. Longworth, 1817. 64 p. MWA; NN; RNR.   42107

Shelton, William
The means of improving Richmond, and the state
of Virginia... Richmond, Pr. by Shepherd and Pollard,
1817. 76 p. Vi.   42108

[Sherwood, Mrs. Mary Martha (Butt)]
The history of little Henry and his bearer... Andover, Mass., Pr. by Flagg & Gould, for Mark Newman, 1817. MSaE; MWA.   42109

[--] -- 2d Amer. ed. Hartford, Hudson and Co.,
1817. 32 p. CtHi; MWA.   42110

[--] -- 2d Amer. ed. Middlebury, Vt., F. Burnap,
1817. 64 p. MWA; Vt; VtMiS; VtU-W.   42111

A short account of the last sickness and death of Maria
Mott, daughter of Richard and Abigail Mott of Mamaro-
neck, in the state of New York. New York, Samuel

Wood, 1817. 28 p. MeU. 42112

A short narrative of the life and death of Mrs. Hannah
Davis... Keene, N. H., Pr. by John Prentiss, 1817.
MWA. 42113

Ein Schon Lied. Ephrata, Pa., 1817. 15 p. MWA;
PHi. 42114

A short history of the Bible and Testament. Hartford,
Pr. by B. & J. Russell, for Cooke & Hale, 1817.
190 p. CtHi; MBeHi; MHolliHi; MWA. 42115

Silliman, Benjamin, 1779-1864
A sketch of the life and character of President
Dwight... New Haven, Pr. by T. G. Woodward, for Malt-
by, Goldsmith & Co., 1817. 47 p. CSansS; CSt; CtY;
CtHT; CtHi; DLC; IC; ICN; ICU; IU; InU; M; MAnP; MB;
MH; MDeeP; MnSM; MWA; MdBE; MiD-B; NN; NjP;
OCHP; PHi; PPPrHi. 42116

-- A sketch of the life and character of Prof. Valentine Mott. New Haven, Pr. by T. G. Woodward, 1817.
47 p. RP. 42117

Simeon, Charles
An appeal to men of wisdom and candor; or, four
discourses preached before the university of Cambridge,
November, 1815. Baltimore, Schaeffer & Maund, 1817.
87 p. MWA; MdBE; MdHi; PPL; PPM; RPB. 42118

Sindbad the sailor.
The history of Sindbad the sailor... Chillicothe,
Ohio, for the publishers, 1817. MWA. 42119

Sir John Denham, and his worthy tenant... New Haven,
Sidney's press, 1817. 30 p. CtHi; CtY; MHA; MWA.
42120

The sisters; and, The rose, or History of Ellen Sel-
wyn... New Haven, Sidney's press, 1817. 46 p. CtY.
42121

Six numbers, (first inserted in the Columbian register
of New-Haven,) on banking, and the shaving operations

of directors; with general remarks, (never before in print.) By "Corrector." New-Haven, Pr. for the author, 1817. 16 p. DLC. 42122

60 dollars reward. Runaway on Thursday morning last, my negro man Charles Oden, about 28 years of age, 5 feet 10 or 11 inches high, grum look, shows the white of his eyes when displeased... Ezra Mantz. Holly Bush tanyard, 2 miles east of New-Market, Frederick county, Md. February 25th, 1817. Fredericktown, Pr. by John P. Thomson, 1817. Broadside.NHi. 42123

A sketch of the life and character of Dr. Poedagogus, the reformer... New York, Pr. by Van Winkle, Wiley & Co., 1817. 71 p. CtSoP; MWA; NBLiHi; PPPrHi. 42124

A sketch of the public life of the Duke of Otranto. Philadelphia, Pr. [by G. Phillips] for M. Carey and son, 1817. 172 p. MB; MWA; P; PHi; PReaAT; PWW; ScU. 42125

Sketches of universal history; compiled from several authors, for the vol. III. 1st ed. New Haven, Pr. by T.G. Woodward, 1817. 259 p. Ct; CtHT-W; DLC; NRHi; NRMA. 42126

Slack, Joshua P.
American orator. Trenton, N.J., D. & E. Fenton, 1817. MWA; RPB. 42127

Smith, Adam, 1723-1790
The theory of moral sentiments; or, An essay towards an analysis of the principles by which men naturally judge concerning the conduct and character... Boston, Wells & Lilly, 1817. 2 v. CBPac; DLC; ICP; KyLoP; KyLx; MA; MAn; MB; MBC; MH; MS; MWA; MiOC; NCH; NWM; NcAS; OAU; OClW; OWoC; PPL-R; PLFM; ViU. 42128

-- -- 1st Amer. ed. Philadelphia, Pr. by J. Maxwell, for Anthony Finley, 1817. 598 p. MNan; MWA; MoSpD; VtU. 42129

Smith, Ebenezer
A vindication of defence for agitation in eight years
cruel contest by the volunteer for the good laws of his
country, as proposed by the author bearing the signa-
ture of Ebenezer Smith of Londonderry, state of Vermont...[Brattleboro] Published by the author [1817?]
46 p. McCorison list.   42130

Smith, Eli, 1787-1839
A funeral sermon on the death of Governor Madison, delivered before the legislature of Kentucky and
the citizens of Frankfort, December 8th, 1816...Frank-
fort, Ky., Pr. by Gerard & Kendall, 1817. 26 p.
CSmH; DLC; MHi; OCHP.   42131

Smith, Elias
Hymns, original and selected, for the use of
Christians by Elias Smith and Abner Jones. Boston,
Pr. by Thomas G. Bangs, 1817. 356 p. MBeHi. 42132

-- Hymns original and selected for the use of Christians...Ed. 8. [Boston] Pr. by Thomas G. Bangs, for
Elias Smith, 1817.   360 p. MWA; RPB.   42133

-- Three sermons on election. Boston, Pr. by T.G.
Bangs, 1817. 126 p. MB.   42134

Smith, Ethan
Episcopacy examined...Concord, N.H., Pr. by
George Hough, 1817. 45 p. MWA; NjR.   42135

Smith, Gamaliel E.
A journal of the proceedings of the convention of
delegates assembled at Brunswick...on the subject of
the separation of Maine from Massachusetts...Kenne-
bunk, Me., Pr. by James K. Remick, 1817. 80 p.
MWA; MeB; Nh.   42136

Smith, Henry More
The mysterious stranger; or memoirs of Henry
More Smith; alias Henry Frederick Moon; alias William
Newman; who is now confined in Simsbury mines, in

Connecticut for the crime of burglary.   New Haven,
Maltby, Goldsmith & Co., 1817. 102 p. NIC-L.   42137

Smith, J. S.
    To the electors of Orange, Person, and Wake.
Fellow-Citizens, I have at last yeilded [sic] to the re-
peated and numerous solicitations of my friends, and
am a candidate to represent you in the Fifteenth Congress of the United States...J. S. Smith, Hillsborough,
N. C., July 4th, 1817. [1817?] Broadsheet. NcD.
                                                    42138

Smith, John
    Two sermons delivered in Salem, N. H. ...Nov. 24,
1816. By John Smith, A. M. after his dismission...
Andover, Mass., Pr. by Flagg and Gould, 1817. 30 p.
Ct; MBC; MSaE; MWA; MeBat; NN; Nh-Hi.   42139

Smith, John Augustine, 1782-1865
    A syllabus of the lectures delivered to the senior
students in the College of William and Mary, on government...Philadelphia, T. Dobson and son, 1817. 118
p. CSmH; DLC; MWA.   42140

Smith, Michael
    Beauties of divine poetry, or appropriate hymns...
Lexington, Ky., Pr. by Worsley & Smith, 1817. RPB.
                                                    42141
-- A narrative of the sufferings in Upper Canada, with
his family, in the late war, and journey to Virginia
and Kentucky of M. Smith, minister of the gospel...
Ed. 3. Lexington, Ky., 1817. 161 p. DLC; OCHP;
WHi.   42142

[Smith, Nathaniel R.]
    Moral miscellanies...By a layman. [1817] Sabin
83667.   42143

Smith, Richard L.
    Oration delivered at Auburn, July 4, 1817...Au-
burn, [N. Y.] Pr. by H. C. Southwick, 1817. 12 p.
NAuHi.   42144

Smith, Samuel Stanhope
    Oratio inauguralis... Trenton, N. J., Edita a D. et E.
Fenton. G. Sherman, excudebat.   32 p. MWA; NjR; RPB.
                                                      42145

-- An oration, upon the death of Gen. George Washington... Ed. 3.   Trenton, N. J., Pr. by G. Sherman,
for D. & E. Fenton, 1817.   MWA.   42146

Smith, Seth
    The prevalence of the Gospel, and the abolition of
war.   A sermon preached in the First Church in Gen-
oa, N. Y., November 14th, 1816,... Auburn [N. Y.] Pr.
by Skinner &Crosby, 1817. 16 p. NN.   42147

Smollett, Tobias George
    The adventures of Ferdinand Count Fathom... New
York, William B. Gilley, 1817.   2 v. MWA; PU. 42148

Smyth, Alexander
    Postcript to an Address to the Freeholders of
Washington, Wythe, Russell, Lee, Scott, Grayson and
Tazewell... Richmond, February 18th, 1817.   Broadside.
NcD.   42149

Snell, Thomas, 1774-1862
    A sermon preached before His Excellency John
Brook, esq. governor... the honorable Council, and the
two houses comprising the legislature of the commonwealth of Massachusetts, May 28, 1817; being the anniversary election.   Boston, Russell & Cutler, 1817.
26 p.   CBPac; CSmH; DLC; ICMe; ICU; M; MA; MBAt;
MH-AH; MNBedf; MNe; MSaE; MWA; MiD-B; NN;
OCHP; PHi; RPB; TxHR.   42150

Snow, Simeon
    Free communion, of all Christians, at the Lord's
table.   Illustrated, and defended, in a discourse...
Keene, N. H., Pr. by John Prentiss, 1817. 48 p.
CSmH; MWA; Nh-Hi.   42151

Snowden, Richard
    The history of North and South America, from its

discovery to the death of General Washington... Philadelphia, Pr. by William Greer, for Benjamin Warner,
1817. 2 v. in 1. DLC; MiU; OC.   42152

Society for the support of the gospel among the poor
in the city of New York.
        Fourth report... New York, Pr. by Daniel Fanshaw,
1817. 16 p. MMeT; MWA.   42153

Society of the Protestant Episcopal church for the advancement of Christianity in Pennsylvania.
        Fifth annual report... Philadelphia, Pr. by William
Fry, 1817. MWA.   42154

Society of the state of Delaware for the promotion of
American manufactures.
        Constitution of the Society of the state of Delaware
for the promotion of American manufactures. [Wilming-
ton? 1817] 4 p. DeGE.   42155

-- ...Resolutions... offered by Mr. Isaac Briggs. [Wil-
mington, James Wilson, 1817?] 4 p. N.   42156

-- To the Honorable the Senate and House of Representatives of the United States, in Congress assembled.
The memorial and petition of the citizens of the state
of Delaware and its vicinity, associated under the name
of the Society for the Promotion of American Manufactures. [Wilmington? Del., 1817?] 8 p. DeGE. 42157

Solemnization of the third centurial jubilee... commenced
by Dr. Martin Luther on the 31st October, 1517... New
York, Pr. by A. Ming, 1817. 41 p. MWA; NHi; NjR.
                                                        42158

Some account of Maria Hughes... [Philadelphia] Wm.
Bradford, Agent, 1817. MWA.   42159

...Some account of the happy death of Peter V. -
[Philadelphia, Pr. by Lydia R. Bailey, 1817] (This is
no. 21 of the Tracts of the Philadelphia female tract society) MWA.   42160

Some account of the Pennsylvania hospital: from its

first rise to the beginning of the fifth month, called
May 1754. Philadelphia, Pr. at the office of the
United States' Gazette, 1817. 145 p. ICU; MB; MiD-B;
NNT-C; NbU-M; RHi; WHi.   42161

Somerville Sunday School Society, New Jersey.
Report...for 1817. 4 p. NjR.   42162

Something curious. [Letter dated at Annapolis, Dec.
12, 1817; and speech of Mr. .....in the Senate chamber, in caucas, delivered Tuesday morning, 9th Dec.
1817] 24 p. MdHi.   42163

Something wonderfull!! [New Haven, 1817] Broadside.
(Federalist campaign literature) CtY.   42164

The songs of Zion; or, The Christian's new hymn book
for the use of the Methodists. Baltimore, Pr. by J.
Robinson, for Joseph Cushing, 1817. DLC; ODaB.
                                                    42165
The songster's miscellany: being a choice selection of
the most approved English, Irish, Scotch, and American songs...Philadelphia, Pub. for the subscribers,
1817. 72 p. DLC; MWA; RPB.   42166

The songster's new pocket companion, embracing the
most popular new songs singing at the different theatres
in the United States. Boston, T. Swan, 1817. 240
plates. (Plates engraved by M. Butler) MHi; RPB.
                                                    42167
... The sorrows of Yamba...[Philadelphia, Pr. by
Lydia R. Bailey, 1817] (This is no. 24 of the Tracts
of the Philadelphia female tract society) MWA. 42168

The soundness of the policy of protecting domestic
manufactures; fully established by Alexander Hamilton,
in his report to Congress on the subject, and by Thomas Jefferson, in his letter to Benjamin Austin. Philadelphia, Pr. by J.R.A. Skerrett, 1817. 24 p. DeGE;
MWA.   42169

-- ... To which are added, Extracts from the address
of the American Society for Promoting Domestic Manu-

factures, established in New York... Philadelphia, Pr. by J.R.A. Skerrett, for the Philadelphia Society for the Promotion of American Manufactures, 1817. 36 p. DeGE; MWA. 42170

South Carolina (State)
Acts and resolutions of the General Assembly of the state of South-Carolina in Dec., 1816. Columbia, Pr. by D. & J.J. Faust, 1817. 145 p. DLC. 42171

-- Acts and resolutions of the General Assembly of the state of South Carolina, passed in March, 1817. Columbia, S.C., Pr. by D. & J.J. Faust, 1817. 16 p. DLC; Nb; Nj; Sc. 42172

-- A collection of the militia laws of the United States and South Carolina, that are of force, with such parts of the Constitution thereof as relate to the militia; also the patrol laws of South Carolina. By John B. Miller ... Columbia, Pr. by D. & J.J. Faust, 1817. 82 p. DNA; ScU. 42173

-- The opinion of the Hon. Judge Cheves, on the act to amend the 3d section of the 10th article of the Constitution... Columbia, S.C., Cline & Hines, 1817. 16 p. CSmH; MiD-B; NN. 42174

-- The opinions of the Hon. Judges Colcock, Nott, Bay and Frimke, on the Act to amend the third section of the tenth article of the constitution, and on the constitutionality of the act entitled, "An act to provide a more expeditious mode of disposing of the cases on the dockets of the Constitutional court in Charleston and Columbia." Columbia [S.C.] Pr. by D. & J.J. Faust, 1817. 12 p. CSmH; MBS; MiD-B. 42175

-- Reports of cases argued and determined in the Court of chancery of the state of South-Carolina, from the revolution to [June, 1817]---By Henry William Desaussure... Columbia, S.C., Pr. by Cline & Hines, 1817- 19. 4 v. DLC; MH-L; LNL-L; NN. 42176

Southbridge, Mass. --Baptist Church.
The confession of faith... Worcester, Mass., Pr.
by William Manning, [1817?] MWA. 42177

Southwark hose company, Philadelphia.
Articles and by laws... Philadelphia, 1817. MWA.
42178
[Spafford, Horatio Gates]
Hints to emigrants, on the choice of lands; particularly addressed to farmers in the north-eastern
states. Albany, Pr. by J. Buel, for the author, 1817.
8 p. MB; MWA. 42179

[--] The mother-in-law... Boston, A. Bowen, and Cummings and Hilliard, 1817. MWA. 42180

Spalding, Joshua
Baptism by sprinkling... Bennington, Vt., Pr. by
Darius Clark, 1817. 16 p. MWA; NNUT. 42181

Spalding, Lyman
Reflections on fever and particularly on the in-
flammatory character of fever. New York, C.S. Van
Winkle, 1817. 43 p. MWA; NNNAM. 42182

The spelling book; or, introduction to reading: compiled at the request of the London Sunday School Union;
for the use of Sunday schools in general and adopted by
the New York Protestant Episcopal Sunday School Society. New York, Pr. by T. & J. Swords, 1817. MWA.
42183
Spirit of the Forum, and Hudson remarker. Conducted
by an association of gentlemen. No. 1. April 16, 1817.
Hudson, N.Y., 1817. 16 p. N. 42184

Spirit of the Times. Carlisle, Pa., John M'Farland,
Nov. 10, 1817, 1st issue. Weekly newspaper. MWA.
42185
-- Shippensburg, Pa., John M'Farland, July 4, 1817,
1st issue. Weekly newspaper. MWA. 42186

-- Wellsburgh, Va., 1817. Newspaper. Brigham, p.
1175. 42187

Spirit of Uion. Richmond, Va., Burling & Gray, 1817.
Newspaper. Brigham, p. 1142.   42188

The spiritual Combat. Philadelphia: Pr. by Lydia R.
Baily, for Bernard Dornin, at the Catholic bookstore,
cor. of Third and Walnut Sts, 1817. 281 p. NcWsS.
    42189
Spooner, Cyrus
    A convenient manual for the practising physician
and surgeon... Zanesville, O., Pr. at the Express office, 1817. 133 p. OClWHi.   42190

Spring, Gardiner, 1785-1873
    The doctrine of election... preached... December,
1816... Cooperstown, N.Y., Pr. by H. & E. Phinney,
1817. NN.   42191

-- -- New York, Pr. by E.B. Gould, 1817. 43 p.
CtHC; ICT; MWA; MiD-B; NjR; PPPrHi.   42192

-- An oration, pronounced on the evening of the 5th
February, before the alumni of Yale college, resident
in the city of New-York, in commemoration of their
late president, Timothy Dwight, D.D., L.L.D...New-
York, Pr. by J. Seymour, for Dodge & Sayre, 1817.
35 p. CtHC; DLC; ICP; MWA; N; NjR; OCHP; PHi.
    42193
Spring, Samuel
    The united agency of God and man in salvation...
Newburyport, Mass., Pr. by E.W. Allen, 1817. 20 p.
MA; MWA; NjP; NjR.   42194

Springer, Moses, Jr.
    Songs of Zion: being a collection of hymns, for the
use of the pious of all denominations... Hallowell, Me.,
Pr. by E. Goodale, 1817. 160 p. Sabin 89839.   42195

Spurzheim, Johann Gaspar, 1776-1832
    Examination of the objections made in Britain a-
gainst the doctrines of Gall and Spurzheim... Article of
the Foreign Quarterly review, by Rich. Chenevix...
with notes by J.G. Spurzheim... 1st Amer. ed., with
improvements by Dr. Spurzheim. Boston, Marsha,

Capen and Lyon, 1817. 112 p. PPPH.   42196

Stafford, Ward
    New missionary field...Ed. 2.   New York, Pr. by
Clayton and Kingsland, 1817. 55 p.   MWA; N; NBuG;
NjR.   42197

-- -- New York, Pr. by J. Seymour, 1817. MWA.
                                                       42198
-- Important to seamen.   Extracts from a report en-
titled New missionary field. [New York, 1817]   8 p.
N.   42199

Stafford's almanack for 1818.   By Hosea Stafford. New
Haven, Steele & Gray [1817]   [24] p. CtY; MWA. 42200

Stanford, John
    An address delivered on request of the managers
to the children of the Union Sunday Schools, convened
in the City Hotel assembly room, on the first anniversary of the society, February, 1817. New York, 1817.
4 p.   MMeT; NjR.   42201

-- The Christian course.   A sermon on the death of
Elijah Hunter, Esq. who departed this life the 22d of
December, 1815...New York, Pr. by J. Gray, 1817.
26 p.   MWA; NRCR.   42202

-- Discourse on the duty and advantages of improving
our baptism.   New York, 1817.   24 p. OCHP.   42203

-- Divine benevolence to the poor; a discourse delivered before the...mayor and corporation of the city
of New York, April 22, 1816, on the opening the chapel in the new alms-house.   New York, Pr. by T. & J.
Swords, 1817.   31 p.   NcU.   42204

Staniford, Daniel, 1766-1820
    The art of reading...Ed. 12.   Boston, West &
Richardson, 1817.   240 p. CSt; CtHT-W; DLC; ICP;
MDeeP; MFiHi; MHi; MPri; MWA; MWHi; NhD; NjN;
NjR; RPB.   42205

Stansbury, Arthur Joseph
The motives, aims and means of a gospel minister
...A sermon preached at Stillwater, on the ordination
of the Rev. Mark Tucker, October 8th, 1817. Albany,
Webster and Skinner, 1817. 17 p. MB; MWA; MWiW;
NcWfc.   42206

The Star. A collection of songs, sentimental, humorous, and patriotic. Pittsburgh, Pa., Butler & Lambdin, 1817. 170 p. CSt; RPB.   42207

Star of Freedom. Newtown, Pa., Asher Miner, May
21, 1817, 1st issue. Weekly newspaper. MWA. 42208

The Star Spangled Banner, being a collection of the
best naval, martial, patriotic songs...chiefly written
during, and relation to the late war...Ed. 2. Wilmington, Del., J. Wilson, 1817. 143 p. DeHi; DeWI; MWA;
MiU-C; NBuG.   42209

State convention...De Witt Clinton for the office of
Governor...[1817] Broadside. NN.   42210

State papers and public documents of the U.S. from the
accession of George Washington to the presidency, exhibiting a complete view of our foreign relations since
that time. Ed. 2. Boston, T.B. Wait and sons, 1817.
10 v. CL; CLSU; CtHT-W; DLC; GS; IaDa; IaB;
KyLxT; MA; MB; MCon; MFi; MHi; MNe; MS; MWA;
MWiW; MdU; MiMus; Ms; NBuG; NNCoCi; NjP; OAU;
OCl; OClW; OCLaw; PPB; RPB; ViAl; ViU; WHi; WaS.
                                                           42211

Statement of faith delivered to Saints- -- Prefixed--
Preamble to the Organization of Churches and Societies. Keene, N.H. [1817] 11 p. MWA.   42212

Statements...from the Pennsylvania, Philadelphia, and
Farmers and Mechanics' Banks. Harrisburg, Pa.,
1817. PPL.   42213

Stearns, Samuel
A discourse delivered at Bedford, July 8, 1817, at
the dedication of the meeting-house...Concord, Mass.,

Pr. by J. T. Peters, 1817. 23 p. CSmH; MWA; MiD-B;
RPB.   42214

Stearns, Silas, 1784-
    A discourse delivered December 31, 1816 at the
opening of the new meetinghouse of the Baptist church
and society in Bath. Portland, Me., 1817. 11 p.
NRAB.   42215

Steel, John Honeywood
    An analysis of the mineral waters of Saratoga and
Ballston. Albany, E. & E. Hosford, 1817. 94 p.
DNLM; MWA; MWiW; NNNAM; OC.   42216

[Stevens, George Alexander]
    A lecture on heads... Philadelphia, Wm. Charles,
1817. MWA.   42217

Stevens, Robert
    An essay on average, & on other subjects con-
nected with the contract of marine insurance... 1st A-
merican, from 2d London ed. Philadelphia, M. Carey,
1817. 304 p. Ct; CtW; DLC; LNL-L; MH; MSaP;
MWA; MdBB; MsU; NNC-L; NNIA; PHi; PPL-R; PU-L;
RNR; ScCC.   42218

Stevens' improved Connecticut calendar or almanack...
New Haven, Steele & Gray, 1817. 36 p. MWA. 42219

Steuben Patriot. Bath, N. Y., April 22, 1817. First
leaf only. (First [or one of the first] of the newspapers of this town in NYPL) NN.   42220

Steward, Joseph
    A sermon delivered at the First Presbyterian
church in Hartford, on the state Thanksgiving, November 28, 1816... Hartford, Pr. by George Goodwin &
sons... 1817. 15 p. CtHi; IEN; IEG; MBC; MWA; O;
PPPrHi; WHi.   42221

Stewart, Dugald
    Dissertation first; exhibiting a general view of the
progress of metaphysical, ethical, and political phi-

losophy, since the revival of letters in Europe. Boston, Wells & Lilly, 1817. 260 p. DLC; GOgU; MB; MH-AH; MNan; MWA; MWiW; MiU; MtBu; NHi; NhD; NjR; PPL-R; PU; ScU; WHi; WaPS.   42222

Stoddard's diary; or, Columbian almanac...1818... Calculated by Andrew Beers. Hudson, N.Y., A. Stoddard [1817] [36] p. DLC; MWA; NHi; NN; PHi. 42223

Stone, Henry
    A Masonic address, delivered at Rensselaerville, on the anniversary of St. John the Baptist, June 24, 1817...Albany, Pr. by E. & E. Hosford, 1817. 16 p. N.   42224

Stone, Micah
    An address, delivered before the Moral society in Brookfield, April 16, 1817...Brookfield, Mass., Pr. by E. Merriam & Co., 1817. MWA.   42225

Storr, Gottlob Christian
    An essay on the historical sense of the New Testament...Boston, Pr. by Wells and Lilly, 1817. 92 p. CBPSR; CtY-D; ICP; InCW; MB; MBC; MH-AH; MWA; MWiW; NCH; NNG; RPB; WHi.   42226

A striking instance of the influence of Divine grace on the mind. Philadelphia, Pr. [by J.R.A. Skerrett] for Benjamin & Thomas Kite, 1817. 12 p. MNBedf; MWA; NcGu; NbU.   42227

Strong, Jonathan
    Sermon, Oct. 27th, 1815, at the dedication of the Meeting-House in the Third Society Abington. Boston, 1817. 24 p. Tuttle S 3363.   42228

Styles, John
    Memoirs and remains of the late Rev. Charles Buck...1st Amer. ed. Philadelphia, Pr. by Wm. Fry, for Anthony Finley, 1817. 366 p. Ct; CtW; IaLyYMA; MH-AH; MWA; NBLiHi; NNUT; Nh-Hi; OClWHi; PWW; RPA; ScCoT; ViRUT; VtU.   42229

The substance of a pamphlet entitled A solemn review
of the custom of war. Showing that war is the effect
of a popular delusion and proposing a remedy.   Hartford, etc. 1817. 24 p. MH-AH; ViRUT.   42230

A succinct account of the disturbance which occurred
at the Charleston Theatre, the evening of the 12th of
March, 1817, with the address to the public Mr. Holman, the manager, and Mr. Caldwell... Charleston, S. C.
A. E. Miller, 1817. 39 p. NN; PU.   42231

Sully, Maximilien de Béthune, duc de, 1559-1641
    The memoirs of the Duke of Sully, prime-minister
to Henry the Great.   Translated from the French by
Charlotte Lennox.   A new ed., rev. and cor. ...
Philadelphia, Pr. by J. Maxwell, for Edward Earle,
1817. 5 v. CSto; CoCsUP; CtW; DLC; FIU; GEU; GU;
KyLo; MB; MBarn; MH; MLy; MSa; MSaE; MWA; MWH;
MdBP; Mi; MiD-B; MsWJ; NNMer; NT; NcAS; NcU;
NcWsS; Nj; OAU; OCU; P; PHi; PPL-R; PPP; RPB;
ScSoh; TMeC; TNP; ViU; WvU.   42232

Summary, or general argument of the last manifesto of
the last servant of Jesus Christ... Wilmington, Del.,
Pr. by R. Porter, 1817. (Added title in French) MWA.
                                                42233
Sunaar Kabischwar
    Le trone enchante conte Indian traduit de Persan.
Par M. Le Baron Lescallier... New York, De l'im-
primerie de J. Desnoues, 1817. 2 v. ArSsJ; DLC;
MWA; NR.   42234

No. I. Sunday School rewards- present for Sunday
school children- Signed W.   Boston, Ezra Lincoln,
1817. MWA.   42235

Sutcliffe, Joseph, 1762-1856
    An introduction to Christianity: designed to pre-
serve young people from irreligion and vice... 2d Amer.
from the 2d (imp.) English ed.   New-York, Pr. by J.C.
Totten, for J. Soule and T. Mason, for the Methodist
Episcopal church in the United States, 1817. 239 p.
CtW; DLC; MWA; MnSH.   42236

Swan, James
    An address to the Senate and House of Representatives of the United States, on the question for an enquiry into the state of agriculture, manufactures and commerce. Boston, Pr. by John Eliot, 1817. 24 p.
MHi.   42237

Swedenborg, Emanuel, 1688-1772
    A compendium of the chief doctrines of the true Christian religion... Philadelphia, Pr. by Lydia R. Bailey, for William Schlatter, 1817. CSmH.   42238

-- Dissertations on the Regenerate life in harmony with the theological views of Baron Swedenborg the undoubted messenger of our Lords second advent to which is prefixed a short account of the life of Baron Swedenborg. Philadelphia, Pr. by Anderson & Meehan, for a member of the New Jerusalem Church, 1817. 102 p.
OUrC.   42239

-- The doctrine of the New Jerusalem concerning the Lord... Philadelphia, Lydia R. Bailey, 1817. 159 p.
P; PHi.   42240

-- "A treatise on the divine Trinity, together with an account of wonderful things seen in the spiritual world." Philadelphia, Pr. by Lydia R. Bailey, for Wm. Schlatter, 1817. 55 p. DeGE; ICBB; MBNC; OClWHi; PHi;
PPL-R.   42241

Swett, Samuel
    An abstract of the Baron de Rogniat's considerations on the art of war. Boston, Cummings and Hilliard, 1817. 24 p. DLC; MBNEH; MH; MSbra; MSo;
MWA; MdAN.   42242

Swinton, William
    New language lessons. New York, Harper Bros.,
1817. MWbor.   42243

Swords' pocket almanack for 1818. New York, T. & J. Swords [1817] 92 p. DLC; MWA; NHi; NNG; NNS;
PHi; PU.   42244

A system of artillery discipline...Boston, Munroe and
Francis, 1817. 60 p. MWA; MeHi.   42245

T

A table for receiving and paying gold coins of Great
Britain. Boston, 1817. MB.   42246

Tacitus, Cornelius
    Opera ex recensione Io. Augusti Ernesti denuo
curavit J.J. Oberlinus. Bostoniae, Wells et Lilly,
1817. 3 v. CU; CtW; GHi; ICU; IEG; IP; MA; MB;
MBC; MBev; MNBedf; MNF; MSa; MWiW; MoS; NhNa;
NjP; NjR; OClW; OMC; PPDrop; PPL; PU; PV; ScCC;
TNV; TxU; VtMiM.   42247

Tappan, Benjamin, 1773-1857
    A review of the question whether the common law
of England, respecting crimes and punishments, is in
force in the state of Ohio, in a letter addressed by a
citizen to a member of the legislature. Pittsburgh,
Pa., Butler & Lambdin, 1817. 44 p. OClWHi. 42248

[Taylor, Isaac] imputed author.
    Gethsemane: or, Thoughts on the sufferings of
Christ...1st Amer., from 2d enl. London ed. Philadelphia, A. Finley, 1817. 208 p. ICP.   42249

Taylor, John, 1750-1824
    Arator; being a series of agricultural essays,
practical and political: in sixty-one numbers...3d ed.,
rev. and enl. Baltimore, Pr. by J. Robinson, for J.
M. Carter, 1817. 220 p. CSmH; DA; DLC; ICU; IaAS;
MB; MH; MWA; MdBE; MdHi; NIC; NcU; NcWfC; OCY;
PPL; PU; TxU; ViU.   42250

Taylor, John Louis
    A charge delivered to the grand jury of Edgecombe
Superior Court, at the spring term of 1817, exhibiting
a view of the criminal law of North Carolina. Raleigh,
N.C., J. Gales, 1817. 47 p. NcAS; NcU.   42251

Taylor, Joseph
   Tales of the Robin, and other small birds selected
from the British poets, for the instruction and amusement of young people...Philadelphia, M'Carty and Davis
for Wm. Charles, 1817. 140 p. MWA; MnU; PP.
                                                        42252
The teachers assistant; or, A system of practical
arithmetic; wherein the several rules of that useful
science...Ed. 3, with improvements...Philadelphia,
stereotyped by B. & J. Collins, for Benjamin Warner,
1817. 198 p. NjR.   42253

The Telegraph. Newtown Village, N.Y., W. Murphy.
September 9, 1817. (Name of town later changed to
Elmira. First [or one of the first] of the newspapers
of this town in NYPL)   NN.   42254

Templi Carmina, Songs of the temple, or Bridgewater
collection of sacred music. Ed. 5, imp. and enl.
Boston, West & Richardson, 1817. 325 p. ICN;
MStouHi.   42255

Tennessee (State)
   Acts passed at the 1st session of the 12th General
Assembly of the state of Tennessee...Sept., 1817...
Knoxville, Pr. by George Wilson, 1817. 238 p. C;
DLC; IU; Ky; L; MH-L; MWA; MdBB; NNB; RPL; T;
TMC; WaU.   42256

-- Journal of the Hosue[!] of Representatives at the
1st session of the 12th General Assembly in Knoxville,
Pr. by George Wilson, 1817. 329 p. (Last p. wrongly
numbered 229.)   MWA; NN; T; TU.   42257

-- Journal of the Senate at the First session of the
12th General Assembly...Knoxville, Pr. by George Wilson, 1817. 220 p. CtY-L; DLC; MWA; NN; T; TU.
                                                        42258
Testis, pseud.
   Expose and review of the vindication. New York,
15th December, 1817. 15 p. DLC; NN.   42259

Thacher, James
    American modern practice... Boston, Pr. by C.
Norris & Co., for Ezra Read, 1817. 744 p.   DLC;
DNLM; ICJ; MB; MBC; MBU-M; MNF; MWA; MdBM;
MiDW-M; NBMS; NBuG; NNNAM; Nh; NhD; OClM; RPM;
TNV.   42260

-- The American new dispensary, containing the gen-
eral principles of pharmaceutic chemistry... Ed. 3.
Boston, Thomas B. Wait & sons, 1817. 724 p. DNLM;
InU-M; MB; MH-M; MnU; NBMS; NBuU-M; NNNAM;
PPC; RPM; ScCMu; TxU.   42261

[Thacher, Samuel Cooper]
    The unity of God... Boston, Repr. by Wells and
Lilly [1817] 24 p. CBPac; MH; MLy; MWA; NjR.
                                               42262
[--] -- 2d Amer. ed. Boston, Repr. by Wells and
Lilly [1817?] MWA.   42263

[--] -- 2d Amer. ed. Worcester, Mass., Repr. by
William Manning, 1817. 24 p. CSt; DLC; ICMe; M;
MB; MBAt; MBrof; MDeeP; MH; MWA; MWHi; MeBat;
NN; NjR; OClWHi; PMA; ScHi.   42264

Thayer, Mrs. Caroline Matilda (Warren)
    Religion recommended to youth... New York, Pr.
by Abraham Paul, for Thomas Bakewell, 1817. 139 p.
MWA;TxU.   42265

Thayer, Elihu
    A summary of Christian doctrines and duties...
Ed. 2, rev., enl. Concord, N.H., Pr. by George
Hough, 1817. MWA.   42266

Thayer, Nathaniel, 1769-1840
    A sermon, delivered at Lancaster, Dec. 29, 1816,
the last Lord's day in which there was religious worship in the old meeting-house... Worcester [Mass.] Pr.
by William Manning, 1817. 39 p. CSmH; CSt; DLC;
ICMe; MB; MBAt; MBC; MH; MSaE; MSo; MWA; MWHi;
MiU-C; NN; Nh; RPB.   42267

-- A sermon, delivered to the Christian Society in
Lancaster, January 1, 1817 at the dedication of their
new house for publick worship...Worcester, Mass.,
Pr. by William Manning, 1817. 24 p. DLC; MBAt;
MBC; MSo; MWA; MiU-C; RPB; WHi.   42268

Thayer, William A.
    A compendium of geography... Portland, Me.,
Mussey & Whitman, 1817. 88 p. DLC; MWA; NN.
                                            42269
Thing, Samuel
    A letter, addressed to the Rev. Enoch Fond...
Worcester, Mass., Pr. by William Manning, 1817. 27
p. ICMe; MBNEH; MH-AH; MWA; MWHi; NN; RPB.
                                            42270
Thomas, Joseph, b. 1791
    The life of the pilgrim Joseph Thomas, containing
an accurate account of his trials, travels and gospel
labours, up to the present date. Winchester, Va., Pr.
by J. Foster, 1817. 372 p. CSmH; DLC; ICBB; MWA;
PPPrHi.   42271

-- The Pilgrim's hymn book offered as a companion to
all Zion travelers. Ed. 2. Winchester, Va., Pr. by
J. Foster, 1817. 216 p. IEG; MWA.   42272

Thomas, Robert, 1753-1835
    The modern practice of physic, exhibiting the
character, causes, symptoms, prognostics, morbid ap-
pearances, and improved method of treating the diseases of all climates...New York, Collins & Co., 1817.
915 p. MWA; NIC; NNNAM; Nh; RPB; WvH.   42273

-- -- Abridged from the 5th and last London ed.
Philadelphia, T. Dobson and son, 1817. 515 p. DLC;
IU-M; KyLxT; MWA; MdBJ; NbU-M; NcD; OCGHM;
OClM; PPC; PPHa; RPM.   42274

Thomond, Charles F.
    Pious lectures. Translated from La Doctrine
chretienne by J. Appleton. Philadelphia, B. Dornin,
1817. MdW.   42275

Thompson, Benjamin
    Stranger; a drama.   New York, D. Longworth,
1817. MWA.   42276

Thompson, Otis
    A sermon, preached at the funeral of Mrs. Free-
love King... Providence, Pr. by Miller & Hutchens,
1817. MWA.   42277

-- A sermon, preached at the ordination of the Reverend Stetson Raymond... Providence, Pr. by Miller &
Hutchens, 1817. MWA.   42278

Thomson, James
    Castle of indolence. New York, Gilley, 1817. MB.
                                               42279
-- The seasons, to which is prefixed a life of the author by Samuel Johnson. Boston, Pr. by T. G. Bangs,
for Charles Ewer, 1817. 264 p. CtHC; ICMe; MAm;
PU.   42280

-- -- Boston, Pr. by T. G. Bangs, for T. Bedlington,
1817. 264 p. CtW; MWA; NN; NNC; PU.   42281

-- -- New York, Pr. [by Daniel Fanshaw] for W. B.
Gilley, 1817. 287 p. MWA; NcAS; NcGr; TSewU.42282

Thomson, John
    Lectures on inflammation... Philadelphia, M. Carey
and son, 1817. 509 p. DNLM; GU-M; InI; IU-M; MB;
MH-M; MWA; MdBM; MoSW-M; NBuU-M; NBMS;
NNNAM; NcU; NhD; OC; OMC; PPC ; PPAN.   42283

Thomson, John Lewis
    Historical sketches of the late war between the U-
nited States and Great Britain; blended with anecdotes
illustrative of the individual bravery of the American
sailors, soldiers, and citizens. Ed 4, greatly enl. and
improved. Philadelphia, Thomas DeSilver, 1817. 367 p.
GS; MB; MLanc; MWA; MiD-B; MiMus; MiU; MnDu;
NWatt; NcD; NcU; TCh; ViU.   42284

-- -- Ed. 4. Richmond, Va., P. Cottom, [1817?]

367 p. DLC; ViU.   42285

Thomson, Samuel
    Address to the people of the United States...[Bos-
ton, 1817] MWA.   42286

Thorburn, Grant, 1773-1863
    Beta cicla, or Mangel Wurzel, its properties and
virtues, with directions for its culture. New York,
the author, 1817. 22 p. MH; N.   42287

-- The gentleman & gardener's kalendar, for the Mid-
dle states of North America...Ed. 3, cor. & imp.
New-York, Pr. by E. B. Gould, 1817. 117 p. DLC; N;
NN.   42288

Thorp, Thomas
    Animadversions upon a sermon, preached by the
Rev. Bennet Tyler...New Haven, Pr. by T. G. Wood-
ward, 1817. 32 p. Ct; CtHi; CtY; MB; MBC; MH;
MWA; MWiW; NNMHi; NNUT.   42289

Thoughts on capital punishment. From the Christ dis-
ciple. [Boston] 1817. MB; NN.   42290

Thoughts of the importance of religion. Philadelphia,
Pr. by J. R. A. Skerrett, for Benj. & Thomas Kite,
1817. 12 p. InRchE; MWA; NcGu; PSC-Hi.   42291

The Times. Hartford, Conn., F. D. Bolles & Co.,
Jan. 1, 1817, 1st issue. Weekly newspaper. Ct; DLC.
                                              42292
To Ephraim Farmer's creditors and correspondents.
[Salem, Mass., 1817] 12 p. MWA.   42293

To Federalists attached to Republican government in
the state of New-York. [1817] 7 p. MWA; N; WHi.
                                              42294
To Isaac Blackford, esquire. Sir, We certainly ex-
pected something from you in reply to our address, for
criminals at the bar generally plead not guilty...Inde-
pendent Freemen, August 2, 1817. In.   42295

To the afflicted. [New York] Pr. by D. Fanshaw, for
the New York Religious Tract Society, 1817. 8 p.
IaHi.   42296

To the electors of the Congressional district composed
of the counties of Washington, Wythe, Grayson, Tazewell, Russell, Scott and Lee...[1817?] Broadside.
NcD.   42297

To the electors of the state of Pennsylvania. Philadelphia, 1817. 11 p. PHi.   42298

To the freemen of the state of Rhode-Island...[1817]
MWA.   42299

To the Honorable the Senate and House of Representatives of the United States in Congress assembled: the
memorial and petition of...manufacturers of woollen
articles in the states of New Jersey, Pennsylvania and
Delaware...[1817?] 6 p. DeGE.   42300

To the patrons of the arts. Elegant museum at the
Washington Hall...over the Columbian Hall, Court-
Street. ...Forty wax figures as large as life...Salem,
Mass., 1817. Broadside. MSaE.   42301

To the people of Connecticut. [Hartford, G. Goodwin
& sons, 1817] MWA.   42302

To the President of the United States. Sir, The under-
signed inhabitants of Mississippi Territory, residing
west of Pearl river, beg leave...[Natchez, 1817]
Broadside. DNA.   42303

To the speakers and members of both houses of the
Virginia legislature. The petition of sundry inhabitants
of the.....respectfully shew, that all the country above
the falls contiguous to James River, is greatly interested in the establishment of a canal on the south side
...[Petersburg? 1817?] Broadside. Vi.   42304

Tobin, John, 1770-1804
     The faro table; or, The guardians. A comedy...

New-York, David Longworth, 1817. 58 p. DLC; MWA; N; NlC; RNR. 42305

Tolland County (Conn.) Association
Reply to Mr. Abbot's statement of proceedings in the First Society in Coventry, Conn. Hartford, 1817. 48 p. MHi. 42306

[Tooke, Andrew]
Tooke's pantheon of the heathen Gods... Baltimore, Pr. by B. Edes, for Coale and Maxwell, 1817. 306 p. MH; MWA; NcD; OSW; PPL. 42307

Toplady, Augustus Montague
A course of family prayer for each day in the week. Boston, Pr. by Thomas G. Bangs, 1817. 36 p. CBPSR; MB; MHi; MWA; RPB. 42308

-- Memoirs of the Rev. Augustus Montague Toplady, A. B., late Vicar of Broad-Hembury, Devonshire, England. Boston, Pr. by Thomas G. Bangs, 1817. 88 p. MBC; MH; MPiB; MWA; MiD-B; WHi. 42309

Torrey, Jesse, jr.
The intellectual torch; developing an original, economical and expeditious plan for the universal dissemination of knowledge and virtue; by means of free public libraries. Ballston Spa, N. Y., Pr. by J. Comstock, for the author, 1817. 36 p. CSmH; DLC; MH; MWA; N; WHi. 42310

Torrey, Jesse, fl. 1787-1834
A portraiture of domestic slavery, in the United States: with reflections on the practicability of restoring the moral rights of the slave, without impairing the legal privileges of the possessor; and a project of a colonial asylum for free persons of colour... Philadelphia, Pr. by John Bioren, for the author, 1817. 94 p. CSmH; CtSoP; DLC; GAU; IHi; IaU; In; InRchE; KU; MA; MB; MBAt; MBC; MBL; MH; MLaw; MLow; MNF; MWA; MWiW; MdBJ; MeBat; MiDW; MiU; MnU; NBuG; NIC; NNC; NNS; NcU; NcWfC; NhD; OClWHi; OO; P; PHi; PP; PPL-R; PSC-Hi; PU; RP; RPB; TxU; Vi;

ViRVU.   42311

Totten, John C., comp.
Hymns and spiritual songs, with the choruses af-
fixed, as usually sung at camp-meetings...Ed. 8. New
York, J.C. Totten, 1817. 192 p. GAGTh; MWA; N.
42312
The touchstone, or a humble, modest inquiry into the
nature of religious intolerance. Whether it ever ex-
isted? Whether it is found in these regions? And the
way to detect it in ourselves. By a member of the
Berean Society...Brattleborough, Vt., Simeon Ide,
1817. 36 p. VtU-W.   42313

Toulmin, Joshua, 1740-1815
A review of the preaching of the apostles; or, The
practical efficacy of the Unitarian doctrine; proved and
illus. from the Acts of the Apostles, and the epistle of
Paul to Timothy and Titus...Utica, N. Y., Pr. by T.
Walker, for the editor, 1817. 59 p. CBPac; CSt; ICMe;
MBAt; MWA; NUtHi.   42314

Townsend, Absalom
Albany, August, 1817. Sir, You will perceive, by
the notice in the last numbers of the American magazine, edited by Mr. Spafford that the subscription to
that work, has been duly assigned to me. -- I must
therefore earnestly request you to send three dollars,
the amount of your subscription to my office, no. 84
State-street, Albany, by mail or otherwise, without delay. [Signed] Absalom Townsend, Jr. Attorney at
Law. [Albany? 1817] Broadside. MHi.   42315

Tract Association of Friends, Philadelphia.
Annual reports. Philadelphia, 1817- PHi.   42316

Tracy, Antoine Louis Charles Destutt de
A treatise on political economy...Georgetown, D. C.,
Pr. by W. A. Rind & Co., for Joseph Milligan, 1817.
MWA.   42317

Train, Charles
A discourse, delivered in Medway, West parish, at

the festival of St. John the Baptist...Dedham, Mass.,
Pr. by Abel D. Alleyne, 1817. 19 p. CSmH; M;
MBAt; MBFM; MH-AH; MWA; PPFM.   42318

A treatise on internal navigation...Ballston Spa, N. Y.,
Pr. by V. F. Doubleday, 1817. 267 p. DLC; MH; N;
NNE.   42319

The trial and conviction of Abraham Casler, for the
murder of his wife Catharine Casler, at the Schoharie
Oyer and Terminer and General Gaol delivery, in September, 1817. Schoharie, N. Y., 1817. 20 p. N; N-L;
NNNAM.   42320

No entry.   42321

Trial of Abraham Kessler, for poisoning his wife with
arsenic. New York, Pelsue & Gould, 1817. MBS.
                                                 42322

The trial of antichrist...New York, William Guthrie...
1817. 166 p. MWA; NCH; NN.   42323

The trial of Episcopacy reported by R. C. C. Poughkeepsie, N. Y., Pr. by P. & S. Potter, for P. Potter,
1817. 200 p. MeBat; MoU; TxDaM.   42324

Trial of Frederick Eberle and others, at a nisi prius
court, held in Philadelphia, July 1816, before the Hon.
Jasper Yeates, justice ... for illegally conspiring...
to prevent the introduction of the English language into
the service of St. Michael's and Zion's churches belonging to the German Lutheran congregation in the city
of Philadelphia. Taken in short hand by James Car-
son...Philadelphia, pub. for the reporter, 1817. 240 p.
Ct; MBS; MSa; MdBB; MeLewB; MnU; N-L; NIC-L;
NRivHi; NTSc; PPA; PPG; PReaHi; WaSp.   42325

Trial of Henry Phillips for the murder of Gaspard Dennegri. Supreme Judicial Court, Boston, January 9,
1817. [Boston] Pr. by Thomas G. Bangs [1817] 24 p.

CSfLow; MBr; MH-L; MHi; MWA; NTSC.   42326

The trial of Robert W. Hauston, versus General John
Dicks, and others, members of a court martial...Be-
ing an action of trespass, instituted in the Court of
Common pleas, of Lancaster County, Pennsylvania...
Philadelphia, Lydia R. Bailey, 1817. 198 p. MBAt;
MH-L; MdBB; MiD-B; P; PLFM.   42327

Trial of William M'Donnough,...for the murder of his
wife...at Boston...1817. Boston, Pr. by Thomas G.
Bangs [1817] 16 p. DLC; MB; MBAt; MDedHi; MH-L;
NHi.   42328

The triangle. Fourth series of numbers by the investigator... New York, Pr. by Van Winkle, Wiley & Co.,
for the author, 1817. 84 p. MeHi; ViRUT.   42329

-- Fifth series of numbers. By the investigator.
New-York, Pr. by Van Winkle, Wiley & Co., 1817. 60
p. IaDaU; NNS.   42330

No entry.

          42331

Troy, N. Y. Sunday school association.
      The...annual report of the Board of inspectors of
the Sunday school association of the city of Troy...1st
(1817) [1817] NBuG.   42332

True stories related by a friend to little children. New
York, S. Wood and sons, 1817. [48] p. MWA; PP.
          42333

Trumbull, Henry
      History of the discovery of America of the landing
of our forefathers at Plymouth...Boston, Pr. by Stephen
Sewell, for the author, 1817. 256 p. MFiHi.   42334

-- Western emigration. Journal of Doctor Jeremiah
Smipleton's tour to Ohio. Boston, Pr. by S. Sewall
[1817?] 36 p. DLC; WHi.   42335

Tudor, William, jr., 1779-1830
A discourse delivered before the Humane society, at their anniversary, May, 1817... Boston, Pr. by John Eliot, 1817. 64 p. CSt; DLC; MB; MBC; MH; MMeT; MWA; MiD-B; NN; NjR; PPAmP; RPB. 42336

Tuhi, John
Life and confession of John Tuhi... [1817] MWA. 42337

Tullidge, H. H.
An inquiry into the nature of pulmonary consumption... New-York, Pr. by C. S. Van Winkle, 1817. 36 p. CtY-M; DNLM; MWA; NNNAM. 42338

Turner
Grammar exercises... of the Latin tongue. 1st Albany ed. Albany, Webster & Skinner, 1817. MWA. 42339

Turner, Edward
A discourse delivered at the dedication of the Universalist meeting-house, in the city of Hudson, New-York, October 23, 1817... Hudson, N. Y., Pr. by S. W. Clark, 1817. 26 p. MMeT-Hi; MWA; N. 42340

-- The gospel visitant, being principally original tracts on moral and religious subjects; in which an illustration of the gospel of God our Saviour, is attempted by arguments drawn from the scripture and reason. The whole directed to the promotion of piety and morality. By Edward Turner and Hosea Ballou. Vol. II. Salem, Mass., Pr. by Warwick Palfray, Jr., 1817. [194-258] p. MMeT-Hi; MSaE. 42341

Turner, George
An oration, pronounced before the Washington Benevolent Society of the County of Washington, Ohio, on the 22d of February, 1817. Marietta, O., Pr. by Royal Prentiss, 1817. 14 p. CSmH; OClWHi; OCHp. 42342

Tuthill, Mrs. L. G., ed.
My little geography. Edited by Mrs. L. G. Tuthill. Philadelphia, Lindsay & Blackiston, 1817. 137 p. PLFM. 42343

Tyler, Benjamin Owen
    Eulogium Sacred to the memory of the illustrious
George Washington... New York, Benjamin O. Tyler,
1817. Broadside. CSmH.   42344

Tyler, Bennet
    The doctrine of the saints' perseverance... New
Haven, Pr. by Nathan Whiting, 1817. 24 p. CU; Ct;
CtHi; CtY; MBC; MH-AH; MWA; OCHP; NN; PLT;
PPPrHi.   42345

Tyler, Royall
    A family discourse, delivered at Coventry Andover
Society, Conn. September 13, 1815. Boston, Pr. by
T.B. Wait and sons, 1817. 16 p. Ct; CtHC; DLC; MB;
MBC; MHi; MWA; NN.   42346

                           U
Umphraville, Angus
    The siege of Baltimore, and the battle of La
Tranche... Baltimore, Pr. by Schaeffer and Maund,
1817. 144 p. CSmH; DLC; MB; MH; MWA; MNBedf;
MdBE; MnU; MdBP; MdHi; RPB; PPHi.   42347

Union College, Schenectady, N. Y.
    Annual catalogues, 1817. Schenectady, N. Y.,
1817. MBC.   42348

United Benefit Society of Journeymen Cordwainers,
N. Y.
    Constitution of the United Benefit Society of Jour-
neymen Cordwainers of the City of New York, agreed
to, October 20th, 1817. 8 p. (Dauber & Pine, Book-
shops, Inc.; Cat. 259 May, 1940 No. 82)   42349

United States
    An account of the receipts and expenditures of the
United States, for the year 1816... [City of Washington,
1817] (Title page missing. Pages [1-24] missing) 25-
168 [169-179] p. MWA.   42350

-- An act to incorporate the subscribers to certain

banks in the District of Columbia...[Alexandria,
D.C.?] 1817. MWA.   42351

-- [Acts passed at the first and second sessions of the
fourteenth Congress of the United States. 1815-1817.
[Washington City, 1817] 311 p. Vi.   42352

-- Acts passed at the second session of the fourteenth
Congress of the United States. Washington City [1817]
199-311 p. MWA; NjR; PU-L.   42353

-- Adjt. and Inspector General's office, November 1st,
1817. General order. 5 p. MdHi.   42354

-- Amendment proposed to the Bill authorizing the commutation of soldiers' bounty lands. [Washington, 1817]
(H.R. 1 [December 30, 1817]) DLC.   42355

-- Amendments proposed by Mr. Lowndes to the bill,
entitled "A bill concerning the navigation of the United
States. No. 32. [Washington City, 1817] 3 p. (H.R.
January 29, 1817) DLC.   42356

-- The annual report of the Commissioners of the sink-
ing fund. February 7, 1817. Printed by order of the
House of Representatives. Washington, Pr. by William
Davis, 1817. 27 p. DLC; MWA; MWiW; MnSH; O.
                                             42357
-- The Army Register for 1817. Adjutant and inspec-
tor general's office. Washington City, January 1st,
1817. Pr. by Edward de Krafft, 1817. 19 p. MdHi;
NcU; Nh-Hi; OClWHi.   42358

-- Articles of war, military laws, and rules and regulations for the Army of the United States. Adjutant and
inspector general's office, September 1816. Rev. September, 1817. [Washington] Pr. by E. de Krafft [1817]
102 p. DLC; MB; MdHi.   42359

-- A bill authorizing the commutation of soldiers' bounty land. [Washington City, 1817] 2 p. (H.R. 46. January 11, 1817) DLC.   42360

-- -- [Washington City, 1817] (H.R. 1. December 8, 1817) DLC.   42361

-- A bill authorizing the deposit of the papers of foreign vessels, with the consul of their respective nations. [Washington City, 1817] 2 p. (H.R. 74. January 25, 1817) DLC.   42362

-- A bill authorizing the establishment of a national armoury. [Washington City, 1816! 1817] 2 p. (H.R. 51. January 13, 1817) DLC.   42363

-- A bill authorizing the opening and working copper mines on Lake Superior, and for other purposes. [Washington City, 1817] 2 p. (H.R. 88. January 28, 1817) DLC.   42364

-- A bill authorizing the payment of a sum of money to Nathaniel Seavey and others. [Washington City, 1817] 1 p. (H.R. 125. February 11, 1817) DLC. 42365

-- A bill authorizing the payment of a sum of money to Teackle Savage and others. [Washington City, 1817] 2 p. (H.R. 139. February 17, 1817) DLC.   42366

-- A bill authorizing the payment of a sum of money to the state of Georgia under the articles of agreement and cession between the United States and that state. [Washington City, 1817] 1 p. (H.R. 124. February 11, 1817) DLC.   42367

-- A bill authorizing the payment of the principal and interest due on the loan office certificates therein named. [Washington City, 1817] 4 p. (H.R. 96. February 3, 1817) DLC.   42368

-- A bill authorizing the secretary of the Treasury to cause repayment to be made of certain alien duties. [Washington City, 1817] 1 p. (H.R. 115. February 8, 1817) DLC.   42369

-- A bill authorizing the secretary of the Treasury to pay to the state of Georgia fifteen per cent upon the

quota of direct tax, for the year one thousand eight
hundred and sixteen, assumed and paid by that state.
[Washington City, 1817] 2 p. (H.R. 62. January 18,
1817) DLC.   42370

-- A bill authorizing the secretary of the Treasury to
remit the duties therein mentioned. [Washington City,
1817] 2 p. (H.R. 72. January 25, 1817) DLC. 42371

-- A bill by which the right of citizenship may be re-
linquished. [Washington City, 1817] (H.R. 15. December 22, 1817) DLC.   42372

-- A bill concerning invalid pensioners. [Washington
City, 1817] 6 p. (H.R. 91. January 29, 1817) DLC.
                                                    42373
-- A bill confirming certain lands in the county of Ar-
kansas, in the Missouri Territory, to the heirs of
Elisha Winter, deceased. [Washington City, 1817] 2 p.
(H.R. 57. January 15, 1817) DLC.   42374

-- A bill confirming certain lands in the Missouri Territory to the legal representatives of Elisha Winter,
and the legal representatives of William Winter. [Wash-
ington City, 1817] (H.R. 21. December 30, 1817) DLC.
                                                    42375
-- A bill confirming certain lands in the Territory of
Illinois to the heirs of Philip Renaut. [Washington
City, 1817] 2 p. (H.R. 144. February 18, 1817) DLC.
                                                    42376
-- A bill confirming the title of Joseph Gillard. [Wash-
ington City, 1817] 1 p. (H.R. 117. February 10,
1817) DLC.   42377

-- A bill confirming the title of Miller and Fulton to a
tract of land on the Bayou Boeuf, state of Louisiana.
[Washington City, 1817] 1 p. (H.R. 90. January 29,
1817) DLC.   42378

-- A bill for erecting a light-house on the west chop of
Holmes' Hole harbour, in the state of Massachusetts.
[Washington City, 1817] 1 p. (H.R. 127. February 11,
1817) DLC.   42379

-- A bill for extending the time for locating Virginia
military land warrants, and for returning the surveys
thereon to the General land office, and for giving further time to complete the surveys and obtain patents
for lands located under Virginia resolution warrants.
[Washington City, 1817] 3 p. (H.R. 40. January 4,
1817) DLC.   42380

-- A bill for organizing, classing, and arming the militia, and for calling them forth to execute the laws of
the Union, suppress insurrection, and repel invasion,
and to repeal the laws heretofore passed for those purposes. [Washington City, 1817]   16 p. (H.R. 60.
January 17, 1817) DLC.   42381

-- A bill for the benefit of the widows and orphans of
the officers, seamen and mariners who were lost in
the United States brig Epervier. [Washington City,
1817] 1 p. (H.R. 68. January 22, 1817) DLC. 42382

-- A bill for the better adminiatration of justice in the
Supreme court, and for the appointment of circuit
judges. [Washington City, 1817] 3 p. (H.R. 28. February 7, 1817) DLC.   42383

-- A bill for the payment of certain militia claims of
the state of Georgia. [Washington City, 1817] (H.R.
16. December 22, 1817) DLC.   42384

-- A bill for the relief of Anthony Buck. [Washington
City, 1817] 1 p. (H.R. 126. February 11, 1817) DLC.
                                                 42385
-- A bill for the relief of certain Creek Indians. [Wash-
ington City, 1817] 1 p. (H.R. 93. January 29, 1817)
DLC.   42386

-- A bill for the relief of certain sufferers in the late
war between the United States and Great Britain.
[Washington City, 1817] 4 p. (H.R. 70. January 23,
1817) DLC.   42387

-- A bill for the relief of Henry Lee. [Washington
City, 1817] 1 p. (H.R. 116. February 8, 1817)

DLC.   42388

-- A bill for the relief of Joel Earwood. [Washington City, 1817] (H.R. 12. December 17, 1817) DLC.
42389

-- A bill for the relief of John Anderson. [Washington City, 1817] (H.R. 19. December 30, 1817) DLC.
42390

-- -- [Washington City, 1817] (H.R. 22. December 31, 1817) DLC.   42391

-- A bill for the relief of John Bate. [Washington City, 1817] 2 p. (H.R. 86. January 28, 1817) DLC.
42391

-- -- [Washington City, 1817] (H.R. 2. December 8, 1817) DLC.   42393

-- A bill for the relief of Robert Burnside. [Washington City, 1817] 1 p. (H.R. 88. January 29, 1817) DLC.   42394

-- -- [Washington City, 1817] 1 p. (H.R. 89. January 29, 1817) DLC.   42395

-- A bill for the relief of Samuel Aikman. [Washington City, 1817] (H.R. 11. December 17, 1817) DLC.
42396

-- A bill for the relief of Samuel H. Harper. [Washington City, 1817] 1 p. (H.R. 96. February 1, 1817) DLC.   42397

-- A bill for the relief of Thomas Malone, Josiah Carney, John Floyd M'Grew, John Johnson, and Rhodominci H. Gilmer. [Washington City, 1817] 3 p. (H.R. 123. February 11, 1817) DLC.   42398

-- A bill for the relief of William Daniel. [Washington City, 1817] 1 p. (H.R. 92. January 29, 1817) DLC.   42399

-- A bill for the relief of Winslow and Henry Lewis. [Washington City, 1817] (H.R. 9. December 15, 1817) DLC.   42400

-- A bill further to regulate the territories of the U-
nited States, and their electing delegates to Congress.
[Washington City, 1817] 2 p. (H.R. 50. January 15,
1817) DLC. 42401

-- A bill in addition to an act, entitled An act for the
relief of John Thompson. [Washington City, 1817]
(H.R. 14. December 19, 1817) DLC. 42402

-- A bill making appropriation for the support of government for the year one thousand eight hundred and
seventeen. [Washington City, 1817] 17 p. (H.R. 64.
January 20, 1817) DLC. 42403

-- A bill making appropriations for the support of the
Navy of the United States for the year one thousand
eight hundred and seventeen. [Washington City, 1817]
2 p. (H.R. 83. January 28, 1817) DLC. 42404

-- A bill making appropriations to defray the expenses
of the army and militia during the late war with Great
Britain. [Washington City, 1817] 2 p. (H.R. 111.
February 7, 1917) DLC. 42405

-- A bill making provision for the establishment of additional land offices in the territory of Missouri. [Wash-
ington City, 1817] (H.R. 13. December 18, 1817) DLC.
42406
-- A bill making provision for the establishment of additional land offices in the Territory of Missouri, and
for the final adjustment of claims to towns and village
lots therein. [Washington City, 1817] 5 p. (H.R. 75.
January 25, 1817) DLC. 42407

-- A bill making provision for the location of the lands
reserved by the first article of the Treaty of the ninth
of August one thousand eight hundred and fourteen, between the United States and the Creek nation, to certain chiefs and warriors of that nation, and for other
purposes. [Washington City, 1817] 4 p. (H.R. 43.
January 9, 1817) DLC. 42408

-- A bill making provision for the support of the mili-

tary establishment for the year one thousand eight hundred and seventeen. [Washington City, 1817] 2 p.
(H.R. 110. February 7, 1817) DLC.   42409

-- A bill more effectually to provide for the punishment of certain crimes against the United States, and
for other purposes. [Washington City, 1817] 34 p.
(H.R. 121. February 10, 1817) DLC.   42410

-- A bill regulating the pay and emoluments of the
pursers and midshipmen of the Navy, and the medical
staff of the army of the United States. [Washington
City, 1817] 1 p. (H.R. 102. February 10, 1817) DLC.
                                                  42411
-- -- [Washington City, 1817] 1 p. (H.R. 120. February 10, 1817) DLC.   42412

-- A bill repealing the act passed on the twenty-second
day of April, one thousand eight hundred and eight and
fixing the command of the marine corps. [Washington
City, 1817] 1 p. (H.R. 140. February 17, 1817) DLC.
                                                  42413
-- A bill respecting the assessment and collection of
the direct tax. [Washington City, 1817] 2 p. (H.R.
73.) DLC.   42414

-- A bill respecting the compensation of the collectors
therein mentioned. [Washington City, 1817] 1 p.
(H.R. 112. February 7, 1817) DLC.   42415

-- A bill respecting the pay and emoluments of certain
officers of the army of the United States. [Washington
City, 1817] 1 p. (H.R. 85. January 28, 1817) DLC.
                                                  42416
-- A bill supplementary to an act, entitled, "An act
to authorize the state of Tennessee to issue grants and
perfect titles to certain lands therein described, and to
settle the claims to the vacant and unappropriated lands
within the same. [Washington City, 1817] 6 p. (H.R.
84. January 28, 1817) DLC.   42417

-- A bill supplementary to "An act providing for the
relief of persons imprisoned for debts due to the United

States. [Washington City, 1817] 2 p. (H.R. 58. January 16, 1817) DLC.   42418

-- A bill supplementary to "an act to regulate the duties on imports and tonnage." [Washington City, 1817] 1 p. (H.R. 156. February 24, 1817) DLC.   42419

-- A bill supplementary to the Act establishing the Mint, and the act concerning the Mint. [Washington City, 1817] (H.R. 4. December 9, 1817) DLC. 42420

-- A bill to abolish the internal duties. [Washington City, 1817] (H.R. 3. December 9, 1817) DLC. 42421

-- A bill to alter and establish certain Post roads. [Washington City, 1817] 7 p. 1 fold tab. (H.R. 155. February 22, 1817) DLC.   42422

-- A bill to alter the flag of the United States. [Washington City, 1817] 1 p. (H.R. 37. January 2, 1817) DLC.   42423

-- A bill to amend an act, entitled, "An act making further provision for military services during the late war, and for other purposes." [Washington City, 1817] 2 p. (H.R. 48. January 11, 1817) DLC.   42424

-- A bill to amend an act, entitled "An act respecting fugitives from justice, and persons escaping from the service of their masters." [Washington City, 1817] (H.R. 18. December 29, 1817) DLC.   42425

-- A bill to amend and explain the "Act for designating, surveying, and granting military bounty lands," passed the sixth May, one thousand eight hundred and twelve. [Washington City, 1817] 1 p. (H.R. 51. January 13, 1817) DLC.   42426

-- A bill to amend the act, entitled "An act, granting bounties in land, and extra pay to certain Canadian volunteers," passed fifth of March, eighteen hundred and sixteen. [Washington City, 1817] 2 p. (H.R. 47. January 11, 1817) DLC.   42427

-- A bill to amend the act "for the government and regulation of seamen in the merchant service and for the relief of distressed and destitute American seamen in foreign ports." [Washington City, 1817] 4 p. (H.R. 77. January 25, 1817) DLC.   42428

-- A bill to appoint an additional judge for the Mississippi Territory, and for other purposes. [Washington City, 1817] 2 p. (H.R. 69.) DLC.   42429

-- A bill to authorize the payment of certain militia claims of the state of Georgia. [Washington City, 1817] 1 p. (H.R. 78. January 27, 1817) DLC.   42430

-- A bill to authorize the sale of the northeast quarter of section number sixteen, in township number four north- range number one west of the third principal meridian. [Washington City, 1817] 2 p. (H.R. 106. February 6, 1817) DLC.   42431

-- A bill to authorize the secretary of the Treasury to subscribe in behalf of the United States for shares in the capital stock of certain canal companies therein mentioned. [Washington City, 1817] 3 p. (H.R. 147. February 20, 1817) DLC.   42432

-- A bill to define and enlarge the boundaries of the land district of Edwardsville in the Illinois Territory. [Washington City, 1817] 1 p. (H.R. 105. February 6, 1817) DLC.   42433

-- A bill to enable the people of the Mississippi Territory to form a consitution and state government, and for the admission of such state into the union, on an equal footing with the original states. [Washington City, 1817] 4 p. (H.R. 61. January 17, 1817) DLC.
42434

-- A bill to establish a national board of agriculture. [Washington City, 1817] 3 p. (No. 149. February 21, 1817) DLC.   42435

-- A bill to establish an uniform system of Bankruptcy throughout the United States. [Washington City, 1817]

(H. R. 6. December 12, 1817) DLC.   42436

-- A bill to extend the charters of certain banks in
the District of Columbia and for other purposes.
[Washington City, 1817] 7 p. (S. 54. In Senate of the
United States. February 22, 1817) DLC.   42437

-- A bill to incorporate the Columbian Insurance Company of Alexandria. [Washington City, 1817] (H. R. 10.
December 16, 1817) DLC.   42438

-- A bill to incorporate the subscribers to certain
banks in the District of Columbia. [Washington City,
1817] 20 p. (S. 55. In Senate of the United States.
February 22, 1817) DLC.   42439

-- A bill to prescribe the effect which certain records
and judicial proceedings of the courts of each state
shall have in every other state, and in the courts of
the United States. [Washington City, 1817] (H. R. 17.
December 23, 1817) DLC.   42440

-- A bill to prevent citizens of the United States from
selling vessels of war to the citizens or subjects of
any foreign power, and more effectually to prevent the
arming and equipping vessels of war in the ports of
the United States, intended to be used against nations
in amity with the United States. [Washington City,
1817] 3 p. (H. R. 55. January 14, 1817) DLC. 42441

-- A bill to prohibit all commercial intercourse with
ports or places into, or with which the vessels of the
United States are not ordinarily permitted to enter and
trade. [Washington City, 1817] 5 p. (H. R. 66. January 21, 1817) DLC.   42442

-- A bill to provide for the due execution of the Laws
of the United States within the state of Mississippi.
[Washington City, 1817] (H. R. 20. December 30, 1817)
DLC.   42443

-- A bill to provide for the erection of a court house,
jail, and public offices within the county of Alexandria,

in the District of Columbia. [Washington City, 1817]
2 p. (H.R. 38. January 4, 1817) DLC.   42444

-- A bill to provide for the redemption of the public
debt. [Washington City, 1817] 5 p. (H.R. 53. January
14, 1817) DLC.   42445

-- A bill to regulate and fix the compensation of clerks
and messengers. [Washington City, 1817] 4 p. (H.R.
119. February 10, 1817) DLC.   42446

-- A bill to regulate the laying out and making a road
from the Ohio river opposite where the Cumberland
road strikes that river, to the state of Indiana. [Wash-
ington City, 1817] 4 p. (H.R. 76. January 25, 1817)
DLC.   42447

-- A bill to regulate the trade in plaster of Paris.
[Washington City, 1817] 2 p. (H.R. 153. February 21,
1817) DLC.   42448

-- A bill to regulate trade and intercourse with the Indian tribes, and to exclude foreigners from a participa-
tion therein. [Washington City, 1817] 3 p. (H.R. 103.
February 4, 1817) DLC.   42449

-- A bill to repeal so much of an act, entitled, "An
act to regulate duties on imports and tonnage, " passed
April twenty-seventh, one thousand eight hundred and
sixteen, as limits the levying and collecting a duty of
twenty-five per centum ad valorem on certain goods to
the thirtieth of June one thousand eight hundred and
nineteen. [Washington City, 1817] 1 p. (H.R. 138.
February 14, 1817) DLC.   42450

-- A bill to repeal so much of any acts now in force
as authorizes a loan of money, or an issue of Treasury
notes. [Washington City, 1817] 2 p. (H.R. 54. January 14, 1817) DLC.   42451

-- A bill transferring the duties of commissioner of
loans to the Bank of the United States, and abolishing
the office of commissioner of loans. [Washington City,

1817] 3 p. (H.R. 122. February 10, 1817) DLC.
42452
-- Collector's office, Portland, January 2, 1817.
Statement of the amounts of internal duties imposed by
the United States (excepting those on...) paid by each
person in the seventh Collection District of Massachusetts, during the year 1816...Woodbury Storer, Collector for the seventh collection district of Massachusetts.
Broadside. MeHi. 42453

-- ...The Committee of claims, to whom was referred the petition of Rachel Dohrman, report...[Wash-
ington City, 1817] 3 p. DLC. 42454

-- The committee on naval affairs, to whom was referred the memorial Edward Shubrick and others, officers of the late United States' brig Chippewa. Report.
[Washington City, 1817] 2 p. DLC. 42455

-- The committee to whom has been referred a bill
from the Senate entitled, "A bill to provide for the
prompt settlement of public account," propose the following amendments. [Washington City, 1817] 7 p.
(H.R. February 7, 1817) DLC. 42456

-- Congressional directory. Issued by U.S. - Congress 1817. MH. 42457

-- The Constitution framed for the United States of
America, by a convention of deputies, from the states
of New Hampshire, Massachusetts, Connecticut, New
York, New Jersey, Pennsylvania, Delaware, Maryland,
Virginia, North Carolina, South Carolina, and Georgia,
at a session begun May 25, and ended September 17,
1787. Schenectady, N.Y., Pr. by I. Riggs, 1817. 27
p. MWA; NSchHi; OO. 42458

-- Copy of Major Kearney's report of November 5th,
1815. February 20, 1817. Printed by order of the
House of representatives. [Washington City, 1817] 14 p.
CtY; DLC; MWA. 42459

-- Correspondence between the chairman of the Commit-

tee of ways and means and the acting secretary of War;
in relation to the expenditures and appropriations for
the ordnance and quartermaster general's departments.
January 31, 1817. Washington City, Pr. by William A.
Davis, 1817. 20 p. DLC; DNA; MWA; MWiW; O. 42460

-- Direct tax for 1816. Notice is hereby given, that
the Direct Tax for the year 1816, laid in conformity
to the acts of Congress passed the 9th of January,
1815, and 5th of March, 1816, upon the following described property, is now unpaid... In Rowley... Ipswich
... Wenham... Hamilton... Given under my hand, this
17th day of Sept. 1817... John Woodberry, Jr. Dep.
Collector, 9th Collection District in Massachusetts.
Broadside. MSaE.   42461

-- -- Notice is hereby given, that the direct tax for
the year 1816, laid in conformity to the act of Congress
passed the 5th of March 1816, upon the following described property is now remaining unpaid... John Kellogg, Deputy Collector for the first collection district
in the state of Vermont. More new books. Fay, Davison & Burt, have just received, in addition to those
recently advertised in their catalogue, the following
books... March 19. [Rutland, Vt., Fay, Davison &
Burt, 1817] Broadside. McCorison list.   42462

-- Documents accompanying a "bill authorizing the appointment of hospital surgeons... [Washington, 1817]
7 p. NNNAM.   42463

-- Documents accompanying a bill respecting the
assessment and collection of the direct tax. January
25, 1817. Printed by order of the House of representatives. [Washington City, 1817] 3 p. DLC; MWA.
                                               42464
-- Documents accompanying a bill to amend the act for
the government and regulation of seamen in the merchant service, and for the relief of distressed and destitute American seamen in foreign ports. January 25,
1817. [Washington City, 1817] 18 p. DLC; MWA.
                                               42465
-- Documents accompanying a bill to prevent citizens

of the United States from selling vessels of war to the
citizens or subjects of any foreign power, etc., etc.
January 14, 1817...Washington City, Pr. by William
A. Davis, 1817. 13 p. DLC; G; MWA; MiD-B.　42466

-- Documents accompanying a letter from the Acting
Secretary of War of the 4th inst. to the chairman of
the ways and means; being detailed statements on which
were founded the estimates for the expenses of the
army for the year 1817. January 10, 1817...Washing-
ton City, Pr. by William A. Davis, 1817. 32 p. G;
MWA.　　　　　　　　　　　　　　　　　　　42467

-- Documents submitted by Mr. Mason, of Virginia,
relative to the unchartered banks of the District of Columbia, February 25, 1817. Ordered to be printed for
the use of the Senate. Washington City, Pr. by William A. Davis, 1817. 8 p. DLC; G; MWA.　　42468

-- Documents presented by the committee on naval affairs, to whom was referred the nomination of John
Heath, of Virginia, to be consul at Teneriffe. December 29, 1817. Printed by order of the Senate of the
United States. Washington, Pr. by E. De Krafft, 1817.
36 p. RHi; ScU.　　　　　　　　　　　　　42469

--[Fragment of list of taxes paid by individuals] Collectors office. Windsor, Jan. 13, 1817, Thomas
Leverett, Col. Designed by the Secretary of the Treasury for the state of Vermont. Broadside. MWA.
　　　　　　　　　　　　　　　　　　　　　42470
-- General view of the internal duties for 1816. [Wash-
ington City, 1817] 5-28 p., 20 charts. MWA.　42471

-- In Senate of the United States. January 2, 1817.
Mr. Lamb submitted the following motion for consideration. [Washington, 1817] 2 p. (For the appointment
of additional agents for the more convenient payment of
persons on the pension list of the U.S.) DLC; MWA.
　　　　　　　　　　　　　　　　　　　　　42472
-- -- January 3, 1817. Mr. Lacock submitted the following motion for consideration. [Washington City,
1817] 2 p. (Regarding the increasing of pay of the regi-

mental and battalion paymasters and giving them rank
in the army.) DLC; MWA.   42473

-- -- January 3, 1817. Mr. Varnum submitted the
following motion for consideration. [Washington City,
1817] 2 p. (To inquire into the expediency of repealing
the act for increasing the salary of sergeant of arms of
the Senate and door-keeper of the House.) DLC; MWA.
                                                    42474

-- -- January 3, 1817. Ordered to be printed for the
use of the Senate under an injunction of secrecy. [A
commercial treaty between the United States and the
King of Sweden and Norway] [Washington City, 1817]
96 p. (Text in French and English) DLC.   42475

-- -- January 3, 1817. To the honourable the Senate
and House of representatives of the United States in
Congress assembled. The petition of Robert Kid, of
the city of Philadelphia, merchant, a citizen of the U-
nited States, respectfully showeth. [Washington City,
1817] 35 p. DLC; MWA.   42476

-- -- January 6, 1817. The joint library committee
beg leave to report. [Washington City, 1817] 34 p.
DLC; MWA; N.   42477

-- -- January 7, 1817. Mr. Goldsborough submitted
the following motion for consideration. [Washington
City, 1817] 2 p. (Requesting the President to give a
report of the amount of money paid by the government
of the U.S. for the services of miltia during the late
war.) DLC.   42478

-- -- January 7, 1817. Mr. Hardin, submitted the
following motion for consideration. [Washington City,
1817] 2 p. (To inquire into the expediency of requiring
attorneys employed in the collection of moneys to give
bond.) DLC; MWA.   42479

-- -- January 7, 1817. Mr. Tait submitted the following motion for consideration. [Washington City, 1817]
2 p. (Regarding surveys and examinations of the Chesapeake Bay in reference to the selection of a site for a

naval depot.) DLC; MWA.   42480

-- -- January 7th, 1817. Read and ordered to be
printed for the use of the Senate. [Report of the secretary of the Treasury on the United States Bank at
Washington] [Washington City, 1817] 3 p. DLC. 42481

-- -- January 7, 1817... To the honorable the Senate
and House of Representatives... The memorial of the
ship owners, and others, interested in foreign commerce, in the town of Portsmouth and state of New
Hampshire. [Washington City, 1817] 5 p. MWA.
                                                           42482
-- -- January 7, 1817... Committee Room. December
26th, 1816. Sir, The committee on Finance... [Wash-
ington City, 1817] 3 p. MWA.   42483

-- -- January 8, 1817. The Committee on roads and
canals, to whom was referred the petition of a number
of the inhabitants of Washington County, Pennsylvania,
praying a change in part of the route of the western
turnpike road, report. [Washington City, 1817] 2 p.
DLC; MWA.   42484

-- -- January 9, 1817. The Committee on public
lands who were instructed, by a resolution of the 25th
ulta. "to inquire into the expediency of authorizing, by
law, an exchange of territory with any of the Indian
tribes. " [Washington City, 1817] 5 p. DLC; MWA.
                                                           42485
-- -- January 10, 1817. Mr. Noble presented the following motion for consideration. [Washington, 1817]
2 p. (To inquire into the expediency of allowing compensation to Peter Winchel, Thomas Bell, and John
Harman) DLC; MWA.   42486

-- -- January 10, 1817. Mr. Williams, submitted the
following motion for consideration. [Washington City,
1817] 2 p. (To inquire into the expediency of purchas-
ing copies of the late ed. of the acts of Congress and
furnishing one copy for use of each county in the U. S.)
DLC; MWA.   42487

-- -- January 10, 1817 read, and ordered to be printed
for the use of the Senate. Treasury department. January 9th, 1817. Sir. In obedience to the resolution of
the Senate of the 19th ult. relative to the administration
of the fund for the relief of sick and disabled seamen,
I have the honour to transmit the papers. [Washington
City, 1817] 11 p. DLC; MWA.   42488

-- -- January 13, 1817. Agreeable to notice Mr.
Barbour, submitted the following motion for consideration. [Washington City, 1817] 2 p. (That the secretary of War be instructed to procure copies of existing
militia laws of the different states.) DLC; MWA. 42489

-- -- January 13, 1817. The committee on the Public
lands, to whom was referred the petition of David
Chambers report. [Washington City, 1817] 2 p. DLC;
MWA.   42490

-- -- January 14, 1817. The military committee to
whom was referred a resolution of the 6th instant, directing the committee to inquire into the expediency of
increasing the pay of the regimental; and battalion pay
masters, and giving them rank in the army report.
[Washington City, 1817] 2 p. DLC; MWA.   42491

-- -- January 14, 1817. The military committee, to
whom was referred a resolution of the 3d instant, directing the "committee to inquire into the expediency
of authorizing by law, the appointment of additional
agents in such states, or territories where it may be
found necessary for the more convenient payment of
such persons, as now are, or may hereafter be placed
on the pension list." Report. [Washington City, 1817]
2 p. DLC; MWA.   42492

-- -- January 15, 1817. The Committee of claims, on
the petition of Louis Charles deBlanc, report. [Wash-
ington City, 1817] 2 p. DLC; MWA.   42493

-- -- January 16, 1817. Mr. Ashmun submitted the
following motion for consideration. [Washington City,
1817] 2 p. (Regarding altering a law imposing a duty

on carriages.) DLC; MWA.   42494

-- -- January 16, 1817. Mr. Taylor submitted the
following motion for consideration. [Washington City,
1817] 2 p. (Regarding establishing a post route from
Vincennes to Fort Harrison.) DLC; MWA.   42495

-- -- January 16, 1817. Mr. Tichenor submitted the
following motion for consideration. [Washington, 1817]
2 p. (Requesting the secretary of War for a statement
of the number of officers, non-commissioned officers,
musicians and privates now composing the military establishments) DLC; MWA.   42496

-- -- January 16, 1817. The Committee of finance,
to whom was referred the petition of James Humes,
collector of the revenue for the 6th district of Pennsylvania. Report. [Washington, 1817] 5 p. DLC; MWA.
                                                     42497
-- -- January 17, 1817. Read. Department of War,
Washington, January 16, 1817. Sir. In compliance
with a resolution... requesting information respecting
the "exchange of lands with any of the Indian tribes"...
I have the honor to inclose the papers marked A. B. C.
and D. [Washington City, 1817] 8 p. DLC; MWA;
MiD-B.   42498

-- -- January 17, 1817. Mr. Wilson submitted the
following motion for consideration. [Washington, 1817]
2 p. (Regarding land bounty to widows of soldiers who
were killed in the service of the United States.) DLC;
MWA.   42499

-- -- January 17, 1817. -- [Washington City, 1817]
2 p. (Regarding increasing the compensation of the
post-master at Newark, N. J.) DLC; MWA.   42500

-- -- January 20, 1817. Documents submitted by the
committee to whom was referred the bill respecting the
heirs and legatees of Thomas, deceased. [Washington
City, 1817] 2 p. DLC; MWA.   42501

-- -- January 20, 1817. The Naval committee of the

Senate, to whom has been referred the memorial of
Frederick Jenkins and Rensselaer Havens, in behalf of
the owners, officers and crew of the late private armed
brig General Armstrong report. [Washington City,
1817] 4 p. DLC; MWA.   42502

-- -- January 20, 1817. Ordered to be printed for the
use of the Senate. Treasury department. January 30,
1816. Sir. I have the honour to transmit herewith a
report on the petition of Henry Malcom. [Washington
City, 1817] 5 p. DLC; MWA.   42503

-- -- January 21, 1817. The Committee of claims, to
whom was referred a resolution instructing them to inquire into the expediency of authorizing, by law, the
payment of the state of Georgia of certain claims for
the services of the militia, called out under the authority of the United States, during the years 1792 and
1793, for the defence of the said state against Indian
invasion. Report. [Washington City, 1817] 3 p. DLC;
MWA.   42504

-- -- January 22, 1817. Ordered, that the documents
Nos. 1 and 2 referred to in the report of the Committee of claims, of yesterday, on the expediency of authorizing payment to the state of Georgia for militia
services during the years 1792 and 1793, be printed
for the use of the Senate. [Washington City, 1817] 9 p.
(Report of secretary of war on Georgia militia.) DLC;
MWA.   42505

-- -- January 22, 1817. Resolved, that 500 copies be
printed of the report of Mr. Jefferson, then secretary
of State dated December 16, 1793, on the privileges
and restrictions of the commerce of the United States
in foreign countries, pursuant to the resolution of the
House of representatives of February 23, 1791. [Wash-
ington City, 1817] 21 p. DLC; MWA.   42506

-- -- January 23, 1817. Ordered to be printed for the
use of the Senate. To the Honourable the Senate and
House of representatives of the United States of America, in Congress assembled: The memorial of Frederick

Jenkins, and Rensselaer Havens, in behalf of the
owners, officers and crew of the late private armed
brig General Armstrong. Respectfully represents.
[Washington City, 1817] 3 p. DLC; MWA.   42507

-- -- January 23, 1817. Ordered to be printed for the
use of the Senate. To the Honourable the Senate and
House of representatives of the United States, in Congress assembled- The memorial of ship-owners, and
others, interested in foreign commerce, convened by
public notice at the Tontine Coffee House, in the city
of New York, the 17th January, 1817. [Washington
City, 1817] 4 p. DLC; MWA.   42508

-- -- January 24, 1817. Mr. Fromentin submitted the
following motion for consideration. [Washington City,
1817] 1 l. (That members of the Senate and House of
representatives at the beginning of each session be supplied with a copy of the acts passed at the previous
session.) DLC; MWA.   42509

-- -- January 27, 1817. Documents accompanying a
"bill authorizing the appointment of hospital surgeons
and hospital surgeon's mates, in the navy of the United
States." Navy department. January 23, 1817. [Wash-
ington City, 1817] 7 p. DLC; MWA.   42510

-- -- January 27, 1817. Mr. Troup submitted the following motion for consideration,   [Washington City,
1817] 2 p. (Regarding the treaty of peace and amity
between His Britannic majesty and the United States.)
DLC; MWA.   42511

-- -- January 27, 1817. Ordered to be printed for the
use of the Senate. Report of the secretary of the Navy,
communicating, in obedience to a resolution of the Senate, information relating to the selection of a site for a
naval department. [Washington City, 1817] 53 p. DLC;
MWA.   42512

-- -- January 27, 1817. The Committee of claims, to
whom was referred the petition of Rachael Dorhman report. [Washington City, 1817] 3 p. DLC; MWA. 42513

-- -- January 29, 1817. [Report of secretary of the Navy on the naval establishments.] [Washington City, 1817] 8 p. DLC; MWA. 42514

-- -- January 30, 1817. The committee to whom was referred the petition in behalf of the representatives of Francis Cazeau report. [Washington, 1817] 23 p. DLC; MWA. 42515

-- -- February 3, 1817. Mr. Campbell submitted the following motion for consideration. [Washington City, 1817] 2 p. (To inquire into the expediency of establishing a new district for surveying public lands south of Tennessee.) DLC; MWA. 42516

-- -- February 3, 1817. Ordered to be printed for the use of the Senate. To the honourable the Senate and House of representatives of the United States assembled, the memorial of the merchants of the City of New York respectfully represents. [Washington City, 1817] 8 p. DLC; MWA. 42517

-- -- February 4, 1817. Mr. Tichenor submitted the following motions for considerations. [Washington City, 1817] 2 p. (To inquire into the expediency of repealing the 2d section of the act establishing the military staff, as related to hospital surgeons and surgeons' mates.) DLC; MWA. 42518

-- -- February 5, 1817. Mr. Roberts, from the Committee of claims, to whom has been referred the petition of Sarah Dewees, report. [Washington City, 1817] 3 p. DLC; MWA. 42519

-- -- February 7, 1817. Mr. Hardin submitted the following motion for consideration. [Washington City, 1817] 2 p. (That the committee on pension inquire into the expediency of granting a pension to the infant child of Captain James Logan.) DLC; MWA. 42520

-- -- February 7, 1817. Mr. Wilson submitted the following motion for consideration. [Washington City, 1817] 2 p. (That instructions from a state legislature

to a Senator, from such state, should be received
and filed in the Senate) DLC; MWA.   42521

-- -- February 7, 1817. Ordered to be printed for
the use of the Senate. To the Honourable the Senate
and House of representatives of the United States, of
America in Congress assembled: The memorial of
the ship owners, and others, interested in foreign commerce, in the town of Portsmouth and state of New
Hampshire. [Washington City, 1817] 5 p. DLC. 42522

-- -- February 10, 1817. Mr. Barbour submitted the
following motion for consideration. [Washington, 1817]
2 p. (To inquire into the expediency of amending the
law to abolish the existing duties on spirits distilled
within the U.S.) DLC; MWA.   42523

-- -- February 10, 1817. Mr. Chace submitted the
following motion for consideration. [Washington City,
1817] 2 p. (Regarding an act to provide for the collection of duties on imports and tonnage.) DLC; MWA.
                                              42524

-- -- February 10, 1817. Mr. Hardin submitted the
following motion for consideration. [Washington, 1817]
2 p. (Regarding establishing a post route through the
town of Bedford, Ky.) DLC; MWA.   42525

-- -- February 10, 1817. Mr. Lacock submitted the
following motion for consideration. [Washington City,
1817] 2 p. (Requesting the President for a report on
the rations, provisions and money spent by the army
from Sept. 1812 until winter 1815.) DLC; MWA. 42526

-- -- February 10, 1817. Mr. Noble submitted the
following motion for consideration. [Washington City,
1817] 2 p. (Regarding establishing a land office in the
eastern part of Indiana.) DLC; MWA.   42527

-- -- February 10, 1817. Mr. Ruggles submitted the
following motion for consideration. [Washington City,
1817] 2 p. (To inquire into the expediency of granting
the right of pre-emptions to the inhabitants settled on
the reservation at Sandusky.) DLC; MWA.   42528

-- -- February 10, 1817. Mr. Taylor submitted the following motion for consideration. [Washington City, 1817] 2 p. (For the establishment of new post-roads.) DLC; MWA.   42529

-- -- February 10, 1817. The committee of claims to whom has been referred the petition of Joseph W. Page report. [Washington, 1817] 2 p. DLC; MWA.   42530

-- -- February 11, 1817. Mr. Daggett submitted the following motion for consideration. [Washington City, 1817] 2 p. (To inquire into the propriety of placing James Gorham, of New-Haven, in Connecticut on the pension list.) DLC; MWA.   42531

-- -- February 11, 1817. Mr. Troup submitted the following motion for consideration. [Washington City, 1817] 2 p. (To inquire into the expediency of establishing by law the town of Darien in Georgia as a port of entry.) DLC; MWA.   42532

-- -- February 11, 1817. The Committee on finance, who were instructed by a resolution of the Senate, to inquire into the expediency of repealing an act, entitled "An act increasing the compensation allowed the sergeant-at-arms of the Senate and House of representatives, and of the door-keeper of the Senate and House of representatives," approved March 13th, 1815, report. [Washington City, 1817] 2 p. DLC; MWA. 42533

-- -- February 11, 1817. The Committee on finance, who were instructed, by a resolution of the Senate to inquire into the expediency of so altering the law imposing a duty on carriages as to exempt from its operation any carriage which is usually and chiefly employed in husbandry, or for the transportation or carrying of goods, report. [Washington, 1817] 2 p. DLC; MWA.   42534

-- -- February 12, 1817. Mr. Tait, from the committee on naval affairs submitted the following motion for consideration. [Washington City, 1817] 2 p. (Survey of the eastern entrance into Long Island sound, the harbor

of Newport and Hampton Roads, ordered.) DLC; MWA.
42535
-- -- February 12, 1817. The committee of claims,
to whom has been referred the petition of Samuel
Brown report. [Washington City, 1817] 2 p. DLC;
MWA. 42536

-- -- February 13, 1817. The Committee of claims,
to whom has been referred the petition of A. J. Villard
report. [Washington City, 1817] 2 p. DLC; MWA.
42537
-- -- February 13, 1817. The Committee of claims,
to whom was referred the petition of Simon Sarrazin
and J. B. Aubert, of Baton Rouge, in the State of Louisiana report. [Washington City, 1817] 2 p. DLC;
MWA. 42538

-- -- February 14, 1817. Read, and ordered to be
printed for the use of the Senate. Copy of the reports
of Messrs. Latrobe and Hoban, on the public buildings.
[Washington City, 1817] 19 p. DLC; MWA. 42539

-- -- February 14, 1817. The committee appointed on
so much of the President's message as relates to
roads and canals, report. [Washington City, 1817] 4 p.
DLC; MWA. 42540

-- -- February 14, 1817. The committee of claims,
to whom has been referred, the petition of Denis de la
Ronde report. [Washington City, 1817] 2 p. DLC;
MWA. 42541

-- -- February 17, 1817. Mr. Mason, of N. H. submitted the following motions for consideration. [Wash-
ington City, 1817] 2 p. (Regarding the establishment of
a bank within the city of Washington) DLC; MWA.
42542
-- -- February 17, 1817. Mr. Mason of N. H. submitted the following motion for consideration. [Washington
City, 1817] 2 p. (Regarding the erecting of suitable
buildings for custom houses.) DLC; MWA. 42543

-- -- -- [Washington City, 1817] 2 p. (To reduce the

military peace establishment to 5000 men.) DLC; MWA.
                                                    42544

-- -- February 18, 1817. Mr. Fromentin, from the
Joint Library committee, reported the following resolutions, which were read and passed to the second
reading. [Washington City, 1817] 2 p. (Regarding the
erecting of a suitable building for the Library) DLC;
MWA.   42545

-- -- February 19, 1817. Mr. Fromentin submitted
the following motion for consideration. [Washington
City, 1817] 2 p. (Regarding the salary of the judge of
the sixth circuit court of the U.S.) DLC; MWA. 42546

-- -- February 19, 1817. Mr. Goldsborough submitted
the following motion for consideration. [Washington
City, 1817] 2 p. (Regarding precautionary measures for
the security of the country watered by the Chesapeake
Bay.) DLC; MWA.   42547

-- -- February 19, 1817. Mr. Williams submitted the
following motion for consideration. [Washington City,
1817] 2 p. (Requesting the President for a copy of
the correspondence between the government of the U.S.
and the government of Spain.) DLC; MWA.   42548

-- -- February 19, 1817. The committee of claims,
to whom has been referred the petition of Joseph C.
Boyd, report. [Washington City, 1817] 2 p. DLC;
MWA.   42549

-- -- February 19, 1817. The committee of claims to
whom has been referred the petition of Thomas Ewell
report. [Washington, 1817] 2 p. DLC; MWA.   42550

-- -- February 19, 1817. The committee to whom was
referred the motion submitted by Mr. Fromentin, on
the 14th inst. with instructions in relation to the Journal report. [Washington City, 1817] 4 p. DLC; MWA.
                                                    42551

-- -- February 20, 1817. The committee on naval affairs to whom was referred the memorial of Edward
Shubuck and others, officers of the late United States

brig Chippewa, report...[Washington City, 1817] 1 p.
MWA.   42552

-- -- February 20, 1817. Read, and ordered to be
printed for the use of the Senate. To the honourable
the Senate and House of representatives of the United
States, in Congress assembled: The memorial of the
merchants of Portsmouth, N.H., and its vicinity, who
have suffered from the depradations of French cruisers,
respectfully represents. [Washington City, 1817] 3 p.
DLC; MWA.   42553

-- -- February 22, 1817. Mr. Campbell, chairman of
the committee on finance, communicated the following
correspondence with the secretary of the Treasury.
[Report of the secretary of the Treasury on the currency.] [Washington City, 1817] 3 p. DLC; MWA.
                                                         42554

-- -- February 24, 1817. The Committee on the post-
office and post-roads, who were instructed by a resolution of the Senate, to inquire into the expediency of increasing the compensation of the Postmaster at Newark, New Jersey, having had the same under their consideration, respectfully submit the following resolution
to the Senate. [Washington City, 1817] 2 p. DLC;
MWA.   42555

-- -- February 25, 1817. Mr. Roberts submitted the
following motion for consideration which was read and
passed to a second reading. [Washington City, 1817]
2 p. (Regarding the payment of the assistants to the
sergeant-at-arms and door-keepers of the Senate.) DLC;
MWA.   42556

-- -- February 25, 1817. Mr. Wilson submitted the
following motion for consideration. [Washington City,
1817] 2 p. (To inquire into the expediency of increasing the pension of Randolph Clarkson.) DLC; MWA.
                                                         42557

-- -- February 25, 1817. Mr. Wilson submitted the
following resolution which was read, and passed to a
second reading. [Washington, 1817] 2 p. (Resolution
on making any future contract for the printing of Con-

gress.) DLC; MWA.   42558

-- -- February 25, 1817. The Committee of claims
to whom has been referred the petition of Frederick
Folley report. [Washington City, 1817] 2 p. DLC;
MWA.   42559

-- -- February 27, 1817. The Committee of claims,
to whom has been referred the petition of William B.
Stokes. [Washington City, 1817] 3 p. DLC; MWA.
                                              42560

-- -- March 1, 1817. Mr. Dana, from the committee
to whom was referred so much of the message of the
President of the United States as relates to weights and
measures, reported the following resolution. [Wash-
ington City, 1817] 2 p. DLC; MWA.   42561

-- -- Dec. 5, 1817. Agreeably to notice, Mr. Daggett asked and obtained leave to bring in the following
resolution, which was read and passed to the second
reading; Resolved...[Washington City, 1817] 1 p. (On
the distribution of state papers and public documents.)
DLC.   42562

-- -- Dec. 8, 1817. Mr. Sanford submitted the following motion for consideration: Resolved...[Washing-
ton City, 1817] 1 p. (On alteration of present system
of collecting duties.) DLC.   42563

-- -- Dec. 9, 1817. Agreeable to notice, Mr. Barbour asked and obtained leave to bring in the following
resolution, which was read and passed to the second
reading. Resolved...[Washington City, 1817] 1 p.
(On the amendment of the Constitution of the U.S. in
relation to internal improvement.) DLC.   42564

-- -- Dec. 10, 1817. Mr. Morril submitted the following motion for consideration: Resolved...[Washing-
ton City, 1817] 1 p. (On surveying several tracts of
military bounty lands.) DLC.   42565

-- -- Ddc. 10, 1817. Mr. Sanford submitted the following motion for consideration: Resolved...[Washing-

ton City, 1817] 1 p. (On the settlement of public accounts.) DLC. 42566

-- -- Dec. 12, 1817. Mr. Campbell submitted the following motion for consideration: Resolved...[Washington City, 1817] 1 p. (Inquiry concerning the ascertainment of boundaries and other land marks of claimed lands.) DLC. 42567

-- -- Dec. 12, 1817. Mr. Daggett submitted the following motion for consideration: Resolved...[Washington City, 1817] 1 p. (Inquiry concerning subject of bankruptcies, punishment of offences in the U.S., and definition of piracy and other offences committed on high seas.) DLC. 42568

-- -- Dec. 12, 1817. Mr. Lacock submitted the following motion for consideration: Resolved...[Washington City, 1817] 1 p. (For the establishment of a district and circuit court in Pittsburgh, Penn.) DLC. 42569

-- -- Dec. 15, 1817. Mr. Barbour submitted the following motion for consideration: Resolved...[Washington City, 1817] 1 p. (On information regarding negotiation with Spain.) DLC. 42570

-- -- Dec. 15, 1817. Mr. Daggett, from the committee to whom was referred the resolution authorizing the distribution of certain public documents, reported it with the following amendment: [Washington City, 1817] 1 p. DLC. 42571

-- -- Dec. 15, 1817. Mr. Morrow submitted the following motion for consideration: Resolved...[Washington City, 1817] 1 p. (On the ascertainment and establishment of the northern boundary line of the Ohio state.) DLC. 42572

-- -- Dec. 15, 1817. Mr. Troup submitted the following motion for consideration: Resolved...[Washington City, 1817] 1 p. (For the restitution of slaves.) DLC. 42573

-- -- Dec. 15, 1817. Mr. Williams, of Mississippi,

submitted the following motion for consideration: Resolved...[Washington City, 1817] 1 p. (On provision
of Laws of the U.S. within the state of Mississippi.)
DLC.   42574

-- -- Dec. 16, 1817. Mr. Morrow submitted the following motion for consideration: Resolved...[Washing-
ton City, 1817] 1 p. (Inquiry concerning location or
surveys on Virginia lands to which the Indian title has
not been extinguished.) DLC.   42575

-- -- Dec. 18, 1817. Mr. Eppes submitted the following motion for consideration: Resolved...[Washington
City, 1817] 1 p. (The extension of time for Virginia
military land warrants.) DLC.   42576

-- -- Dec. 18, 1817. Mr. Noble submitted the following motion for consideration: Resolved...Washing-
ton City, 1817. 1 p. (The expediency of establishing
a land office in eastern Indiana.) DLC.   42577

-- -- Dec. 18, 1817. Mr. Ruggles submitted the following motion for consideration: Resolved...[Washing-
ton City, 1817] 1 p. (For the appointment of commissioners to survey, lay out, and mark a road from the
west bank of the Ohio river to Columbus.) DLC. 42578

-- -- Dec. 22, 1817. Mr. Noble submitted the following motion for consideration: Resolved...[Washington
City, 1817] 1 p. (For the payment of three per cent
to the state of Indiana from the net proceeds of sales
of U.S. lands lying within the said state.) DLC. 42579

-- -- Dec. 23, 1817. Agreeably to notice given yesterday, Mr. Morril asked and obtained leave to introduce the following resolution, which was read, and
passed to the second reading: Resolved...[Washington
City, 1817] 1 p. (On the description of the quality of
lot given to each soldier.) DLC.   42580

-- -- Dec. 23, 1817. Mr. Dickerson, agreeably to
notice given yesterday, and in obedience to instructions
received from the legislature of New Jersey, asked and

obtained leave to introduce a resolution, proposing an
amendment to the constitution and the appointment of
electors of President and Vice President of the U.S.
Resolved... [Washington City, 1817] 2 p. DLC.   42581

-- -- Dec. 23, 1817.   Mr. Smith submitted the follow-
ing motion for consideration: Resolved... [Washington
City, 1817] 1 p. (On duties in 1815, 1816, and 1817)
DLC.   42582

-- -- Dec. 24, 1817.   The Committee of Claims to
whom has been referred the petition of Silas Willard,
report... [Washington City, 1817] 1 p. DLC.   42583

-- -- Dec. 29, 1817.   Mr. Tait submitted the following motion for consideration: Resolved... [Washington
City, 1817] 1 p. (On the expediency of augmenting the
pay of the militia.) DLC.   42584

-- -- Dec. 29, 1817.   Read and ordered to be printed.
To the Congress of the United States.   The General
Assembly of the State of Tennessee, begs leave to ad-
dress your honorable body, on the unsatisfied claims
for land in this state... [Washington City, 1817] 6 p.
DLC.   42585

-- -- Dec. 30, 1817.   The Committee of Claims, to
whom was referred the petitions of William Edwards
and John G. Stubbs, report... [Washington City, 1817]
1 p. DLC.   42586

-- -- Dec. 30, 1817.   Mr. Daggett submitted the following motion for consideration: Resolved... [Washing-
ton City, 1817] 1 p.   (On an act to set apart and dispose of certain public lands.) DLC.   42587

-- -- Dec. 30, 1817.   Mr. Smith submitted the following motion for consideration: Resolved... [Washington
City, 1817] 1 p. (On duties during the years 1815 and
1816.) DLC.   42588

-- -- Dec. 30, 1817.   Read, and ordered to be printed
...A statement showing the amount of duty which ac-

crued on salt imported during the years 1815 and 1816
...[Washington City, 1817] 1 p. DLC.   42589

-- -- Dec. 31, 1817. Mr. Burrill submitted the following motion for consideration: Resolved...[Washing-
ton City, 1817] 1 p. (For the erection of centre building of the Capitol.) DLC.   42590

-- -- Dec. 31, 1817. Mr. Burrill submitted the following motion for consideration: Resolved...[Washing-
ton City, 1817] 1 p. (On the subject of the African
slave trade.) DLC.   42591

-- -- Memorial of the directors of the Chesapeake and
Delaware canal company. January 9, 1817. Read and
ordered to be printed for the use of the Senate. [Wash-
ington City, 1817] 6 p. DLC; MWA.   42592

-- -- Report of the secretary of the Treasury on the
petition of William Edwards. January 9, 1817. Read
and ordered to be printed for the use of the Senate.
[Washington City, 1817] 3 p. DLC; MWA.   42593

-- -- Report of the secretary of the Treasury relative
to the survey of military bounty lands. January 2,
1817. Read...[Washington City, 1817] 2 p. DLC;
MWA.   42594

-- The infantry exercise of the United States army,
abridged for the use of the militia of the United States.
Ed. 2, cor. and imp. Poughkeepsie [N.Y.] P. Potter,
and Sheldon Potter, Philadelphia, 1817. 156 p. CSmH.
                    42595
-- Joint resolution for abolishing the traffick in slaves,
and the colonization of the free people of colour of the
United States. February 11, 1817. Read, and committed to a committee of the whole House on Monday
next. [Washington City, 1817] 2 p. DLC; MWA. 42596

-- Joint resolutions submitted by Mr. Forsyth, concerning a violation of the charter of the National Bank
by its directors, and requiring the secretary of the
Treasury to withdraw the public deposits therefrom.

January 14, 1817. [Washington City, 1817] 2 p. CtY;
DLC; MWA.   42597

-- Journal of the House of representatives of the U-
nited States, at the second session of the Fourteenth
Congress... Washington City, Pr. by William A. Davis,
1816! [1817] 658 p. CSmH; DLC; MWA; MWiW; NjP.
                                                     42598
-- Journal of the Senate of the United States of America, being the second session of the Fourteenth Congress, begun and held in the city of Washington, December 2d, 1816... Washington, Pr. by William A.
Davis, 1816! [1817] 533 p. DLC; MWA; MWiW; MdBE;
MnU.   42599

-- Laws of the United States of America. Vol. VI.
Published by authority. Washington City, Pr. for the
Department of State, 1817. 311 p. KyLxT.   42600

-- Laws of the United States, resolutions of Congress
under the Confederation, treaties, proclamations, and
other documents, having operation and respect to the
public lands. Collected, digested, and arranged, pursuant to two acts of Congress, passed April 27, 1810,
and January 20th, 1817. City of Washington, Jonathan
Elliot, 1817. 377 p. CU; DLC; IaU-L; MWA; MiDSH;
NNC-L; NNLI; NSyHi; Nh; Nj; NjR; OClWHi; OWoC;
PU; TChU; THi.   42601

-- -- Collected, digested, and arranged, pursuant to
two acts of Congress, passed April 27, 1810, and January 20th, 1817. City of Washington, Pr. by Edward
De Krafft, 1817. 377 p. Ar-Hi; CSmH; DLC; MS; MWA;
MeBat; MsWJ; PPAmP; RPB.   42602

-- ... Letter from His Excellency David Holmes, governor of the state of Mississippi, transmitting a copy
of the constitution and form of government of the said
state... Washington City, Pr. by E. De Krafft, 1817.
23 p. ([U.S. 15th Cong., 1st sess. House. Doc.] 2)
(Read, and ordered to lie upon the table. December 4,
1817) CSmH; DLC; G; MH-L; MsJS; NjP; O; OCLaw;
VtMiM.   42603

-- Letter from the acting secretary of War, relative
to the collection of military fines, in compliance with
a resolution of the House of representatives of the 7th
instant. February 14, 1817. Washington City, Pr. by
William A. Davis, 1817. 3 p. DLC; MWA.   42604

-- Letter from the acting secretary of War to the chairman of the committee of ways and means, enclosing detailed statements on which are founded the estimates
for the expenses for the year 1817, including arrear-
ages. January 6, 1817. Washington City, Pr. by
William A. Davis, 1817. 43 p. DLC; G; MWA. 42605

-- Letter from the acting secretary of War, transmitting a statement of the officers and privates comprising the whole military establishment of the United
States: made in pursuance of a resolution of the House
of representatives of the 11th inst. January 13, 1817.
Washington City, Pr. by William A. Davis, 1817. 7 p.
DLC; DNA; MWA; MWiW.   42606

-- Letter from the acting secretary of War, transmitting a statement of the probable of annual expense of
the military academy from the year 1801 to 1816; the
number of students educated at said Academy, and of
those now retained in the army; as also of the appropriation for buildings, and for books, plans, &c. &c. February 15, 1817. Washington City, Pr. by William A.
Davis, 1817. 21 p. DLC; G; MH; MWA; MeB.   42607

-- Letter from the acting secretary of War, transmitting a statement showing the actual number of the army
of the United States, and the stations of each corps; in
compliance with a resolution of the Senate of the United
States, of the 21st instant. January 23, 1817. Washington City, Pr. by William A. Davis, 1817. 8 p.
DLC; DNA; In; MWA; MWiW.   42608

-- Letter from the acting secretary of War, transmitting a statement showing the expediture of the moneys
appropriated for the contingent expenses of the military
establishment, for the year 1816. February 24, 1817.
Washington City, Pr. by William A. Davis, 1817. 78 p.

United States

DLC; DNA; IaHi; MWA; MWiW.   42609

-- Letter from the acting secretary of War, transmitting an official report of the adjutant and inspector general relative to a mutiny said to have taken place at Norfolk, of a part of the 38th regiment United States infantry. February 20, 1817. Washington City, Pr. by William A. Davis, 1817. 6 p. DLC; G; MWA; Vi.
42610

-- Letter from the acting secretary of War. Transmitting his report on the letter of Major Gen. Harrison, and the accompanying documents; referred to the Secretary of War, on the 30th of April, last... December 31, 1816. Read and referred to a select committee. Washington City, William A. Davis, 1817. 15 p. In; InHi; KyLoF.   42611

-- Letter from the acting secretary of War, transmitting information relative to the claims of the state of Massachusetts for the payment of the expenses of the militia, ordered out by the executive authority of the state during the late war. February 20, 1817. Washington City, Pr. by William A. Davis, 1817. 90 p. DLC; G; MWA; MeB; Nh-Hi.   42612

-- Letter from the acting secretary of War, transmitting statements of contracts made at the War department in the year 1816, on behalf of the United States. January 11, 1817. Washington, Pr. by William A. Davis, 1817. 7 p. DLC; MWA; MWiW; O.   42613

-- Letter from the acting secretary of War transmitting statements of the clerks employed in the department of War, and the compensation allowed to each. January 15, 1817. Washington City, Pr. by William A. Davis, 1817. 12 p. DLC; G; MWA; MeB; O; PMA.
42614

-- Letter from the Commissioner of the public buildings, transmitting an estimate for enclosing and improving the Capitol square. February 3, 1817. Washington City, Pr. by William A. Davis, 1817. 5 p. DLC; G; MWA; MeB; MiD-B.   42615

-- Letter from the Comptroller of the Treasury transmitting a statement of balances remaining on the books
of the Treasury which have been due more than three
years prior to September 30, 1816, and remaining un-
settled on that day... Feb. 5, 1817. Washington City,
Pr. by William A. Davis, 1817. 21 p. DLC; DNA;
MWA; MWiW; O.   42616

-- -- ... On the books of the Accountant of the Navy.
February 19, 1817. Washington City, W. A. Davis,
1817. 21 p. DLC; MWA; MWiW; O.   42617

-- Letter from the post-master general, transmitting a
list of contracts made by him in the year 1816, for
transporting the mails February 15, 1817. Washington
City, Pr. by William A. Davis, 1817. 12 p. DLC;
MWA; MWiW; MnSH; O.   42618

-- Letter from the Post-master general, transmitting
a list of unproductive post roads for the year 1817.
February 20, 1817. Washington City, Pr. by William
A. Davis, 1817. 14 p. DLC; MWA; MWiW; MnSH.
                                                    42619

-- Letter from the Post-master general, transmitting
a report of the clerks employed in his office during the
year 1816; and the compensation allowed to each. February 18, 1817. Washington, Pr. by William A. Davis,
1817. 4 p. DLC; G; MWA.   42620

-- Letter from the secretaries of the several departments respecting the accountability of public officers
and agents and the duties and emoluments of the Attorney General. January 21, 1817. Washington City,
Pr. by William A. Davis, 1817. 8 p. DLC; G; MWA;
MeB; TU.   42621

-- Letter from the secretary of State, transmitting a
list of the names of persons to whom patents have been
issued, for the invention of any new or useful art, or
machine, manufacture, or composition of matter, or
any improvement thereon, from January 1st, 1816, to
January 1st, 1817. January 6, 1817. Washington, Pr.
by William A. Davis, 1817. 12 p. DLC; DeGE; MWA;

MWiW; O.   42622

-- Letter from the secretary of the Navy, transmitting
a statement and application of the moneys drawn from
the Treasury on account of the Navy, from October 1,
1815 to September 30, 1816. January 7, 1817. Washington City, Pr. by William A. Davis, 1817. [6] p.
DLC; MWA; MWiW; O.   42623

-- Letter from the secretary of the Navy, transmitting
a statement of contracts made by the Navy department
during the year 1816. January 14, 1817. Washington,
Pr. by William A. Davis, 1817. [6] p. DLC; MWA;
MWiW; O.   42624

-- Letter from the secretary of the Navy, transmitting
a statement of moneys transferred during the last re-
cess of Congress, from sundry specific appropriations
to the other specific appropriations, by the authority
of the President of the United States. January 3, 1817.
Washington City, Pr. by William A. Davis, 1817. 6 p.
DLC; MWA; MWiW.   42625

-- Letter from the secretary of the Navy, transmitting
lists of the names of the clerks in the Navy department,
and in the office of the Commissioners of the Navy during the year 1816; and the amount of compensation allowed to each. January 9, 1817. Washington City, Pr.
by William A. Davis, 1817. 7 p. DLC; G; MWA. 42626

-- Letter from the secretary of the Treasury, communicating his reason for not transferring the public
moneys deposited in certain state and other local banks,
to the Bank of the United States. Dec. 12, 1817...
Washington City, Pr. by E. De Krafft, 1817. 16 p.
DLC; G; NjP; O.   42627

-- Letter from the secretary of the Treasury to the
chairman of the Committee of ways and means, in relation to transfers of appropriations by the President of
the United States. January 6, 1817. Washington City,
Pr. by William A. Davis, 1817. 6 p. DLC; G; MH;
MWA.   42628

-- Letter from the secretary of the Treasury to the chairman of the committee of ways and means, relative to the collection of duties. February 24, 1817. Washington City, Pr. by William A. Davis, 1817. 4 p. DLC; MWA; MeB.   42629

-- Letter from the secretary of the Treasury, transmitting a report made in pursuance of a resolution of the House of representatives of March 9, 1816, requiring the secretary of the Treasury to report to the next session of Congress, whether any, and if any, what alterations are necessary to equalize the duty on the capacity of stills, boilers, and other instruments used in distillation. January 13, 1817. Washington City, Pr. by William A. Davis, 1817. 58 p. DLC; G; MWA.
42630

-- Letter from the secretary of the Treasury, transmitting a statement of goods, wares, and merchandise exported from the United States, during the year ending September 30, 1816. February 3, 1817. Washington City, Pr. by William A. Davis, 1817. 17 p. DLC; MWA; MWiW.   42631

-- Letter from the secretary of the Treasury, transmitting a statement of the emoluments and expenditures of the officers of the customs in the year 1816. February 25, 1817. Washington City, Pr. by William A. Davis, 1817. 2 l. 6 fold tab. DLC; MWA; MWiW; MnSH; O.   42632

-- Letter from the secretary of the Treasury, transmitting a statement of the names of the clerks employed in the Treasury department during the year 1816; and the amount paid to each. January 7, 1817. Read and ordered to lie upon the table. Washington City, Pr. by William A. Davis, 1817. [6] p. DLC; MWA; MWiW; O.   42633

-- Letter from the secretary of the Treasury, transmitting a statement showing the quantity of public lands sold and the receipts therefor, in the states of Ohio and Indiana, and the Illinois and Mississippi territories, during the year ending on the 30th of September, 1816.

February 14, 1817. Washington City, Pr. by William
A. Davis, 1817. [6] p. DLC; MWA; MWiW; MiD-B;
MnSH; O.   42634

-- Letter from the secretary of the Treasury, transmitting an estimate of the appropriations for the service of the year 1817. January 6, 1817. Washington
City, Pr. by William A. Davis, 1817. 59 p. DLC; G;
MWA; MWiW; O.   42635

-- Letter from the secretary of the Treasury, transmitting an estimate of the appropriations for the service of the year 1818. Dec. 17, 1817...Washington
City, Pr. by E. De Krafft, 1817. 57 p. DLC; NjP.
                                                 42636
-- Letter from the secretary of the Treasury, transmitting his annual report on the state of the finances.
Prepared in obedience to the "Act supplementary to an
act to establish the Treasury department." December
8, 1817. Washington City, Pr. by E. De Krafft, 1817.
24 p. DLC; G; N; NjP; O.   42637

-- Letter from the secretary of the Treasury, transmitting statements of the internal duties for 1815; of
the amount of direct tax, &c. &c. &c. February 11,
1817. Washington City, Pr. by William A. Davis,
1817. 27 p. DLC; MWA; MWiW; MnSH; O.   42638

-- Letter from the secretary of the Treasury, transmitting statements of moneys paid at the Treasury during the year 1816; for the miscellaneous claims not
otherwise provided for, &c. &c. &c. January 27, 1817.
Washington City, Pr. by William A. Davis, 1817. 6 p.
DLC; ICJ; MWiW.   42639

-- Letter from the secretary of the Treasury, transmitting statements of the importations of goods, wares,
and merchandise in American and foreign vessels and
an aggregate view of both, from the 1st of October,
1814, to the 30th of September, 1815. February 28,
1817. Washington City, Pr. by William A. Davis,
1817. 60 p. DLC; G; IaHi; MWA; MWiW.   42640

-- Letter from the secretary of the Treasury, transmitting statements relating to the internal duties and direct tax; and an abstract of the official emoluments and expenditures attending the collection of the same. December 5, 1817. Washington City, Pr. by E. De Krafft, 1817. 28 p. DLC; NjP; O.   42641

-- Letter from the secretary of the Treasury, transmitting sundry statements relative to the operations of the Mint of the United States. February 28, 1817. Washington City, Pr. by William A. Davis, 1817. 10 p. DLC; MWA; MWiW; MnSH; O.   42642

-- Letter from the secretary of the Treasury, transmitting the annual statement of the district tonnage of the United States, on the 31st of December, 1815; with and explanatory letter from the Register of the Treasury. January 17, 1817. Washington City, Pr. by William A. Davis, 1817. 7 p. DLC; MWA; MWiW.
42643

-- Letter from the secretary of War, transmitting a list of the officers who held brevet rank in the army of the U.S., at the close of the late war...Dec. 29, 1817. Washington City, Pr. by E. De Krafft, 1817. 12 p. DLC; NjP.   42644

-- Letter from Thomas Tudor Tucker, treasurer of the United States, transmitting his accounts for 1816. February 25, 1817. Washington City, Pr. by William A. Davis, 1817. 283 p. DLC; G; KyLxT; MWA; MWiW.
42645

-- Letters patent to Nathan Read for the invention of a machine for threshing wheat and other small grains, signed by James Monroe, President of the United States and John Quincy Adams, secretary of State, on December 23, 1817. MSaE.   42646

-- Memorial of B. Henry Latrobe, surveyor of the Capitol of the United States. February 26, 1817. [Washington City, 1817] 5 p. DLC; MWA.   42647

-- Memorial of sundry citizens of Baltimore praying of the general government aid and protection to commerce

and manufactures.   February 23, 1816.   Referred to
the committee of commerce and manufactures.   [Washington City, 1817]   13 p.   CtY; DLC; MWA.   42648

-- Memorial of the American society for the encouragement of domestic manufactures.   January 29, 1817.
Referred to the committee of commerce and manufactures.   [Washington City, 1817]   5 p.   DLC; MWA.
                                                        42649
-- Memorial of the merchants of the City of New York
to... Congress... Feb. 3, 1817.   [Washington City,
1817]   8 p.   NcD; PHi.   42650

-- Memorial of the Mississippi convention, praying an
extension of the limits of that state.   December 17,
1817.   Washington City, Pr. by E. De Krafft, 1817.
8 p.   DLC; G; NjP; R.   42651

-- Memorial of the president and board of managers
of the American society for colonizing the free people
of colour of the United States.   January 14, 1817.
[Washington City, 1817]   5 p.   DLC; MWA.   42652

-- ...Message from the President of the United States,
communicating information of the proceeding of certain
persons who took possession of Amelia island and of
Galvezton, during the summer of the present year, and
made establishments there.   December 15, 1817...
Washington City, Pr. by E. de Krafft, 1817. 46 p.
([15th Cong., 1st session. House. Doc. no.] 12) DLC;
NjP; O; OO; PHi.   42653

-- Message from the President of the United States,
communicating, pursuant to a resolution of the House of
Representatives of the eleventh inst.   A report of the
present strength of the army of the U.S. ...Dec. 22,
1817.   Washington City, Pr. by E. De Krafft, 1817.
5 p. 3 fold. charts.   DLC; NN; NjP.   42654

-- Message from the President of the United States,
complying with the resolution of the Senate, of the
eleventh of this month.   December 18, 1817.   Printed
by order of the Senate of the United States.   Washing-

ton City, Pr. by E. De Krafft, 1817. 5 p. DLC; G;
MiD-B; O; R.   42655

-- Message from the President of the United States,
in compliance with a resolution of the sixteenth inst.,
relative to the restitution of slaves under the first article of the Treaty of Ghent. December 29, 1817. Pr.
by order of the Senate of the United States. Washington City, Pr. by E. De Krafft, 1817. 5 p. DLC; G; O;
R.   42656

-- Message from the President of the United States,
to both Houses of Congress, at the commencement of
the first session of the fifteenth Congress, Dec. 2,
1817. Pr. by order of the Senate of the United States.
Washington City, Pr. by Edward De Krafft, 1817. 11 p.
DLC; G; MWA; MiD-B; MoU; O; PHi; R.   42657

-- Message from the President of the United States, to
both Houses of Congress, at the commencement of the
first session of the fifteenth Congress. December 2,
1817. Read, and committed to the Committee of the
House on the state of the Union. Washington City, Pr.
by Edward De Krafft, 1817. 11 p. DLC; G; NjP; O.
                                                 42658
-- Message from the President of the United States,
transmitting a report of the director of the Mint, of
the operation of that establishment during the year 1816.
January 7, 1817. Washington City, Pr. by William A.
Davis, 1817. 8 p. DLC; G; MWA.   42659

-- Message from the President of the United States,
transmitting agreeably to a resolution of the Senate of
the 8th instant, the claims of certain states for the services of militia during the late war. January 23, 1817.
Washington City, Pr. by William A. Davis, 1817. 7 p.
DLC; MWA.   42660

-- Message from the President of the United States,
transmitting an account of the contingent expenses of
the government for the year 1816. January 18, 1817.
Washington City, Pr. by William A. Davis, 1817. 6 p.
DLC; G; MWA; MeB.   42661

-- Message from the President of the United States, transmitting documents relative to the execution of the first article of the late treaty between the United States and Great Britain. February 7, 1817. Washington City, Pr. by William A. Davis, 1817. 103 p. CSmH; DLC; G; MWA; Nh-Hi.   42662

-- Message from the President of the United States, transmitting the correspondence between the United States and the government of Spain, relative to the subject of controversy between the two nations. February 22, 1817. Washington City, Pr. by William A. Davis, 1817. 77 p. DLC; G; MH; MWA; Nh-Hi; ScC.   42663

-- Message from the President of the United States, upon the subject of discriminating duties payable in the ports of Great Britain and the United States, by vessels of the respective nations. February 3, 1817. Washington City, Pr. by William A. Davis, 1817. 3 p. DLC; MWA; MeB.   42664

-- Mr. Rich's motion. February 6, 1817. Read and committed to a committee of the whole House, tomorrow. Washington City, Pr. by Roger C. Weightman, 1817. 3 p. O.   42665

-- Petition of Gurdon S. Mumford and others, shipowners, in New-York. January 23, 1817. Referred to the committee of the whole House, on the "bill to prohibit all commercial intercourse with ports and places, into, or with which the vessels of the United States are not ordinarily permitted to enter and trade." [Washington City, 1817] 4 p. DLC; MWA.   42666

-- ... Petition from the citizens of the counties of Clarke, Monroe, Washington, Mobile, and Baldwin, in the Alabama Territory. October, 1817. December 30, 1817. Referred to the select committee... on a memorial of the Mississippi convention, relating to an extension of the limits of that state. [Washington? 1817] 12 p. CtY; DLC; G; NjP.   42667

-- -- Washington City, Pr. by E. De Krafft, 1817.

12 p. R.   42668

-- The Post-office law, with instructions and forms,
published for the regulation of the Post-office. 1817.
City of Washington, Pr. for the General Post-Office,
1817. 106 p. Ct; DLC; MWA; NRivHi.   42669

-- Post Offices in Vermont...January 1, 1817. N.B.
The first column contains the distance by the nearest
post road to Washington City. The second column contains the distance to Montpelier...[Montpelier? 1817]
Broadside. McCorison List.   42670

-- Proposed amendments to the bill, authorizing the
commutation of soldiers' bounty lands. [Washington,
1817] (H.R. 2. [December 8, 1817]) DLC.   42671

-- Register of all officers and agents, civil, military,
and naval, in the service of the United States...1817-
Washington, 1817-   MH; MdBP; NIC; PPAmP; PPL.
                                             42672
-- Register of the commissioned and warrant officers
of the navy...Washington, 1817-   MH.   42673

-- Regulations established by the secretary of War,
for substantiating claims to pensions...War Department,
Pension Office, December 23, 1817. [Washington,
D.C., 1817] Broadside. NcD.   42674

-- Report from the secretary of the Treasury, of the
amount of receipts in the treasury of the U.S., from
imports, internal taxes, and other sources of revenue,
within the District of Columbia...Dec. 30, 1817...
Washington City, Pr. by E. De Krafft, 1817. 6 p. DLC;
NjP.   42675

-- Report, in part, of the Committee on so much of
the President's message as relates to roads, canals,
and seminaries of learning. December 15, 1817. Read
and committed to a committee of the whole House on
Friday next. [Washington City, 1817] 11 p. DLC; G;
NjP.   42676

-- Report in the case of Winslow and Henry Lewis.
December 15, 1817. Read, and with a bill for their
relief. Committed to a committee of the whole House,
tomorrow. [Washington City, 1817] [1] p. DLC; G;
NjP.   42677

-- Report of a select committee appointed to inquire
into the claims of certain detachments of the militia of
Georgia, during the years 1793 and 1794. December
22, 1817. Washington City, Pr. by E. De Krafft,
1817. 3 p. DLC; NjP; R.   42678

-- Report of a select committee on the memorial of
William Tatham. Made February 10, 1817. [Washing-
ton City, 1817] 4 p. DLC; MWA.   42679

-- Report of a select committee on the petition of the
Berkshire association for the promotion of agriculture
and manufactures. Feb. 21, 1817.   [Washington
City, 1817] 2 p. DLC; MWA.   42680

-- Report of a select committee on the subject of
claims for services of militia of the state of Georgia,
performed during the years 1793 and 1794, by order of
the executive of that state, under a discretionary power by the War department; accompanied with "A bill to
authorize the payment of certain militia claims of the
state of Georgia. January 27, 1817. Read and ordered to be printed. [Washington City, 1817] 4 p.
DLC; MWA.   42681

-- Report of the claim of the heirs of Philip Renaut,
accompanying a bill confirming certain lands in the
Territory of Illinois, to the heirs of Philip Renaut.
Made February 18, 1817, and ordered to be printed.
[Washington City, 1817] 3 p. DLC.   42682

-- Report of the Commissioners of the Navy pension
fund, containing sundry statements in relation to the
state of that fund; made in obedience to the act for the
better government of the Navy of the United States.
January 17, 1817. Washington City, Pr. by William A.
Davis, 1817. 22 p. DLC; MWA; MWiW; O.   42683

-- Report of the committee appointed by the citizens of
Pittsburgh, at a meeting held at the court-house on
the 21st of December, 1816, to inquire into the state
of the manufactures in the city and its immediate vicinity. Made February 17, 1817. In the House of
representatives of the United States. [Washington City,
1817] 24 p. DLC; MWA; PHi; PPi.   42684

-- Report of the Committee appointed to inquire what
amendments are necessary to the act granting bounties
in land and extra pay to certain Canadian volunteers.
January 11, 1817. Read and together with the bill
herewith reported, ordered to be printed. [Washing-
ton City, 1817] 4 p. DLC; MWA.   42685

-- Report of the Committee of claims on the case of
John I. Pattison. Dec. 18, 1817...[Washington City,
1817] 1 p. DLC; NjP.   42686

-- Report of the Committee of Claims on the petition
of Alexander Worster. December 29, 1817. Washington City, Pr. by E. De Krafft, 1817. 2 p. DLC; NjP;
R.   42687

-- Report of the Committee of Claims on the petition
of Bowie, Kurtz, and others. January 14, 1817.
[Washington City, 1817] 6 p. DLC; MWA.   42688

-- Report of the Committee of claims on the petition
of Caleb Nichols, accompanied with a bill for his relief. January 27, 1817. [Washington City, 1817] 4 p.
DLC; MWA.   42689

-- Report of the Committee of claims on the petition
of John Anderson, with a bill for his relief. December 31, 1817. Committed, with the bill to a Committee of the whole House on Friday next. [Washington
City, 1817] 2 p. DLC; G; NjP.   42690

-- Report of the Committee of claims, upon the petition of Paul Robinson, of Vermont, February 7, 1817.
[Washington City, 1817] 2 p. DLC; MWA.   42691

-- Report of the Committee of claims upon the petition of Renner and Heath.   January 17, 1817.   [Washington City, 1817]   3 p.   DLC; MWA.   42692

-- Report of the Committee of commerce and manufactures, on the expediency of making Cincinnati, on the river Ohio, a port of entry, February 13, 1817.   [Washington City, 1817]   4 p.   DLC; MWA.   42693

-- Report of the Committee of commerce and manufactures on the petition of Anthony Buck.   February 5, 1817.   [Washington City, 1817]   8 p.   DLC; MWA. 42694

-- Report of the Committee of commerce and manufactures on the petition of Henry Lee, accompanied with a bill for his relief.   Made February 8th, 1817, and ordered to be printed.   [Washington City, 1817]   2 p. DLC; MWA.   42695

-- Report of the committee of public lands on the petition of Joseph Gillard.   Made February 10, 1817.   Accompanied with "a bill confirming the title of Joseph Gillard. "   [Washington City, 1817]   2 p.   DLC; MWA.
                                                    42696
-- Report of the Committee of revisal and unfinished business.   December 12, 1817.   Read, and ordered to lie upon the table.   [Washington City, 1817]   3 p.   DLC; G; NjP.   42697

-- Report of the Committee of the House of representatives, in pursuance of the joint resolution of the two Houses, to ascertain and report a mode of examining the votes for President and Vice-President of the United States, and of notifying the persons elected of their election.   February 15, 1817.   [Washington City, 1817] 4 p.   DLC; MWA.   42698

-- Report of the Committee of ways and means, accompanying a bill to abolish internal duties.   Dec. 9, 1817.   Read and committed to a committee of the whole House tomorrow.   [Washington City, 1817]   2 p. DLC; NjP.   42699

-- Report of the Committee of ways and means on petitions from the collectors of Plymouth, N. C., Kennebunk, in Maine, Edgartown, in Massachusetts, and Middletown, in Connecticut. February 7, 1817. [Washington City, 1817] 3 p. DLC; MWA. 42700

-- Report of the Committee of ways and means, on the expediency of making an appropriation to satisfy the claims of the friendly Creek Indians, whose property was plundered by the hostile Creeks, in consequence of their attachment to the United States. January 29, 1817. [Washington City, 1817] 4 p. DLC; MWA. 42701

-- Report of the Committee of ways and means on the expediency of repealing or modifying the act laying duties on licenses to retailers. February 11, 1816. [Washington City, 1817] 8 p. DLC; MWA. 42702

-- Report of the Committee of ways and means on the expediency of repealing the duty on carriages. Made February 11, 1817. [Washington, 1817] 8 p. DLC; MWA. 42703

-- Report of the Committee of ways and means on the petition of Charles H. Saunders and Manuel Judah. January 2, 1817. [Washington City, 1817] 4 p. DLC; MWA. 42704

-- Report of the Committee of ways and means, on the petition of Robert Burnside. January 29, 1817. [Washington City, 1817] 2 p. DLC; MWA. 42705

-- Report of the Committee of ways and means, to whom was referred the annual report of the secretary of the Treasury, on so much thereof as relates to an addition to the sinking fund. January 14, 1817. [Washington City, 1817] 6 p. DLC; MWA. 42706

-- Report of the Committee of ways and means, who were instructed to inquire into the propriety of allowing to the state of Georgia fifteen per cent, out of her quota of direct tax of 1816, assumed by the state. January 18, 1817. [Washington City, 1817.] 3 p. DLC;

GU-De; MWA.   42707

-- Report of the Committee on elections, to which was
recommitted their report of the 31st ult. on the petition of Rufus Easton, contesting the election of John
Scott.   January 10, 1817.   [Washington City, 1817] 5 p.
DLC; MWA.   42708

-- Report of the Committee on Indian affairs.   Made
February 4th, 1817, and committed with the bill "to
regulate trade and intercourse with Indian tribes, " &c.
to committee of the whole House tomorrow. [Washing-
ton City, 1817] 4 p. DLC; MWA.   42709

-- Report of the Committee on pensions and revolutionary claims on the petition of Sarah Deweas and
others for payment for property destroyed by the ene-
my in the revolutionary war.   January 17, 1817...
[Washington City, 1817] 4 p. DLC; MWA.   42710

-- Report of the Committee on private land claims, on
the petition of Gabriel Winter and others, accompanying
a bill "confirming certain lands in the county of Arkansas, in the Missouri Territory, to the heirs of Elisha
Winter, deceased. " January 15, 1817.   Read and ordered to be printed.   [Washington City, 1817] 10 p.
DLC; MWA.   42711

-- Report of the Committee on private land claims, on
the petitions of Gabriel Winters and others, accompanying a bill "confirming certain lands in the county of
Arkansas, in Missouri territory, to the heirs of Elisha
Winter and to the heirs of William Winter.   December
30, 1817...[Washington City, 1817] 3 p. MWA.   42712

-- Report of the Committee on public expenditures on
the memorial and accounts of Colonel James Thomas,
quarter-master general February 15, 1817.   [Washing-
ton City, 1817] 16 p. DLC; MWA.   42713

-- Report of the committee on public lands, accompanying a bill making provisions for the establishment of an
additional land office in the Territory of Missouri, and

for the final adjustment of claims to town and village
lots.   January 25, 1817.   [Washington City, 1817] 2 p.
DLC; MWA; MoSHi.   42714

-- Report of the Committee on so much of the Presi-
dent's message as relates to roads and canals. Made
February 7, 1817.   [Washington City, 1817] 18 p.
DLC; MWA; N.   42715

-- Report of the Committee on so much of the public
accounts and expenditures, as relate to the War department.   March 1, 1817.   [Washingtln City, 1817] 15 p.
DLC; MWA.   42716

-- Report of the Committee on the Judiciary who were
instructed to inquire whether any, and if any, what
legal provisions are necessary to prescribe the effect
which the public acts, records, and judicial proceedings of each state shall have in the courts of every
other state.   December 23, 1817.   Washington City,
Pr. by E. De Krafft, 1817. 1 p. DLC; NjP; R. 42717

-- Report of the committee on the national currency,
instructed by a resolution of the House of representatives, to inquire whether the President and directors of
the Bank of the United States, have adopted any ar-
rangement by which the specie part of the second installment can be evaded or postponed.   January 10,
1817.   [Washington City, 1817] 12 p. DLC; MWA.
                                                  42718
-- Report of the Committee on the post-office and post-
roads, to whom was referred the memorial of the
"American Bible Society." January 25, 1817. [Wash-
ington City, 1817] 3 p. DLC; MWA.   42719

-- Report of the committee on the public buildings.
Made February 18, 1817. [Washington City, 1817] 40 p.
DLC; MWA.   42720

-- Report of the Committee on the public buildings,
relative to Daniel Pettibone's petition.   February 19,
1817.   [Washington City, 1817] 10 p. DLC; MWA.
                                                  42721

-- Report of the committee on the public expenditures.
Made March 3d, 1817. [Washington City, 1817] 7 p.
DLC; MWA.   42722

-- Report of the committee on the public lands on the
petition of Chew and Relf, owners, and representatives
of the owners of the claim of the Marquis de Maison
Rouge. Made February 10, 1817. Accompanied with
a bill confirming the title of the Marquis de Maison
Rouge. [Washington City, 1817] 2 p. DLC; MWA.
                                                   42723
-- Report of the committee on the public lands, on the
petition of William Miller and others, by their attorney,
Josiah S. Johnston. January 29, 1817. [Washington
City, 1817] 5 p. DLC; MWA.   42724

-- Report of the committee to whom was referred a
Memorial of a convention of delegates from fifteen
counties in the Mississippi Territory, praying that the
said territory may be admitted as a state entire and
without division; accompanied with a bill for the admission of the people of the Mississippi Territory into the
Union, &c. January 17, 1817. [Washington City,
1817] 7 p. DLC; MWA.   42725

-- Report of the committee to whom was referred so
much of the President's message as relates to the re-
organization or classification of the militia of the United
States. January 17, 1817. [Washington City, 1817]
16 p. DLC; MWA.   42726

-- Report of the joint committee of the two Houses,
appointed to examine and report to their respective
Houses what business is pending between them and what
is indispensable to act upon previous to the adjournment. February 27, 1817. [Washington City, 1817]
7 p. DLC; MWA.   42727

-- Report of the military committee upon the subject of
allowing the non-commissioned officers and privates
who enlisted for and during the late war, or who died
or were killed previously to obtaining an honourable dis-
charge, their balance of pay and bounty land. February

5, 1817. [Washington City, 1817] 4 p. DLC; MWA.

42728

-- Report of the President and directors of the Washington canal company, of the amount of their expenditure, and the clear profits thereof; made in pursuance of a requisition of their charter. January 31, 1817. [Washington City, 1817] 2 p. DLC; MWA.   42729

-- Report of the secretary of War, of the number of warrants for military bounty land, issued to soldiers who served during the late war, and the quantity of land included in such warrants. December 12, 1817. Washington City, Pr. by E. De Krafft, 1817. [3] p. DLC; G; NjP; O.   42730

-- Report of the select committee appointed on the 4th of December last, on so much of the message of the President of the United States, as relates to roads and canals. February 20, 1817. Printed by order of the House of representatives. [Washington City, 1817] 8 p. DLC; MWA.   42731

-- Report of the select committee appointed on the 20th December, last, on the petitions of inhabitants of Buffalo, and the Niagara frontier, in the state of New York, accompanied with a "Bill for the relief of certain sufferers in the late war, between the United States and Great Britain. January 23, 1817. [Washington City, 1817] 4 p. DLC; MWA.   42732

-- Report of the select committee appointed on the 20th instant, on a memorial of the legislature of North Carolina, remonstrating against the act of Congress, passed in the year 1806, "authorizing the state of Tennessee to issue grants and perfect titles to certain lands therein described, and to settle the claims to the vacant and unappropriated lands within the same." January 28, 1817. [Washington City, 1817] 9 p. DLC; MWA.

42733

-- Report of the select committee appointed on the 12th ult. to inquire into the expediency of altering the flag of the United States. January 2, 1817. [Washington City, 1817] 3 p. DLC; MWA.   42734

-- Report of the select committee on the President's message of the 6th February, 1817. February 11, 1817. [Washington City, 1817] 2 p. DLC; MWA.42735

-- Report of the select committee, to which was referred sundry petitions, remonstrating against the practice of transporting and opening the mails on the Sabbath, and praying a discontinuance thereof. March 1, 1817. [Washington City, 1817.] 9 p. DLC; MWA.
42736

-- Report of the select committee, to whom were referred the petition of Samuel Thompson and John Dailey. January 14, 1817. [Washington City, 1817] 2 p. DLC; MWA. 42737

-- Report on colonizing the free people of colour of the United States. February 11, 1817. Read, and committed to a committee of the whole House on Monday next. [Washington City, 1817] 5 p. DLC; MWA. 42738

-- Report on the claim of the heirs of Philip Renaut, accompanying a bill confirming certain lands in the territory of Illinois, to the heirs of Philip Renaut. Made February 18, 1817... [Washington City, 1817] 3 p. MWA. 42739

-- Resolutions offered by Mr. Johnson, of Kentucky, and Mr. Walker, of North Carolina. December 9, 1817. Read and committed to a Committee of the whole House, on Monday next. [Washington City, 1817] 2 p. DLC; G; NjP; R. 42740

-- Rules and regulations for the field exercise and manoevres of infantry... Concord, N.H., Pr. by Isaac Hill, 1817. MWA. 42741

-- Rules of the federal courts, within the Vermont district... Rutland, Vt., Pr. by Fay & Davison [1817?] (Apparently set up in 1816 but not issued until 1817 at which time the firm was Fay, Davison & Burt) 23 p. MWA; VtU-W. 42742

-- Statement accompanying a bill respecting the pay and

emoluments of certain officers of the army of the U-
nited States.   January 28, 1817.   [Washington City,
1817] 2 p.   DLC; MWA.   42743

-- Statement of the amount of internal duties imposed
by the United States, (except those on household furniture, on watches and stamps) and paid by each person
in the first collection district of Vermont during the
year one thousand eight hundred and sixteen. ... Isaac
Burton, collector for the first collection district of Vermont. [Rutland, Vt., 1817] Broadside. McCorison
List.   42744

-- Statement of the amount of internal duties imposed
by the United States, (excepting those on household
furniture, on watches and on stamps) paid by each person in the third collection district of Vermont, during
the year 1816. ... Thomas Leverett, collector for the
3d collection district of Vermont.   February 24th, 1817.
[Windsor, Vt., 1817] Broadside. McCorison List.
                                                 42745
-- Statement of the amounts of internal duties... in the
4th collection district of Vermont, during the year
1816...[Middlebury, Vt., Pr. by F. P. Allen, 1817?]
7 p. MWA.   42746

-- Statement of the annual expense of the military
academy from 1801 to 1816; the number of students
educated, etc. Washington City, Pr. by William A.
Davis, 1817. (Cat. of J. Pierson, Bronxville, N. Y.,
"Interesting Americana" [1939] No. 24)   42747

-- Table of post-offices in the United States, with the
names of the post-masters, the counties and states in
which they are situated, and the distances from the city
of Washington. Washington City, J. Elliot, 1817. 88 p.
MH; MLexHi; MWA; NIC; PPAmP.   42748

-- Tariff, or rates of duty after 30th June, 1816, on
all goods, wares and merchandise, imported into the
United States of America. Boston, Andrew J. Allen
[1817] 28 p. MSaP.   42749

-- Tariff, or rates of duty, on all goods, wares, and merchandizes imported into the United States. [New York? 1817?] 21 p. MH.   42750

-- $10 reward: deserted the service of the United States, on or about the 24th instant, Isaac Holbrook, a Corporal in Company D, corps of Artillery, stationed at Fort Preble, harbor of Portland. By order of the Major commanding, [Signed] N. G. Dana, Lt. of Artillery. Fort Preble, Nov. 27, 1817. Portland, Me., [1817] Broadside. MHi.   42751

-- To all people to whom these presents shall come... Greeting. Know ye, that I, Thomas Leveret, of Windsor, in the state of Vermont, and one of the Collectors of internal duties for the United States of America...[Windsor, Vt., 1817?] Broadside. McCorison List.   42752

-- Translations of Elisha Winter's warrant of concession. Made January 25, 1817. Printed by order of the House of representatives. [Washington City, 1817] 4 p. CtY; DLC; MWA.   42753

The United States almanac, for the year of our Lord 1818...by David Young, philom. Elizabeth-Town, N. J., Shepard Kollock [1817] [36] p. MWA; NHi; NjR; NjMo.
42754

Universal death in Adam, and life in Christ. Containing a refutation of the doctrine of total depravity and endless misery. By a layman. Salem, Mass., Pr. for the author, 1817. 16 p. MMeT; MWA; NjR. 42755

The universal dream book... Philadelphia, 1817. MWA.
42756

Universalist church in the U. S. A.
     Statement of the faith delivered to the saints... Keene, N. H., [1817] MWA.   42757

[Upham, Thomas Cogswell]
     The home in the West... Hanover, N. H., David Watson, Jun., 1817. MWA; RPB.   42758

Urbana Gazette.   Urbana, Ohio, Allen M. Poff, May,
1817, 1st issue.   Weekly newspaper. MWA.   42759

The Utica directory.   Containing the village census, of
1816...Utica, N. Y., William Williams, 1817. [50] p.
MWA; NN; NUt.   42760

Utica Observer.   Utica, N. Y., E. Dorchester, Jan. 7,
1817, 1st issue.   Weekly newspaper. MWA.   42761

                              V
Valpy, Richard, 1754-1836
     The elements of Greek grammar, with notes. By
R. Valpy...2d Amer. from the last London ed., with
cor. and additions.   Boston, Cummings and Hilliard,
Univ. press, Hilliard and Metcalf, 1817. 276 p. CtW;
ICU; MB; MBAt; MBC; MH; MWA; MWelC; MeBa;
MoSpD; NCH; OCl; ViU.   42762

Vanderlyn, John
     A description of the principal paintings in Mr.
Vanderlyn's exhibition. Chamber-street. [New York,
1817?] [7] p. N.   42763

VanHorne, James
     A narrative of the captivity and sufferings of James
VanHorne, who was nine months a prisoner by the Indians on the plains of Michigan. Middlebury, Vt., 1817.
18 p. TWS.   42764

Varte, Charles
     Map of the United States partly from new surveys
dedicated to the citizens thereof by their humble servant
Charles Varte, engineer and geographer. Baltimore,
Charles Varte, 1817. MdBP.   42765

-- -- Baltimore, Charles Varte, 1817. 110 x 146 cm.
MdBP.   42766

Vattel, Emmerich de
     The law of nations...Philadelphia, Abraham Small,
1817. 500 p. C; CU; GU-L; KyBgW; MH-L; MWA;

MdAS; NGH; NR; NcU; Nj; PP; TxU.   42767

Vaux, Frances Bowyer
    Henry; a story, intended for little boys and girls,
from five to ten years old... 1st Amer. ed.   Philadelphia, Wm. Charles, 1817. [60] p. PP.   42768

Vaux, Roberts, 1786-1836
    Memoirs of the life of Anthony Benezet... Philadel-
phia, Pr. by Merritt, for James P. Parke, 1817. 136p.
DLC; IC; ICU; ICN; InRchE; MB; MSaE; MWA; MdBJ;
MiD-B; MiU; NBF; NBLiHi; NBuG; NNG; NNS; NhD;
NjP; OC; OClWHi; OMC; P; PHi; PHC; PFal; PP; PPF;
PPAmP; PPL; PPLT; PPWa; PSC-Hi; PU; TNF; ViHaI.
                                                   42769
-- -- York [S. C.] Repr. for W. Alexander, 1817.
156 p. NcD.   42770

The veil withdrawn, or Presbyterian vindicated, and
the character of its enemies.   In a letter to a re-
vered gentleman, by a minister of that church. Charleston, S. C., Office of the Patriot, 1817. 38 p. NN.
                                                   42771
Vergilius Maro, Publius
    Opera... Philadelphia, A. Small, 1817. 711 p.
CBe; CtW; MMhHi; MNotnW; MNBedf; MWA; MtStJosC;
WU.   42772

-- -- Philadelphia, Pr. by A. Small, for M. Carey &
son, 1817. 711 p. GAU; MWA.   42773

-- Works... selected by William Stoughton.   Baltimore,
J. Cushing, 1817. MWA.   42774

Vermont (State)
    General list of the state of Vermont, for the year
1817. [1817] 5 l.   McCorison List.   42775

-- Governor's speech.   ... Jonas Galusha.   Montpelier,
Oct. 10, 1817. [Montpelier? 1817] Broadside. Mc-
Corison List.   42776

-- Journals of the General Assembly of the state of

Vermont... Oct., 1817. Rutland, Pr. by Fay, Davison & Burt [1817] 250 p. CSmH; DLC; MWA; Nb; Vt; VtHi; VtU-W; VtMiS. 42777

-- Laws of the state of Vermont, to the close of the session of the Legislature in the year 1816; with an Appendix, containing the titles of local acts, and an Index of the laws in force. Vol. III. Rutland, Fay, Davison & Burt, 1817. 336 p. C; Ct; ICLaw; IaU-L; In-SC; M; MH; MSaEC; MWA; MdBB; Mi-L; NN; Nc-S; Nj; Nv; OClW; Or-SC; PPHmP; R; RPL; VtMiM; VtHi; VtU-W; W; WaU. 42778

-- Laws passed by the Legislature of the state of Vermont... 1817. Middlebury, Pr. by Frederick P. Allen for William Slade, Jr. [1817] 144 p. Ia; In-SC; MH-L; MWA; MdBB; Mi-L; NNLI; Nb; Nj; RPL; Vt; W; VtU-W; 42779

-- Rules of the Supreme Court... of Vermont. Rutland, Vt., Pr. by Fay, Davison & Burt [1817] 12 p. MH-L; MWA; Vt. 42780

Vermont & New-York almanack for the year of our Lord 1818... By Andrew Beers, philom. [Burlington] Pr. for A. Pritchard [1817] 24 p. DLC; MWA; VtMiS. 42781

Vermont Bible Society
   Fifth report of the Vermont Bible Society, communicated to the society, at their annual meeting. At Middlebury, October 15, 1817. Montpelier, Vt., Pr. by E. P. Walton, Oct., 1817. 32 p. VtHi. 42782

Vermont Intelligencer. Bellows Falls, Vt., Bill Blake & Co., Jan. 1, 1817, 1st issue. Weekly newspaper. MWA. 42783

The Vermont register and almanack for the year of our Lord 1818... Burlington, Vt., Pr. by S. Mills, for Saml. Mills and Wm. Slade, [1817] 108 p. DLC; MH; MWA; NN; VtHi. 42784

Verses to the memory of Richard Reynolds, &c. New York, 1817. PSC-Hi. 42785

A view of exertions lately made for the purpose of colonizing the Free people of colour, in the United States, in Africa or elsewhere. City of Washington, Pr. by Jonathan Elliot, 1817. 23 p. CU; G; LNH; MBC; MWA; MdHi; MeBat; OrPD. 42786

A view of the principles upon which the Independent Society for Public Worship, under the ministry of the Rev. Mr. Frey, is established. New York, July 1817. 8 p. MH. 42787

Vigilant Fire Society, Boston.
Constitution of the Vigilant Fire Society, instituted at Boston Jan. 12, 1817. Boston, Pr. by Chester Stebbing, 1817. 8 p. MBB. 42788

The village harmony. Ed. 8. Boston, [1817] MB. 42789
-- Or, New-England repository of sacred musick... Ed. 14. Boston, West & Richardson [1817] RPB. 42790

The village songster: containing a selection of the most approved patriotic and comic songs. Haverhill, Mass., Pr. by Burrill and Tileston, 1817. 72 p. MWA. 42791

Vincent, Thomas
Christ's sudden and certain appearance to judgment... Philadelphia, Probasco and Justice, 1817. 354 p. ICU; MWA; NRAB; PSC-Hi; PPPrHi. 42792

Vindication of the captors of Major Andre. New York, Kirk & Mercein, T. & W. Mercein [1817] 99 p. MdCatS. 42793

Virginia (State)
Acts passed at a General Assembly of the Commonwealth of Virginia, begun... 11th day of November, 1816... Richmond, Pr. by Thomas Ritchie, 1817. 219 p. DLC. 42794

-- Circular [regarding the duties of county clerks] Richmond, Council Chamber, December 31, 1817. [Signed] William Robertson, Clerk of the Council.

[Richmond, 1817] Broadside. ViU.   42795

-- Journal of the House of Delegates of the Commonwealth of Virginia, begun... 11th day of November,
1816. Richmond, Pr. by Thomas Ritchie, 1816[!]
[1817] 250 p. NN.   42796

-- Journal of the Senate of the Commonwealth of Virginia, Nov., 1816. Richmond, Pr. by Thomas Burling,
1816[!] [1817] 76 p. NN.   42797

Virginia almanac for 1818. By John Sharp. Alexandria,
Va., Pr. by E. L. Bogan, for J. A. Stewart [1817]
MWA.   42798

Volksfreund und Hagerstauner calender, auf das Jahr
1818... Hagerstaun, Md., Gruber & May [1817] 36 p.
DLC; MWA; MdHG; MdHi; PHi.   42799

Der Vollstandige Pferde-Arzt. Herausgegeben von
Sage und Rietze. Reading, Pa., Pr. by H. B. Sage,
1817. (Samuel Ward, La Plata, Md. [Letter of July
18, 1962])   42800

W

[W., M. B.]
    An die Gott suchende und Jesus liebende seelen.
Lancaster, Pa., Pr. by Joseph Ehrenfried, 1817.
MWA; P; PHi.   42801

W., S.
    A visit to London... A new ed. Philadelphia, Pr.
by Wm. Greer, for Benjamin Warner, 1817. MB; MWA;
MWiW.   42802

Wadsworth, Benjamin, 1750-1826
    Female charity an acceptable offering. A sermon
delivered in the Brick meeting house in Danvers, at the
request of the Charitable female cent society in Danvers
and Middleton, for promoting Christian knowledge, Nov.
7, 1816. Andover, Mass., Pr. by Flagg and Gould,
1817. 32 p. CSt; MB; MBC; MWA; NjR.   42803

Waldo, J.
    Child's pronouncing spelling book.   Georgetown,
S. C. , 1817. MWA.   42804

Walker, John
    A critical pronouncing dictionary, and expositor of
the English language... Ed. 6, imp.   Philadelphia,
Pr. by Griggs & Co., for Benjamin Warner and Thom-
as & William Bradford, 1817. 413 p. MWA; MiHi.
                                                           42805
-- A sermon from Ps. CV. 2, and Letters to the Rev.
T. D. Baird... Cadiz, Ohio, J. W. White, 1817. 72 p.
PPPrHi.   42806

Walsh, Michael
    A new system of mercantile arithmetic, adapted to
the commerce of the United States in its domestic and
foreign relations... 4th Pittsburgh ed.   Pittsburgh, Pa.,
Cramer & Spear, 1817. 249 p. InU; PPi.   42807

Walton, J.
    The life of Robert Sanderson... New York, 1817.
MLanc.   42808

Walton's Vermont register and almanac, for the year
of our Lord 1818... Montpelier, Vt., E. P. & G. S. Walton, [1817] 132 p. DLC; MBNEH; MB; MH; M; MWA;
NHi; NN; Vt; VtHi; VtU-W.   42809

Wanastrocht, Nicolas
    Abridgment of French grammar.   Georgetown,
D. C. , W. Duffy, 1817. 55 p. DWP; MWA.   42810

-- Grammar of the French language, with practical exercises.   4th Amer., from 13th London ed.   Boston,
Pr. by Joseph T. Buckingham, for West & Richardson,
1817. 468 p. CU; ICU; KyU; MB; MEab; MH; MMeT;
MWA; MeB; MsU; NNC; OOxM; PHi; PPF.   42811

Warden, William, 1777-1849
    Letters written on board His Majesty's ship the
Northumberland, and at Saint Helena; in which the conduct and conversations of Napoleon Buonaparte, and his

suite, during the voyage, and the first months of his
residence in that island, are faithfully described and
related.   Albany, Repr. by Websters and Skinners,
1817. 132 p. MWA; MoS; NN.   42812

-- -- Boston, Pr. [by Nathan Hale] at the office of the
Daily Advertiser, 1817. 140 p. MB; MBMHiM; MH;
MWA; RPA.   42813

-- -- New Haven, Pr. [by S. Converse] at the Journal
office, [1817] 110 p. CtW; CtY; MBC; MNF; MWA;
NSyU; NjR; PPM.   42814

-- -- Newbern, N. C., 1817. MH.   42815

-- -- Philadelphia, Pr. by J. Maxwell, for M. Thom-
as, 1817. 244 p. CSmH; CtHT; DLC; GEU; LNMus;
LNStM; MWA; MdCatS; MdHi; MoKU; NNS; PMA; PU;
RPB; ScU; TxCsA; Vi; ViU; WM.   42816

-- -- Philadelphia, Pr. by W. Brown, for Mitchell and
Ames, 1817. 240 p. GDC; MNBedf; MdBJ; MtHi; OAU;
ScNC.   42817

-- -- Pittsburgh [Pa.] Pr. by Butler & Lambdin, for
Robert Patterson and Cramer & Spear, 1817. 182 p.
CSmH.   42818

-- -- Winchester, Va., John Heiskell, 1817. 114 p.
ViWin.   42819

Wardlaw, Ralph, 1779-1853
     Unitarianism incapable of vindication: a reply to
the Rev. James Yates's vindication of Unitarianism.
Andover [Mass.] Pr. by Flagg and Gould, for Mark
Newman, 1817. 351 p. CSansS; CSt; DLC; ICMe; ICP;
LNB; MH-AH; MWA; MWiW; NN; NcMHi; PPiXT; RPB.
                                                         42820
Ware, Ashur, 1782-1873
     An oration delivered before the Republicans of
Portland, July the fourth 1817... Portland [Me.] Pr. by
Francis Douglas, at the Argus office, 1817. 14 p.
CSmH; DLC; MWA.   42821

Ware, Henry, 1764-1845
A sermon, delivered at Northborough, October 30, 1816, at the ordination of the Reverend Joseph Allen ...Cambridge, Mass., Pr. by Hilliard and Metcalf, 1817. 33 p. MWA; NjR.   42822

-- A sermon delivered January 1, 1817, at the ordination of the Reverend Henry Ware, to the pastoral care of the Second church in Boston, by his father Henry Ware...Boston, J.W. Burditt, 1817. 35 p. CSt; IC; ICMe; MAnP; MBAU; MH; MMeT-Hi; MNF; MWA; MdHi; MeB; MeHi; NcD; OO; RPB.   42823

Ware, Henry, Jr.
A sermon, preached at the interment of the Rev. Thomas Prentiss...Charlestown, Mass., Pr. by Samuel Etheridge, 1817. 16 p. DLC; ICMe; MBAt; MBC; MBD; MH; MHi; MSaE; MWA; NN; WHi.   42824

Warner, Thomas
A brief outline of the history of the Bible... New York, 1817. 35 p. MH-AH; M; N; NNG; PPPrHi.
42825
Warner's almanac, for the year of our Lord, 1818... Calculated by Joshua Sharp. Philadelphia, Benjamin Warner [1817] [36] p. MWA; NCH.   42826

-- Philadelphia, Benjamin Warner [1817] [44] p. NCH.
42827
Washington, Thomas, Jr.
Masonic oration; delivered on the 24th June, 1817, in Nashville...[Nashville, Tenn., Pr. by T.G. Bradford [1817] 32 p. DLC.   42828

Washington, D.C. (City)
Acts of the corporation of the City of Washington; passed by the Fourteenth Council. Printed by order of the Council. Washington, Pr. by Edward De Krafft, 1817. 64 p. In-SC.   42829

Washington almanac for 1818. Calculated by John Sharp...Baltimore, Cushing & Jewett [1817] MWA.
42830

Washington circulating library, Boston.
    Catalogue of the Washington circulating library...
[Boston] Pr. by T. G. Bangs, 1817. MWA.   42831

Washington Examiner. Washington, Pa., John Grayson, May 28, 1817, 1st issue. Weekly newspaper.
DLC.   42832

Washington fire club, Roxbury, Mass.
    The rules and regulations...Boston, Pr. at the
Chronicle press, 1817. 8 p. MWA.   42833

Washington hose company. Baltimore.
    Constitution...Baltimore, Pr. by Pomeroy & Toy,
1817. 13 p. MiD-B.   42834

Washington Orphan Asylum Society
    Report of the Washington Orphan Asylum Society.
Instituted on the tenth of October, 1815. Washington,
D. C., Pr. by William A. Davis, 1817. DLC.   42835

Washington Society
    Ode for the fourth of July, 1817. By a member.
Tune - "Columbia Land of Liberty." ...[Boston] Pr.
by T. G. Bangs, [1817] Broadside. MHi.   42836

The watch-word; or, Quito-gate; a melodrama in two
acts...New York, D. Longworth, 1817. 28 p. MBr;
MH; MMal; MWA; NCH.   42837

Waterhouse, Benjamin, 1754-1846
    A circular letter, from Dr. Benjamin Waterhouse,
to the surgeons of the different posts, in the Second
Military Department of the United States' Army. [Cam-
bridge, Mass. ? 1817] 24 p. DNLM; IEN-M; MBM;
MWA; NNNAM; PPL.   42838

Waterloo Gazette. Waterloo, N. Y., George Lewis,
May 28, 1817, 1st issue. Weekly newspaper. MWA.
                                               42839
Waters, Samuel, 1750-1828
    A sermon, delivered in Worcester jail, July, 1817.
By Samuel Waters...Worcester, Mass., Pr. by William

Manning, 1817. 12 p. CSt; DLC; M; MB; MBAt; MWA;
MWiW; MiD-B; NN; NRAB.   42840

Watkins, John
   Scripture biography... Albany, George Lindsay,
1817. MWA.   42841

Watson, Richard
   Anecdotes of the life of Richard Watson,   Philadelphia, 1817. MB.   42842

Watterston, George, 1783-1854
   A memoir of the history, culture, manufactures,
uses, &c. of the tobacco plant... Washington City, Pr.
by Jonathan Elliot, 1817. 12 p. DLC; MB; PPL-R.
                                                   42843
Watts, Isaac, 1674-1748
   Watts' divine songs for the use of children. (A-
dorned with cuts) New-Haven, Sidney's press, 1817.
[47] p. MWA.   42844

-- Hymns and spiritual songs.   In three books. Haverhill, Mass., stereotyped by B. & J. Collins; pub. by
Burrill and Tileston, 1817. [313]-585, [4] p. (Bound
with The Psalms of David imitat... by I. Watts, Haverhill, Mass. 1817. Pub. by Burrill & Tileston, stereotyped by B. & J. Collins) MSaE; MWA.   42845

-- -- New York, Pr. by J. Seymour, 1817. 320-596 p.
(Bound with Psalms carefully suited... new ed., cor.
New-York, Pr. by J. Seymour, 1817) MWA; PPPrHi.
                                                   42846
-- -- Philadelphia, Pr. by W. Hill Woodward, for Wil-
liam W. Woodward, 1817. 389 p. (Bound with Psalms
carefully suited... Philadelphia, 1817. W. Hill Wood-
ward, printer.) MWA; NRAB; NjP; P; PBa; PPPrHi.
                                                   42847
-- Dr. Watts's plain and easy catechisms for children:
Together with a collection of prayers and hymns. 1st
Brattleboro' ed.   Brattleborough [Vt.] Pr. by J. Holbrook, 1817. 48 p. MWA.   42848

Wauby, Isaac
    The water of life free... Philadelphia, Pr. by D.
Dickinson, 1817. MWA.   42849

... Way of salvation. [Hartford, Pr. by Hudson & Co. ?
1817] MWA.   42850

[Webb, Mrs. Eliza (Bowen)]
    The female marine... Ed. 5. Boston, Pr. for the
purchaser, 1817. MWA.   42851

Webster, Noah, 1758-1843
    American spelling book. West's ed. Boston, West
& Richardson, 1817. DLC; MWA.   42852

-- -- Containing the rudiments of the English language,
for the use of schools in the United States... The rev.
impression. Brattleborough, Vt., John Holbrook, 1817.
168 p. Ct; MWA; NN; NNC; OO; VtMiS.   42853

-- -- Brattleborough, Vt., Holbrook and Fessenden
[1817] MWA.   42854

-- -- Hartford, Hudson & Co., 1817. 168 p. CtHi;
MWA.   42855

-- -- 13th revised impression. Utica, N.Y., William
Williams, 1817. 168 p. NN.   42856

-- Dictionary of the English language: compiled for the
use of common schools in the United States. Hartford,
Pr. by George Goodwin & sons, 1817. 366 p. CtHi; IU;
ICU; MA; MH; MWA; NIDHi.   42857

-- A letter to the Honorable John Pickering, on the sub-
ject of his vocabulary; or, Collection of words and
phrases, supposed to be peculiar to the United States of
America. Boston, West and Richardson, 1817. 60 p.
CtSoP; DLC; ICU; MA; MB; MH; MHi; MNBedf; MWA;
NNF; NNS; RPJCB; WHi.   42858

Webster's calendar, or the Albany almanack for 1818.
By Andrew Beers. Albany, Websters and Skinners

[1817] MWA; NCanHi; NNebg; NN; NWattJHi; NjR.
42859

The weekly monitor; moral, entertaining, and instructive. Vol. I, No. 1, (June 5, 1817) Boston [1817]
MB; MBC; MH.   42860

Weekly visitor. New York, Alexander Ming, Nov. 1,
1817, 1st issue. Weekly newspaper. CtY; MWA; NN;
NjR.   42861

Weems, Mason Locke, 1759-1825
    Hymen's recruiting-serjeant... Greenfield, Mass.,
Pr. for the public, 1817. 40 p. MDeeP; MWA. 42862

-- Das leben des Georg Waschington, mit sonderbaren
anecdoten sowohl ehrenvoll für ihn selbst als auch
nachahmungswürdig für seine jungen landsleute... Baltimore, Schäffer & Maund and M. Carey & Son, Philadelphia, 1817. 240 p. CSmH; DLC; DeGE; ICN; MB;
MH; MWA; MdHi; MdBE; MdBP; MdU; NN; NjMoW;
PHi; PPL; PReaHi.   42863

-- The life of Benjamin Franklin, written chiefly by
himself; with a collection of his best essays, humorous,
moral, and literary. New ed., rev. and enl. Philadelphia, M. Carey, 1817. 264 p. MB; MH; MWA;
PHi; PPAmP; PPF; PPL-R.   42864

-- The life of George Washington; with curious anecdotes, equally honourable to himself, and exemplary to
his young countrymen... Ed. 18, greatly improved.
Philadelphia, Pr. by Mathew Carey, 1817. 228 p. DGU;
DLC; GU; IHi; MB; MWA; NN; PHi.   42865

Weiser, Conrad, fl. 1817
    An address to the free & independent German elec-
tors of the commonwealth of Pennsylvania. Philadelphia, 1817. PP.   42866

-- To the citizens of Dauphin County, and the friends of
Harrisburg... [Harrisburg, 1817] Broadside. DLC.
42867

Wesley, John
The beauties of the Rev. J. Wesley, containing
the most interesting passages selected from his whole
works... Philadelphia, Jonathan Pounder, 1817. 254 p.
CtY-D; MH; MWA; MoSW; OPosm; PHi; PPLT; PU.
42868
-- The doctrine of original sin, according to Scripture,
reason and experience, in answer to Dr. Taylor, by
the Rev. John Wesley,   New York, J. Soule and T.
Mason, 1817. 377 p. MWA; NcD; OAU; OHi.   42869

-- Sermon on duty of constant communion. Hartford,
1817. MB; MWA.   42870

[West, Mrs. Lucy (Brewer)]
The female marine, or adventures of Miss Lucy
Brewer, a native of Plymouth County, Mass. ... Ed. 5.
Boston, Pr. for the purchaser, 1817. CSmH.   42871

West, Elizabeth
Memoirs on spiritual exercise of Elizabeth West...
1st Amer. ed. Exeter, N.H., Pr. by C. Norris,
1817. 282 p. MWA; Nh.   42872

West-Jersey Gazette. Salem, N.J., I.A. Kollock,
Aug. 13, 1817, 1st issue. Weekly newspaper. NjHi.
42873
Western Register. Washington, Pa., Robert Fee, Feb.
1817, 1st issue. Weekly newspaper. PPiHi.   42874

Western almanack, for... 1818... by James R. Stubbs.
Cincinnati, Williams & Mason, and Morgan, Lodge &
Co. [1817] 36 p. DLC; ICN; MWA; OCHP; OClWHi.
42875
The Western Reserve almanac, for the year of our
Lord, 1818... Pittsburgh, Pa., Pr. by Butler & Lamb-
din [1817] 16 p. OClWHi.   42876

Western Telegraph. Eaton, Ohio, C. Vanansdal & Co.,
Aug. 1, 1817, 1st issue. Weekly newspaper. MWA.
42877
Westminster Assembly of Divines
The shorter catechism of the... assembly... Chilli-

cothe, O., Pr. by John Andrews, 1817. 60 p. (Harlow Lindley, Columbus, O.)   42878

-- -- New York, Pr. by J. C. Totten, for T. A. Ronalds, 1817. 36 p. MWA; NN; WGrNM.   42879

Westminster Observer. Westminster, Md., George
Keatinge, 1817, 1st issue. Newspaper. Brigham, p.
270.   42880

Wharton, Charles Henry
    A concise view of the principal points of contro-
versy between the Protestant and Roman churches...
New York, Pr. by Clayton & Kingsland, for David
Longworth, 1817. 8 p. GEU; InID; MWA; MWH; NjP.
                                                     42881
-- A letter to the Roman Catholics of the city of Wor-
cester... New York, Pr. by Clayton & Kingsland, Re-
pub. by David Longworth, 1817. 40 p. (Bound in -
His - A concise view of the principal points of contro-
versy between the Protestant and Roman churches...
New York, 1817) InID; MB; MWA; MWH.   42882

[--] A reply to An address to the Roman Catholics of
the United States of America... New York, Pr. by Clayton & Kingsland, Repub. by David Longworth, 1817.
(Bound in - His - A concise view of the principal
points of controversy between the Protestant and Roman
churches... New York, 1817) MWA.   42883

-- A short answer to "A true exposition of the doctrine
of the Catholic church touching the sacrament of pen-
ance... New York, Pr. by Clayton & Kingsland, Repub.
by David Longworth, 1817. 130 p. (Bound in - His - A
concise view of the principal points of controversy between the Protestant and Roman churches... New York,
1817) MWA; MWH.   42884

-- Some remarks on Dr. O'Gallagher's "Brief reply"...
New York, Pr. by Clayton & Kingsland, for David Longworth, 1817. (Bound in - His - A concise view of the
principal points of controversy between the Protestant
and Roman churches... New York, 1817) 76 p. MWA;

MWH; MoSpD.   42885

[Whelpley, Samuel] 1766-1817
    Letters addressed to Caleb Strong, esq. late gov-
ernor of Massachusetts: showing war to be inconsistent
with the laws of Christ, and the good of mankind. Ed.
2. Philadelphia, Pr. by J. Rakestraw, for Benjamin
& Thomas Kite, 1817. 127 p. Ct; CtHC; CtSoP; DLC;
ICN; MBAt; MH; NNS; NNUT; Nj; NjP; PHC; PHi;
PPM.   42886

[--] The triangle. Fourth series... New York, Pr. by
Van Winkle, Wiley & Co., 1817. MWA.   42887

[--] -- in five series of numbers... New York, Pr. by
Van Winkle, Wiley & Co., 1817. (Five parts in one
vol.) MWA.   42888

-- -- Part 1. In five series of numbers. By the investigator (pseud.) New York, the author, 1817. MB.
                                             42889
[Whitcomb, Chapman]
    Patent medicine in Mob-Town... [1817?] MWA.
                                             42890
White, Charles
    A catalogue of the materia medica, and of pharma-
ceutical preparations. The articles enumerated in this
catalogue. Boston, Pr. by Giles E. Weld, 1817. 35 p.
DLC; DNLM; MBM.   42891

White, Elihu
    A specimen of printing types, from the foundry of
E. White. New York, Pr. by J. Seymour, 1817. 52
unnumbered leaves. MWA; NN.   42892

White, John
    An address, delivered before the Dedham auxiliary
society for the suppression of intemperance... Dedham,
Mass., Pr. by Abel D. Alleyne, 1817. 18 p. MBAt;
MWA; RPB; VtMiM.   42893

White, Joseph
    Annual address to the Medical Society of the state

of New York. Cooperstown, N. Y., 1817. DNLM.
42894

White, William, bp., 1748-1836
Comparative views of the controversy between the
Calvinists and the Arminians... Philadelphia, Pr. by E.
Bronson, for M. Thomas, 1817. 2 v. ICBB; MH;
MWA; MdBD; OrP; PHi; PPAmP; PPL-R; PPP; PPPrHi;
PU; ViAlTh.
42895

-- An essay, containing objections against the position
of a personal assurance of the pardon of sin, by a di-
rect communication of the Holy Spirit... Philadelphia,
Pr. at the office of the United States' gazette, for
Moses Thomas, 1817. 67 p. CSt; CtHC; DLC; IES;
MWA; MdBD; NNG; NjR; PHi; PPL-R; PPM; PU;
TxDaM; ViAlTh.
42896

Whitefield, George
A letter from the Rev. Mr. George Whitefield, to
the Rev. Mr. John Wesley. Hartford, Pr. by George
Goodwin & sons, 1817. 24 p. CtHC; CtHi; MWA; NN;
NcD.
42897

Whitman, Ezekiel Cheever
Our days few, uncertain, and full of trouble...
Northampton, Mass., Pr. by Ephraim Whitman, 1817.
16 p. CSmH; MWA; NN.
42898

Whitman, Samuel, 1751?-1826?
Blessedness of those who shall ascend to Glory
without dying. A sermon, delivered before the Hamp-
shire Missionary Society, at their annual meeting in
Northampton, August 21, 1817. Northampton, Mass.,
Pr. by Ephraim Whitman, 1817. 40 p. DLC; MB; MBC;
MDeeP; MH-AH; MWA; NN; NjR; RPB; TxHR. 42899

-- Parachrema; or, Baptism by immersion not scriptural. A sermon, preached at Goshen in April, 1816.
Northampton, Mass., Pr. by E. Brooks, at the Register office, 1817. 23 p. CSmH; CSt; MNF; MWA. 42900

Whiton, John Milton
Youth called upon to remember God... Concord,

N. H. , Pr. by Isaac Hill, 1817. MWA. 42901

Whitsitt, James
Infant baptism... Nashville, Tenn., Pr. by Norvell & M'Lean, 1817. 66 p. MB. 42902

Who is the hero of Saratoga... General Dearborn or Brooks? Let the official report of the Commander in Chief of the Republican army answer!! Extract of a letter from Major General Gates, to his Excellency the President of Congress, dated - "Camp at Saratoga, Oct. 12, 1777...[Signed] A plain farmer. [1817?] MHi. 42903

Widows and single women's society, Philadelphia.
Constitution for the Widows and single women's society of Philadelphia. Instituted the 9th of January, 1817. Philadelphia, William Fry, 1817. 18 p. GDC; PPPrHi. 42904

Wigham, John
Christian instruction, in a discourse as between a mother and her daughter... Philadelphia, Benjamin & Thomas Kite, 1817. 24 p. MNBedf; MWA; NbU; NjR; OClWHi; PPM; PSC-Hi. 42905

Wilbur, Hervey, 1787-1852
A short Biblical catechism, containing question historical, doctrinal, practical and experimental... Ed. 9. Greenfield, Mass., Pr. by Denio and Phelps, 1817. 198 p. CSt; CtSoP; MBC; MDeeP; MWA; NNUT; NbOP; NjP. 42906

[Wilkinson, Rebecca?]
Sermons to children: to which are added, short hymns, suited to the subjects. By a lady. Composed for the New-York Widow's Society. Albany, Pr. by Websters & Skinners, 1817. 93 p. MWA. 42907

Willard, S.
Hebrew grammar. Cambridge, Hilliard & Metcalf, 1817. MWA. 42908

Willetts, Jacob, (1785-1860)
    An easy grammar of geography, for the use of
schools...Ed. 4.   Poughkeepsie, Pr. by P. & S. Potter, for Paraclete Potter, 1817. 204 p. MWA; N.
                                                      42909
-- The scholar's arithmetic.   Ed. 2.   Poughkeepsie,
Paraclete Potter, 1817.   DLC; MH; MWA; NP.   42910

--[-- Philadelphia, 1817] (Greenwood and Martin, p.
821.   Martin (1898)]   42911

William Henry
    Chemistry. 1 vol. Philadelphia, 1817. MdAS.
                                                      42912

No entry   42913

William and Mary College, Williamsburg, Va.
    The officers, statutes and charter of the College of
William and Mary. Philadelphia, Repr. by William
Fry, for the University, 1817.   61 p. MWiW; MeHi.
                                                      42914
...William Bryant...[Philadelphia, Pr. by Lydia R.
Bailey, 1817] (This is no. 25 of the Tracts of the
Philadelphia female tract society) MWA.   42915

Williams, Peter, 1780?-1840
    A discourse, delivered on the death of Capt. Paul
Cuffe, before the New-York African institution, in the
African Methodist Episcopal Zion church, October 21,
1817...New-York, Pr. by B. Young and co., 1817.
16 p. DLC; MBC; MWA.   42916

Williams, Thomas
    Discourse at a public meeting of the Singers in the
North Parish in Wrentham, 13th May, 1817...Dedham,
Mass., Abel D. Alleyne, 1817. ICN; MAtt; MBC;
MWA; RPB.   42917

Williams College
    Catalogue of the faculty and students. Albany, J.

Buel [1817] MWiW.   42918

William's return, or good news for cottagers. Ed. 2.
Boston, Munroe & Francis, 1817. MWA.   42919

Willison, John
    A treatise concerning the sanctification of the
Lord's day. Philadelphia, A. Walker, 1817. 336 p.
NcCJ; NjR; PMA.   42920

-- -- Philadelphia, D. Hogan, 1817. 336 p. KyLoP;
MWA; PPiXT; VtMiS.   42921

Williston, Seth
    A vindication, of some of the most essential doc-
trines of the Reformation...Hudson, N. Y., Pr. by
Ashbel Stoddard, 1817. 264 p. MWA; NN; NSyU.
                                               42922
Willson, James Renwick, 1780-1853
    A historical sketch of opinions on the atonement,
interspersed with biographical notices of the leading
doctors, and outlines of the sections of the church
from the incarnation of Christ to the present time...
Philadelphia, Pr. by Wm. Fry, for Edward Earle,
1817. 351 p. GDC; GMM; ICP; ICU; MBAt; MBC;
MeBat; NNUT; PPLT; PPPrHi; PPiRPr; PPiW; PPiXT;
TxAuPT; WU.   42923

Wilmer, William Holland
    A sermon delivered in Christ Church, Alexandria,
on the occasion of the death of the Right Rev. T. J.
Claggett, Bishop of the Protestant Episcopal Church of
Maryland...Alexandria, Va., Pr. by B. L. Bogan,
1817. DLC; MH; MWA; MdBD; NNS; TJaU; ViAlTh.
                                               42924
Wilson, George M.
    Catalogue of prints, and books of prints, just re-
ceived from London, and for sale by George M. Wilson, No. 81 Pine-street, New-York. January, 1817.
[New York, 1817] NN.   42925

Wilson, James Patriot, 1769-1830
    An essay on grammar; the principles of which are

exemplified and appended in an English grammar...
Philadelphia, Pr. by W. Fry, 1817. 230 p. CSmH;
CtHT-W; CtW; DLC; ICU; MB; MH; MWA; MeBat; NNC;
NNUT; NPSta; NcU; NhD; NjR; PPL; PMA; PP; PHi;
PPAmP; PPPrHi; PU; TNP; ViRU; VtMiM; WU. 42926

Wilson, Peter
Compendium of Greek prosody... New York, Pr.
by T. and J. Swords, 1817. 21 p. MWA; MdBD;
PPPrHi. 42927

Wilson, Robert G.
Satan's wiles, a sermon delivered July 13, 1817,
in the Presbyterian Church, Chillicothe. Chillicothe,
O., Pr. by John Andrews, 1817. 16 p. NHi; OCHP;
PPPrHi. 42928

[Wilson, Sir Robert Thomas] 1777-1849
A sketch of the military and political power of
Russia, in the year 1817... New-York, Kirk and Mer-
cein, 1817. 208 p. CSfCW; DLC; DeGE; KyLo; KyLx;
MBAt; MWA; Md; Nh; NjP; MoSM; PMA. 42929

Wilson, Thomas
The biography of the principal American military
and naval heroes... New York, John Low, 1817-19.
2 v. CtHT; DLC; MNe; MWA; MdW; NN; NcWfc. 42930

Wilson, Thomas, bp. of Sodor and Man, 1663-1755.
A short and plain instruction for the better understanding of the Lord's supper; with the necessary preparation required... 1st Amer., from 16th London ed.,
adapted to the use of the Protestant Episcopal church
in this country. Fredericktown, Md., Pr. by Samuel
Barnes, for Charles Mann, 1817. 209 p. CSmH; DLC;
ICU; MH; MWA; MdBD; MdHi; NNG; NRCR; NjMD;
PPiXT; PU; ViAl. 42931

Wilson's farmers almanac for 1818... By Joshua Sharp.
Trenton, J.J. Wilson, 1817. MWA; NjR. 42932

Winter... New York, Samuel Wood & sons, [1817?]
MWA. 42933

Winthrop, James
    A scriptural notice to the believers in Christianity
...[Cambridge, Mass., 1817] MWA.   42934

Winyaw Intelligencer. Georgetown, S.C., Eleazer
Waterman, Sept. 6, 1817, 1st issue. Semi-weekly
newspaper. MWA.   42935

[Wirt, William] 1772-1834
    The letters of the British spy. Ed. 6, with the
last corrections of the author. Baltimore, Pr. by J.
Robinson, for Fielding Lucas, jun., 1817. 186 p. DLC;
MB; MWA; MWHi; MdBE; MdBLC; MdHi; NcAS; PHC;
PP; PNt.   42936

-- Sketches of the life and character of Patrick Henry.
By William Wirt...Philadelphia, Pr. by William Brown,
for James Webster, 1817. 427 p. DLC; DeGE; GEU;
ICMcHi; MWA; MdAN; MdHi; NjR; PCC; PLFM; RPB;
Vi; ViRVal; ViWR.   42937

Wistar, Caspar, 1761-1818
    A system of anatomy for the use of students of
medicine...Philadelphia, T. Dobson and son, 1817. 2 v.
CSt-L; DLC; KyLoJM; KyLxT; KyU; LNT-M; MWA;
MdBJ; MdBM; MnRM; MoKSJH; MoSMed; NBMS;
NNNAM; NNU-M; NcU; OC; OCU-M; OClM; OCo; P;
ScCMeS; TNV; TU-M; TxU-M.   42938

Witherell, George
    A sermon, on the subjects and mode of baptism...
Plattsburgh, N.Y., Pr. by A.C. Flagg, 1817. 28 p.
MWA.   42939

Witherspoon, John
    Letters on the education of children and on mar-
riage. Andover, Mass., Flagg & Gould, 1817. 81 p.
MB; MBC; MSaE; MWA; NjP.   42940

-- A series of letters on education...Hallowell, Me.,
Pr. by E. Goodale, 1817. MB; MWA.   42941

Wolcott, T.
    Hymns and spiritual songs.   Portland, Me., A. &
J. Shirley, 1817. (Fairbanks Museum) VtStjF.   42942

Wood, Benjamin
    A sermon, delivered in Holliston, July 30, A.D.
1817.   At the funeral of Mrs. Mary I. Wheaton...
Providence, Pr. by William C. Goddard, 1817. MWA.
                                                 42943
Wood, Jacob
    A brief essay on the doctrine of future retribution
...Worcester, Mass., Pr. by William Manning, 1817.
32 p. MMeT; MWA.   42944

Woodhouselee, Alexander Fraser Tytler, lord
    Elements of general history.   From British ed. 5.
New York, Nicholls, 1817. 184 p. MB; MWA; NNG;
PHi.   42945

-- -- ...Ancient and modern, to which are added a
table of chronology etc.   Philadelphia, Pr. [by S.
Marks] for Francis Nichols, 1817. 737 p. NjR. 42946

Woods, Leonard
    A sermon, preached at Haverhill, [Mass.] in re-
membrance of Mrs. Harriet Newell...Ed. 7.   Boston,
Samuel T. Armstrong, 1817. 192 p. KBB; MPax;
MSaE; MWA.   42947

[Woods, Samuel]
    New-York Preceptor.   New York, S. Wood & sons,
1817. MWA.   42948

Wood's almanac for 1818.   Calculations by Joshua
Sharp.   New York, Samuel Wood & sons [1817] [34] p.
MWA; NNA.   42949

Woodstock Herald.   Woodstock, Va., Williams & Bogan,
Dec. 24, 1817, 1st issue. Weekly newspaper. Shenan-
doah Herald Office, Woodstock.   42950

Woodward, John
    Claim against Holland.   Opinion of John Woodward,

Esq. of the city of New-York, in the case of the St.
Michaels and cargo of Baltimore, vs. the King of Hol-
land (now styled the King of the Netherlands) New
York, 1817. 32 p. MB; MH; NN. 42951

Woodworth, Samuel
The champions of freedom; or, The mysterious
chief. A romance of the nineteenth century, founded
on the war between the United States and Great Britain... New York, Charles N. Baldwin, 1817. 2 v.
MWA. 42952

[--] The complete coiffeur... New York, 1817. MWA.
42953
-- Ode for the fourth March, 1817. [New York, D.
Longworth, 1817] MWA. 42954

Woolman, John
Memoir of John Woolman... Ed. 2. Philadelphia,
Pr. [by J. R. A. Skerrett] for Benjamin & Thomas Kite
...1817. 31 p. MWA; MiD-B; NjR; PSC-Hi. 42955

Woolworth, Aaron, 1763-1821
Prayer for ministers, a Christian duty. A sermon.
Delivered October 23, 1816 at the ordination of the
Rev. Henry Fuller... Sag-Harbor, N. Y., Pr. by Sam-
uel A. Seabury, 1817. 18 p. DLC; MWA; NB;
NHuntHi; NSmB; NEh; RPB. 42956

Worcester, Joseph Emerson, 1784-1865
A geographical dictionary, or universal gazetteer;
ancient and modern... Andover, Mass., Pr. by Flagg
and Gould, for the author. Pub. by Henry Whipple,
Salem, 1817. 2 v. CSt; Ct; CtW; DLC; KyU; MB;
MBC; MH; MSaP; MWA; MiOC; MiU; NNC; Nh-Hi; NjP;
NjR; OUrC; THi; TJoT; ViL. 42957

[Worcester, Noah] 1758-1837
A candid and conciliatory review of the late corre-
spondence of the Reverend Dr. Worcester, with the
Rev. William E. Channing, on the subject of Unitarian-
ism, by a serious inquirer... Boston, Pr. by Lincoln &
Edmands, for the author, 1817. 88 p. MAnP; MB;

MH-AH; MWA; MWeyHi; MiD-B; NhD; RHi; WHi. 42958

[--] The friend of peace. No. X. By Philo Pacificus.
Boston, Pr. by Joseph T. Buckingham, 1817. 40 p.
MMeT-Hi; MNBedf. 42959

[--] -- No. 7. by Philo Pacificus [pseud.] Boston,
Wells and Lilly, 1817. CSmH. 42960

[--] -- No. 1-4. by Philo Pacificus [pseud.] Browns-
ville [Pa.] J. Dingee, D. Cattell, and W. M'Girr,
1817. 128 p. CSansS; CSmH; DLC; ICU; MWA;
OClWHi; PSew. 42961

[--] -- Cincinnati, O., Williams & Mason, for the
Warren County Peace Society, 1817. 160 p. CSmH;
OCHP; OClWHi. 42962

[--] -- [Nos. I-VII]. Greenfield, Mass., Ansel Phelps,
1817. 281 p. MDeeP; MWinchrHi; MWA; MeBat; NBu;
NCH; NN; NjP; OClWHi; RPB. 42963

[--] -- New York, Pr. by Samuel Wood & sons, 1817.
40 p. NjR. 42964

[--] ... The friend of peace, in a series of numbers:
together with A solemn review of the custom of war,
as an introduction to said work. By Philo Pacificus
[pseud.] ... [Schenectady, N. Y.] Pr. by I. Riggs, for
Isaac Stevens, [1817] [277] p. DLC; ICJ; ICN; IaHi;
MWA; N; NGH; NN; NNC; OO. 42965

[--] A solemn review of the custom of war; showing
that war is the effect of popular delusion, and proposing a remedy. By Philo Pacificus. Schenectady, N. Y.,
Pr. by I. Riggs, 1817. 205 p. CSmH; IaU; MA; MAJ;
MWA; MiD-B; MoKU; N; NGlo; NN; NNC; OO. 42966

Worcester, Samuel
    Christian psalmody in four parts... Ed. 2. Boston,
Pr. by Samuel T. Armstrong, 1817. 630 p. LNH;
MMhHi; MWA; MHard; NBuG; NNUT; OO. 42967

-- -- Ed. 2.   Boston, Pr. by Samuel T. Armstrong,
1817.   239 p. MLexHi; MWA; MWiW; Nh-D; PPPrHi.
42968
-- The drunkard a destroyer; a discourse delivered
before the Massachusetts society for the suppression of
intemperance, at their anniversary meeting, May 30,
1817. Boston, J. Eliot, 1817. 24 p.   Ct; DLC; MBev;
MH; MHi; MMeT; MWA; MeB; WHi.   42969

-- -- Boston, Pr. by John Eliot, 1817. 28 p.   CSt;
MBC; MH-AH; MHi; MScitHi; MWA; MiD-B.   42970

[--] Memoirs of the life, conversion, and happy death,
of Mrs. Eleanor Emerson. New York, Pr. by D.
Fanshaw, for C. Dodge, 1817. MWA.   42971

-- Select harmony: the fourth part of Christian psalmody,
consisting of a variety of tunes... suited to the various
subjects and metres of the psalms and hymns.   Ed. 2.
Boston, 1817. 79 p. MB; MH-AH.   42972

-- Select hymns: the third part of the Christian psalmody. Ed. 2.   Boston, Samuel T. Armstrong, 1817.
48 p. MWA; RPB.   42973

-- -- Ed. 2.   Boston, Samuel T. Armstrong, 1817.
198 p. MWA.   42974

Worcester, Thomas
    A new chain of plain argument, deemed conclusive
against Trinitarianism.   Addressed to a Trinitarian
writer for the Panoplist... Boston, Pr. by John Eliot,
1817. 46 p. CSt; Ct; IEG; M; MAnP; MB; MBAt;
MBAU; MBC; MH; MNBedf; MSaE; MWA; MeBat; MeHi;
NN; Nh-Hi; RPB.   42975

[Worth, Gorham A.]
    A New-Year's day.   Dedicated to the patrons of
Liberty Hall and Cincinnati Gazette, January 1st, 1817.
[Cincinnati, 1817] 9 p. MWA.   42976

Worthington Manufacturing Co.
    Articles of association... Columbus, O., P.H. Olm-

sted, 1817. 23 p. OClWHi.   42977

Wright, Chester
    A sermon, preached before the Female foreign mis-
sion society in Montpelier, 1816...Montpelier, Vt., Pr.
by E. P. Walton, 1817. 14 p. MBC; MWA; VtHi.42978

Wright, Nathaniel Hill
    The fall of Palmyra...Middlebury, Vt., William
Slade, Jun., 1817. 143 p. CSmH; DLC; ICU; IU;
MBAt; MH; MWA; MiD-B; NBuG; RPB; Vt; VtHi;
VtMiS; VtU-W; WU.   42979

[Wright, Thomas H.] d. 1856?
    Letters critical and pathological, by Paetus [pseud.]
remote descendant of Thrasea Paetus. Baltimore, Pr.
by J. Robinson, for Cushing & Jewett, 1817. 55 p.
DNLM; PU.   42980

                    X-Y-Z
Yale University
    Catalogue of the faculty and students of Yale Col-
lege November, 1817. New-Haven, Pr. at the Journal
office, 1817. 14 p. CtY; MWA.   42981

-- Catalogus Senatus Academici, et eorum qui munera
et officia academica gesserunt, quique aliquovis gradu
exornati querunt in Collegio Yalensi...Novi - portus:
Execudebat Thomas Green. Woodward, 1817. 58 p.
Ct; MH-L; ScU; TNP.   42982

-- The laws of Yale college, in New-Haven, in Con-
necticut, enacted by the president and fellows. New-
Haven, Pr. at the Journal office, 1817. 46 p. Ct;
DLC; MNF; N; NSyHi; RPB.   42983

Yankee fire society, Dover, N. H.
    Rules and regulations to be observed by...insti-
tuted at Dover, Nov. 29, 1802. Revised, 1817. NhDo.
                    42984
The Yankee traveller...Concord, N. H., George Hough,
1817. MWA.   42985

[Yates, Christopher Columbus]
An exposition of a most villainous attempt at extortion. [Albany, 1817] 16 p. MB; MBAt; N. 42986

Young, Edward
Devout thoughts of a retired penitent... Pittsburgh, Pa., Pr. by Butler & Lambdin, 1817. 24 p. MWA. 42987

Young, Peter
A brief account of the life and experience, call to the ministry, travels and afflictions of Peter Young... Portsmouth, N.H., Pr. by Beck & Foster, 1817. 168 p. DLC; MH; MWA; MWH; NNC; NRAB; Nh; Nh-Hi; NjMD. 42988

[Young, Samuel]
A treatise on internal navigation... Ballston Spa., N.Y., Pr. by U.F. Doubleday, 1817. 267 p. MH; MWA. 42989

Young cottager: an authentic narrative. New York, J. Seymour, 1817. MWA. 42990

Young men's missionary society of New York.
The constitution of the young men's missionary society of New-York: formerly called the Assistant New-York Missionary society; founded on the twenty-third day of January, A.D. 1809. New-York, Pr. by Daniel Fanshaw, 1817. 16 p. MBC; NNUT; NjR. 42991

-- History of the Young men's missionary society of New York, containing a correct account of the recent controversy respecting Hopkinsian doctrines. New York, the author, 1817. 40 p. CtHC; MWA; NB; NjR; PPPrHi. 42992

Zeugniss von der taufe... Harrisburg, Pa., Laurentz Wartmann, 1817. MWA. 42993